—— THE ——
PERSPECTIVE

WHAT THE HELL ARE THEY THINKING?

The 100 debates that govern your life, written in a way that tells both sides of every story.

EDITED BY
DANIEL RAVNER

Copyright @ Daniel Ravner, Perspective Media LTD.

All rights reserved. No part of this book may be reproduced, in any forms or aby any means, electronic, printed or otherwise, without written consent from The Perspective LTD except in the case of brief quotations for the sake of articles, or reviews. Perspective Media LTD and the big-debates authors has made every effort to ensure the quality and accuracy of its content and the arguments presented in this book. They are, however, not accountable for the claims and content made by the publishers and authors displayed in the references or changes to the content of the links made since it was originally used. The perspective LTD, through this book, aims to show the different points of view that exist on a specific subject matter that are prevalent in society. We do not hold or advocate for any specific argument.

U.S. Copyright Office's DMCA Designated Agent Directory - DMCA-1001226

Print Version ISBN 978-965-92950-8-1

e-book ISBN 978-965-92950-9-8

For further inquiries: info@theperspective.com

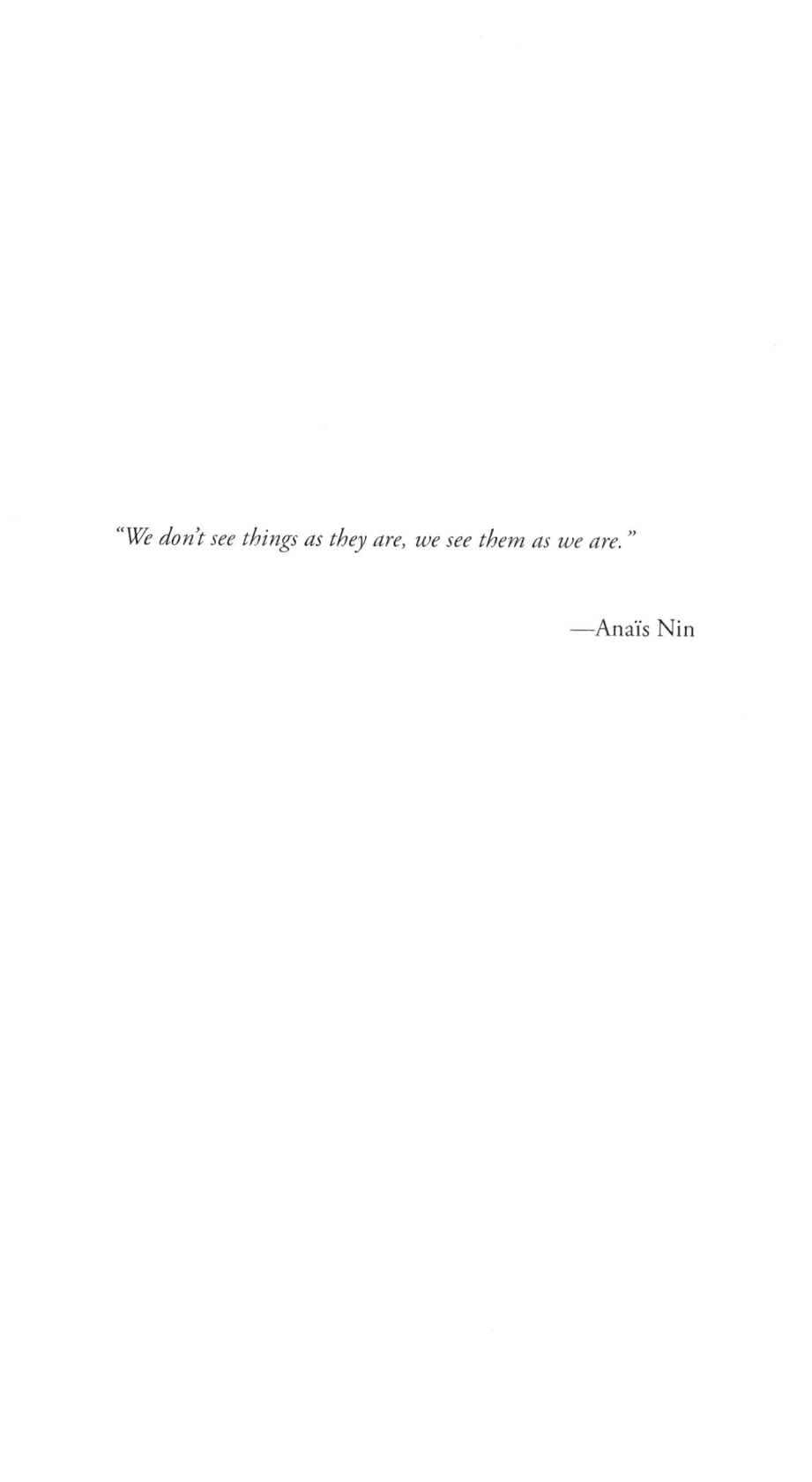

"We don't see things as they are, we see them as we are."

—Anaïs Nin

CONTENTS

You are encouraged to read this book in whatever order sparks your interest

Preface ix
Politics chapter 1
  Should we legalize marijuana? 2
  How similar are the far-left and the far-right? 6
  Should the US accept refugees? 9
  Is China the next superpower? 13
  The perspective on gun control 17
  The perspective on Donald Trump 21
  Do protests work? 25
  America first? Should the us intervene militarily in foreign conflicts? 30
  The perspective on Putin 34
  Should 'Black Lives Matter' fight for all lives? 38
  The perspective on single-payer health care 42
  Should the First Amendment cover racism and hate speech? ... 46
  Should Puerto Rico become the 51st state? 50
  The perspective on gerrymandering 54
  The perspective on the United Nations (UN) 58
  Edward Snowden – hero or traitor? 62
Living chapter 65
  Is happiness a choice? 66
  Is there life after death? 70
  Is there life outside Earth? 74
  The perspective on having kids 77
  Which came first, the chicken or the egg? 80
  Should adopted children be involved with their birth families? 83
  Cats or dogs: who makes a better companion? 87
  City vs. suburbs: where is better to live? 90

Are humans inherently violent? 94
Is fear beneficial or damaging to our lives? 98
Is honesty the best policy? 102
The perspective on time – is it linear or cyclical? 105
The perspective on religion 109
The perspective on working from home. 112

Entertainment chapter **117**
Harry Potter vs. Harry Potter: are the books better than the movies? 118
Do artists with seriously questionable morals deserve fame? 121
Should celebrities expect privacy?. 125
Hamilton – overrated or worth the hype? 129
(Titanic) Could Jack have been saved? 132
The Kardashians: inspiring or damaging to women? 135
The perspective on binge-watching 139
The perspective on Fox News 143
Throwback TV: Seinfeld or Friends? 147
Which is better: *Star Wars* vs. *Star Trek*? 151

Society chapter **155**
The perspective on animal testing 156
Is the death penalty justified or should it be abolished? 160
The perspective on fracking 164
Social welfare: do its advantages outweigh its disadvantages? 167
The perspective on the royal family 171
Can people change their minds? 175
The perspective on political correctness 179
Can the use of torture be justified? 182
Should we negotiate with terrorists? 185
The perspective on circumcision 189
Should we depend on fossil fuels or renewable energy? 192
The perspective on abortion. 196
Does reverse racism exist in America? 199
Should prostitution be legalized? 203
Should the burqa be banned? 207
Should convicted criminals have the right to vote? 211

    The perspective on surrogacy 214
    The perspective on unions 217
    Do vegans have the moral high ground?. 221
    Are whistleblowers heroes or traitors?. 225
    Should women serve in combat units? 229

Sports Chapter **233**
    Is Roger Federer the best tennis player of all time? 234
    Are the NFL "Concussion Rules" ruining the Game? 238
    Messi or Ronaldo – who is truly the best? 241
    Should college athletes get paid? 245
    Should sports betting be legal?. 249
    Should women compete against men in sports? 252
    Lebron vs. Jordan: Who's the greatest of all time?. 256
    Should instant replays (VAR) be used in sports? 259
    Should the NHL ban fighting in hockey? 262

History chapter **265**
    The perspective on Diana, Princess of Wales 266
    The perspective on Christopher Columbus 270
    The bombings of Hiroshima and Nagasaki: Plain evil or a necessary
        evil?. 274
    The perspective on Che Guevara 278
    The perspective on Ronald Reagan 281

Finance chapter **285**
    Should we raise taxes on the rich? 286
    Should we raise the minimum wage? 290
    The perspective on Bitcoin. 293
    Are entrepreneurs born or made? 297
    The perspective on the American dream. 300
    Should you fly traditional or low-cost airlines?. 304
    Is home ownership still worthwhile? 307

Education chapter **311**
    Redshirting: should parents delay kindergarten for a year?. 312
    The perspective on school uniforms. 315
    How great is 'great literature' if it needs to be studied to be
        understood?. 318

Should we allow smartphones in school? 321
Should we distribute condoms in high schools? 324
Health chapter **329**
   Are antidepressants a good solution? 330
   Is obesity a disease? 333
   Milk: Is it healthy or harmful to drink? 337
   Are vaccines safe or risky for your kids? 340
   Are vitamin supplements helpful or harmful?................. 344
   The perspective on cosmetic surgery........................ 348
Technology chapter **353**
   The perspective on Jeff Bezos.............................. 354
   The perspective on digital marketing 358
   Can Facebook maintain dominance? 362
   The perspective on Steve Jobs.............................. 366
   Ios or Android – which smartphone is better? 370
   The perspective on Elon Musk............................. 373
   The perspective on Google................................ 377
Acknowledgements... **381**
Endnotes 383

All debates were updated for this book
by Rachel Segal and Zoe Jordan

PREFACE

Thanks for reading this book.

At the end of 2016, I set out to start The Perspective.

Back then, I felt (and still do) that the world I will eventually leave my three girls is in a worse condition than the one I inherited from my parents, and I wanted to do something about it.

The righteous, often violent, one-sided discourse that was—and still is—prevalent on social media (and which has since seeped into real life) seems like a particularly destructive side effect of the digital revolution. The binary "us vs. them" rhetoric has extended to everything, and if you can't talk about anything, then you can't solve anything either.

The echo chamber that surrounds us and constantly affirms our existing views became my focus five years ago. And providing an alternative, practical, designed-for-actual-humans-with-regular-ordinary-messy-lives solution became my goal.

I wanted to get people to listen, to acknowledge that EVERYTHING has nuance and that NOTHING is black or white. I wanted to push the pendulum back to the center and away from extremism. It's a bit much, I know, but at that time, I had just turned 40, and these goals were what my midlife crisis had transformed into.

It should be noted, I'm not the world's most moderate guy. I get seriously annoyed with some of the things I see and hear people say on TV. So how did I end up with the motto, "There are at least two sides to every story"?

I come from the worlds of content and marketing. I've built a career on my ability to carve a story and generate emotions. Still, I used to be horrible in political debates! I could see how the more heated I became, the less I was able to reach the person in front of me, who had also become more heated, and also could not stop preaching.

At some point, though, it dawned on me that if I ever wanted to get people to see things the way I do, I would have to take a risk. I would have to truly open myself up to try and see things the way "the other side" sees them. (After all, it can't be that so many people are ALL idiots, right?) I realized that while being just and fair doesn't bring change, being smart might. And the price to pay for affecting change, is to truly try and see the other side's point of view, take a risk agreeing with (some) of it and maybe, even, sometimes admit that I am wrong (or, at least, not wholly right).

I subsequently dove deeply into the worlds of social psychology and behavioural science to better define the reasons why people hold on to their opinions the way they do. I also surveyed ways to circumvent people's rejections of ideas that are different from their own. My team and I then started building a methodology based on how to approach debates when one's goal is not to inform both sides (although that can also happen) but to get people to open their minds to the other side's point of view.

How does that look?

Picture a heated discourse in which you throw the strongest argument you have at your counterpart. For example: "Climate change is real. Science says so…" While that argument may sound strong to you, your counterpart may not necessarily think so. He/she may have heard this particular argument a million times before and is now immune to it. Therefore, using an objectively weaker yet fresh and different argument may give you a better chance of getting your adversary to listen. For example: "Relying on oil makes our country and economy dependent on foreign countries. Therefore, alternative energy makes our country stronger."

Remember, we are in the business of opening minds, not changing them.

Another concept that our methodology incorporates has to do with how conservative and liberals react differently to the same values. The Moral Foundation Theory says that we (conservatives and liberals) care about the same things but not necessarily in the same order of importance. For the sake of a clear example, I'm going to grossly overgeneralize here: Democrats care more about hurt (e.g., Is someone getting hurt as a result of a certain act?). While Republicans care more about loyalty (e.g., Is a certain act tarnishing the values that defines our group?).

Let's take the issue of flag burning. For Democrats, while seeing such a sight is uncomfortable, they might say "There's no need to overreact; it's a piece of cloth." For Republicans, however, the same act might be seen as a sign of aggression against the values that they hold dear, an act of disrespect toward the people who died to realize these values. They may react fiercely based on this view.

Going back to The Perspective and how it can make a difference – Its idea is to write and present an argument in such a way that would appeal to the values of whichever group that you are trying to persuade.

Based on research and works of smarter (than myself) men and women, we set up and modified The Perspective Methodology, which included ideas like:

1. The only way to write an objective piece of content is by bringing two equally subjective points of view to the same place (same big debate article in our case).
2. The same author writes both sides of the debate. We found that it is more effective, for the cause of opening minds, to have one writer and one editor in charge of each debate's balance, rather than using two different writers as each one would most likely speak to his or her audience instead of to the people on the other side.
3. Each writer is different, with his/her own tone (which we have safeguarded) and opinions. Our way to create balance was to adhere to the specific big debate methodology and format we created, through research, writing, editing and presentation.

I'll fast forward through a lot of our startup's founding story (i.e., UI innovation, gathering a brilliant team of writers, getting many no's, finding the angel that invested money to get the venture off the ground, A/B testing our ideas, finding some that worked and many more that didn't, work, work, work and so much more work…).

Long story short: It worked.

A year after our launch, The Perspective won the WebAward in the News category and an Eppy Award for Best Innovation Project. It was also a highly commended finalist for The Drum Award for Editorial Innovation.

More importantly, research [1] conducted by Herzliya Inter Disciplinary college in May 2019, led by Dr. Gali Einav and Ofir Allen MA, probed into the effectiveness of The Perspective's content. The research team found that 58.46% of readers opened their minds to different points of view after reading our signature big debates (the readers moved to the center of a "views scale"). This prompted research on a larger scale in March 2021 (that is still being written) but already shows that our big debates have an especially significant effect on people who are defined as extreme.

This book comprises our most popular, most engaged-with debates on our site, all updated especially for this book. Plus, there are 30 debates that are exclusive to the book. The subjects of these exclusive debates are based on popular searches.

It's an "everything you need to know about everything you need to know" kind of book. It provides a broader sense of the hot topics that come up in the news or around the dinner table but in a way that's easy to read and challenging (in a good way). At the very least, you'll be smarter about stuff.

The Perspective was created by a small group of people on a tight budget. It's a media startup with a social cause, and like any startup, everyone who is part of it serves as both the president and intern of the venture. Everyone is crucial, from the designer all the way to the reader. A list of acknowledgments is available at the end of this book, but I want to start by saying to the team, and to you, our reader – Thanks.

And now,

Are you willing to put your mind where your mouth is? Are you confident enough to open your mind to a view that's different from your own? If so, read on...

Daniel Ravner

---

1 https://www.theperspective.com/effectiveness-study/

POLITICS CHAPTER

- Should we legalize marijuana?
- How similar are the far-left and the far-right?
- Should the US accept refugees?
- Is China the next superpower?
- The perspective on gun control
- The perspective on Donald Trump
- Do protests work?
- America first? Should the US intervene militarily in foreign conflicts?
- The perspective on Putin
- Should Black Lives Matter fight for all lives?
- The perspective on single-payer health care
- Should the First Amendment cover racism and hate speech?
- Should Puerto Rico become the 51st state?
- The perspective on gerrymandering
- The perspective on the United Nations
- Edward Snowden – hero or traitor?

SHOULD WE LEGALIZE MARIJUANA?

Original debate written by Chaya Benyamin

Long regarded as a social ill, support for recreational marijuana use has been gaining traction across the United States and the globe. Eleven states[1] have legalized it for recreational use, and 33 states[2] allow the drug for medicinal purposes. With Canada[3] [4]having legalized marijuana in 2018 and the potential for other countries [5]to follow suit, it is more important than ever to understand the possible economic, social, and health impacts – good and bad – that may accompany increased access to marijuana. While proponents of legalization believe marijuana's biggest drawback to be increased calorie intake, health professionals and lawmakers have offered less optimistic analyses.

In this article, we'll explore the question of whether legalized marijuana is a pitfall to be avoided, or the inevitable recognition of the non-criminal nature of one of America's most popular pastimes.

Just Say No

Growing green isn't green

Federal law, security concerns, and desire to produce plants with higher levels of THC have driven domestic cannabis producers to grow their crops indoors at a truly hefty price for the environment. Indoor pot production has a massive carbon footprint. The energy used to produce just one joint [6]is equivalent to leaving a light on for over a day. Denver's indoor pot farms are estimated to account for almost 4%[7] of the city's total electricity consumption. In total, cannabis production is estimated to cost $6 billion[8] in energy expenditures each year and predicted to hit $50 billion by 2026. As the globe's second biggest producer of carbon emissions, the US should not support the rise of another industry with unsustainable energy demands.

Legalized weed is detrimental to the poor

Various studies have established a connection between the risk factors of poverty and substance use[9] and abuse. Liquor store owners have either exploited or contributed to this reality; most low-income neighborhoods have a disproportionately high[10] number of liquor stores. California marijuana dispensaries took notes from urban liquor stores and have been setting up shop in Los Angeles's poorest neighborhoods[11] for over a decade. The same phenomena repeated itself in Denver[12], where over 200 grow and sell operations flooded low-income areas since weed became legal.

Legalized marijuana poses real threats to public health and safety

Just like smoking cigarettes, smoking pot contributes to the development of respiratory diseases and increased risk of lung cancer.[13] In addition, doctors and health officials assert that there is a direct connection between marijuana use and psychosis and schizophrenia[14]. With the legalization of marijuana use, the prevalence of marijuana-related illnesses may grow with the number of people who use it. For example, following legalization, Colorado health professionals[15] noted a surge in cases of extreme illness in children who ingested marijuana edibles (it is no help that many such edibles look exactly like gummy bears). Law enforcement, too, has complained of the difficulty of identifying drugged drivers[16], whose level of intoxication cannot be easily verified as with alcohol.

Don't Criticize It, Legalize It

Prohibition is extremely expensive

In America, the number of addicts has hovered just above 1%[17] for the last 30 years, while costs associated with drug control surged to $820 billion[18] and growing. On the other hand, municipalities that supported decriminalization (legalization's half-sister) policies, saved money in spades on drug enforcement. For instance, sources estimate that local and state governments annually spend $29 billion[19] on drug prohibition, with an additional $18 billion spent by the federal government. However, full drug legalization would bring in $19 billion[20] in state and local tax revenue and $39 billion in federal tax revenue. Clearly, legalization of marijuana can cut government spending, consequently saving resources for other societal uses. Not to mention, legalization can generate tax revenue that could go towards transferring income from drug producers and consumers to public funds.

Legalization is correlated with lower rates of drug abuse

Somewhat counterintuitively, one of the more effective ways to discourage drug use is to legalize it. When Portugal decriminalized all drugs, the country's drug abuse rates were cut in half[21] and there was no increase[22] in use of weed or any other substance. Other drug-tolerant nations, like the Netherlands, show significantly lower rates[23] of lifetime and occasional marijuana use. One year after Colorado legalized recreational pot use for adults, a survey of 17,000 high school students showed a decline[24] in teen marijuana use. The rate is still below the national average[25] even in 2019. It seems marijuana legalization may have stripped the drug of its rebellious appeal and returned Colorado teens to other means of weekend thrills.

The pot industry creates jobs and bolsters the economy

The global legal marijuana market size is estimated to reach $66.3 billion by the end of 2025, according to a Grand View Research, Inc[26]. report. If that's not telling enough, a study conducted by the Marijuana Policy Group concluded that Colorado's legalized pot industry created 18,000 jobs and generated over $2 billion[27] in economic activity in 2015. Since then, the marijuana industry has boosted a number of business sectors[28], from agriculture to materials to transportation. Moreover, the industry is bringing US veterans[29] back to work through security positions on farms and in dispensaries. In an economy where workers regularly lose jobs to overseas operations and automation, governments cannot afford to turn their backs on industries that create new opportunities for their citizens to earn a decent living.

The Bottom Line: There is plenty of evidence to suggest that marijuana legalization has been a boon for the states that have introduced it, and an effective, low-risk anti-anxiety remedy[30]. But as *South Park* creator Trey Parker[31] cautioned, the consequences of marijuana use might be different than we expect: "Pot makes you feel fine with being bored and it's when you're bored that you should be learning a new skill… If you smoke pot you may grow up to find out that you're not good at anything." Does that ring true for you? How do you think marijuana legalization will affect people?

HOW SIMILAR ARE THE FAR-LEFT AND THE FAR-RIGHT?

Original debate written by Chaya Benyamin

Do the far-left and the far-right ever seem hopelessly similar to you? As odd as this question may sound at first, Horseshoe Theory[32] suggests that the political spectrum is not a straight line with ideologies moving across a line from left to right, but rather a horseshoe, with its farthest outliers bending in toward each other and sharing a number of beliefs. In recent years, violent clashes between the far-left and far-right, at UC Berkeley[33], in Charlottesville, North Carolina,[34] in Portland, Oregon[35], and most recently during the George Floyd protests[36], have challenged society to take a look at the actions of both extremes and ask: To what extent does similarity in action mean similarity in character?

The Far-Left and the Far-Right Are Two Peas in a Pod

Victim complex

People on the outermost poles of the political spectrum, meaning on both the far-left and the far-right, often view themselves as aggrieved parties. Interestingly, one study found that having faced adversity – namely violence, loss of a loved one, or experiencing illness or disability – is indeed a predictor of extreme political views[37]; the more adversity people faced, the more likely they were to lean to the far right or far left in their ideologies. Experiencing adversity may explain the rhetoric of victimization that permeates the far-left as well as the far-right. White Nationalists complain[38] of cultural and economic obliteration at the hands of multicultural movements and affirmative action, while proponents of the far-left demand restitution for the silencing of minority groups via discriminatory legislation, the recent rise in popularity of white nationalists[39], police brutality[40] and micro-aggressions[41].

By any means necessary

Militancy pervades the ranks of the far-left and the far-right. More than idolizing violent purveyors of their ideologies (think far-right's Mussolini[42] to the far-left's Che Guevara[43]), many far-right and far-left movements are vehement in their rejection of non-violence[44] and employ it regularly. Right-wing groups are said to have carried out 150 attacks[45] on US soil – from shooting to bombings – since 1993. Similar crimes have been perpetrated by militant offshoots of left-wing groups, beginning with the 1960's Weathermen[46] and continuing until today with the Antifa[47] movement.

An idle mind is the devil's playground

Scientists have connected boredom[48] to the adoption of extreme political stances, calling youth, wealth, and education the most common risk factors of extremism. Before the coronavirus pandemic hit, it could be argued that without families to support or even necessarily the need to support themselves, the average college student[49] has more free time than others to develop defined political views. As such, it is hardly surprising that constituents on the far-right and far-left are overwhelmingly educated and even well-off (a trend that held even for the Hezbollah[50] fighters of the 1980s and 90s).

The Far-Left and Far-Right Are as Different as Night and Day

Different hard-wiring

Psychologist have determined that liberal and conservative brains literally function quite differently[51]. For example, an examination of the possessions of liberal and conservative college students revealed that the former had more books and travel-memorabilia, while the latter had more items relating to cleaning and organization. This investigation suggested key differences in liberal and conservative mindsets – with one leaning toward the discovery of new experiences and the other emphasizing self-discipline and order. This hard-wiring gives rise to dramatically different value systems[52] – systems that view the basic ideas like fairness, equality, and even right and wrong in radically different terms.

History is in the eye of the beholder

The far-right and the far-left have dramatically different interpretations of the past[53] – interpretations which dictate their political stances and calls to action. The far-right expresses nostalgia for the past and actively works to preserve their history, regardless of what that might mean in today's context. For right-wing Southerners, this means protecting statues of famous Confederates and decrying the removal of the Confederate flag[54] from public buildings or the removal of Confederate monuments. Conversely, the far-left (and in this case, many liberals) associates the past with its ills[55] – slavery, sexism, and other injustices. History and its institutions are not to be preserved and cherished, but rather, an embarking point from which to begin reform.

Superficial similarities

When two groups utilize similar tactics, it does not necessarily mean that the groups are one and the same. The Antifa[56] and white nationalist movements exemplify key ideological differences that should not be overlooked. While Antifa and white nationalist movements both express distaste for the government (and even a will to overthrow[57] it), their reasons for these sentiments are rather opposite. Antifa, whose members also frequently identify as anarchists, view government as an instrument of inequality, while white nationalists express hostility toward government because they believe it facilitates equality – a notion that offends those whose identity is built upon a defined racial hierarchy.

....

The Bottom Line: Both the far-left and the far-right have a victim-like mentality and employ militant strategies, yet each group has contrasting views on history and personal values. What do you think? Do overlapping tactics and stances in the far-right and far-left amount to a hegemonic portrait of extreme personalities, or is each extremely distinct?

SHOULD THE US ACCEPT REFUGEES?

Original debate written by Andrew Vitelli

The UN Refugee Agency estimates the global number of 'forcibly displaced' people to have surpassed 80 million[58] in 2020, the largest number since World War II. More than two thirds of all refugees come from five countries[59]: Syria, Venezuela, Afghanistan, South Sudan and Myanmar, in that order.

The longtime world leader in resettling asylum-seekers, the US is at a crossroads. While the Trump administration slashed the number of refugees admitted to the US, to the relief of some and the chagrin of others, Biden promised to raise the limit[60], before backtracking[61], Between humanitarian values and looking out for number one, the USA seems to be trying to find the balance.

This article looks at three arguments in favor of accepting more refugees and three arguments against doing so.

The US Should Not Accept Refugees

Terrorists will slip into the country

Syrians have comprised the striking majority of global refugees since 2014[62]. In 2015, polling showed that 13 percent of Syrian refugees held a positive view of ISIS. It's a low percentage, but is it worth risking it? Even if America's rigorous vetting process is effective, out of 10,000 Syrian refugees, hundreds could be sympathetic to the terror group. After all, it took just 19 terrorists to carry out the 9/11 attacks, killing thousands of Americans and launching two decades of war. Even a single terrorist can do horrific damage, as the terrorist attack [63]in Strasbourg, France, proved.

ISIS will certainly look to exploit any opportunity to infiltrate the US. Former CIA director John Brennan[64], the commander of NATO[65], and German intelligence officials[66] have all warned of ISIS fighters disguised as refugees entering western countries.

The money could be spent helping Americans

Resettling refugees is not cheap – one think tank estimates that resettling a refugee in the US costs more than $60,000[67]. The Office of Refugee Resettlement spends upwards of $1.5 billion[68] a year, and adding more refugees will likely drive these costs up. Also, refugees are likely to need government assistance, at least in the first years after their arrival in the country.
Were the US flush with cash, this kind of spending may be reasonable. But with over $28 trillion in debt[69], almost 40 million Americans[70] living in poverty, the US is not in a position to spend billions of dollars on refugee resettlement. Our primary moral responsibility – and the opinion of many Americans[71] – is to take care of Americans already in the country; it seems unfair to spend billions on refugees while veterans sleep in the streets.

Neighboring countries should bear the responsibility

In the case of Syria, countries like Lebanon and Jordan[72] have taken in many refugees, and even Israel provides medical care[73] for Syrian refugees. But others in the region [74] could do much more. Saudi Arabia[75], for example, is ten times Syria's size and has a per capita GDP comparable to the US. This is preferable, not just in the interest of American self-preservation but that of the refugees themselves; culture shock would be considerably less than relocating to American culture and they would have a greater chance of success in other Arab countries.[76]

The US Should Accept Refugees

Refugees can make American stronger

Welcoming refugees into the US isn't simply a matter of good will. Refugees make America a stronger country – culturally and economically. The latter point has been the conclusion of several studies[77] on the economic impact of refugees worldwide. With America's population aging, and Baby Boomers hitting retirement, absorbing refugees of working age will, in the long term, be beneficial. Adding young workers into the labor force will boost GDP and prevent stagnation that is seen in countries like Japan, as a report[78] by the National Academy of Sciences determined.

Just as previous generations of immigrants from around the world have helped the US become an economic superpower, the contributions made by immigrants could also strengthen 21st century America.

The US must play its part in alleviating the refugee crisis

Of the world's 80+ million displaced people, over half of them are children[79]. And while 2018 numbers show that 14% of refugees[80] were hosted by developed nations, the other 86% are taken in by developing nations, whose institutions, economies and systems are already under greater strain. COVID-19[81] has not improved this disparity.

Meanwhile, for the first time in over three decades, the US has lost its top spot[82] as world leader in resettling refugees. But what does this say about America's values? The US has always prided itself on its diversity, morality and history and historically, America has always been a place of [83]refuge.

Refugees are very unlikely to be terrorists

Fears of terrorist groups infiltrating America through refugee resettlement programs are overblown. In fact, refugees are less likely to commit a terrorist attack than non-refugee immigrants or native-born Americans. Since 1980, the US has accepted around 3 million refugees[84] and none of them[85] have committed acts of terrorism. Terrorists have found other ways into the country – the 9/11 hijackers, for example, entered on student or tourist visas. Refugees to the US undergo a rigorous vetting process,[86] lasting up to two years and including interviews with the UN, US State Department and US Department of Homeland Security. As one Homeland Security analyst wrote in commentary published by the conservative Heritage Foundation[87], "The U.S. refugee system can be, should be, and is being picky at who we allow to enter the U.S. as a refugee."

The Bottom Line: America's response to the global refugee crisis evokes questions of American ideals, security, and the country's place in the world. With civil unrest, famine and climate crises[88] showing no sign of ending any time soon, should the US restrict caps on refugees or allow in more people after intensive vetting? What do you think?

IS CHINA THE NEXT SUPERPOWER?

Original debate written by Kira Goldring

A superpower[89] is defined as a country that has global influence over others in cultural, technological, military[90] and political spheres, and China, whose Communist party recently celebrated its 70th anniversary[91], is emerging as a strong contender for the position. While the US has been the world's superpower for decades, escalating political tension between the US and China, especially the renewed trade war [92]and criminal charges against Chinese company Huawei[93], leads many to wonder: Is China the Next Superpower?

Here are three arguments suggesting that China is becoming the next world superpower, and three arguments against it.

China Will Replace the US as Superpower

Embraces globalization

It's rare to pick up a knick-knack in the US without seeing the words "Made in China" written on it. That's because China is the world's top exporting and trading country[94], having exported $435.45 billion worth of goods into the US in 2020. In fact, the US is China's top trading partner, receiving 19.2% of all Chinese imports. China has also taken strong steps to make global connections, trying to solidify relationships with some of America's previous allies. It is also running an effective public-relations game[95], representing itself as a globalist world power. China's One Belt and One Road[96] initiative seeks to stimulate economic growth across Asia by investing billions of dollars into building ambitious amounts of infrastructure[97] to connect China with the rest of the world. China also has the distinct advantage of riding high, being among the first to bounce back economically[98] since the start of the coronavirus pandemic.

Additionally, China is a huge investor in the US, owning over $1.123 trillion[99] of US debt, and snapping up[100] US-born startups. The fact that President Trump considered rejoining the TPP[101] (Trans-Pacific Partnership) only a year after withdrawing from it – on what was, at the time, the brink of a trade war[102] with China, which is still continuing[103] – demonstrates the "strategic threat[104]" China poses to the US.

The West wants in

It's not just exports that set China apart; China boasts a market of which the West wants a piece. Its economic growth has surpassed every other country's at an average of 10% per year[105]; the sheer size of its population (over one billion people), combined with a growing middle class, has given the country unrivaled buying power[106]. Consequently, American companies are itching to get involved. Facebook and Google have repeatedly tried[107] to re-enter China, with each company changing policies and creating new products to try to get into the Chinese game. Some of Hollywood's biggest films have also been reworked[108] just for the chance of being allowed in, not to mention that popular TV shows have been censored[109] for fear of seeming critical of China.

Technologically dominant

China checks the technological domination[110] box on the list of superpower qualifications. Once notorious for being the "copycat" nation, it now boasts strong entrepreneurial spirit[111] nearly akin to that of Silicon Valley. Its digital payments market[112] is far more developed and prevalent than that of the US. By 2021, it is projected that nearly 80%[113] of all of China's smartphone users will be using their phones instead of cash or credit cards at points of sale, compared to only 31% of Americans. Its eCommerce sales account for over 50%[114] of its retail sales, compared with around 30%[115] of US sales. Its two largest internet companies – Alibaba Group[116] and Tencent Holdings[117] – are leaders in online gaming, social media and ecommerce not to mention TikTok[118], the most downloaded non-gaming app in 2020, with an estimated net worth of $50 billion[119]. From the lightweight, cutting-edge Mavic Pro[120] drone (which controls over 70% of the commercial drone market), to the rise and fall[121] of its bike-sharing industry [122]and all-inclusive app WeChat[123], the technological innovation emerging from China that once would have been met with skepticism from the West is now met with due admiration.

China Isn't Made of Superpower Stuff

Government intervention stifles potential

Soaring economic growth isn't enough to propel a country into superpower status. China's financial system lacks credibility[124], as it is largely underdeveloped and subject to government meddling. Additionally, the financial sector[125] rarely provides investors with real, profitable returns, and has been accused of limiting competition. For example, Uber[126] failed in China after government preferences for state-owned enterprises gave Chinese rideshare company Didi a competitive edge. Although China has kept its pledge[127] to open up its finance sector to foreign investment[128], including in VPN services[129], to counter said accusations, the level of government involvement in the economy overall puts China out of the running in the superpower race.

The world isn't on board

China needs global support to become a superpower, which it lacks in the current political climate. With its documented human rights [130]violations of the Muslim Uyghur minority in the Xinjian province, and its silencing[131], censoring[132] and mishandling of the Covid-19 outbreak to minimize accountability, the world is rightly wary of trusting China.

Additionally, take currency: Part of America's rise to power was due to the post-WWII Bretton Woods Conference[133] of 1944, in which delegates from around the world agreed that exchange rates would be rooted in gold, with the US dollar being the reserve currency. This rendered the dollar the most important currency in the world, and as a result, the US became the world's foundation for economic stability. China, however, doesn't have the trust[134] that the world showed the US after WWII; the country's persistent straying from Western ideals will keep the world at large from getting too close.

Problems at home

China's current population of over one billion people [135] puts a large strain [136] on its natural resources. Efforts to curb explosive growth – such as the one-child policy[137], which had been in place for over 30 years – have backfired, resulting in an aging population that's predominantly male[138]. Much of China's youth has gone abroad to seek opportunity, and China's labor force is shrinking[139] as a result. While their middle class may be growing rapidly, the income inequality[140] outside of big cities is rampant by unparalleled standards. Until China's demographics are adjusted to reflect a more balanced society across age, genders and socioeconomic status, their rise to superpower status is likely to be nonexistent.

....

The Bottom Line: It's true that China is making great strides towards globalization, with booming technological and economic sectors. Yet its world standing and domestic issues seem to indicate that it still isn't ready for world domination. Would you bet on China as the world's next superpower?

THE PERSPECTIVE ON GUN CONTROL

Original debate written by Rachel Segal

America – land of the free, home of the brave and protector of constitutional rights. The great nation of opportunity, where dreams and guns are both within reach, boasts higher levels of gun ownership than other developed countries. Around 40%[141] of Americans say they or someone in their household owns a gun. During the Covid-19 pandemic, gun sales boomed (for example, sales in May 2020 increased 80%[142] year over year). Research by the Swiss-based Small Arms Survey[143] in 2018 showed that Americans owned 393 million guns[144], both legally and illegally. This means that roughly for every 100 residents in America, there are 120.5 guns. That being said, as the law doesn't allow a country-wide database for people to register the guns they own, there is no official number[145], only those produced by various polls. And yet, in 2020, 20,000 Americans[146] were killed by gun violence.

Here are three arguments in support of gun control laws and three more in support of gun ownership.

Arguments for Gun Control

Gun control laws don't diminish the Second Amendment

Gun control proponents aren't interested in taking away citizens' guns. They cheer the Second Amendment[147], which states: "A well-regulated Militia, being necessary to the security of a free State, the right of the people to keep and bear Arms, shall not be infringed." They support the Supreme Court 2008 decision[148], which validates the interpretation of the amendment that protects an individual's right to own a firearm unrelated to serving in a militia, and to use that arm for lawful purposes, such as self-defense within one's home.

But this same Supreme Court decision also emphasizes that, in former Justice Antonin Scalia's words: The Second Amendment is "not a right to keep and carry any weapon whatsoever in any manner whatsoever and for any purpose whatsoever." Regulating deadly machinery (as we do with cars) is not about denying access but about oversight in the interest of safety for the community at large.

Gun restrictions prevent selling to the wrong hands

If anything, gun restrictions[149] are aimed at making the world safer by limiting guns from getting into the wrong hands. This leads to fewer deaths. Universal background checks[150] on private and gun show sales, an issue that survivors of the February 2018 Parkland massacre helped push legislators[151] to prioritize, can help prevent criminals and the mentally ill from getting guns. Research[152] asserts that federal checks could cut gun deaths by an estimated 90%. And let's not forget about mandatory safety features. Installing safety devices[153] on guns would minimize accidental gun deaths, especially of and by children. Think about it: We have childproof caps on medicine bottles, so why not have childproof firearms?

Such laws help prevent selling the wrong guns

High-capacity magazines enable a shooter to fire multiple times without reloading, turning murderers into mass murderers. An investigation into mass shootings[154] found that high-capacity magazines were used in at least 50% of the 62 mass shootings that were analyzed. For example, the 2018 school shooting in Parkland, Florida[155], saw 17 people dead and 14 wounded, thanks to a semi-automatic AR-15 – a deadly, military-inspired rifle that has been the weapon of choice for many mass shooters. After the deadly mass shooting in Las Vegas[156] in October 2017, the Trump administration banned bump stocks[157], a device that lets semi-automatic rifles function like machine guns.

So, while banning the purchase of such technology, magazines or assault weapons won't prevent gun crime from happening, it will greatly reduce the carnage.

Arguments for Gun Ownership

An enhanced sense of safety

Law enforcement agencies are constantly protecting civilians[158]. Countless policemen[159] have heroically saved others during shootings even at the expense of their own lives. Still, the police can't always protect everyone everywhere all of the time, so firearms significantly contribute to gun owners' sense of – and actual – safety. In a 1982-83 study[160], almost 2000 imprisoned felons in 10 states were surveyed about whether gun control prevented crime. More than half (57%) said that most criminals feared armed citizens more than the police. Additionally, 40% said they were deterred from carrying out their crime when they thought their potential victim was armed. It's no surprise, then, that 57% of people[161] feel that possessing a gun prevents them from being victimized.

Exercises civil liberties

Gun ownership exercises a fundamental individual right under the U.S. Constitution. For most upstanding citizens, owning a gun is as important to them as maintaining freedom of speech, the press, religion, among others. In fact, three quarters of gun owners[162] believe that the right to bear arms is paramount to their freedom. No wonder gun owners take it personally when gun control laws appear to infringe on this right, thus impeding efforts to acquire firearms and protect themselves and their families. Plus, there's the risk that certain proposed background checks may require government databases to keep gun owners' personal information indefinitely. This could lead to future database searches unrelated to the information when it was first collected. This understandably can be perceived as an unfair invasion of privacy.

Unintended consequences of ineffective gun restrictions

When the law meant to protect you, instead, turns you into prey, it's understandable to want to take self-defense into your own hands. In Chicago, where there are bans on assault rifles[163] and high-capacity magazines, and where gun shops were banned until 2012, gun control laws are not proving effective. Though the city has some of the toughest gun restrictions[164] in place, it suffers from rising gun and gang violence[165]. The city's mayor, Lori Lightfoot, is working to increase public safety, but has an uphill battle[166]. Chicago[167] is just one example of many cities where law-abiding citizens are paying the price – with their lives – of ineffective gun control laws.

....

The Bottom Line: Gun control laws keep people safer[168], and self-preservation is why gun owners have guns to begin with. With that, law-abiding gun owners still have the constitutional right to protect themselves against crime and should not be penalized for the actions of others. How would you feel about keeping a gun in your house?

THE PERSPECTIVE ON DONALD TRUMP

Original debate written by Chaya Benymin

Not many presidents in American history have garnered as much attention or generated as many strong opinions amongst the American and global public as former President Donald Trump. After being elected in 2016 and redefining presidential norms during his one term in office, the world is asking whether his legacy lived up to his famous campaign promise to "Make America Great Again."

Below, we'll discuss three ways in which he met the mark, and three ways he fell short of the bar.

Fair Gains

No more bloodshed

The Trump administration's foreign diplomacy advanced peace in many parts of the world. He borrowed a page from Obama's[169] rapprochement playbook and engaged North Korea in talks for the first time in history, emerging with the US-North Korea Singapore Statement[170]. Trump's administration struck a deal with the Taliban[171], bringing the USA's 18-year conflict in Afghanistan, which cost over 2,000 US soldiers their lives and tens of thousands of Afghani casualties, to a close. His work fostering official diplomatic ties[172] between long-time Middle Eastern outsider, Israel, and Arab states, such as the UAE[173], Bahrain and Morocco, in addition to Sudan[174], is the biggest advance for regional peace in the last 25 years.

A man of the people

Trump made the working-class central[175] to his vision for reviving America, and reflected their concerns and experiences back to them, complimenting their value system and its place in American society in clear language[176]. Whereas liberal platforms have tended to focus on issues faced by minorities and marginalized groups, Trump recognized that there is a large contingency of Americans[177] who do not fall within those definitions, whose concerns nevertheless deserve the nation's attention. Whether or not he effectively addressed Middle America's needs, he did something all politicians should do by responding to voices that had fallen by the wayside.

America first

Throughout his one term as president, Trump was true to his promise to ensure that America got the most out of its international partnerships. He sought to fend off the rise of a non-democratic country to global economic supremacy by implementing tariffs and other trade regulations on China[178] and the decline of America's industrial activities by withdrawing from the Trans-Pacific Partnership[179]. He openly questioned the legitimacy of NATO's contribution structure, catalyzing reforms[180] that will see the US shouldering less of the financial and human resource burdens of protecting European member-states. Trump also implemented policies, however controversial, that slowed illegal immigration[181] into America. In being unafraid to reevaluate every contract, even those with longstanding partners, Trump drove the message that America expects fair terms and accountability.

Steep Losses

Virtue matters

The US presidency, morality, and the notion of setting an example are intertwined, by the design of the Founding Fathers. Trump's personal example was hardly virtuous and far from one that children, let alone an entire nation, should emulate. He abandoned duty to country by dodging the Vietnam draft; decades later, in a moment of exceptional insensitivity, he called his efforts to avoid sexually transmitted illnesses his "personal Vietnam." Trump's extramarital exploits and his track-record of misogyny[182] are well-known. For instance, FBI documents suggest that he was actively involved in orchestrating the payment of hush-money to a porn star[183] before the 2016 election. He was also accused of countless shady business dealings, including defrauding innocent Americans through a fake university[184] that bore his name and using his charitable foundation[185] as his personal piggy bank. And he lied during his campaign and term. A lot[186]. In fact, many feel that Trump's lies about the severity of the coronavirus[187] and the effectiveness of masks significantly contributed to the steep American death toll.

What about the little guy?

On the 2016 campaign trail, Trump was the working family's champion, boldly promising to protect their jobs. In reality, the Trump years didn't add prosperity to America's middle- and working classes. Trump's promised punishment for companies offshoring operations never materialized[188]. Despite his pledge to protect blue-collar workers in ailing industries such as coal, the industry is rapidly shrinking[189]. His tax cuts mostly benefited wealthy individuals and corporations[190], who used the breaks to enhance their dividends[191], rather than investing in job creation. It was also revealed that thanks to government loopholes, the billionaire president paid just $750.00 in income tax[192] during his presidency, less than the nation's poorest[193] taxpayers.

America, with a capital 'I'

Trump degraded ties and civility between America's citizenry. In his bid for power, Trump cynically erected a narrative of "two Americas," frequently pitting groups against each other[194] and pandering to anti-social, even violent sectors of his voting base, such as the KKK and the Proud Boys. Trump's offensive on American social cohesion was expressed in the nation's rise in hate crime[195]s, increased participation in anarchist groups, the highest levels of political polarization the US has ever seen, and the wholesale erosion of citizens' trust in each other. This divisiveness culminated after the 2020 election, when Trump refused[196] to accept defeat and subsequently played a large role[197] in encouraging the violent riot that erupted at the US Capitol

Building, which ended in 5 deaths[198], multiple arrests and Trump's historic second impeachment[199].

....

The Bottom Line: Former President Trump's accomplishments are as controversial as his failures, but countless intelligent people standing on both sides of the political divide know that no presidency can be declared "perfection" or "total loss." Where do you see shades of grey? Tell us in the comments.

DO PROTESTS WORK?

Original debate written by Chaya Benyamin

From Ghandi's Salt March to the faceoff at Tiananmen Square[200] to the March for Our Lives[201] protesting America's lack of gun control to the protests in Hong Kong[202] that got the world talking about an extradition bill to the George Floyd protests[203] erupting across America, humanity buzzes with protest movements every year. And while nothing is as captivating as a crowd, especially when the crowd is storming the US Capitol building[204] with lawmakers inside, a comparison of the number of protests held yearly to governmental or society changes suggests that the actual success rate of this cornerstone of non-violent (and sometimes violent[205]) resistance is, in fact, rather low. This begs the question: Do protests work?

Here are three reasons why protests are effective, and three reasons they are not.

Say It Loud, Say It Proud

Protests bring socially and economically marginalized groups to the foreground

Throughout history, coal miners have been unlikely champions of protest movements. As global economies began shifting away from coal, miners suffered from downsizing, colliery closures, and loss of benefits. In the US[206] and UK[207], miners used protests to bring their struggles to the public – and won. In 2016, coal workers of the China's Longmay[208] coal firm prompted the government to admit financial struggles and demand back payment of thousands of workers. The 2011 Occupy Wall Street[209] movement was similarly effective in giving America's lower income bracket a voice, shedding light on the growing chasm between the top 1% of American earners and the rest of the nation. More recently, the nationwide protests across America in response to the murder of George Floyd at the hands of a police officer have brought police brutality and racism[210] into the spotlight, forcing Americans to address the ongoing disparate treatment of African Americans[211], especially by law enforcement.

Protests promote solidarity

Protests are not merely coalitions of the aggrieved, but can be understood as an expression of a shared fate. Protests like the Women's March on Washington[212] and Standing Rock[213], as well as Parkland high schoolers against gun violence[214] and Tea Party[215] protests saw participation by individuals who are not directly affected by the core grievances of women, Native Americans, victims of school shootings and government spending. Why? Because people's identities are governed as much by their values as they are by their color, class, age and education. Case in point: The 2019 protests in Hong Kong against China's encroaching influence inspired solidarity protests[216] in the United States and elsewhere around the world. More recently, people of all races, colors and religions are protesting across America and the world[217] against police brutality and have even come together to protest coronavirus lockdowns[218]. Protests offer the opportunities to use values as their main identifiers, allowing for greater identification across diverse groups. Such intersectionality[219] was seen during the Women's March on Washington, whose expansive platform [220]drew an estimated one million participants[221] from 670 protest events across the country – likely the largest non-violent protest in history[222].

Protests produce results

Protests have been shown to exert influence over politics. Serbians ousted a dictator[223] through nonviolent resistance and Egyptians[224] followed suit ten years later. In recent American politics, the grassroots protests that sprung up at American airports in in reaction to Trump's 2017 executive order barring refugees and citizens of several Muslim-majority countries from entering the US might be credited[225] for prompting swift legal action that allowed many visa-holders to remain in the country. Also, in 2018, teachers throughout West Virginia went on strike during a nine-day protest that resulted in, among other demands[226], a 5% increase in pay – not to mention inspiring additional teacher strikes[227] in other states. It may be too soon to tell the final outcome, but the teenage survivors of the Parkland high school shooting in 2018 created a national discussion and movement[228] that is holding government officials and businesses[229] accountable when it comes to measures that would increase responsible gun control.

Don't Waste Your Energy
Protests hardly ever achieve their ends

Protests aren't as effective as demonstrators like to think. Thousands of protests[230] are constantly taking place around the world. While the George Floyd protests across America[231] and the world[232] may have changed how Americans view each other and how the world views America[233], most protest efforts pass without remark, revealing the miniscule impact[234] of protests in general. Though the mob of pro-Trump protestors that stormed the US Capitol building[235] in an attempt to overturn the 2020 presidential election results drew the world's attention (and condemnation[236]), it did not succeed in meeting its aims; the constitutional ceremony to certify the election results was interrupted, but Joe Biden's presidential victory has been confirmed[237].

A Princeton study[238] found that public opinion hardly comes to bear on legislation, and the results of most protests confirm this. The anti-war movement against US military involvement in Vietnam that was popularized on college campuses[239] in 1965 had no effect[240] on war activities, which,e in fact, ramped up[241] until the war's end in 1973. Protests in the US and the UK[242] against the Iraq war did nothing to curb the invasion. The Women's Day March of 2016 was even confronted by results that ran counter to their goal of ensuring reproductive rights for women worldwide. Just two days after the protest, former President Trump signed an executive order[243] stripping US aid from foreign institutions that offer abortion services, and further rollbacks on reproductive rights [244]in the foreign and domestic arena continue.

Protests alone do not achieve change

Dr. Martin Luther King's "I Have a Dream" speech bookended the Civil Rights Movement[245]'s march on Washington, yet the march itself cannot be credited for the civil rights legislation that followed it. Protest was just one part of a layered nonviolent resistance[246] tactic employed by the movement for a decade before any legislation was signed. Protests can win exposure for a cause, but they do not fight legal battles that make change possible. Consider the 2016 Standing Rock protest[247] against the Dakota Access Pipeline. While media attention may have hastened legal decisions on the matter of building on Sioux lands, the final battle was ultimately decided in the Oval Office [248]and in the courtroom, and the protest lines[249] were swiftly shut down. Additionally, the Hong Kong protest movement[250], which grabbed the world's attention in 2019 as it pushed back against the Chinese government, has since fizzled out [251]as it has become evident that it lacks options and opportunities for keeping China's government at arm's length.

Protests are win-lose propositions that highlight ideological differences and sow discord

The ethos of protest is rooted in conflict[252], not conflict resolution – resistance, even nonviolent resistance, is an act of war intended to change a political reality. To many, protest rhetoric is more about preaching to the choir than it is about changing hearts and minds. The one-voice-no-debate approach may be perceived as a zero-sum game that pits protesters against their environment, and to an extent, against anyone who is not protesting. This charged atmosphere often leads to violence that proves counterproductive to protest goals[253]. Look no further than the pro-Trump protesters who violently overran[254] the US Congress. For an older example, Antifa[255] protestors and their embrace of violence [256]tend to undermine their aims of fighting against fascism. This light being shone on the (mis)actions of the extreme left lessens the focus on or impact of the extreme right, and widens national discord[257], as was shown after Charlottesville[258] in 2017.

The Bottom Line: While protests can do much to direct attention toward controversial issues[259], attention is not necessarily all that is required to effect change. Do you believe that protests lead to change?

AMERICA FIRST? SHOULD THE US INTERVENE MILITARILY IN FOREIGN CONFLICTS?

Original debate written by Andrew Vitelli

The debate over when the US should intervene militarily in foreign countries dates back more than a century, and the US will have to confront this question as long as it remains a world superpower. In 2016, President Trump was elected, in part, on his promise to avoid military engagements overseas. But evidently, it was virtually impossible not to engage. Indeed, his foreign policy[260] over the years shows – with strikes against the Assad regime in Syria, tensions that gave way to talks[261] over North Korea's nuclear program, increased US troops[262] in Afghanistan in 2017 and military confrontation with Iran[263] – that isolationism is not necessarily possible. Meanwhile, Biden's withdrawal of troops from Afghanistan[264] by September 11, 2021, has been met with criticism.

Here are three reasons for intervention abroad and three against, focusing on cases in which there is no direct and immediate threat to US security.

The US Should Not Get Involved in Foreign Countries

Intervention rarely benefits the US

The last large-scale US intervention came in 2003, when American forces overthrew the Saddam Hussein[265] regime in Iraq and began an eight-year occupation. That war alone cost the US more than $2 trillion[266] and the lives of nearly 4,500 American soldiers. It's been estimated that since 2001,

America's post-9/11 wars and military action in the Middle East and Asia have totaled $6.4 trillion[267], a number that will surely grow.

When it comes to American wars of choice, the Iraq experience is no outlier. Though the US is capable of defeating any enemy, the cost of doing so in both human lives and money is usually far greater than anticipated. Wars like Iraq and Vietnam[268], the latter of which saw nearly 60,000 American soldiers killed, are a case in point. But even smaller-scale interventions, like President Clinton's 1993 mission in Somalia[269] or the overthrow of Libyan dictator Moammar Gaddafi in 2011, have had unintended consequences[270]. (And let's not forget that Americans paid higher gas prices[271] after airstrikes killed Iran's top military commander at the beginning of 2020.)

When core US interests, such as the security of its citizens, are at stake, Americans may have no choice but to bear these consequences. But more often, the consequences of military action outweigh the benefits.

It rarely benefits the country of the intervention

From the invasion of Hawaii[272] in 1893 to the bombing of Syria in 2017[273], it is the norm for US intervention to be justified on humanitarian grounds. In some cases, this may truly be the motive. Case in point, punishing the Assad regime for its use of chemical weapons[274] against civilians. But rarely does military action improve the lives of ordinary citizens.

The US mission in Libya was aimed at stopping a civilian massacre by the government. It may have done just that, but Gaddafi's death[275] in 2011 led to civil war and chaos[276] in the country, with ISIS gaining[277] a foothold. Post-occupation Iraq looks no better, while Afghanistan remains unstable 19 years after the US invasion[278]. And if we go back a generation, wars in Southeast Asia devastated the region while bringing little benefit to its people.

America should not be the world's police

Beyond weighing the pros and cons of each intervention, supporters of US action overseas must answer a broader question: When does a country have the right to intervene[279] in another country?

The UN Charter, signed after World War II, requires authorization from the UN Security Council[280] to use force. Respecting an internationalized body's authority to decide on such issues is preferable to allowing any one country to act alone. Also, American foreign adventures make it more difficult for the US to criticize aggression by other powers, such as Russia's invasions of Crimea[281] and Georgia[282] over the past decade or Iran's involvement in Syria[283] and Lebanon[284].

America Can Be a Force for Good

Inaction also has consequences

Too often, US military action is judged against a perfect alternative. Yet, while intervention has its drawbacks and complications, failing to act often carries an even steeper price.

Avoiding confrontation sometimes puts American citizens at risk. President Clinton had the chance to kill[285] Osama bin Laden several times but did not pull the trigger. A strike that killed al-Qaeda's leader but resulted in civilian casualties may have earned criticism – indeed, it may have ended up in the other half of this column – but it could have prevented[286] the 3,000 lives lost on 9/11 and avoided a wider war in Afghanistan.

Then there are the humanitarian costs of inaction. Clinton called his failure to stop the genocide in Rwanda, where 800,000 people were killed in just two months, one of his biggest regrets[287]. And what do Presidents Obama and Trump think about Syria, where around half a million people [288]have been killed since the civil war began in 2011?

Intervention sometimes helps

Opponents of US intervention often point to cases in which American forces arguably made the situation worse. But Americans have also fought to prevent genocides, dethrone brutal dictators and uphold global norms, not to mention the crucial role[289] in defeating the Nazis in World War II.

In 1991, Operation Desert Storm [290]prevented Saddam's permanent annexation of Kuwait, an act that otherwise would have encouraged any dictator to snatch up smaller neighbors without fear of consequence. In 1995, NATO's campaign in Bosnia following massacres in Srebrenica and Markale brought Bosnian Serbs to the negotiating table[291], leading to the

Dayton Peace Accord. US forces left a decade later, without a single American killed by enemy fire.

The alternative is worse

It may be nice to imagine a world in which differences between nations are resolved only through diplomacy. But were the US to take a step down from the international stage, it would not be the UN that would fill the void. Russia and China, both countries less committed to democratic ideals[292] than the US, would step in – as Russia is said to be doing in the Middle East[293]. We need only to look back at the last time another superpower – the Soviet Union – challenged the US for global supremacy; only because of US protection was Western Europe able to thrive without falling to the grasp of Soviet rule. Meanwhile, regional hegemons like Iran[294] would be free to impose their will on smaller nations without the credible threat of sanctions[295] and force[296] from the US.

....

The Bottom Line: US intervention overseas is never ideal and rarely uncomplicated, but the alternatives could potentially be worse. If you had the job and were facing the current threats from North Korea, Syria and Iran[297], what would you do?

THE PERSPECTIVE ON PUTIN

Original debate written by Kira Goldring

Vladimir Putin has been Russia's dominant political leader since the turn of the millennia, and since his 2018 re-election secured a fourth six-year term, he's shown no signs of slowing down. This may be changing, evidenced by his United Russia party losing a third of its seats[298] in recent Moscow legislative elections. Having been referred to as the world's most powerful person[299], Putin has certainly earned a reputation for himself – but is it a good one?

Below, we'll explore three reasons that support the image of Putin as a positive political leader, and three reasons claiming that his actions in office have been questionable thus far.

Putin Has Been a Positive Influence

He established order in an unstable region

After the fall of the Soviet Union, what Russia needed most was stability and security. Putin stepped in, raised a shaky country off its feet, and got it to stand on solid ground. During his first two terms as president, Russia's GDP increased by 70%, and investments rose by 125%[300]. His many domestic reforms – such as tax cuts and expansion of property rights[301] – further provided Russia with the stability it was looking for. Aside from giving his people someone to believe in, he made active changes that resulted in a much stronger, secure country than had been for decades.

He is a beloved leader

Putin has been voted into office as President again and again[302]. He exceeded expectations by winning 73% of the vote[303] in the 2018 elections, surpassing the 65% voter turnout in his 2012 victory. Although the numbers have fluctuated[304] throughout his presidency, 2021 approval ratings showed that 65% of Russians[305] have confidence in Putin's ability to do the right thing with regards to world affairs. This has even proved true through times of war, with 94% of Russians [306]having supported the 2014 annexation of Crimea. They similarly supported the war with Chechnya[307], which occurred when Putin was still establishing himself as president.

According to his predecessor, Boris Yeltsin[308], the public's confidence in Putin was because "people believed that he, personally, could protect them." A recent #superputin exhibition[309] in Moscow, which portrayed Putin as a superhero[310], only further emphasizes the admiration the Russian people have maintained for their country and leader.

He sticks to his guns

It's clear that Putin refuses to be bullied[311]. He stands up to Western hegemony[312], as evidenced by his decision to annex Crimea[313] against Western wishes. Even after being hit with economic sanctions[314], he didn't back down. Such sanctions fueled nationalistic pride[315], and Putin seems to be putting Russian interest at the forefront of his decisions, regardless of whom he aggravates in the process. In fact, to emphasize his theme of putting Russia – and its security – first, no matter the consequences, the 2018 Election Day was moved to March 18[316], the fourth anniversary of Russia's seizure of Crimea. Although it may be infuriating for other world powers, this refusal to be intimidated is arguably an important quality for a country of millions to see in their leader, and has elevated Russia's status[317] in the world order.

Putin Is on a Power Trip

His character is shady

As a former member of the KGB, Putin still shrouds parts of himself in secrecy[318], and has done a number of questionable-bordering-illicit things. Though not from former President Trump[319], Putin is facing accusations[320] over meddling in the U.S. elections[321], and he's previously been voted "Person of the Year" by the Organized Crime and Corruption Project[322], due to his alleged engagement with the mafia to launder money and promote interests abroad[323]. Additionally, suspicious deaths[324] seem to happen to people who oppose Putin or try to expose political corruption. Such an incident in 2018 involved the poisoning of a Russian ex-spy and his daughter[325] in England, while opposition leader Alexey Navalny's August 2020 poisoning has likewise been attributed to Russia[326]. Meanwhile, thanks to economic sanctions and too much faith in oil, millions of Russians[327] are living below the poverty line, while Putin may be the richest man in the world[328], with an estimated net worth of $200 billion. What kind of leader is rolling in such dough when the people who follow him have trouble affording bread[329]?

Russia needs help at home

While a powerful player in the world game, Putin is lacking when it comes to managing Russia's current domestic affairs. For example, the current average life expectancy for men in Russia is only 66.5 years. While this is a record high[330], it fuels the need for more social protection for older adults[331]. There is reportedly poor quality of air and water in many areas, hurting the overall health of the nation, with limited resources allocated to preventative healthcare. Also, the country's economy is largely dependent on the price of oil – which is dangerous given the falling oil prices – and they manufacture little outside of gas and guns. While support for Putin may be high at home, it doesn't mean he's giving his people what they need.

More a corrupt czar than a democratically elected president

Politically, Putin's tactics to mitigate the opposition's chances in recent municipal elections in Moscow have prompted allegations against him of corrupting democracy[332], and not for the first time. As one way to retain a tight grip on power, Putin has long been accused of employing a campaign of intimidation[333] against activists who oppose his politics and policies, such as lawyer Lyubov Sobol, or the aforementioned Skripal and Navalny. Journalists[334] have regularly been jailed to be silenced, and, under Putin, the press is anything but free. Putin also makes use of the systems at his service to extend his tenure[335]; in 2020 he proposed constitutional reforms to limit a president to serving two terms (which had already been extended from four to six years) – so long as the term count begins now – meaning that Putin, already in power for two decades, could conceivably rule Russia until 2036.

....

The Bottom Line: Popular among many of his own people and frightening to almost everyone else, Putin is both respected and suspicious in his political and personal dealings. What do you think? Has Putin been a good world leader, or is he just another corrupt politician?

SHOULD 'BLACK LIVES MATTER' FIGHT FOR ALL LIVES?

Original debate written by Talia Klein Perez

As the George Floyd protests[336] in the US sparked a continuing nationwide[337] effort[338] to protest police brutality and racial inequality, Black Lives Matter[339] (BLM) has taken center stage. In fact, some call it the largest movement in US history[340]. However, long before this current social awakening, social media networks were full of hashtag battles between #BlackLivesMatter and the #AllLivesMatter response. Strong opinions on both sides insist that they are fighting for justice and human dignity.

Here, we'll take a look at both sides of the debate, asking whether it is effective for the BLM movement to protest only for Black Lives, or if the call for justice should instead be All Lives Matter.

Three Reasons Why Black Lives Matter Should Focus Only on Black Lives

Black Americans shouldn't be expected to speak on behalf of other people of color

Every minority has its own unique experience of marginalization, exclusion and abuse that differs from one group to the next. Because the prejudice and racism suffered by each minority takes a different form, it is unrealistic and unfair[341] to both Black Americans and other American minorities to expect that the BLM movement speak for everyone. BLM activists know the experience of living as Black people in America, especially regarding issues of police brutality[342]; therefore, it is not[343] the role of BLM to speak for Latin-Americans, Asian-Americans or Hispanic Americans. Moreover, saying that all lives matter can be seen as downplaying the racism[344] specifically targeted at Black Americans or shifting attention away from them to other groups. Why take the microphone away from BLM activists when doing so can be interpreted as a form of silencing[345]?

Fighting for the cause that matters most to you doesn't undermine other causes

There are many causes to fight for in the world. It is natural for each of us to feel the most passionate about whatever cause hits closest to home. The recent George Floyd protests have put the spotlight on discussions regarding systemic racism[346] in America toward Black people. BLM's overwhelming desire to save Black families from abuse, inequality and murder (especially of unarmed victims, like Trayvon Martin[347], Breonna Taylor[348], or Ahmaud Arbery[349] – not to mention George Floyd[350]) lends power to the cause, which we cannot expect to feel equally for any other. The BLM's focus on Black Lives does not undermine the worthiness of any other minority's fight against racism or of any other social justice issue; it merely indicates that this is the primary issue right now.

It extends privilege to other groups at the expense of Black Americans

Although everyone on both sides agrees that all lives matter, the "All Lives Matter[351]" slogan is frequently used to hijack and undermine the BLM message in favor of other people. When a #BlueLivesMatter hashtag was added to support policemen, it was used to oppose #BlackLivesMatter." This was further shown in 2016 when 10,000 people[352] protested in support of Peter Liang, a Chinese-American policeman who was jailed for killing Akai Gurley, an unarmed Black man. Many of Liang's supporters shouted, "All Lives Matter," claiming that he was a scapegoat because he was not white and that he should not be jailed. However, Black activists pointed out that Liang was tried by a jury of his peers and deserved to be jailed for his actions. Using "All Lives Matter" to demand freedom for someone who was convicted of murdering an unarmed Black man is nothing more than demanding that white privilege be extended to all people of color except for Black Americans.

Three Reasons Why All Lives Matter Is a Better Call to Arms

It recognizes the persecution of other minorities

Black Americans are not the only minority group to suffer discrimination. The slogan "Black Lives Matter" ignores the way that the lives of other minorities have also been treated as cheap and unimportant over the centuries. By shouting "Jews will not replace us" at the 2017 Neo-Nazi march[353] in Charlotteville, racists and fascists showed that they don't distinguish between minorities. It is adding insult to injury to single out only one minority as deserving of protests, rallies and hashtags of support. Furthermore, there is a better chance of succeeding in the overall fight against racism if anti-racist activists can bring a unified voice, resources and action to the struggle.

It focuses attention on the problem of white privilege

White privilege[354] is not only a problem because it discriminates against Blacks but because it discriminates against anyone who is not a white heterosexual male. Shouting "Black Lives Matter" could move the focus away from dealing with white privilege as a source of social inequality. Because the hashtag seems to reiterate that what matters are Black lives, it risks shining the spotlight on only one small aspect of a much bigger issue. The "All Lives Matter" motto can serve as an umbrella slogan that opposes restricting privilege to just one group, instead of potentially implying that the problem could be solved if only Black Americans were included in the said privilege.

#BlackLivesMatter can hurt the cause

When Martin Luther King Jr[355]. led the Civil Rights movement in the 1960s he called for equal rights for everyone[356]. All Lives Matter promotes this message of shared humanity. In contrast, Black Lives Matter seems to imply that Black Lives may matter more than those of other lives. It could even create more harm than good by giving the impression that to Black activists, non-Black lives matter less. Politics have also become entwined in the movement, distracting from its cause. For instance, some BLM activists have been accused of espousing anti-Semitic sentiments[357] in the media and/or on social media, [358]instead of speaking up for Black civil liberties. If the BLM were to embrace the #AllLivesMatter slogan, it would show that they care for all minorities, who would then be less cautious about embracing their cause.

....

The Bottom Line: The Civil Rights Movement of the 1960s was both smart and just, and it was successful in its struggle, though the work is far from being done, as civil rights leader John Lewis[359] eloquently said before he died. It remains to be seen which is the best path for change in 2020. Which concept do you think is more effective, Black Lives Matter or All Lives Matter?

THE PERSPECTIVE ON SINGLE-PAYER HEALTH CARE

Original debate written by Andrew Vitelli

Since the 2016 US presidential election, single-payer health care has moved from a fringe position into the mainstream[360]. A single-payer plan, sometimes summarized as "Medicare for all," entails the government providing every citizen with health insurance, which is paid for through taxes. During the 2018 midterm elections[361], health care became a central issue. While existing US policy sees the government providing health care to the elderly and the poor, with a patchwork of subsidies and tax benefits helping to cover the remaining citizens, even the value[362] of that is not unanimously agreed upon.

Can single-payer health care work in the United States, or would it cost too much while limiting consumer choice? We take a look at three arguments for each side of the debate.

Pro Single-Payer

It will help the middle class and entrepreneurs

While everyone stands to benefit from a more efficient health care system, the groups that may gain the most are the middle class and small business owners and workers. The current system provides government-sponsored health care for the poor and elderly through Medicare and Medicaid[363]. Meanwhile, most workers in large corporations receive health care as part of their compensation[364] as required under Obamacare[365]. The people left behind are those between jobs, those working for small businesses and those looking to start or grow their own small business.

Government-provided health care would make it easier for entrepreneurs to leave their jobs and start their own businesses, since they would not be putting their families' health care at risk. It would make it easier to hire workers early on, since employees would be more willing to take a risk working at a new firm knowing that health care is provided. And if the business takes off, it would no longer face the threat of the employer mandate[366] once it crosses a certain threshold, which Obamacare set at 50 workers.

It will save money

Americans are paying more than other developed countries for their health care. Let's look at Canada,[367] France, Sweden and Switzerland, for example. These are all countries that have a similar GDP per capita to the US but offer single-payer health care systems. According to OECD data[368], these countries spent between 10 and 12 percent of their GDP on health care costs compared to a whopping 17 percent of the United States' GDP. There are several reasons for this. Cutting the massive administrative costs associated with private health care, for example, would reduce overall health care spending by around 15 percent, according to one study[369].

It will produce better results

Compared to other countries, Americans are paying the most for their health care, yet their investment is not paying off. Study after study[370] shows that Americans achieve worse health results than their peers in the developing world. A report[371] published in the summer of 2017 compared the US with 11 similar countries and found that it fared the worst[372] of the bunch. On access to care, equity and health care outcomes, the US ranked last, while only France was worse in administrative efficiency. Meanwhile, if Americans had been guaranteed healthcare in time for the coronavirus pandemic, this may well have improved health outcomes by removing barriers to testing and treatment.[373]

At 77.9 years, US life expectancy is near the bottom[374] of the OECD, behind poorer countries such as Chile. Nearly every developed country has some form of universal health care. In the OECD, only the US and

Mexico[375], one of the group's poorest nations, fall short. From Israel to Australia to the UK, wealthy nations outside the US have embraced the single-payer system and have seen better results. Not to mention that Obamacare also guarantees coverage for people with pre-existing medical conditions[376].

Single-Payer Is Not Feasible

It means long wait times, worse care

Sure, it may be nice to envision single-payer health care as a means to ensure that care is available to everyone. The problem, as Canadians can attest, is that, in practice, it can mean that while more citizens are covered[377], their standard of care is lower. Under the Canadian system, a typical patient can expect to wait 20 weeks[378] after seeing a doctor to begin treatment with a specialist. As imperfect as the US health system is, American patients rarely[379] see wait times this long. Too often these delays can mean the difference between life and death. Perhaps that is why many Canadians end up crossing the border[380] for US medical treatment. In this sense, the quality of healthcare in the US surpasses[381] that of Canada and Western Europe.

The private market drives innovation

America's profit-driven health care market has its flaws, but it has also contributed to making the US the most innovative country in the world in the field of medicine. In the last 10 years, nearly half of the winners[382] of the Nobel Prize in Physiology or Medicine have hailed from the US, a far higher rate than any other country. This trend dates back decades[383] and Nobel Prizes are just one measurement. In 2009, 40 percent of articles[384] published in biomedical journals came from the US, three times as many as its nearest competitor. And more than 40 percent of new drugs[385] are developed in America. Were the US to abandon its private sector model, the country and the wider world would lose out on this innovation.

It is unaffordable

Americans may be willing to spend a little more money for the security of knowing they would receive quality healthcare. According to some estimates[386], the costs of enacting a single-payer system, though, would not just be high. They would be astronomical. Examining a past proposal by Senator Bernie Sanders, the non-partisan Urban Institute found that it would increase spending by $32 trillion over 10 years[387]. The Committee for a Responsible Federal Budget pegged the number even higher[388]. According to the Washington Post[389], such a spending hike would require "a tax increase so huge that even the democratic socialist Mr. Sanders did not propose anything close to it." The only way to square his proposal, as New York Times columnist Paul Krugman noted, was with a "huge magic asterisk.[390]"

The Bottom Line: Single-payer health care in the US would require an increase in government spending but would allow for wider coverage across the population. Would the quality of care decrease, and if so, is that a worthwhile trade-off to ensure everyone is covered? What do you think?

SHOULD THE FIRST AMENDMENT COVER RACISM AND HATE SPEECH?

Original debate written by Talia Klein Perez

In an era of racial tension[391], when the nomination of the first woman of color to the office of vice president elicits hate-filled and sexist statements[392] from others on news outlets and social media, one has to wonder where the First Amendment comes into play. While it legally protects the freedom of religion, speech, press, petition, and assembly, can it be interpreted to include racism and hate speech as well? Or, should the First Amendment be understood as protecting Americans' rights to speak and act, but within boundaries, which leaves racism and hate speech out of its protection?

Let's examine why the First Amendment should and should not be interpreted to include racism and hate speech.

Racism and Hate Speech Should Be Understood as Protected by the First Amendment

Who draws the line?

If all speech is protected by the First Amendment, then there is less room for government restrictions. On the other hand, if we allow the government to regulate free speech, then we open the door for greater government involvement in every aspect of our lives. This, much like McCarthyism, which sought to eradicate values viewed as a threat to the American way of life, could wind up as a grandiose witch hunt and likely hurt America in the long run.

Moreover, a democracy is not measured by its mainstream, law-abiding citizens. A democracy allows people to go against its modes and norms. When we shut down what we are not comfortable hearing, that's a dictatorship[393].

Why bother defending something indefensible?

It's hard to stand up and defend[394] the morally repugnant expressions of racists and haters. In certain circumstances, it is pretty clear that what extremists[395] are doing or saying is wrong. However, outlawing the rhetoric does not change the way people think. A look beyond the law is needed, and measures such as raising awareness[396] and launching education[397] programs and changing policy should be taken to root out hate and teach tolerance.

Inciting a call to civil war

The First Amendment, as it is understood today, protects people's right to say what they want[398], not do what they want. Free speech does not absolve people from responsibility for their actions. Aristotle believed that the law binds men together into a "cohesive and just community."[399] However, in today's more Libertarian America, the law must be upheld as is to keep minimal order, without inciting more hatred and aggression. It is not unthinkable to assume that banning some voices by law would just make those voices fester in darkness, rather than disappear. Every action has a re-action, and excluding extreme voices might push people to a bigger clash[400] than the one we are seeing.

Racism and Hate Speech Should Not Be Protected by the First Amendment

The First Amendment should protect all

The U.S. Constitution aims to shape the American nation and give it character. It is the everlasting written spirit of the United States. Let's look at the Founding Fathers, however questionable[401] their personal lives and decisions were back then. Did they think that racism should be included in the Constitution? It's fairly evident that the answer is no. The First Amendment is not so much about speech as it is meant to ensure that everyone inhabiting

America feels safe and can express themselves. American ethos is that of a melting pot and being multiracial is one of its core features[402]. As such, honoring the First Amendment and the Founding Fathers' decrees means disavowing racism in all of its forms.

Words hurt – and infringe on our right to safety

Those who commit criminal acts are tried and sentenced. In addition, those who commit racist and hateful acts or articulate slurs should be punished as well. Hate speech is violent by nature and can cause direct and indirect[403] physical and psychological harm. Professor Lisa Feldman Barrett of Northeastern University took a scientific approach to understanding how hate speech affects the human brain. She explained that[404] "if words can cause stress, and if prolonged stress can cause physical harm, then certain types of speech can be a form of violence."

Words also create an atmosphere that incites physical harm, as evidenced in the systematic murdering of millions at the hands of the Nazis, made possible after propaganda[405] laid the groundwork of hate. Some offensive remarks may seem harmless, but they can snowball into more volatile forms. Once speech reaches an extreme, it becomes too late to avoid its dangerous consequences.

A red line must be drawn for hateful speech and conduct

The purpose of law is not just to regulate bureaucracies, but also to establish common norms and values. On a dynamic issue such as free speech, where different interpretations have far-reaching implications on character and on the safety of its citizens, the law needs to take a stand. The government needs to draw a red line on principle against hatred and intolerance. The "value-neutral state," i.e., a country which does not take a stand, as described by Jeremy Waldron in his influential book[406], is detrimental. If America is to remain the prosperous leader of the free world, tolerance, freedom and respect must be distinguished from hatred, racism and acts of violence.

The Bottom Line: Excluding racism and hate speech from the free speech protected under the First Amendment of the US Constitution could cause the government to cross a line, and may actually incite more racism and hate. However, the Founding Fathers would have wanted *everyone* to be protected under this Amendment, and hate speech is threatening to people's safety. How do you see it?

SHOULD PUERTO RICO BECOME THE 51ST STATE?

Original debate written by Talia Klein Perez

Puerto Rico became a U.S. territory in 1898[407] as a result of the Spanish-American War, and thanks to the Jones Act of 1917[408], babies born in Puerto Rico are automatically granted U.S. citizenship. Yet despite their citizenship, which enables them to serve in the American Army, Puerto Ricans are limited in the benefits they receive as U.S. citizens. They receive limited federal funding and are unable to vote in U.S. federal elections. It's long been asked why Puerto Rico shouldn't become a U.S. state. This question becomes increasingly poignant following natural disasters[409] and the consequent bipartisan disagreements[410] over how much relief funding[411] should be allocated to the territory.

Here are three reasons why Puerto Rico should become the 51st U.S. state and three reasons why it shouldn't.

Three Reasons Puerto Rico Should Become the 51st State

Puerto Ricans would live better, on their own turf, a win-win for all

The current situation is holding Puerto Ricans back. As of 2021, Puerto Rico's unemployment rate rested at 8.8%.[412] Before Hurricane Maria hit Puerto Rico in September 2017, an estimated 46% of Puerto Ricans[413] were living below the poverty line; in addition, the number of Puerto Ricans who immigrated to mainland U.S. increased by a third[414] in 2018. Those leaving over the past decade are in search of better employment opportunities[415].

In becoming a U.S. state, Puerto Ricans could enjoy both the benefits associated with statehood[416] and the tools needed to develop their own industry and workforce on the island. Statehood would increase local job opportunities[417], bring about income creation benefits and enable locals to receive better health care[418], which they are already paying for, but do not currently benefit from. What's more, with Puerto Ricans enjoying statehood benefits from the comfort of their own homes, they would be able to pursue – and live – the American Dream in their own country.

Puerto Ricans deserve a say in the laws that affect them

If, according to American history, "all men are equal in the eyes of the law," then why don't Puerto Ricans have equal say in the laws they must uphold? The U.S. currently controls[419] Puerto Rico's external affairs and federal regulations, yet Puerto Ricans are ineligible to vote[420] in the U.S. presidential elections and have only one non-voting representative in the House. With almost three million citizens[421] living in Puerto Rico, U.S. statehood would enable Puerto Ricans to be represented by two Senators. They would also be allowed to vote in U.S. federal elections and on issues, bills and reforms that affect them.

The U.S. would be able to fight tax evasion more effectively

The United States does not require any federal income tax[422] from U.S. citizens who are residents of Puerto Rico and profit from the island's sources. Adding Puerto Rico to the U.S. state register would require these citizens residing and working in Puerto Rico to pay federal income taxes[423], significantly boosting the Federal Reserve's annual revenues. This would also mean that American companies would no longer be able to move their businesses offshore[424] to Puerto Rico to evade taxes[425], a current and significant problem in the U.S. Making Puerto Rico a state would limit accessible corporate corruption channels significantly. It might also make it easier to oversee and/or control how U.S. government funds are actually being utilized there and could prevent local government corruption[426].

Three Reasons Puerto Rico Should Not Become a U.S. State

Many Puerto Ricans don't really want statehood

Despite the pro-statehood vote[427] in the November 2020 referendum, Puerto Ricans have to wait indefinitely for Congress to actually do anything about it.[428] Meanwhile, many citizens are concerned about their rights and independence as a U.S. state. They do not want to lose their unique cultural [429]heritage and Spanish language, with more in common with Latin America than the U.S. Puerto Ricans are also concerned that they will lose their international standings, including their recognition as an individual Olympic team or participant in world pageants and competitions if they become a U.S. state.

The U.S. would inherit Puerto Rico's debt

The Commonwealth filed for bankruptcy[430] in May 2017 and is still in the process of reaching a deal with creditors[431]. However, since Puerto Rico is not currently a U.S. state, it is unable to access Chapter 9 of the U.S. Bankruptcy Code[432], when it falls on financial hardship. What's more, even if Puerto Rico could access these rights, the island's $49 billion[433] of unfunded pension liabilities and $74 billion[434] debt, held by the territory's government as well as by local public corporations, is so great that they would only be able to cover one-third of the accrued debt. If granted statehood, the U.S. would inherit this debt. The question is, can the U.S. cope with the challenges that making Puerto Rico a state would impose, or would America drown in the process? Having been hit hard by the economic downturn, Puerto Rico might just be considered too much of a burden[435] on the U.S. national treasury.

The aftermath[436] of Hurricane Maria brings up another serious aspect to consider. If Puerto Rico becomes a U.S. state, it would require a lot of money and resources from FEMA every time a natural disaster occurs. Due to hurricanes Harvey, Irma and Florence, FEMA is already stretched too thin, and several communities within the U.S. are still awaiting assistance. Adding Puerto Rico to the mix would cause much-needed federal funding to be directed away from other U.S. states, at a time where natural disasters are on the rise[437] in America. Plus, worrying about non-U.S. states in times of tragedy and stress can contribute to a growing partisan divide, not to mention international fallouts[438], which distract[439] government officials from focusing on core issues and those in need.

Forget statehood, Puerto Rico should be fully independent

Puerto Rico should not be the 51st U.S. state but, rather, a fully independent[440] country. As already discussed, because Puerto Rico is a U.S. colony, it is dependent on *and* constrained by U.S. federal regulations and laws. Transitioning into independence would let Puerto Rico address its debt crisis on its own terms and grant its inhabitants the right to self-determination. Doing so would give more power to the people, as they would be able to hold accountable elected representatives at all levels of government. This constant state of limbo is eroding Puerto Rico's ability to stand on its own feet, as many other nations have successfully done.

....

The Bottom Line: Puerto Rico becoming a U.S state could potentially provide an impoverished island with a fighting chance at equality, but at hefty costs to local industry and U.S. funds. Do you think Puerto Rico should become America's 51st state?

THE PERSPECTIVE ON GERRYMANDERING

Original debate written by Kira Goldring

An age-old practice, gerrymandering[441] is the manipulation of political elections through redrawing the boundaries of a district to favor one political party over another. This way, a district includes either more or less of the people who traditionally vote a certain way. Both Republicans and Democrats have used gerrymandering to their advantage in the past and present, but many see it as a form of voter suppression[442], and the issue has even made its way to the Supreme Court[443]. But the question stands: Is gerrymandering a threat to America's democracy?

Below are three reasons it's okay to continue the practice of gerrymandering, and three reasons it should be eliminated from the political system.

Eliminate Gerrymandering

Inaccurate representation

Redistricting often misrepresents the political leanings of the people living in the districts being reorganized. Take swing-state North Carolina, which narrowly leaned in favor of Donald Trump as president despite electing a Democratic governor in 2016. North Carolina is a "purple" state (i.e., a state with a nearly equal amount of Republican and Democrat voters), yet while Democrats won 49% of state House votes[444] in 2019, they only took 42.5% of its seats. For the first time in history, a federal court wet its feet in the gerrymandering issue and ruled the state's redistricting plan unconstitutional in that it unduly favored one party over another. As long as redistricting continues to disproportionately favor one party, a large percentage of voters won't have their political interests appropriately represented.

Non-democratic

A strong democracy should not allow for partisan abuses of election rules, yet gerrymandering does just that. A recent study[445] suggests that the practice has increasingly affected election cycle's results, culminating in 16-17 seats in Congress that are thanks to gerrymandering alone. Gerrymandered districts allow for elected officials to choose their constituents[446], rather than giving voters the basic right to appoint their own representatives. If America is to call itself a true democracy, then the vote needs to be brought back to the citizens. Gerrymandering warrants the same kind of checks and balances that have been established to keep America's government from veering from democracy in the first place.

Redistricting should be neutral

A recent poll[447] gauging the American attitude toward redrawing Congressional districts found 85% of responders in favor of using a non-partisan commission to do so. As they stand now, many states' elections are biased in favor of the dominant political parties, thanks to said parties' ability to waste the votes of the opposing party. California, the current gold standard of redistricting, gave the job to its non-partisan citizens[448] rather than the state Legislature in 2008; this generated many more competitive districts in the area and incorporated public feedback into every aspect of the district maps. More states should follow in California's lead – as the experts say[449]: The more independent the body, the better the result.

Keep Gerrymandering Around

The big sort

Opponents of gerrymandering often cite the practice as the reason there is a lack of competition in the political system. Yet, there is another factor that plays a much bigger role: Bill Bishop recognized the phenomenon of Americans self-segregating into politically like-minded communities, coining the term "The Big Sort.[450]" This describes how Democrats tend to move into cities[451], while Republicans gravitate more towards rural communities, making it more difficult[452] to draw competitive districts. Whether or not this is a favorable practice, studies show that voters are actually physically sorting themselves; in other words, we are doing the partisan gerrymandering on our own, before political parties even have to.

Neither side suffers

There is a reason that the Supreme Court avoids[453] tackling cases of partisan gerrymandering; it aids both Republicans and Democrats, and preserves order in our government. Both parties[454] have access to technology that allows them to reorganize districts in a way which gives themselves a competitive advantage, leading neither party towards political setback. Additionally, fewer competitive races is beneficial for everyone[455], as it means less need for staff and fundraising. A number of analyses[456] show that anyone can take more seats in the House when they gerrymander; the point of democracy is that people elect other people to represent and promote their causes in any legitimate way possible. Gerrymandering is legitimate, and if everyone can use it equally – so, why not?

Gerrymandering is not to blame for extremism

While gerrymandering may highlight America's growing polarization[457] and thus, its lack of an ideological middle, it is certainly not the cause. Gerrymandering gets a bad rap[458] due to the increasing amount of extremist members in Congress. This is because people automatically think that the shifting or redrawing of Congressional boundaries create a homogeneous district that will lead to blowouts for one party or the other. In fact, as a study[459] examining America's partisan divide shows, there is growing evidence of polarity among citizens across counties, states and regions. For example, there was an 8% increase in polarization[460] between 2008 and 2012, irrespective of redistricting changes. In other words, Americans themselves are becoming more extreme in their political views, and are, therefore, voting in more extreme candidates. Diversity within each party is sharply narrowing and Americans are less tolerant than ever[461] of their political opponents.

The Bottom line: Gerrymandering is far less of a threat to our political system than it's made out to be, yet it still contributes to election bias and inaccurate voter representation. Do you think it is unfair to gerrymander, or are there other political issues America should focus on?

THE PERSPECTIVE ON THE UNITED NATIONS (UN)

Original debate written by Talia Klein Perez

Established in 1945[462] to prevent future world wars, the United Nations (UN) currently has 193 member-states. It works to develop and enforce international laws and policies to achieve peace, social progress and economic development worldwide. But is the UN a well-functioning contributor to international development, or is it ridden by bureaucracy and limited in its ability[463] to help nations with ongoing conflicts?

Here are three reasons why the UN is effective and three more why it's failing.

Three Reasons the UN Is a Failure

Human rights continue to be violated

The UN promotes and fights for human rights globally, yet these rights continue to be violated[464] by many countries. It's not the UN's fault that international human rights are trampled on, but the organization seems powerless to stop it. Take the genocide in Rwanda[465], where the UN had an "Assistance Mission" established in 1994. Its members were aware of the impending genocide, but UN peacekeepers failed to stop the majority Hutus from murdering almost a million minority Tutsis. Another example is the 2005 rape and sexual abuse[466] against Congolese children, perpetuated by UN peacekeepers themselves. Subsequent reports[467] found similar allegations in other countries.

Lots of committees, little change

The United Nation's bodies and their committees and sub-committees, such as the General Assembly, Security Council and Human Rights Council, are plagued with bloated bureaucracy and an imbalance of power. These can cause important UN resolutions with widespread support and impact to be stymied by a single veto from one of the Security Council's permanent five-member states. The Human Rights Council has also faced repeated criticism[468] over allowing member countries who themselves have a history of human rights abuses (such as China and Saudi Arabia) – a fact which prompted the US to recently withdraw from the committee, not for the first time. Or, take the Geneva-based Conference on Disarmament[469], which recently appointed Syria – a country well-known for using chemical weapons against its civilians – as its temporary president. The hypocrisy of such committees has led to little change regarding key human rights issues and general ineffectiveness overall.

Peacekeepers' good intentions have led to fatal consequences

Despite its noble mission, the deployment of 125,000 peacekeepers in troubled nations has sometimes caused unintended negative side effects on host societies. Take, for example, the issue of peacekeepers fathering and abandoning babies[470]: there is no exact number of abandoned children known, (a dozen paternity claims were received in 2014), but the phenomenon motivated the United Nations to initiate a DNA collection protocol. Additionally, a 2013 report also discussed the danger of corruption in peacekeepers'[471] missions.

Also, the world's most recent outbreak of cholera in 2010, after an earthquake rocked Haiti, points to the United Nations. Genome testing demonstrated that the source of the plague, which infected[472] over one million people and killed 10,000, was most likely a Nepali UN peacekeeping force. A UN-appointed panel of experts[473] found that the cholera strain diagnosed in Haiti was "a perfect match" for a strain found in Nepal. According to NPR, Nepalese peacekeepers were staying at the UN camp in Haiti during the earthquake, and poor sanitation flooded[474] local waterways with sewage from the camp. Such unintended consequences show that the UN has done more harm than good in parts of the world it has tried to help.

Three Reasons Why the UN Is Effective

It has the greatest international authority of any organization

The United Nations is currently the only active and respected international forum[475] with such widespread clout among the world's nations. One of its six bodies[476], the Security Council, is charged with maintaining global peace and security. World leaders, even extremely disliked ones, are welcome to speak at the UN, making it a beacon of democracy. Countries who belittle the UN must still respond to its resolutions.

Its peacekeepers are deployed to sensitive regions to keep enemy armies apart[477] and can impose sanctions[478] against hostile countries. Its International Court of Justice, ("World Court"), is the main forum for resolving international conflicts, such as the trial of war criminal Charles Taylor[479], in accordance with international law. The United Nations also created the Universal Declaration of Human Rights[480] – *the* standard the world is supposed to follow. No other organization holds this much global authority.

It has succeeded in strides to eradicate world hunger

Intervention by the UN's World Food Programme, the Food and Agricultural Organization and UN-sponsored emergency aid management are credited with reducing the number of people dying from malnutrition[481] annually. (Although world hunger has recently risen[482] for the first time in the past decade, as one of the UN's Sustainable Development Goals[483] – SDGs – the UN is committed to its goal of ending hunger and continues to make progress to that end.)

Continuing its success of mitigating worldwide hunger[484], former UN Secretary-General Ban Ki-moon set a further challenge of ending extreme poverty by 2030. Thanks to the UN's efforts, only 12.9% of the 23.3%[485] of people suffering from malnutrition between 1990 and 1992 are still going hungry. Northern Africa has even cut local poverty in half. With its international resources and influence, the UN will continue to establish new targets that encourage sustainable development[486] to end world hunger.

It has been instrumental in ridding some countries of 'The Bomb'

Thanks to the International Atomic Energy Agency (IAEA), a number of countries, including South Africa[487] and Kazakhstan[488], have willingly ended their nuclear weapons research programs and have submitted to regular IAEA inspections. And just last year, more than 120 countries adopted a UN treaty to ban nuclear weapons, requiring[489] non-nuclear signatory nations to avoid pursuing atomic weapons in exchange for a commitment by the five powers to move toward nuclear disarmament. The treaty further seeks to guarantee non-nuclear states' access to peaceful, energy-producing nuclear technology.

The Bottom Line: The United Nations provides a great basis for international relationships and progress, but it is also a complex body that has experienced many failures. As former President Obama said, the UN is imperfect[490], but it is also indispensable. How do you feel about it?

EDWARD SNOWDEN – HERO OR TRAITOR?

Original debate written by Rachel Segal

Ever since Edward Snowden leaked documents[491] containing classified US intelligence in 2013, he's been called both a traitor and a hero. While some believe he was heroic for showing Americans that their government was illegally spying on them, others maintain that what he leaked and the way he did so prove his motives were far from patriotic. Snowden's 2019 memoir[492] may provide more insight into his motives, or may just provide more attention to his status as a pop culture icon[493].

Here are three arguments why Edward Snowden is a hero and three why he's a traitor.

Edward Snowden Is a Hero

His revelation of illegal US government activity sparked a global debate

Edward Snowden leaked documents that showed the existence and shocking extent of a global mass surveillance system that the US government[494] used to spy on the personal communications of millions – if not hundreds of millions – of Americans and foreign citizens with no links to terrorism. This system included private emails, phone conversations, web histories, etc. – all without consent or court warrants. Snowden's decision to share this information consequently prompted a global debate over surveillance techniques and protecting citizens' privacy[495]. This, in turn, resulted in the US government passing laws[496] for the first time in decades restricting government surveillance. As part of the far-reaching consequences of Snowden's actions, technology companies like WhatsApp and Apple have also done more to encrypt[497] and protect users' personal information. Snowden catalyzed a global reckoning with the side effects of the digital age.

He acted responsibly with the leaks

Snowden acted responsibly when he revealed that the NSA's surveillance program[498] was unconstitutional. He was careful in not leaking any details about the algorithms that the NSA used in its operations. Nor did the leaks reveal the identities of the groups or individuals that the agency had targeted or the US agents involved. The leaked data also didn't contain any details of US military plans or conversations between US or foreign officials. Therefore, Snowden's leaks added value[499] without doing any harm to US national security, unlike the 2016 WikiLeaks data dumps[500].

He paid a steep price to defend civil liberties

Snowden risked his own freedom to bring information into the public domain about the US government endangering its citizens' civil liberties. Even former US Attorney General Eric Holder, who believes Snowden is a traitor, admitted that he "performed a public service[501]." He knew acting upon his conviction to uphold the sanctity of American values would force him into a life on the run[502], but he leaked the information anyway.

Edward Snowden Is a Traitor

The way he leaked the information was dubious

If Snowden had been a patriotic whistle blower, he would have first found legal avenues for his pursuit in reigning in the NSA. For instance, he could have appealed to members of Congress, who are elected to represent the American people. Instead, he went straight to largely foreign journalists and newspaper editors[503] and burdened them with the responsibility of deciding which of the stolen documents should be kept secret and which should reach the public domain. Snowden may have argued that he was acting nobly, but it was actually careless, as journalists and their editors aren't qualified to decide such legal matters, especially when their interests are about selling newspapers, not protecting U.S. national security.

He damaged US foreign relations

Contrary to Snowden's claim about wanting to stand up for his fellow Americans, the information he leaked actually created more harm than good[504]. The majority of the information that he shared is about the U.S. spying on foreign nations [505]and not its domestic operations. As such, he risked damaging America's relationship with foreign countries. By doing so, Snowden not only undermined U.S. alliances around the world but also U.S. efforts to undermine enemies that operate in countries where citizens have less ability to protect themselves from tyranny. If he had been a true patriot interested in protecting the American constitution, as he claims he is, he would have focused on collecting and leaking only the information that documented the NSA's overreach in domestic spying operations.

A patriot believes in his cause enough to be willing to face the consequences

If Snowden genuinely believed in the righteousness of his cause and actions, he would have been confident enough to remain in the United States and face the consequences[506] of stealing and leaking the NSA documents. He could have had his day and court and attracted further attention to his cause. Instead, he escaped to Hong Kong and then Moscow[507], seeking refuge in places whose motivation to protect him is self-interested at best.

....

The Bottom Line: While Edward Snowden illegally stole and leaked classified NSA documents, he sparked a global debate about surveillance that prompted the US government to change laws that better protect Americans' right to privacy. However, his actions also endangered US foreign relations and revealed secrets to US enemies. Do you think he is a hero or traitor?

LIVING CHAPTER

- Is happiness a choice?
- Is there life after death?
- Is there life outside Earth?
- The perspective on having kids
- Which came first, the chicken or the egg?
- Should adopted children be involved with their birth families?
- Cats or dogs: who makes a better companion?
- City vs. suburbs: where is better to live?
- Are humans inherently violent?
- Is fear beneficial or damaging to our lives?
- Is honesty the best policy?
- The perspective on time – is it linear or cyclical
- The perspective on religion
- The perspective on working from home

IS HAPPINESS A CHOICE?

Original debate written by Kira Goldring

Traveling, falling in love, watching SNL[1], getting a dog — all of these pursuits stem from humans' basic desire to be happy. But do we truly understand where our own happiness comes from? Which circumstances, if any, dictate our ability to consistently feel joy? These questions are particularly relevant in today's unprecedented times, as people worldwide are striving to stay healthy, both physically and mentally[2].

Below, we'll explore three arguments supporting the idea that happiness is a choice, and three arguments against it.

Happiness Is a Choice

We survive the worst through choosing to find meaning

Throughout history, disaster[3] has struck humankind with varying degrees of force. While it's too soon to tell the health and economic implications of the current coronavirus pandemic, we can take comfort in looking at past outcomes to tragedies. The outcomes have always been the same: We are adaptable, and we can survive against all odds. In his book "Man's Search for Meaning[4]," Holocaust survivor Victor Frankl quotes Nietzsche's perspective on resilience: "Those who have a 'why' to live, can bear with almost any how." Frankl argues that our ability to choose to find meaning within suffering is what keeps us alive. This can be achieved through finding loved ones, a sense of humor, and even nature; as long as we choose to find purpose and positivity[5], we can make it through any pain, even in today's times of prolonged self-quarantine[6] and social distancing.

A push-up a day keeps depression away

Happiness stems from chemicals in our bodies, which we choose to increase by proactively exercising, eating chocolate, and achieving small goals. Exercise causes us to release endorphins[7], a chemical responsible for alleviating depression[8] and pain; those who spend free time[9] doing physical activity activate more pleasant feelings than those who don't. Meanwhile, eating chocolate [10]means eating literal happiness, as chocolate stimulates serotonin in the brain, which then produces feelings of joy. Also, when we set short-term, achievable goals, we choose a one-way ticket down happiness lane by releasing dopamine[11], a feel-good chemical that motivates us to succeed. In our day-to-day lives, we can consistently choose to act in ways that nudge our brains to make us feel happy.

Gratitude attitude

Many find Thanksgiving to be one of the happiest U.S. holidays of the year, and it turns out there's a science to that: Happiness is all about the gratitude attitude[12]. According to psychologists Alex Wood, Jeffrey Froh, and Adam Geraghty, habitually focusing on the positive aspects of life[13] is strongly related to all aspects of well-being.

We can proactively practice behaviors that make us happier. This includes doing things to increase gratitude, such as keeping a list of things you're grateful for (a "gratitude journal") or writing a letter[14] to someone who has changed your life for the better and delivering it in person. These actions increase feelings of happiness[15] and optimism among people compared to those who don't do them. So, the next time you're drooling over a Thanksgiving turkey, remember to be grateful for it!

Happiness Isn't a Choice

Our brains search for problems

Part of the set of survival skills we've acquired over time includes defending ourselves against environmental threats. We are constantly, subconsciously scanning for problems[16] in our immediate surroundings to recognize potential threats and avoid danger, and we release cortisol[17] when we find these threats. Cortisol is the "stress hormone" that our bodies automatically produce when we're faced with warning signs that our needs are in danger of not being met. Because of this, we can and do consistently feel pain and discomfort by simply going outside and interacting with the world. This is especially the case in our era of 24-hour news cycles that constantly show and tell us of school shootings[18], natural disasters[19], global pandemics[20], and ongoing political discord.

Money buys security

While the phrase "money doesn't buy happiness" slides easily off the tongue, it forgets to include "but it does buy time." Using money to acquire services that allow people to have more free time, a recent study[21] suggests, increases life satisfaction and promotes emotional well-being. While that's quite convenient for those able to afford au-pairs, cooks and personal secretaries, the average person doesn't rake in enough money to have the choice of affording such services. As a result, people with less money may feel stressed, pressed for time, and less satisfied overall.

Not all people are happy

If happiness were truly a choice, wouldn't it be the obvious one? Yet, there are external factors at play which affect happiness levels and are out of our control. For example, an OECD-administered survey asked countries to rate their overall life satisfaction[22] on a 0-10 scale. It found that countries with relative wealth and security had an average score of 5.5 or less. As life satisfaction is the average degree to which people are content with their lives, it seems as though there are whole countries that are lacking the ability to select "happy" on their list of consistent moods. Happiness, or depression for that matter, is often not a choice; this is exemplified strongly in people with Seasonal Affective Disorder[23], which causes winter blues that don't budge until the spring comes around. No one enjoys suffering, but unhappiness may just be an inevitable part of the human condition[24].

The Bottom Line: There are methods through which humans can choose to be happy, yet our physical and material limits may automatically cause us to have a negative disposition. Are you able to choose happiness, or is your temperament naturally decided for you?

IS THERE LIFE AFTER DEATH?

Original debate written by Kira Goldring

Living with purpose and meaning is a goal that many strive to achieve. However, the motivation for that goal differs. Some people are focused on their current existence, while others believe that positive actions in this world will buy them a ticket to the next one[25] – heaven. This brings us to a question that everyone from religious authority to soul-searching Sally has asked: Does life continue after death? This may be a question on people's minds nowadays as the global death rate[26] from Covid-19 keeps climbing.

Here are three reasons to consider that there may be life after death, and three reasons to believe that death is the end of the road.

A Permanent Sleep

What we know, we know

By definition, death is the cessation of life[27] – so, by all logic, there is no life after death. In this vein, physics professor Sean Carroll[28] contends that life after death is impossible. While there are many things we don't know about the world, he says, we *do* know about the particles that make up the human body – and those don't go anywhere after the body dies. Because consciousness is part of the physical body, it dies along with the rest of a person. Unlike other uncertainties in life, this concept is relatively straightforward: With death, life ends.

Misinterpretation

While people may have the sensations of near-death experiences, a group of scientists believes that they aren't afterlife-related. According to Australian-based neurologist Dr. Cameron Shaw, the tunnel vision [29]some report experiencing after a close encounter with death is a result of the brain failing to receive oxygen[30], which distorts our perceptions. Other researchers[31] have found elevated levels of CO2 in the bloodstreams of those who had out-of-body sensations – which has been linked to visual hallucinations. Similar to the effect of hallucinogenic drugs[32], these sensations may be created by the chemical changes[33], sometimes drug-related[34], happening in a body on the brink of death. Unfortunately, the "white light" some claim to see happens only in our minds: Death, sadly, is what's at the end of the tunnel.

The side with proof

Proving that life after death is feasible has been faulty, at best. Aside from our dreams and feelings, we don't see or hear of anyone who has supposedly passed on to another world. We do, however, see exactly what happens to the human body[35] after it stops working; the process of body decomposition may be a gruesome one, but it is also telling. Archaeologists and coroners will agree on this fact: It doesn't look like there is life after death.

To a Better Place

Near-death experiences

A man – who was declared clinically dead[36] for six minutes after drowning – reported to the Near-Death Experience Research Foundation[37] that he had a joyful, out-of-body experience in which he could see and hear everything from above while unconscious. In addition, in the memoir *Dying to be Me*[38], Anita Moorjani describes[39] learning about the cause of her cancer while she was unconscious. Testimonies[40] like these are not uncommon, as studies around the world estimate that these "near-death" experiences[41] are reported by an estimated 4-8%[42] of the US population.

According to a recent study[43] that lends credence to near-death experiences, even when the brain shows no sign of electrical activity, it's quite possible that a person can remain conscious. Lead researcher Pim van Lommel[44] of the Hospital Rijnstate in the Netherlands, says that scientists should look beyond molecules and cells when studying consciousness. He asserts in the study that people can be conscious of events taking place around them even if or when they are physically unconscious.

Living memories

Life is more than just your physical presence; people live on through the imprint they have on others. Personal legacies keep people alive long after their physical bodies deteriorate. Headstones, stories, newspaper clippings, diaries, videos and photographs are all ways we preserve the lives of those who have perished. Cultures around the world also offer myriad ways of keeping the dead alive: Mexico's Day of the Dead[45] has been around for centuries, and it celebrates the lives of those who have passed (and was featured in the film *Coco*[46]); the *Egyptian Book of the Dead*[47] – a personalized book of spells that helps souls navigate death – has existed for thousands of years; Korea's three-day harvest festival, Chuseok[48], is celebrated by honoring the memories (and gravestones) of ancestors; and Bali's Galungan[49] honors the spirits of loved ones with big feasts. We may stop moving and breathing at some point, but legacies never die, thus, there is life after death.

Bodies that won't quit

We usually focus on the question of whether life stops, not necessarily *when* does life stop. Sources suggest that death may be a more gradual process than previously thought. For instance, research has found that our cells work hard at keeping us alive – perhaps even after we die. According to a recent study[50] in the journal Open Biology, animal cells continued to perform "gene expression" – which is the process necessary to build proteins that are vital for life – subsequent to the death of the animals in the study. This means that following brain death, these animal cells produced activity for several days; in some cases, this cell activity even increased after the animals had died. What's more, the researchers in the study believe that their results may extend to humans[51] as well. Although the brain stops working, our bodies may still be alive after they are declared dead – and they make a huge effort to keep themselves that way.

The Bottom Line: People's lives will always continue in memory and in spirit, but from a physical standpoint, death may be the end of their journey. What do you think? Do you believe in some kind of afterlife?

IS THERE LIFE OUTSIDE EARTH?

Original debate written by Kira Goldring

With two trillion[52] galaxies in the universe, it's easy to speculate that we're not the only intelligent species to exist in all of space. The recent discovery of a potentially habitable super-Earth[53] gives credence to this concept. The idea of celestial beings living outside of our little planet dominates our movies[54], TV shows[55], news, books, and even music[56], because we all want to know the truth: Is there life outside of Earth? Or are we loners in this vast, expansive universe?

Here are three reasons for and against life existing outside of Earth.

Forever Alone

One in a billion

The conditions under which complex life on Earth was created are almost impossible to replicate. An emerging theory from Germany posits that life on Earth may have started from a meteorite impact[57] – one that had to have been incredibly precise to generate the molecules that now make up our world. Other theories, while differing in the "how," agree that the merging of cells responsible for Earth's intelligent beings is extremely rare[58] – most likely a one-time event. Merely having the potential to support life may not be enough; Mars[59], for example, once had *potential* to harbor life – yet we still haven't seen any evidence of this life.

Fermi's Paradox

Italian physicist Enrico Fermi raised the following point, known as Fermi's Paradox[60], in the '50's: If the universe is indeed billions of years old[61], and it's only taken humans a couple hundred thousand years to create technology advanced enough for space travel, then older species in the universe should have been able to colonize the galaxy by now. Human beings are a relatively "young[62]" civilization, and our technology is already sophisticated enough to reach planets hundreds of light years [63]from Earth. Alien civilizations older than ours should have far surpassed us in technological advancement. Yet, as far as we know, no galaxy-domination attempts have been made by the interstellar powers that be – because they probably don't exist.

The Great Filter

Our lone existence in the universe can be explained by The Great Filter[64]. The theory contends that before a civilization is able to reach the level of intelligence necessary for space colonization, it gets "filtered" by some external circumstance and ceases to exist. On Earth alone, there's been evidence of at least five mass extinctions[65], and there are plenty of logical reasons this happens: disease outbreak, climate change[66], natural disaster – the list goes on. While humans may (or may not[67]) have dodged this inevitable filter, it's unlikely that our alien counterparts could have done the same. If they did – where are they?

We Share the Universe

The potential is there

Around a billion Earth-like planets[68] are estimated to inhabit our galaxy, making the potential for life extremely high. The recent discovery of a super-Earth planet 31 light-years away[69] suggests that there could be a potentially habitable world outside of our solar system. Even within our own solar system there are several celestial bodies boasting the potential to support life. Jupiter's icy moon, Europa[70], for example, contains both a source of radiation strong enough to lead to chemical reactions and evidence of an ocean similar to Earth's. Similarly, the conditions of Saturn's moon, Enceladus[71], could already support an Earth-born microbe (a microscopic organism that is too small to be seen with the naked eye), what with its liquid ocean and hydrothermal reactions. While many speculate that the life we uncover on these moons will likely be microbial[72], it would be the first step in learning how to search for more complex life forms within our galaxy.

UFO sightings

As reported by The New York Times[73] and the The Washington Post[74], the Pentagon quietly allocated $22 million toward the investigation of various unidentified flying objects for a number of years. While much of what they saw is classified, video evidence[75] from a US Navy Jet shows that our skies have indeed been permeated by the unknown. These UFO sightings[76] have ranged from bizarre lights over the New Jersey Turnpike to aircrafts moving faster than sound and hovering around the coast of San Diego. Perhaps a lone UFO could have been explained away by human error, but enough sightings to open a five-year investigation? It seems that someone or something is flying those vehicles – and it's not us.

We don't know how to look

We may utilize different ways of communication than our extraterrestrial counterparts, which explains why we haven't yet made contact with one another – our technologies may not have developed to be compatible with one another. Bacteria and neurons, for example, existed long before we had the means to acknowledge them; it just took a while for us to learn how to see them. Also, while radio signals have been our go-to method for reaching out into interstellar territory, we've only had access to this technology for a relatively short amount of time[77]. Radio travels at light-year speed; meaning, if we've been sending out signals for 100 years, only planets within 100 light-years of us would have been able to receive said signals. Just because we don't yet know how to make contact with species outside of our own doesn't mean they don't exist.

The Bottom Line: While there is exciting potential of life-supporting solar bodies in our galaxy, we're still lacking the evidence – and odds – necessary to prove that life outside of Earth exists. What do you say? Is there a real-life E.T. out there somewhere for us to discover?

THE PERSPECTIVE ON HAVING KIDS

Original debate written by Chaya Benyamin

"Be fruitful and multiply" is one of the Bible's first directions to mankind, and until recently, humanity has followed without question. Childlessness in America[78] and across the West is at an all-time high[79]. Over the years, more and more men and women have been opting not to become parents – a trend which ultimately calls into question the conventional path of becoming parents in the first place.

Below, we'll explore three reasons to give parenthood a second thought, and three reasons to keep on starting families.

Less is More

It's irresponsible to bring children into a world with an uncertain future

We're living in uncertain times. But even before the coronavirus pandemic, the world was already in bad shape. Global warming[80] threatens food security and economic prosperity, and fuels conflict. At present, war[81] is widespread, though most nations are now coming together to fight against a common enemy[82]. Political, gender, racial[83] and economic inequality pervade every society. With no answers to these quagmires or pandemics readily available, or even the promise of breathable air[84], how can we justify introducing more humans[85] into our collective calamity?

Life is plenty fulfilling without children

Many of humanity's most inspiring leaders were not parents. Jesus, Gandhi, and Oprah (among countless others[86]) prove that parents do not hold the monopoly on self-actualization or contribution to society. In fact, most achievements which advance society have little or nothing to do with parenting skills, as Susan B. Anthony[87] demonstrated in leading women to the vote in 1926, and as Nikola Tesla[88] proved through his many inventions. Whether these figures chose to forego becoming parents in order to dedicate themselves to the betterment of society or simply for lack of want, they show that fulfillment is available in equal measure to parents and non-parents alike.

Children require a tremendous amount of resources

Parenting is an enormous responsibility. The average American family spends between $12,000 and $14,000[89] each year to raise one child. Multiply that by 17 years[90], and you've bought a house. This is to say nothing of the physical and emotional demands of child-rearing. Parents worry more[91] and sleep less; the latter of which can have significant consequences[92] on health, productivity, and even income. When one looks objectively at the material and emotional resources required to responsibly care for a child, passing on parenting is a completely logical conclusion.

The More the Merrier

Parents are more productive and live longer

It's easy to understand how the challenges of parenting – sleep-deprivation, increased worry, and less time and money for self-care, to name a few – might contribute to a shorter lifespan. But somewhat counterintuitively, a number of studies[93] have shown that people with children live longer than those without them. In addition to enjoying longer lives, mothers in particular seem to receive a competitive edge with regard to workplace productivity when they have children. One writer for Quartz calls motherhood "the ultimate efficiency hack" and explains that a 30-year review of productivity of female economists (mothers and non-mothers alike) revealed that mothers outperformed[94] their childless counterparts. Not a bad trade for a few (hundred) sleepless nights!

Children are an excellent contribution to society

Children are quite literally the hope of the future. Those without children who lament the price society pays to send them to school forget that those children will later be the scientists who patent new technology to treat their ailments, the doctors, nurses and caregivers who'll administer them, and the bankers who will help them to finance it all. China's infamous one-child policy[95], initially intended to curb its population bulge, has revealed itself to be short-sighted, as China now struggles to cope with a large aging population and a lack of youngsters to support them. More than ensuring safe passage of the elderly and securing the future, children anchor the economy. The US Bureau of Labor Statistics reports that the Educational Services sector accounts for more than 3.6 million jobs[96]. With education expanding in every country on the planet, children propel the movement of trillions of dollars in the global economy[97].

Children bring out the best in us

Any parent can testify to the intense admiration young children have for their parents – they are wowed by the way you effortlessly remove candy wrappers and are dazzled by how you tie shoes. Children (well, the little ones, at least) believe their parents know all and that their kisses have magical healing powers. And guess what – being admired makes parents want to be admirable. Parenting asks men and women to model the behavior they'd like to see in their children. Parents look both ways when crossing the street, share, eat their vegetables, and (attempt) to speak kindly to their partners. Children promote emotional growth by reminding their parents that life is not solely about them, and by shining a light[98] on their parents' weaknesses and therefore providing an opportunity to improve upon them.

....

The Bottom Line: While there is no clear-cut evidence to suggest that parenting leads to a happier or more meaningful life, children bring out many positive sides of humanity. What would you say to a friend who is considering having kids? Would you have children?

WHICH CAME FIRST, THE CHICKEN OR THE EGG?

Original debate written by Kira Goldring

Roman philosophers[99] like Aristotle and Plutarch spent much time grappling over the circle of life. They raised the long-lasting question of whether the chicken or egg entered the world first. Ever since, humanity's fascination with our origins hasn't waned; even we of the twenty-first century still spend time ruminating over issues like Adam and Eve, the Big Bang theory and the nature of time[100]. It's no surprise, then, that the chicken-and-egg debate has continued to interest both scientists and laymen alike. So, the question still stands: which came first, the chicken or the egg?

Here are three arguments for the egg as the original Earth-dweller, and three reasons the chicken was actually the first one standing.

Eggs in the Lead

Context Matters

As the question which came first, the chicken or the egg, is paradoxical in nature, the answer may lie in the context. For instance, a look at our nutritional regimen, where eggs and chickens play their most dominant role in our lives, provides a clear answer: the egg came first. Our token first meal of the day typically consists of eggs, with poultry only nearing our plates during lunch or dinner. This basic breakfast etiquette originated with the Ancient Romans[101], and humans worldwide have been carrying on the sensible tradition ever since.

Evolution

A theory endorsed by both Bill Nye the Science Guy[102] and Neil deGrasse Tyson[103], evolution is on the side of the egg as coming before the chicken. This is because there was once a proto-chicken[104] – a bird resembling a chicken, but not quite of chicken status – that went about its business laying and fertilizing an egg. However, this egg carried some sort of genetic mutation[105] that turned it into the chicken we have now come to know and love. Because the parents of the first chicken egg were birds that weren't yet chickens, it appears that the egg did, indeed, come first.

In addition, eggs of other birds predated chickens by millions of years, and there are fossils to prove it. The Archaeopteryx – largely accepted as the world's oldest and first bird[106], and the closest living being of ancient times to resemble a chicken – left behind fossils from 150 million years ago, give or take. So, in comparison to other types of birds, chickens came rather late to the evolutionary party.

Genetically Modified Eggs

The recent advent of genetically modified chicken eggs[107] suggests that in matters of science and medicine, eggs precede the chicken. Not intended for consumption, these eggs have been genetically engineered[108] and contain a protein that plays a key role in fighting diseases like cancer, hepatitis and other immune-related illnesses. Japanese researchers have discovered a complex process to fertilize eggs that, long story short, produce male chicks that are crossbred with females to lay eggs containing the protein-producing cancer-fighting genes. The result, stemming solely from the egg, may reduce medicine production costs[109]. This goes to show than when humans recreate nature, they have to start with the egg.

The Chicken Wins

Protein

British scientists from Sheffield and Warwick universities are now convinced that the chicken preceded the egg, and they have the research[110] to back it up. Their study[111] follows the development of a chicken's egg, concluding that chicken eggs can only form with the help of a protein found solely in the ovaries of a chicken. Additionally, chickens create eggs more quickly[112] than other animals do, but they need the protein to help speed up the process. In other words, it is impossible for a chicken egg to form unless it has emerged from within a hen's body.

The Bible

Whether you believe the Bible[113] is divinely inspired or written by man, the world's oldest, most-read and most oft-purchased book [114]had enough wisdom to solve this chicken-egg mystery from the get-go. Right in the beginning of Genesis[115], the following is written: "And God created great whales, and every living creature that moveth, which the waters brought forth abundantly, after their kind, and every winged fowl after his kind.... And God blessed them, saying, Be fruitful, and multiply, and fill the waters in the seas, and let fowl multiply in the earth." In other words, before they could procreate, fowl – which includes chickens– had to already exist. So, to answer which came first, the chicken or the egg, look no further than the Bible: animals came from nothing, and eggs came from animals.

Instincts

Chickens – like other birds – sit on their eggs[116] for over three weeks to keep them warm and to protect them from external elements. In fact, baby chicks only form [117]in eggs that have been incubated. Research shows that non-mother hens don't take interest in eggs that aren't their own and that they're even inclined to destroy eggs[118] of other species. In other words, chicken eggs need a mother hen to sit on them in order to hatch. If the egg had come first, who would have kept it warm enough to hatch?

....

The Bottom Line: While evolution would suggest the egg's victory in the who-came-first battle, genetics seem to declare the chicken victorious. As biological arguments can be made for both sides, the answer to this puzzling question may always remain a mystery. What do you think – which came first, the chicken or the egg?

SHOULD ADOPTED CHILDREN BE INVOLVED WITH THEIR BIRTH FAMILIES?

Original debate written by Chaya Benyamin

Adoption has transformed dramatically over the past century. Whereas adoptions used to forbid contact between birth and adoptive families, most of today's adoptions are open. This means they include some level of contact between families – ranging from yearly emails to shared holidays. With the majority of America's adoptions[119] being conducted with some level of contact with birth families, open adoption is certainly in vogue. But it is as beneficial for children as its advocates claim?

Below, we'll look at three reasons why open adoption is the most suitable approach, and three reasons why adoptive parents shouldn't feel obliged to have contact with their child's birth family.

Open the Door

Knowledge is power

Open adoption allows access to genetic and family medical history that is unavailable in closed adoptions. For adoptive families, knowledge of any medical[120] or developmental problems among the birth family can help them to prepare and give better care to their child. This is especially the case if the birth mother engaged in an activity that may have adversely (or positively!) affected her baby's health. Without accurate family medical history, adoptees risk making crucial decisions about their health blindly, or could end up paying for expensive diagnostic procedures[121] or genetic testing in order to gain information that could be easily ascertained from biological family.

Open adoptions help adoptees become well adjusted

Before the advent of open adoption, adoptive families often worried that contact with a placed child's birth family would hinder the development of relationships with their adoptive family. Decades-long studies[122] have shown that this fear was unfounded. Adopted children who interact with their birth families feel integrated into their adoptive families and regard their adoptive parents as their mother and father. Whereas closed adoptions have been shown to promote birth-family fantasies in children and adolescents, an adoptee's interaction with biological family helps the placed child develop a realistic idea of their birth family, and thereby form a more authentic and positive self-identity as an adopted person[123].

Stress reduction

Contact between adoptive families and birth families has been shown to relieve stress for parents[124], birth and adoptive alike. Open adoption allows for the burning questions that so often accompany adoption to find real answers – Did the child I placed go to a good home? Is our child's biological mother happy with her decision?

Two-time adoptive mother Courtney Zimbelman describes the stress-reducing benefits for all: "[My daughter] will never have to wonder where she came from or what her birth family is like… it's [also] beneficial for her birth family. They did not place a child for adoption and have that child just disappear from their lives. They get to see her grow and, I hope, that gives them comfort knowing that the adoption decision they made was the right one."

To be sure, the confidence supplied to all parents through open adoption creates a positive environment for adoptees.

Close the Door

Show me the science

Ninety-five percent of American adoption agencies offer some form of open adoption, and advocates and bloggers are quick to tout its benefits. However, there is little science to prove that children in open adoption scenarios are better off emotionally than adoptees with no connection to their birth families. A longitudinal study[125] of adoptees at UMass Amherst revealed that there was no notable difference in self-esteem between children in closed and open adoptions. Additionally, an adoptees' degree of preoccupation with their adoption had no correlation to the level of openness in their adoption.

Risk of rejection

Simply put, birth parents of children put up for adoption have not signed on to be parents. As such, there is no guarantee that even if they desire some contact with the child they placed, that they will commit to the relationship (or be a source of emotional comfort to the child) in the long-term. Birth parents withdraw from open adoption relationships with much more frequency than adoptive parents. When a birth parent is only sporadically involved or disappears altogether, the emotional consequences for children can be devastating. As one adoption advocate[126] puts it, "A child whose biological parent disappears experiences a double whammy. He wonders why he was placed to begin with, then feels rejected again because a birth mother no longer visits."

There is no silver bullet

Open adoption is not a panacea for all emotional issues surrounding adoption. While open adoption does answer important questions of origin for adoptees, it does not necessarily abate a person's grief about having been placed. It also does not make one immune to emotional complications that can arise from the adoptees' relationship with his or her birth family. One adoptee recalls the anger and confusion she felt when her birth mother informed her that she would raise her biological sister. Another expressed fears of alienation and abandonment[127] despite her positive views of being raised in an open adoption. When it comes to mitigating the emotional consequences of adoption, there simply is no silver bullet.

....

The Bottom Line: The outcomes of open adoption are as varied as the families involved. Where do you stand? Is it right that open adoption be the accepted standard, or is better for the door to swing both ways?

CATS OR DOGS: WHO MAKES A BETTER COMPANION?

Original debate written by Rachel Segal

The world is divided into cat people and dog people. Having a certain preference has been known to strain or even break up relationships. As more than half[128] of American households (almost 80 million homes!) own a pet and spent $95.7 billion [129] on them in 2019, the debate between cats and dogs is one that will likely continue until the end of time. Today, in times of forced sheltering in place, the companionship[130] of these furry friends (whether canine or feline) is of great comfort, with animal shelters nationwide seeing a sharp jump[131] in the number of pet adoptions.

Here are three arguments why dogs make better companions and three arguments why felines as pets are the "cat's pajamas."

Why Dogs Make Better Companions than Cats

Dogs love to play (and work)

While you can play with some cats, nothing measures up to the sheer, infectious joy your dog shows for playtime. Inside or outside, dogs are always eager to join any game and will happily play with kids and adults for hours on end. And, unlike cats, dogs can play interactively; they'll catch a ball and bring it back to you. Not only can dogs be easily trained to play and do tricks, they can also be trained to do actual jobs [132]that make a real difference in society. It helps that dogs are scientifically proven to be as smart as 2-year-old kids.[133]

Dogs are more adaptable than cats

While both dogs and cats prefer routine and don't like uncertainty, dogs are much more adaptable than cats. This is because dogs usually bond with their owner[134] rather than with a specific place. So, unlike cats, dogs are more likely to be happy wherever their owner is and will therefore better handle relocating to new places. You can even take your dog on vacation and know that he'll enjoy it rather than be stressed.

Dogs will protect you

No matter the dog breed, all dogs feel protective[135] and defensive of their owners. Whereas cats will typically run off and hide at the first sense of danger, dogs will stay around out of duty and loyalty, protecting and defending you against any threats to your safety. Moreover, a dog's sense of smell can also save lives[136]. Another way that dogs are good for your health is that they motivate their owners to exercise more. New research shows that dog walkers (i.e., most dog owners) are more physically active[137] than people who don't own dogs.

Why Cats Make Better Companions than Dogs:

Cats are independent

The independent spirit of cats[138] is a virtue, especially when you're busy or expecting company. Dogs work themselves into a frenzy, barking, jumping, and drooling on you and your visitors. In their excited bid for attention, dogs' nails scratch clothes and their drool soils them (which is just as unwelcome for owners as it is for guests.) Meanwhile, cats make themselves scarce when the doorbell rings. Maybe, they'll discreetly check out your guests by rubbing up against their leg[139], but there won't be any overbearing leaping or leg humping.

Cats are low-maintenance

You can leave your cat inside when you're not home and be mostly assured that everything will still be in one piece when you get back. More importantly, cats aren't dependent on their owners to go to the bathroom. Sure, kitty litter can smell if it isn't changed regularly, but you can store and change it at your convenience[140]. Not to mention, some cats can be trained to actually use the toilet[141]. In contrast, dogs don't care if there's rain, snow or extreme heat outside. When they need a walk, there's no avoiding it. And even if you have a yard, you'll still need to do constant poop-control outside. Plus, cats groom themselves and don't emit a bad smell. Not even the most ardent dog lover can deny that their furry companion has a distinctly strong odor, which often remains on clothes, furniture and in cars after they've gone.

Cats are quiet

Unlike dogs that will always vocalize their moods with loud barks or endless whining, most cats will (mostly) keep their moods to themselves. Even when cats do protest, their meows or hisses are usually not as loud as barks and can't be heard from the neighbor's house. There's also an added benefit[142] of your cat's low-decibel purring is that it's been shown to reduce stress levels and blood pressure, among other things.

The Bottom Line: Both cats and dogs make wonderful pets for different reasons. While cats are low-key and low-maintenance, dogs are active and adoring. Which type of furry companion to you prefer to live with, especially in times of stress and uncertainty[143]?

CITY VS. SUBURBS: WHERE IS BETTER TO LIVE?

Original debate written by Lee Mesika

Where you choose to live[144] is a major contributor to who you are as a person. The area in which you live evidently becomes a part of you, shaping or even changing your life view. US cities are home to more than 80%[145] of the American population, though rural and suburban living is still seeing growth[146], year after year. While cities are hot spots for culture, they tend to be noisier, dirtier and more crowded. S So the question remains as to where is preferable to live regarding health and overall quality of life.

Here are three arguments in favor of living in the city and three arguments in favor of living in the suburbs.

Suburbia

Cheaper

By choosing to live in the suburbs, as opposed to a city, families are able to save more money each year. On average, it was found that city-based families in the US spend at least around $9,000 more[147] per year (in many cases, the number is significantly higher[148]) just on basic housing and childcare costs. Homes in the suburbs[149] are also cheaper. Not to mention they are usually bigger than real estate options in any city. Therefore, in many cases and especially for millennials, suburban living offers a higher value for money[150].

Space

On average[151], living in the suburbs grants you an additional 300 square feet (about 30 square meters) of living space. What would you do with an extra 300 square feet of[152] real estate? Create a guest room? A home office? The possibilities are endless. More important than design, though, is the fact that these extra feet provide a feeling of space. This matters because living in small spaces, like in New York, where micro-apartments[153] have become increasingly prevalent, can negatively impact your mental health[154] and how your children are raised[155]. There's also the additional concern that overcrowded city life can wreak havoc on your physical health[156], especially during a pandemic[157], with its lack of room for social distancing, and overabundance of polluted air, noise and stress.

Crime

Blame it on TV series, like *The Wire*[158], or flashy news headlines[159], not to mention high-profile cases of cities with police brutality[160], but we associate crime more with city areas[161] than suburban ones. FBI stats[162] and data from the National Center for Victims of Crime[163] confirm our fears. According to these sources, major cities have higher property crime rates, household burglaries, theft and violent crime rates than surrounding suburban areas. Living in the suburbs can be a lot safer crime-wise.

Big City Life

Cultural Diversity

During the last few centuries, the "American Dream[164]" and promises of other riches and a better life attracted immigrants[165] from all around the world to the United States. These immigrants settled in urban areas as opposed to the countryside[166], with the city offering them a better and wider variety of jobs. This trend wasn't just visible in the United States, but also all over the major European cities.

Back in 1900, only 12 cities worldwide had more than 1 million people[167]. Today, more than half[168] of the world's population lives in cities. Cities have grown a lot, and with all these newcomers come new cultures and social diversity. Many cities around the world even have areas that are based on these settlers: Chinatown[169], Little Italy[170], Little India[171], etc. This "melting pot" effect allows us to try foods from different cultures, meet new people from diverse backgrounds, see arts from around the world, and get exposure to different cultures that wouldn't otherwise be available to us without hopping on an airplane.

Transportation

Living in the suburbs requires families to have at least one car. Kids and teens who don't yet have a driver's license or access to a car are completely reliant on their parents for commuting. Whether it's to school, after-school activities, or even to the grocery store, there is heavy reliance on private transportation when growing up in the suburbs. Not to mention the distances or traffic involved in driving from your home to wherever you need to be. Oh, and let's not forget about the added monthly costs of car insurance[172] and gasoline.

In contrast, commuting from point A to B in urban areas is far easier and cheaper[173]. City living allows more flexibility and freedom in getting around, given easily accessible public transportation. New York's subway[174] system has been running since the early 20th century. Underground subways, and above-ground trains, trams[175] and light-rails are in use in almost every European city. In fact, most cities are designed around public transportation. Buses have special lanes, while trains and metros are not subject to traffic. This enables faster commutes. Plus, public transportation riders have the added benefit of being able to hop off and easily explore new areas of their city that would otherwise pass them by if traveling by car. Pre- and post-coronavirus, public transportation is a safe, efficient, and convenient way to get around and/or explore one's surroundings.

A lot more to do

It's no secret that cities attract more tourists than suburban areas do. Let's face it, wouldn't you rather travel to Los Angeles than to the LA suburb of Pacoima[176] (which most people have never heard of)? And with tourists come businesses and attractions, including restaurants, parks, shops, nightlife, etc. Therefore, living in a city may provide a wider variety of entertainment, educational and cultural options than what can be found in suburbia. Besides the museums, public galleries, educational centers found in US cities[177], there are also numerous public events[178] that are often free or affordable for city residents. City dwellers not only have outlets where they can learn about art, culture and history but public transportation that makes diverse cultural opportunities accessible.

....

The Bottom Line: Living in the suburbs can provide more real-estate space and, perhaps, a safer environment while saving you money. However, living in a city exposes you to new cultures and entertainment that are more easily accessible with public transportation. Where would you prefer to live?

ARE HUMANS INHERENTLY VIOLENT?

Original debate written by Josh Gabbatiss
Written as part of a cooperation with Sapiens Magazine

World leaders exchanging nuclear threats[179] across the Pacific Ocean. Police brutality[180], peaceful protests turning violent[181] – or, in the case of Charlottesville[182] in 2017, starting out with the intent of violence[183]. The wars in Afghanistan, Iraq, and Syria[184] (to name just a few). Mass shootings, at schools[185], outdoor concerts[186], places of worship, and public gatherings[187], stretching from America[188] to New Zealand[189]. Terrorism, both domestic and international[190].

You could be forgiven for thinking that this is the natural order of things and that humanity is doomed to eternal conflict because this is just who we are: an innately violent species, still controlled by primitive urges. In fact, the debate around whether we have a built-in predilection for violence has raged among scholars for centuries, and the answer is far from a foregone conclusion.

Here are three arguments suggesting we are naturally violent, and three suggesting we are not.

Humans Are 'Naturally' Violent

Our closest relatives are very violent

Since "wars[191]" between chimpanzee communities were first described in the 1970s, there has been speculation about why these conflicts take place, and what they can teach us about our own capacity for violence. Biological anthropologist Richard Wrangham argues that[192] attacks by groups of male chimpanzees on smaller groups increase their dominance over neighboring communities, improving access to food and mates. Ancestral men might have similarly established dominance by killing rivals from other groups, thus securing greater reproductive success and endowing our species with a desire for violence.

We are molded by conflict

In his 2002 book *The Blank Slate*[193], psychologist Steven Pinker[194] wrote that human bodies and brains have "direct signs of design for aggression," and that men in particular bear the marks of "an evolutionary history of violent male-male competition." As such, men are seemingly more likely to go to war, to murder, or to assault. Moreover, distinguishing anatomical features[195], such as greater physical strength, could well be adaptations for inter-male fighting. But does this mean that men evolved to be violent? Anthropologist Napoleon Chagnon[196] asserted in 1968 that for the Yanomami of Venezuela and Brazil, men who kill have more wives and therefore father more children. This has been described as evidence of selection for violence in action.

Humans have always been like this

The 17th-century thinker Thomas Hobbes [197]famously described the lives of humans in their "natural condition" prior to the development of civil society as "nasty, brutish, and short." The idea that humans are more violent without the architecture of the state to control them is supported by both archaeological and contemporary observations[198]. The chances of dying at the hands of another human is generally higher in non-state societies, and one widely quoted estimate by Pinker places the death rate[199] resulting from lethal violence in ancient non-state societies, based on archaeological evidence, at a shocking 15% of the population. This is compared to 3% in the modern era[200].

We Do Not Have a Tendency toward Violence

We are related to peaceful apes

Primatologist Frans de Waal reckons[201] that primate behavior has been cherry-picked to suit a more violent narrative for humanity. While chimp behavior may well shed light on human male tendencies for violence, de Waal points out that the other two of our three closest relatives, bonobos and gorillas, are less violent than us. It is plausible that instead of descending from chimp-like ancestors, we come from a lineage of relatively peaceful, female-dominated apes, like bonobos[202]. Chimpanzees might be ultra-violent outliers.

Not all humans are violent

While it may seem that violence is universal, our perception can be biased. Biological anthropologist Agustín Fuentes makes the point[203] that while we wouldn't bat an eyelid at the headline "4 Killed in New York City Today," we're unlikely to ever read one declaring "8,299,996 People in New York City Got Along Today." Most people aren't violent, so why do we think violence is innate? Similarly, while most assume that all human cultures are violent, the anthropologist Douglas Fry has documented[204] over 70 societies that don't make war at all, from the Martu of Australia, who have no words for "feud" or "warfare," to the Semai of Malaysia, who simply flee into the forest when faced with conflict.

Cooperation, not conflict, is the key to our success

Contrary to the suggestions of Pinker and others, there is actually very little archaeological evidence for group conflict in our distant past. This suggests that war only became common as larger, sedentary civilizations emerged around 12,000 years ago. Many anthropologists dispute the notion that non-state societies today provide evidence that conflict is part of the human condition, accusing academics like Napoleon Chagnon [205]of distorting results to suit their ideologies. Humans have been responsible for terrible acts of violence throughout our history, but the study of human cultures past and present shows that we are defined far more by cooperation and the avoidance of conflict than by violence. Otherwise, we would not have got where we are today.

The Bottom Line: No one would deny that humans are capable of immense violence[206]. Think Oklahoma City[207], 9/11[208], Sandy Hook[209], Las Vegas[210], Parkland[211], Christchurch[212], and all the other attacks in between and since, not to mention the bombing of Nagasaki and Hiroshima[213]; the list of incidents of mass violence only grows longer. But is the solution to accept violence as part of human nature and look for ways to deal with it, or do we need to rid ourselves of this misguided notion altogether?

IS FEAR BENEFICIAL OR DAMAGING TO OUR LIVES?

Original debate written by Rachel Segal

President Roosevelt first introduced us to the soothing concept that the only thing we have to fear is fear itself[214]. He also reminded Americans that freedom from fear[215] was one of four essential freedoms. However, almost a century later, it seems that Roosevelt's advice has been ignored. Before the pandemic, Americans were living in the safest era in history[216]. However, 2020 brought with it many new causes of fears, both politics[217]-based and health[218]-based. Not to mention the media's constant barrage of fear-based news and advertisements demonstrate that fear[219] still governs American lives.

Whether or not we realize it, fear plays a significant role in shaping our world view, decisions, behavior and way of thinking[220]. This is especially relevant today, when fear of contracting the coronavirus – and its mutations[221] – has changed lives around the world. The ultimate question is whether we are better or worse off because of our fear.

Here are three reasons why fear is beneficial to our lives and three reasons why it is damaging.

Fear Is Damaging to Our Lives

Instructional fear makes us focus on the wrong risks

As we fear what's available in our memory, and the media tends to keep images of terror and death fresh, we seem to be extremely fearful of miniscule risks despite the minute chances of personally experiencing any of the vivid examples we see. This is because the media can easily exacerbate our exaggerated fears. For instance, a study[222] showed that a rise in violence portrayed in TV dramas since the late 1990s has made Americans more afraid of crime despite a fall in actual crime rates[223].

Additionally, after 9/11, Americans were afraid to fly even though driving to the airport is more dangerous. In the year after 9/11, it was calculated[224] that an estimated 1,500 Americans died on the road while trying to avoid the fate of the 246 victims killed in the four deadly flights. And, again, after the 2014 Ebola outbreak[225], the media stoked nationwide paranoia[226] about the disease that turned out be unjustified; as of the 11 total cases[227] in America, only two were contracted within America.

It limits how we live

Being afraid of failing to meet family or even society's expectations plays a big role in shaping our life choices. Whether blatantly or subtly conditioned[228] by family or societal pressures and norms, these fears often linger in our unconscious, influencing our career and relationship choices. For example, people may embark on a particular education and career path solely out of fear[229] of disappointing or being rejected by their parents. Yet even if pursuing your genuine passion and dream job, fear of failure[230] can limit your career potential – as can fear of success. The latter, clinically deemed Imposter Syndrome[231], is the crippling yet common[232] phenomenon of doubting one's abilities and decisions.

On a personal level, being afraid of going against social convention can make people forsake true love for marriages[233] that bring material stability. On the flip side, this same fear can also keep people trapped in doomed marriage[234]s instead of divorcing[235]. Health-wise, fear of contracting the coronavirus has kept people from seeking other critical health treatments[236], which may have negative long-term effects on their lives.

Fear can be manipulated by others

Being afraid of death can also influence people's political choices. For example, two post-9/11 studies[237] found that subjects in a group that had a higher awareness of death favored a political candidate who was perceived as a savior and who preferred an aggressive strategy against their enemies over one who opted for diplomacy.

Additionally, dictators[238] like Adolf Hitler[239], Joseph Stalin[240] and Saddam Hussein, to name just a few, rose to power by exploiting people's fears. When gripped by fear, whether it is real or imagined, it can slow or disrupt people's rationale and abilities to make cognitive decisions[241]. This can make them easy targets for manipulation or even harm by fake news[242] or by leaders who promise protection from a perceived threat.

Fear Is Beneficial to Our Lives

It instills protective self-preservation

Maybe you were bitten by a dog when you were younger and you've been afraid of dogs ever since. This fear conditioning[243] can be life-saving[244], as it tells us when we are in danger and can therefore keep us out of harm's way. As fear generates an instinctual state of heightened awareness within us, it alerts us to be cautious even in split-second decision-making. After all, once you've burned yourself by touching a hot oven, or almost drowned by venturing too far out in the ocean, you'll never do it again. Not to mention that fears of catching the coronavirus has caused people to cancel their travel plans[245], a preventative move that have saved many from getting sick. Research suggests that babies in their first few days can learn fear through the odor[246] of their distraught mothers, which can happen even if a mother experienced a specific fear before pregnancy. This shows us that even before we are old enough to comprehend terror, we are introduced to a fight or flight instinct, which will help us develop tendencies for life-long self-preservation.

It drives personal growth and meaning

While many – if not most – people are afraid of death, we are motivated by our mortality to live as fulfilling a life as possible. According to terror management theory[247], many people manage their fear of death by searching for life-long meaning that will continue to exist after death. This can derive from having kids, participating in a group, like religion, that will endure beyond its members' lives, or by producing art, music[248] or other works that have a lasting legacy.

It can transform us to save others' lives

Life is unpredictable, and danger can come out of nowhere. In such instances, when we are terrified by something staring us in the face, the body's response can transform us and move us to staggering acts of selflessness. When under intense pressure, fear can enable people to summon enormous energy or power reserves[249] that are normally inaccessible. The result can seem nothing short of a superhuman response[250], like lifting a car to save the person squashed underneath. "Under acute stress, the body's sympathetic nervous system prepares the body for sustained, vigorous action. The adrenal gland dumps cortisol and adrenaline into the bloodstream. Blood pressure surges and the heart races, delivering oxygen and energy to the muscles. It's the biological equivalent of opening the throttle of an engine," explains Jeff Wise in Scientific American[251].

The Bottom Line: Experiences in our lives may leave us with intense fears that affect our values and life choices. However, while fear can affect us negatively, it can inspire us to find and create meaning and can save us – and others – from mistakes and even harm. How does fear affect your life?

IS HONESTY THE BEST POLICY?

Original debate written by Kira Goldring

"Honesty is the best policy" is an idiom that pervades countless childhoods and cautionary tales. It may seem like a throwback in today's age of fake news and alternative facts[252]. Yet sometimes it's all too tempting to lie our way out of trouble or to bend the truth enough to avoid hurting someone else. So, which is it? Is honesty really the best policy, or are there reasons to question this well-acknowledged phrase?

Here are three reasons to stick with the truth, and three reasons why bending the truth on occasion is acceptable.

Honesty Is the Best Policy

Mental peace

Anyone who has told a lie knows the uncomfortable feelings of guilt[253] that may soon follow the fib. Not being honest can often have unintended consequences, and if those consequences are worse than we anticipate, we are prone to feeling incredibly distressed. There's no way around this; even telling half-truths[254] can actually be worse than lying outright, studies from the Journal of Personality and Social Psychology show. "Partial confessors" feel higher regret, guilt and shame than do "full confessors" of a lie. Consequently, other research[255] points to improved physical and mental health following reductions in lie-telling. It's a no-brainer; honesty is the best policy. So, stick with honesty, and your mental health will remain in much better shape.

Slippery slope

Lying is a tangled web, and it's hard to stop lying once you've started. Studies done in the experimental psychology department of University College London[256] show that lying one time makes it physically easier to lie in the future. This is because while we experience initial conflict when trodding on the truth, this discomfort subsides over time, making it easier to be dishonest and serve our own self-interests. Yet, the more lies we tell, the harder it is to unravel the web; the odds of getting caught are high, which means we're risking severely negative consequences[257] if discovered – like ruining our reputation and reducing the chance of others trusting us in the future.

Honesty = reliability

Society is built on trust. We go to stores expecting clerks to give us the true prices of merchandise. We believe food is okay to eat when there's an expiration date listed by a reliable company. Trustworthy communities[258] allow people to work together, communicate effectively and openly engage with "the other[259]." Building trust by separating fact from fiction[260] is especially important today when communities may be wary about receiving the coronavirus vaccine. This shows how if honesty weren't a basic tenet of society, whole chunks of our social fabric would crumble. Look no further than the Flint water crisis[261] in Michigan as an example of dishonesty posing health risks to society; thousands of people were lied to [262]about the unhealthy, lead-ridden state of their water, and many got sick as a result. This also applies on an individual level; lying kills relationships[263], where honesty protects integrity. Bearing this in mind, honesty is the best policy – it is also the necessary one.

Other Policies Are Better

Self-indulgent

While honesty is often hailed as a virtue, our motivation for truth-telling is often more self-serving than it is pure. Sitting on a pent-up thought can be difficult to do, and we may feel great relief in letting go of our secrets, no matter at what cost. In fact, social media[264] has exacerbated this self-indulgence by giving people a platform through which to share. It may also force intimacy of their every innermost thought and feeling – ones that everyone else may not want to hear about[265]. Rather than accepting from the get-go that honesty is the best policy, we should evaluate every situation and question whether our motives are pure in telling the truth.

Little white lie

She doesn't really want to hear that she looks fat; he would like to continue believing that his joke was funny. The white lie[266] – a small lie told to avoid hurting a person's feelings – originated somewhere, and for good reason: Not everyone is prepared to hear the truth. In fact, honesty can wound the people closest to us[267]; sometimes, it doubles as a subtle form of assault, by allowing us to unload our angry feelings onto our loved ones through lashing out with true – yet brutal – criticism. In the long run, this kind of honesty may harm our relationships more than it will benefit them.

Benefits of deception

People often derive joy from being deceived. Kids adore hearing stories about Santa Claus[268] and the Tooth Fairy; movie-goers enjoy films the most when the acting is believable. In fact, celebrities win prestigious awards for faking identities and emotions. In addition to the entertainment factor, however, deception often puts us at ease. Imagine the panic that would have ensued if, for example, Americans had known how close they were to war during the Cuban Missile Crisis[269]. In fact, research on dishonesty in the workplace[270] corroborates the important and calming effects of lying; it found that duplicity can both help breed trust during difficult times and boost morale. While lying may not be the best policy, it benefits us enough to lose the bad rap.

....

The Bottom Line: Complete honesty can preserve relationships and keep society peaceful, yet there are instances in which a little fibbing may be required to put out potential social fires. What's your best policy – honesty, or something else?

THE PERSPECTIVE ON TIME - IS IT LINEAR OR CYCLICAL?

Original debate written by Stephen Nash
written as part of a cooperation with Sapiens magazine

Astronomers, archaeologists and theologians, among many others, have pondered the nature and meaning of "time." We all know what time is, until someone asks us to define it. Then we're at a loss for words. Worse yet, the more we think about time, the more complicated the subject becomes, especially if we let the fantasies of science fiction creep into our minds.

These days, with 90% of Americans[271] staying at home in varying degrees of self-isolation[272], we have nothing but time on our hands to ponder the nature of time as we perceive it. Is it linear, meaning it moves in only one direction, or is it cyclical, evolving around cycles, such as seasons? While many people in the modern era seem to agree that time is linear, for most of humankind's existence, time has been considered cyclical and rhythmic.

Below are three arguments stating that time is linear and three more stating that time is cyclical.

Three Reasons Time Is Linear

Time is irreversible

Much to the chagrin of H.G. Wells[273] and other writers, not to mention movie fans of characters like Marty McFly[274], it's simply impossible to travel back in time[275]. As living beings, we are born, we age, and we die, in that order. We know about the past, but we can't, by definition, know about the future. This is because time is unidirectional. This is not perception, it's physical reality.

Things fall apart

The Second Law of Thermodynamics[276] suggests that time is linear and unidirectional because things in our universe go from a state of order to a state of (increasing) disorder. My hot cup of tea becomes cold, it doesn't heat up. A dead body decays, it doesn't come back to life. Cars wear out. And I'm ageing. I can deny that these things happen, but one day I won't be around to deny them anymore.

Time is cumulative

Time is linear because of the different and cumulative ways we can record and measure it. Our smartphone stopwatches measure time in milliseconds. This may be an absurd level of precision for daily life, but it is increasingly important as we push the limits of human athletic performance. We can also measure time by counting the number of times the earth goes around the sun, just as humans have done for thousands of years. If counted, this shows linear progress from a starting point onward. Or we can measure the vibration of cesium-133 atoms, as is done to set International Atomic Time[277]. That global standard is so accurate that it will take 1.4 million years for it to be off by a full second. These natural phenomena can be recorded in long, cumulative and linear sequences.

Three Reasons Time Is Cyclical

The earth, moon, and sun move in repeating, elliptical patterns

All of our most common time measurement systems that we use in daily life are cyclical: the repetition of 60 seconds into a minute, 60 minutes into an hour, 24 hours into a day, seven days into a week, (roughly) four weeks into a month, (roughly) three months into a season, and four seasons into a year. As well, don't our feelings of déjà vu[278] and the idea that history repeats itself support the notion that time is cyclical? If time were truly and naturally linear, wouldn't we use linear, metric counting measures that proceed from a single starting point towards infinity, like distance measurements do?

Humans haven't really needed structured, linear ways to measure time

Until recently, the lives of agricultural, nomadic, and even urban peoples were governed by the endlessly repeating seasonal round. Calendars[279], which portray time as a linear concept, are a recent phenomenon when compared to the long-term existence of our species. The earliest calendar may have developed as early as 10,000 years ago[280]; well-documented calendar systems don't become common in the archaeological record until within the last 5,000 years. Our species is 200,000 years old; for at least 95% of humankind's existence as a species, time was cyclical and circadian.

Before the coronavirus hit, a familiar refrain was we "never have enough time," so we never "take the time" to stop and smell the roses. Today, being forced to stay at home while social distancing has indirectly helped all of us to slow down[281]. Not only did our human ancestors smell those roses, they watched them germinate, grow, reproduce, and die, year after year, without a sense that they were wasting a precious and finite resource in doing so.

Calendars are cultural, man-made constructs

Have you noticed that our calendar years, i.e., linear timeframes, are counted as cumulative units from a particular starting point? This is because annual calendars are used by the political and religious powers to mark events they deem important, like the birth of Jesus, not natural or physical events or processes, like the origin of life on earth.

What's the difference between the Hebrew, Chinese[282], Gregorian, and Mayan calendars? Ultimately, and from the perspective of time itself, not much. These calendars have different origins, starting points, counting systems, and holidays that are relevant only to people, not animals, plants, or the planet. In the end, each of these calendars is nothing more than a cultural construct based on local political, religious, scientific, and economic systems created by humans.

The Bottom Line: Humans have a complicated relationship with time. Our modern lives are almost ridiculously structured by linear time and its precise measurement. However, our human ancestors, and some of our relatives today, live by a different understanding of time, one that it is cyclical, circadian, and rhythmic. There may be wisdom in that. Do you have a linear or cyclical view of time?

THE PERSPECTIVE ON RELIGION

Original debate written by Dimitris Xygalatas

Religion is a universal human experience. All societies, past and present, have some sort of shared beliefs and practices related (to some degree) to the supernatural. For millions of people around the world, religion is paramount to their individual and collective identity, and an important factor in how they live their lives. But not everyone agrees that this is best for society.

Here are three reasons why religion[283] is good for society and three more reasons why it may not be as good as we think.

Religion Is Good for Society

Religion motivates people to do the right thing

All major religions are preoccupied with morality, and all encourage people to be more righteous. Whether through providing inspiration, the promise of rewards in the afterlife, or the threat of punishment, religion can be a powerful social force. Great leaders like Mahatma Gandhi[284], Martin Luther King Jr.[285], Desmond Tutu[286], and Ruth Bader Ginsburg[287] were all empowered by their faith to help those in need and stand up to injustice. Through their actions, they managed to change cultural attitudes, put a stop to oppressive governmental policies (or sexist government policies, in the case of Ruth) and give voice to the underprivileged. Inspired by religion, these leaders, and many more like them, improved the lives of millions and changed the modern world for the better.

And even if religion does not always inspire such grand contributions to society, it still can make a difference on a smaller scale. After all, religion provides comfort and meaning to many by instilling within them an outlook on life that is bigger than their day-to-day challenges or hardships. For instance, there has been a 24% increase[288] in the number of Americans turning to religious faith since the coronavirus pandemic began since religion is a way to cope with the mental health challenges posed by virus.

Religion has inspired great cultural achievements

Some of humankind's highest forms of expression have been inspired by religion. The pyramids in Egypt, the Parthenon in Greece, the Taj Mahal in India, and so many other architectural wonders were built as religious monuments. What's more, Bach's compositions were written as religious hymns. And Michelangelo[289]'s masterpieces depict religious scenes. Centuries later, these masterpieces continue to be sources of awe and inspiration, not just for believers but for all of humanity, adding richness and meaning to the world at large.

Religion promotes social cohesion

One of religion's most important functions is that it acts as social glue. Religious beliefs provide a sense of shared meaning to many people. Moreover, religious rituals bring people together, allowing them to socialize, forget about their problems to a certain degree, and feel part of something greater than themselves. During global coronavirus lockdowns, people felt comforted that they could still turn to their religious communities, even on Zoom[290]. Doing so has enabled otherwise isolated people to stay connected and spiritual[291]. Anthropological studies show that participation in religious events increases group bonding and promotes prosocial behaviors[292]. Through this ability to promote cooperation, religion has been instrumental in holding human societies together and has contributed to the rise of human civilization[293].

Religion Is Bad for Society

Religion promotes prejudice

While religion may foster prosocial behavior, it tends to be towards other members of the same religious group. At the same time, it has been known to promote prejudice and suspicion towards outsiders. Martin Luther[294], credited as the founder of Protestantism, called for the extermination of the Jewish people because of their religious beliefs.

By cultivating arbitrary moral standards, religion has often led to the discrimination or scapegoating of large parts of the population. This is why, in many countries, women are treated as second-class citizens, homosexuals[295] fear for their lives, and atheists[296] face widespread prejudice.

Religion often leads to atrocities

Some of the most violent crimes in human history have been motivated by religious fanaticism. From the Crusades and the Holy Inquisition to the September 11th attacks, religion can often fuel violence, war, and massacres. Indeed, psychological studies show that people are more likely to justify acts of violence[297] and aggression when they are provided with a religious justification[298].

Religion is the opium of the people

Some people think that religion privileges blind faith and obedience over reason and critical thinking. This line of thinking can promote ignorance or denialism on scientific issues and can hinder scientific progress. By promising rewards in another life, religion can also distract people from the problems they face in the life they are actually living. That makes religion a dangerous tool in the hands of certain religious and political elites, who may use it to maintain their privileged status or to convince others to sacrifice their lives. Remember what happened in 1978 in Guyana, when 900 members of Jim Jones[299]'s People's Temple committed mass suicide by drinking cyanide-laced juice[300]? Or David Koresh[301]'s Branch Davidians' cult in Waco, Texas, which also ended in disaster? In these and other extreme cases, believers may live in poverty, risk their lives by trusting others' questionable judgment or even agree to wear suicide vests. All the while, their religious leaders tend to enjoy a worry-free life of wealth and luxury.

....

The Bottom Line: Religion has been with us since the dawn of humanity. Deeply linked to identity, morality, and many of the things that matter to us the most, it is a powerful motivator of human behavior, for better or for worse. Do you think religion brings out the best or worst in people? Does it unite or divide society?

THE PERSPECTIVE ON WORKING FROM HOME

Original debate written by Chaya Benyamin

If you commute to work in a large city, chances are you've fantasized about the potential perks of working from home; professional flexibility, greater work-life balance, a low-stress environment and more autonomy all sound pretty good. Now that Covid-19 has made working from home a reality for many Americans, (71% of those who say that remote work is possible[302]), some are touting it as the new normal.

With the decay of traditional work structures and the rise of a new gig economy[303], work-from-home was on the rise even prior to the pandemic. But while some employers and employees alike are thrilled with the shifting status quo, others insist that dedicated work environments are crucial to mentorship, collegiality, collaboration and more, and are not going anywhere.[304]

Is working from home really all it's cracked up to be? Let's explore some of the advantages and drawbacks of working from home.

Drawbacks of Working from Home

Working from home blurs the line between personal and professional life

For a workaholic, working from home is roughly equivalent to conducting an AA meeting in a distillery – the tools to feed your addiction are precariously close by. And those who are not addicted to work still admit difficulties in setting boundaries[305] between work time and personal time. Conversely, there are also telecommuters who are unable to snap out of "personal mode" when working from home. Those who dream of working in their pajamas often meet the fretful reality that they were about as productive in their waking hours as they were in their sleep. Working at home may actually make it harder to achieve a healthy work-life balance[306] and, therefore, is simply not suitable to all personality types[307].

Freelancers suffer an endemic lack of security

Traditional employment was at one time the cornerstone of a secure future for most Americans: Companies and organizations provided health insurance programs and retirement plans[308] which were, for the most part, financed by the employer. When workers step away from traditional employment, their "buying power" with respect to health care and retirement plans decreases significantly. In addition, freelancers, who comprise the largest segment of telecommuters, are not protected by labor laws[309]. Unlike traditional workers, they are not entitled to overtime pay[310], minimum wage, worker's compensation, or even anti-discrimination protections.

Working from home contributes to professional stagnation

A study from MIT's[311] Sloan Business School confirms that the adage "out of sight, out of mind" is the governing wisdom that gets people ahead, or keeps them in place, at work. The study shows that presence and productivity seem to be inextricably linked in the human psyche, even if there is no actual correlation between presence and output. (Most businesses rely on subjective reviews[312] over performance data).

Simply put, telecommuters are less likely to receive positive performance reviews or receive raises and promotions. Freelance telecommuters have the added challenge of establishing the brand recognition, visibility, and consumer trust that would allow for job promotion or the leverage to demand higher compensation. Furthermore, freelancers incur both time and monetary costs[313] of professional development, making such endeavors less appealing, especially without the same guarantee of advancement that professional development offers in traditional employment.

Advantages of Working from Home

Working from home increases worker productivity

Ninety-one percent[314] of telecommuting employees surveyed reported that they believe they are more productive[315] at home than in the office. Data from a Stanford study[316] that monitored call center employees who worked work from home revealed that this impression has merit: Employees who worked from home answered 13.5% more phone calls than their office-bound counterparts. Homes are largely devoid of typical workplace distractions, engendering deeper concentration for workers and increases in overall productivity for those who employ them. In fact, a recent State of Work Productivity Report found that 65%[317] of full-time employees surveyed thought a remote work schedule would increase productivity.

Work from home is economical for individuals and companies alike

For individuals, working from home means significant savings[318] in transportation costs, like gas and automobile upkeep, and access to affordable (and arguably, healthier) food from their own kitchens. Not to mention, in times of global pandemics, working from home can turn into a protective measure[319]. Time economy[320] for telecommuters is also a distinct advantage – hours not spent commuting can be applied to work, household upkeep, or even exercise or sleep. Work-from-home opportunities increase overall household incomes by providing opportunities for individuals who are not able to get to traditional jobs[321], like parents with young children, retirees, and the disabled[322]. Companies who employ telecommuters save money on real estate, utilities, training. Plus, work-from-home arrangements have even been proven to encourage employee retention[323]. What's more, a recent survey showed that 34% of US workers were willing to take a pay-cut of up to 5%[324] just for the opportunity to work remotely.

Working from home increases the value of work

The gig economy has been particularly useful in connecting talent[325] from around the world to jobs. Freelance platforms like Fiverr and freelancer.com allow freelancers across the globe to network with service seekers and set their own prices, in many cases allowing them to exceed the price they could ask in their local market. A freelancer from India doing business with a company from England need not be confined to the value his service or product might garner in his local market. As such, in the long-term, telecommuting[326] might prove a valuable tool for standardizing the value of labor across markets.

The Bottom Line: It's easy to take a romantic view[327] of working from home – prioritizing flexibility for a greater work life-balance. In reality though, both corporate and independent telecommuters make substantial trade-offs for this flexibility. So where is your next career move taking place?

ENTERTAINMENT CHAPTER

- Harry Potter vs. Harry Potter: are the books better than the movies?
- Do artists with seriously questionable morals deserve fame?
- Should celebrities expect privacy?
- Hamilton – overrated or worth the hype?
- (Titanic) Could Jack have been saved?
- The Kardashians: inspiring or damaging to women?
- The perspective on binge-watching
- The perspective on Fox News
- Throwback TV: Seinfeld or Friends?
- Which is better: Star Wars vs. Star Trek?

HARRY POTTER VS. HARRY POTTER: ARE THE BOOKS BETTER THAN THE MOVIES?

Original debate written by Talia Klein Perez

Though it's been a decade since the last *Harry Potter* movie was released and even more since the final book, J.K. Rowling's magical world still holds a special place in the hearts of fans. While both the films and the books were enormously successful, (the books broke numerous records[1] and the movie '*Harry Potter* and the *Deathly Hallows Part Two* held the record of highest American box office opening[2] for four years[3]), the books versus movies question remains as divisive as ever.

Following, we examine three arguments that the *Harry Potter* books are better and three in favor of the movies.

The Books Are Better Than the Movies

Movies grow old but books never do

No matter how many years pass, when you read the books, the characters, scenes and action that you see in your imagination will be relevant to your time period. In contrast, the movies get dated, and their special effects eventually look old-fashioned. It happened with *Star Wars*[4], after all. Plus, the images of the characters you create in your head remain unchanged, keeping the stories timeless. The actors in all of the *Harry Potter* movies, however, inevitably age[5] and move on to other roles. Seeing a grown-up Daniel Radcliffe and Emma Watson in other movies or entertainment news takes away part of the charm of their original roles when we go back to view them again.

Stuff is left out of the movies

It's inevitable that, for time's sake, the movies can't include the full range of parallels and references that make the books so fabulous. But the parts that are cut out[6] aren't irrelevant. For example, the movies leave out the sassy strength of Ginny Weasley's character and what was in Dumbledore's last letter to Petunia Dursley. Most drastically, the entire plotline with Dobby and the other house-elves is dropped from all the movies. Also, in the movies, we don't get to hear[7] what Harry – or anyone else – is thinking. Perhaps viewers are meant to deduce his thoughts from the music, framing and expression on the actor's face. However, that intimacy is a lot more accessible when thoughts are written out on the page.

Imagination is more powerful than a movie

When you read the *Harry Potter* books, you can picture the characters looking and behaving in the exact way that makes the most sense to you. However, in the movies, the directors and actors force their interpretations onto you. For instance, the movies' assumption that Hermione was white was not implied[8] in the book. This became clear when black actress Noma Dumezweni[9] was cast for the West End production of the play[10] *Harry Potter and the Cursed Child.*

The Movies Are Better Than the Books

The characters come to life

When you read the books, it takes time to learn each character's traits and features until they appear in your mind. When you watch the movies, however, you get the full force of each character's persona the first time they appear on screen. Plus, while not all characters are fully developed in the book, the actors' personalities shine through in each movie, no matter how minor their parts. Not to mention the inspired casting for the movies. Kenneth Branagh[11] as Gilderoy Lockhart in book two, for example, makes more[12] of the phony teacher than Rowling could. Ralph Fiennes as Voldemort gave more menace[13] to the part than the print villain. And Julie Walters[14] made Molly Weasley into everyone's dream mother.

Background music and special effects provide new depth

The movies' music and special effects are among their added value. The soundtrack to each movie enhances the drama, comedy and pathos of the storyline in a way which a book can't convey. John Williams' iconic 'Hedwig's Theme'[15] became the leitmotif of all the *Harry Potter* movies; his magical music set the tone for movies one through three.

Let's not forget that *Harry Potter* is all about magic, and isn't magic meant to be seen, not just read? This is where the movies' special effects[16] enhance the books' magic scenes, action and mystical creatures. While the Quidditch matches[17] are fun in the books, they are downright exhilarating when you watch Harry soar around the goals in the movies. Similarly, Dumbledore's duel with Voldemort[18] in *Harry Potter* five heightens the plot's tension. Plus, the stories' creatures[19], such as Hippogriffs, house elves and dragons, are more spellbinding in the movies thanks to CGI.

Some changes are for the better

By adapting certain parts of the storyline, the changes in the *Harry Potter* movies make the series more intense. (spoiler alert) One example is the death of Hedwig[20]. In the book, she accidentally dies, and no one gets any opportunity to mourn her, especially not Harry. In the movie, Hedwig sacrifices herself[21] to protect Harry when he's ambushed by Death Eaters. It gives a non-human character the ending that she deserves and lets Harry – and all the viewers – mourn her properly. Another example is the decision to cut Blast-Ended Skrewts[22] from the movies. Doing so made the storyline tighter. And the movie's decision to show the torture of Hermione by Bellatrix Lestrange[23] adds to the tension of the cinematic moment.

....

The Bottom Line: Whether you prefer *Harry Potter* as books or movies depends on your imagination and life experiences. What matters is that *Harry Potter* lovers get to enjoy the story twice over, on screen and in writing. Which version do you prefer?

DO ARTISTS WITH SERIOUSLY QUESTIONABLE MORALS DESERVE FAME?

Original debate written by Talia Klein Perez

Every time an artist of any stripe is accused of abuse, crime or immorality, the question is asked: should we separate an artist's accomplishments from the person? From the Michael Jackson[24] and R. Kelly[25] documentaries, which explore respective accusations of sexual misconduct and pedophilia against the singers, to Bill Cosby's retrial guilty verdict[26] to Roman Polanski's growing line of sexual abuse accusers[27], the problem of enjoying the art produced by someone whose acts you abhor keeps rearing its head.

Does the movie *Shakespeare In Love* deserve less love since you learned of its producer, Harvey Weinstein's, sexually abusive behavior[28]? Is *House of Cards* less interesting or *American Beauty* less compelling because of Kevin Spacey's[29] alleged sexual misconduct?

Here are three reasons why we should separate an artist's character from his art and three reasons why we shouldn't.

Art Lives Separately from the Artist That Created It

We would be giving up on a considerable amount of great art

If we start to investigate the private lives of every artist, there'd be much less artwork left. To sin and cause suffering is as much a part of human nature as is to love and express creativity. After all, Richard Wagner[30] was an anti-Semite, the painter Caravaggio was allegedly a murderer[31] and Charles Dickens took a teenage lover[32].

A more recent example is Bill Cosby, whose contribution to television and the positive portrayal of African American families is immeasurable. However, he's been found guilty[33] in his retrial of aggravated indecent assault for drugging and sexually assaulting a woman at his Philadelphia home in 2004.

There's no question that this is very disturbing, but should his cultural contribution to the bettering of society be ignored or erased due to this verdict? We have to separate the artist from their art because if we don't, we'll be missing some great art. Not to mention, is it fair that other actors[34] associated with the work of the accused (be it Bill Cosby, Kevin Spacey, or Louis C.K.) suffer collateral damage? Why should their hard work disappear from the public eye for sins they didn't commit?

Rejecting art leads to censorship

You might feel moral and high-minded for rejecting the movies of Roman Polanski[35], Woody Allen[36] and anything produced by Harvey Weinstein[37], but throwing out art because we disapprove of the artist is the thin end of the wedge. To reject the artwork for any reason other than its artistic merit echoes of censorship. Given that different people have different sensitivities, once you permit any censorship, you don't know where it will end. Besides, the standards of moral decency change over the centuries. What was once acceptable can become unbearable, and vice versa. (Let's not forget that 12 American presidents were slave owners[38]). Holding art to the standards of a fictional 'common decency' is too simplistic.

Art stands alone

Art should be separated from the artist's character because it stands on its own. Many people enjoy listening to the music of Kanye West even though they find his opinions distasteful. The same can be said for the music of R Kelly[39], despite long-standing sexual misconduct allegations against him, and Chris Brown[40], even after he beat up Rihanna. People also appreciate movies starring or directed by Mel Gibson[41] despite their disgust for his apparent anti-Semitism.

Music and movies are not inherently affected by the personal opinions or even the actions of their creators. If you go to a museum and you are moved by a painting by Picasso[42], does it become less moving if you know it was painted by a man who was abusive to his wives[43]? Even Martin Luther King's known adultery[44] didn't undermine the power and pathos of his oratory. Perhaps we need artists to live the tortured lives of self-destruction which produce great art — in which case, we have no right to disown them when they manifest the darkness that so fascinates us.

Why Immoral People Don't Deserve Fame for Their Art

It's unethical to the victims

Celebrating the art of someone accused (or guilty) of abuse of any sort sends the message of caring more for the artist than for their victim(s). This is especially true when both artist and victim are still alive. Woody Allen's daughter Dylan, who claims that Allen molested her[45], wrote an open letter[46] expressing her pain that Allen was honored by people who know what he did to her. Meanwhile comedian Louis C.K.[47] also has a list of victims he exposed to sexual harassment, who deserve consideration before society welcomes his comeback attempts[48]. So, watching a TV show, or paying to watch a movie, enter an exhibition or download a song inevitably means giving certain artists money and recognition that they don't deserve.

Art is too personal to be separated from the artist

It's impossible to separate the artwork from artists' lives because the artwork is shaped and molded by their experiences and actions, by what they value and what they reject. Without knowing the artist's personal life, we miss out on an entire level of understanding their art and symbolic references. For example, without knowing the real history of the Marquis de Sade, all his stories are just adolescent fantasies.

Meanwhile it turns out that Maria Schneider's tears in the rape scene[49] of *Last Tango in Paris* were real because of director Bernardo Bertolucci's off-screen choices, namely, not to inform her in advance[50]. An artist and his art are inextricably linked, a connection that artists profit from. Therefore, it stands to reason that when an artist devalues norms of society, their art loses its value as well.

It glorifies their illegal actions

Ignoring artists' wrongdoings gives them legitimacy to continue their unethical and illegal actions. On a smaller scale, we might glorify a Rock 'n' Roll lifestyle that teens will emulate as a result, but this debate doesn't stop at trashing hotel rooms. As long as rapists, racists and murderers are still being lauded for their work, and artists keep getting the recognition they want, then we, as a society, will be paving the path for others to do the same. Case in point: It has taken 25 years[51] for R Kelly to face some consequences for his alleged sexual misconduct. Would Michael Jackson still be considered the king of pop had we seen *Leaving Neverland*[52] earlier? If we stop consuming art by abusers, perhaps other artists will think twice before doing something illegal or behaving unethically.

The Bottom Line: Should art be enjoyed as a separate entity from the artist or are an artist and his art indistinguishably linked? Next time you learn of a scandal that tarnishes a beloved artist's legacy, will it change their art in your eyes?

SHOULD CELEBRITIES EXPECT PRIVACY?

Original debate written by Chaya Benyamin

Anyone who casually turns on the television or passes by a magazine stand can't help but notice humanity's obsession with celebrities. Cover stories like "A private investigator paid to dig up private information on Meghan Markle[53] and her family" and "Brad Pitt and Ellen DeGeneres[54] Dated the Same Woman" reveal that the public is not nearly as interested in celebrity's work as they are with the gritty details of their personal lives. But does having a public career mean your life belongs to the public?

Here are three arguments for why celebrities deserve privacy, and three reasons why they shouldn't expect much privacy.

Want Fame? Kiss Your Privacy Goodbye

Revealing personal details is an important part of celebrity branding

Before making himself odd by jumping on Oprah's couch, Tom Cruise cultivated a reputation as Hollywood's quintessential do-gooder[55], the kind of guy who saved 8-year-old fans from being trampled and pays for the medical care of complete strangers – the ultimate "good guy."

Gwyneth Paltrow[56] combatted a lull in her star power by launching a lifestyle blog, Goop[57], that revealed (albeit, selectively) her diet, exercise regimen, and parenting techniques. Paltrow capitalized on the public's curiosity about her life to push her lifestyle brand, and she, like other stars, parlays this curiosity into million-dollar movie contracts and endorsement deals. Let's not forget Taylor Swift[58], whose celebrity has helped her evolve from wholesome country singer into pop icon and folk hero, into feminist crusader and equal rights activist.

Infatuation with celebrity isn't about celebrities – it's about society

In her explanation of the public's infatuation with the famed love triangle between Elizabeth Taylor, Eddie Fisher and Debbi Reynolds, gossip scholar (yes, it's a real thing) Anne Peterson writes that public interest was mainly about society wrestling with its norms and values[59]: "The attraction was not to the actual people involved, but to the conflicts they embodied." Spectators work through their own challenges and anxieties alongside people they admire. Who can motivate lifestyle changes like Oprah[60]? Or inspire acceptance like Ellen DeGeneres? Society sees itself in its celebrities, and really, it's not such a bad thing.

Invasions of privacy are not very damaging

Celebrity sex tapes have been a staple of Hollywood scandal since the personal camcorder became popular in the 1980s. Invariably, most of these intimate videos or private nude pictures were stolen and released without the stars' consent, and are brazen invasions of privacy. But careers are rarely ruined by sex tapes or other personal or legal scandals. Martha Stewart remained as popular as ever following a 5-month jail sentence for insider trading[61]; Hugh Grant[62] is still king of the romantic comedy even after cheating on Elizabeth Hurley with a prostitute.

While the MeToo movement changed the landscape for the likes of Harry Weinstein[63] and other celebrities[64] who got away with systematic sexual harassment and abuse, not everything has changed. Actors accused of domestic violence, like Johnny Depp[65], or actresses who have broken the law in other ways, like Felicity Huffman[66], may not retain their titles as Hollywood's popular leading men and women, but they haven't disappeared altogether. Indeed, the public airing of dirty laundry seems to endear the public more than it repels them.

Do Not Disturb

All people are entitled to privacy

All humans need privacy[67]. Privacy allows us to mitigate our social environment and our internal world – a person cannot reflect or grow without freedom from the scrutiny of others. This age of social media and cyber surveillance has brought important questions surrounding privacy to the fore. We are asking what kind of information and data[68] government and businesses are entitled to vis-à-vis our online history[69], but these same considerations are pushed aside in the case of celebrities, whom society rather arbitrarily deems unworthy of privacy at all.

Fame does not necessitate a loss of privacy

The notion that privacy is the natural price of fame is false – even illogical. There are, in fact, plenty of famous people whose private lives are not routinely invaded by the media. Ever seen an article making fun of the Dalai Lama's "dad bod"? Why has MTV neglected to add mega-philanthropist and billionaire Melinda Gates[70] to its list of celebrity MILFs?
Even Hollywood A-listers like Matt Damon and Julia Roberts have managed to avoid the gossip mill. These cases of famous people whose lives are, for the most part, still private, prove that it's possible for fame to be based on achievement rather than intrigue – and all celebrities should be treated this way.

Obsessing over celebrities' personal lives is damaging political awareness

Us gossip zombies helped the celebrity rumor mill[71] generate $3 billion [72]in 2011, a number that has only risen given the pronounced evolution of celebrity journalism in the age of social media. The more celebrities occupy space in public discussion[73], the less space there is for other issues to take center-stage. If celebrities have traded privacy for fame, the general public has traded rudimentary political awareness for juicy gossip. This video[74] depicting university students who are unable to answer basic questions about American government— but ace every entertainment question— broadly illustrates the problem.

The Bottom Line: Celebrities need to be aware that the public's curiosity has no convenient "on/off" button. That said, it might be unfair to expect them to give up their rights to privacy and completely let the public into their private lives. Do celebrities deserve their privacy, or is being in the public eye an inevitable part of the lifestyle they signed up for?

HAMILTON – OVERRATED OR WORTH THE HYPE?

Original debate written by Talia Klein Perez

The winner of 11 Tony Awards[75], *Hamilton*, Lin Manuel Miranda's Broadway sensation, has been the subject of much popular and political excitement since its 2015 debut. Despite rave reviews, including by world leaders[76], fans have asked whether the musical was really worth the $849[77] premium seat (a price that some considered a bargain[78] in the years after its original debut) or close to $200[79] for regular seat ticket fees (even for traveling companies of the show). Now that the filmed version is out, and has been greatly successful[80], a wider audience will be able to see and decide for themselves whether Broadway's most expensive show ever[81] is deserving of praise or largely overrated.

Here are three reasons why *Hamilton* is worth the hype and three reasons why it's not.

Three Reasons Why Hamilton Is All That

Great music and acting

Combining rap, hip-hop, R&B, jazz and Broadway tunes, *Hamilton*'s score and lyrics[82] are innovative, fresh and catchy. In fact, *The Atlantic* made a case for it being the album of the year[83] in 2016. As proof of the songs' impact on pop culture, former President Obama joined in a recording of a *Hamilton* re-mix that was released in 2018. It's a contemporary soundtrack that became the best-selling cast album in Nielsen history. The cast, in best Broadway tradition, is well-versed and alternates between the genres without missing a beat… or a breath. It's no wonder the show sold $30 million[84] in advance ticket sales upon its move to Broadway and has since become a $1 billion franchise.

You actually learn something

Barring some minor tweaks to the storyline, *Hamilton*'s plot generally sticks to the real story of Alexander Hamilton. This means that audiences are learning valuable and unforgettable lessons about the history of the United States of America, all from the comfort of a theater (or living room) seat. Not to mention, the tunes will make your toes dance with glee.

Reflective of current times

Even though the story of Alexander Hamilton took place centuries ago, certain themes strung through the performance are reminiscent of recent events in American society. These include the "repeated effects of speaking one's mind[85]," the clash of immigrants, and the elite and the promise of the "American Dream[86]." In today's era of "a society divided," the musical, with its symbolism of resistance and inspiration for artists of color[87], particularly resonates today and may serve as a comfort or even a springboard towards action and change.

Three Reasons Why Hamilton Is Overrated

Not as 'revolutionary' as it's made out to be

While the show does have a cast comprised of all races, *Hamilton* is not the first production to do so. Is it more impressive this time, because the original characters were all white men? Perhaps. However, when you figure that most of the cast[88] are men and the female cast mates on stage are merely pawns revolving around the main character, the plot seems less "revolutionary" and more patriarchal.

Furthermore, where are historical people of color who most undoubtedly lived in America at the time? As Lyra Monteiro [89]asks in the *Public Historian* journal, "Is this the history that we most want black and brown youth to connect with—one in which black lives so clearly do not matter?"

The alternatives

Hamilton has long been the most expensive ticket out there, by a wide margin. However, instead of spending hundreds of dollars on a single *Hamilton* ticket, before the coronavirus shut down Broadway,[90] you could have spent only $99 of your hard-earned money on a good seat to *Wicked* or *The Lion King* (both classics, easily outdoing *Hamilton* in the scenery/spectacle department). Or, since its 2015 debut, you could have enjoyed the brilliant *Matilda* or laugh-out-loud searing satire which is *Book of Mormon*. Broadway is teeming with great musical performances: from *Chicago* to *42nd Street* to *Oklahoma* or *Dear Evan Hansen* to *Les Miserables*, there was no shortage of alternative top-notch theatre seats.

Not everyone's a fan

Apart from cost and the fact that not everyone might have the patience to sit through a 2 hour and 45 minute[91] history lesson, let's also not forget that the musical is a fast-talking one[92], which means that some viewers, especially those for whom English is not their first language, might have a problems following the show's most celebrated aspect. Indeed, some 20% of Broadway theater-goers are international tourists[93]. So, while it's totally fine not to be a *Hamilton* fan, keep in mind that this show, like opera, might be more enjoyable if you know the story and music before seeing it for the first time.

....

The Bottom Line: It seems as though everyone wants to see *Hamilton*, but is the musical worth the hype, or is it overrated? What do you think?

(TITANIC) COULD JACK HAVE BEEN SAVED?

Original debate written by Talia Klein Perez

With news that a full-size exact replica of the original Titanic[94] is scheduled to hit the seas in 2022, fans of the famous movie can't help but think back to its moving climax, when the hero Jack sacrifices himself to save Rose. He remains submerged in the icy water and inevitably dies of hypothermia while Rose is saved by lying on a wooden door floating on the ocean. But was his sacrifice necessary? This is a question that many viewers are still contemplating[95], more than two decades later.

We examine three arguments that Jack could have joined her, and three that his heroic death was inevitable.

Three Reasons Why Jack Could Have Fit on the Door with Rose

There was enough space – just

After the movie, a lot of *Titanic* (and specifically Jack) fans spent a lot of time recreating[96] the size and shape of the door that Rose was lying on in the movie, and then trying out ways to fit both people onto it. This image[97] shows various ways that two adults could have squeezed onto the same jagged-edged door so that Jack could have been saved. In fact, in 2016, Kate Winslet, who played Rose, admitted[98] to late-night TV host Jimmy Kimmel in an interview that there had been enough space on that door for Jack.

The raft could have been made buoyant enough

For years, *Titanic* director James Cameron rebuffed fans who insisted that there was enough space for Jack by telling them that the issue wasn't space, but rather buoyancy. However, a 2012 episode of *Mythbusters* recreated[99] this famous scene in slightly warmer surroundings. They showed that by tying Rose's life jacket underneath the raft, it could have been made buoyant enough to support their combined weight.

They should have tried anyway

Fans of the movie have insisted on one unanswerable argument. Even if there wasn't enough space or buoyancy in the raft for Jack, Rose should still have tried harder to save him[100]. Perhaps the raft could have held up just long enough to save them both from hypothermia? We'll never know, but thousands of viewers blame Rose for not trying.

Jack is also not off the hook. As Neil DeGrasse noted on Huffington Post[101], "Whether or not he could've been successful, I would've tried more than once... The survival instinct is way stronger than that in everybody, especially in that character."

Three Reasons Why Jack Could Not Have Fit on the Door with Rose

It wasn't buoyant enough

The movie clearly shows[102] that Jack tries to get onto the door with Rose, and then stops as soon as he sees it begin to capsize. It's obvious that it's not buoyant enough to support the weight of both of them. The only options are for one of them to die, or for both of them to die. Jack did the heroic thing by sacrificing himself.

It was too cold

Director James Cameron points out[103] that although the *Mythbusters* might be correct about improving the buoyancy of the raft, their hypothesis isn't possible in the freezing waters[104] of the North Atlantic. Jack would have succumbed to hypothermia. He would be as good as dead anyway by the time he'd swum under the raft in 28-degree (Fahrenheit) waters and tied the lifejacket into place. Moreover, since Rose would have to get off the raft and wait in the water while he did that, she'd probably die of hypothermia as well.

It's not in the script

Although there have been many attempts to prove[105] that Jack could have been saved, Cameron slaps them all down. As he pointed out in an interview[106] with the Daily Beast, the script says "Jack gets off the board and gives his place to her so she can survive." Jack was doomed to die because that's what the script says, and no amount of space or buoyancy research can change that.

The Bottom Line: Having examined the argument on both sides of this debate, we have to conclude that since *Titanic* is a scripted movie, Cameron gets the last word. That being said, if you were Rose, and you were floating on a door with your love interest freezing to death after trying to board it once, and it almost capsized, what would you do? With the launch of the new ship Titanic II[107] approaching, this debate is worth considering.

THE KARDASHIANS: INSPIRING OR DAMAGING TO WOMEN?

Original debate written by Talia Klein Perez

Love them or hate them, the Kardashian family is constantly at the forefront of pop culture. Their social encounters, physical appearances, embrace of gender transitioning[108] and transgender issues, and all-female powerhouse business empire continue to capture the world's attention. Their looks and endeavors, both social and political[109], are always making headlines and prompting discussion both on and offline. In light of the fact that after 14 years and 20 seasons, the Kardashian family has decided to end their reality TV show, *Keeping Up With The Kardashians*[110], we thought it was timely to discuss its – and their – impact.

Here are three reasons why the brand set forth by the Kardashian clan is inspiring to girls and women and three reasons why it is damaging to them.

The Kardashians Serve as a Source of Female Empowerment

Redefining the meaning of power

Utilizing social media and the "selfie," the Kardashian women have taken the reigns when it comes to expressing their selves and their sexuality. By choosing the circumstances of how to document and broadcast their everyday lives, the Kardashians have greater control over how they are viewed and perceived. They choose to advertise their personas at over $1 million[111] per sponsored Instagram post, rather than being exploited by others. Instead of allowing the paparazzi and gossip rags to spin any story they fancy, the

Kardashians are the first to break news of their goings and comings, not to mention new births[112], including raising awareness about surrogacy.[113] The women, themselves, nurture and release the dialogue and stories they want to be heard.

The Kardashians are also harnessing their influence to raise awareness for political issues. Kim has been no stranger to the White House, meeting with President Trump multiple times to advocate for prison reform[114], a cause that has inspired her to study to become a lawyer[115], a career move that reminds everyone of the possibility to reinvent oneself. Her siblings have also used their platforms to shine the spotlight on various social causes[116] ranging from homelessness to surrogacy, Planned Parenthood to the Armenian genocide.

Teaching women to overcome obstacles

Sadly, the Kardashian women are no strangers to hard times. From losing their patriarch to enduring violation in the form of "revenge porn[117]," robbery[118], pregnancy-related health issues[119], and cheating scandals[120] days before giving birth, the Kardashians have a history of turning lemons into lemonade. They are stupendous models of compassion while overcoming a messy divorce[121], learning to co-parent and coping with loved ones' (i.e., Kanye West) mental health issues [122]and romantic partners' addictions[123]. Not to mention, their public acceptance[124] of step-dad Bruce Jenner's very public transition into Caitlyn Jenner[125] did wonders for normalizing transgender issues and raising awareness for the trans community.

Serving as the poster-women for female-led empires

Despite many breakthroughs in the female working world, corporate America is still largely a male-dominated arena[126]. By launching and managing their careers, companies and public appearances, the Kardashian women[127] serve as an inspiration to girls and women looking to make it up the ostensibly testosterone-filled ranks. Spearheaded by mom-ager[128] Kris (Kardashian) Jenner, Khloe, Kourtney, Kim, Kylie and Kendall have launched and continue to run an impressive line of products, endorsement deals and ventures[129], with a collective net worth estimated to be worth more than $1.6 billion[130]. If that's not inspirational to girls and women, what is?

The Kardashians' Public Image Is Damaging to Girls and Women

Unrealistic beauty standards create body dissatisfaction

Reality television shows such as *Keeping up with the Kardashians*, the Kardashian Beauty[131] line of cosmetics, their fashion brands[132], and the ladies' individual[133] social media accounts set high standards of beauty that are unrealistic and unattainable[134] by the average American woman. Failing to emulate[135] the popular Kardashian women's body shapes, hair and makeup regimen (who among us mere mortals can afford a $4,500 skincare routine[136]?) and clothing choices can lead girls and women to overly focus on their exterior, developing body and self-image issues.

Promote compromising behavior

A sex tape, nude selfies, cocktails, shopping... let's face it, the Kardashian women are not exactly the epitome of modern model female behavior. From Kim dressing her young daughter in a corset dress [137]to her endorsing appetite suppressants[138] to Kendall's tone-deaf Pepsi commercial[139], rather than using their corporate prowess to demonstrate how women can do the same as their male counterparts, the Kardashians have shown the public how clichéd feminine wiles can get you ahead in life.

Are totally self-obsessed

The Kardashians are deeply narcissistic,[140] self-obsessed[141] women. It's what they built their careers on; see Kim's 445-page book of selfies[142]. Yet, because they are always in the public eye, the public is constant witness[143] to and enablers of their egocentric follies. Is this the message we want girls and women to observe and internalize? That unilaterally focusing on yourself will lead to success and satisfaction? Will such observed narcissism[144] teach girls and women that it's good to love yourself[145] or that there are consequences[146] to only looking out for "Number One?"

The Bottom Line: Are the Kardashian women the epitome of the feminist movement or are they capitalizing on women's insecurities and displaying backward behaviors? What do you think – do the Kardashians inspire feminism[147] or are they harming it?

THE PERSPECTIVE ON BINGE-WATCHING

Original debate written by Kira Goldring

Before the coronavirus ushered everyone indoors to help flatten the curve, more than 70%[148] of television watchers in America identified as "binge-watchers," with 90%[149] being millennials. Today, when streaming[150] has become a mainstay activity while staying at home, the number of binge-watchers may rise. Binging, when it comes to TV, is usually defined as watching a number of episodes of a single TV show in quick succession.

Binge-watching tends to instill a mixture of pleasure and self-hatred[151] in most people who partake; watching a show you love can be a delightful experience, yet hours go by without your having accomplished anything productive – which most people beat themselves up for later. So, is this newly celebrated tradition one that should be preserved, or are there side effects of binge-watching that may be undesirable?

Here are three arguments in favor of binge-watching, and three arguments against it.

Boycott Binging

The unhealthy choice

It's 1 a.m. and your pillow is calling, but the next episode of your favorite TV show just started automatically, and you *need* to know what happens after the last episode's cliffhanger. The problem? A study in the Journal of Clinical Sleep Medicine[152] links being a self-proclaimed binge-watcher with a 98% amplified risk of poor sleep quality, including fatigue and insomnia.

In the moment it may seem like a good idea but binge-watching before bed can make the next day a difficult one to get through. A recent survey shows that 88%[153] of US adults and 95%[154] of 14 to 44-year-olds have lost sleep because of staying up late to binge-watch multiple episodes of a TV show or streaming series.

Binge-watching doesn't only impact your sleep. A Scottish study from the University of Glasgow[155] asserts that watching more than 2 hours and 12 minutes of television a day is not only bad for your health but can actually lead to an early death. In addition, University of Austin study[156] found that binge-watchers are more likely to be depressed and experience loneliness. Spending long periods of time sitting in one place can slow your metabolism[157] and contribute to developing potentially fatal blood clots. Not to mention that binge-watching may lead to binge-eating[158]. While binge-watching may feel good in the moment, your body may disagree long-term.

Most shows aren't designed for binge-watching

Though the popularity of Netflix[159], and streaming in general, is growing exponentially while people stay at home to avoid coronavirus, the majority of TV shows have been written with the intention of building anticipation[160]; their writers have historically relied on the fact that there is a week between each episode in which you'll be waiting to see what happens next. (Remember *Game of Thrones*[161]?) Binge-watching, by contrast, doesn't provide the time needed for after-thoughts and discussions, central to the community-building experience. Viewer discussions around mystery or action TV shows, like *Lost* or the ultimate *Dallas*-related question of "Who Shot JR?" not to mention questions like "Did Daenerys Targaryen[162] really have to destroy Kings Landing?" or "Did Tony Soprano[163] live or die?" are less likely to happen when the mystery is solved or reasoning explained minutes after the question was posed.

Additionally, the binge-watching phenomenon attests to the lack of patience that characterizes modern society.[164] We're used to getting everything immediately and aren't good at waiting for things we want. Our need for instant gratification (and our inability to delay gratification) may not be good for people over time[165], and binge-watching is a major example of this problem.

Replaces socializing

Many periodic binge-watchers[166] will choose a night with their TV over a night out with friends. A study found that 56% of bingers[167] prefer to watch alone, and 98% of people prefer to watch at home. Though Netflix asserts that 84% of pet owners[168] binge-watch with their pets, what is concerning is that 71% think their furry friend is the best partner to watch with. After all, research from Brigham Young University demonstrates that social isolation is a risk factor for having a shorter life, in ways that are comparable to obesity[169]. Separating yourself from the outside world in order to binge-watch, with or without a pet, may be a sign that things have gone too far.

Bring on the Binge

Enhancing our art

Bingeing on TV makes it easier to enjoy and understand plot complexity, which has led to the creation of complex fiction, and by extension, greater art in our television shows. Shows have never been more creative, suspenseful and thought-provoking than they are today, with a record number of dramas produced in recent years. (Think *The Queen's Gambit, Handmaid's Tale* and *Black Mirror*.) Additionally, newer shows are now written with binge-watching in mind[170] thanks to Netflix; for example, *Ozark, Stranger Things* or Amazon Prime's *The Marvelous Mrs. Maisel*, to name just a few, release all of the episodes from a season at the same time, suggesting that the episodes are intended to be watched quickly and together. Such a canvas of uninterrupted plot lines has allowed creators to be more complex, resulting in better cinematic and more challenging art.

A better viewing experience

Binge-watching makes the entire viewing experience better. It's similar to picking up a book that you absolutely can't put down until you've read it from cover to cover. There's something intensely gratifying about finishing a story from start to finish; gorging on TV shows[171] provides such an effect.

Being completely immersed in a story's plot line puts viewers in a state of "flow,"[172] which is an experience categorized by positive psychology as an important contributor to creativity and well-being. Thanks to binge-watching, we don't have to wait between various parts of a show's narrative (and therefore we don't forget it), which means we can handle and enjoy the intricacies of today's shows, with their multiple plot lines and subtle twists.

Better than drugs

Everyone has addictions, some more serious than others. For those with an addictive personality, binge-watching may be a more harmless urge to give in to than others when soothing an itch. Psychologist Dr. Bea[173] contends that when you watch a show, you release the feel-good chemical dopamine[174] in your brain. Streaming shows keeps the dopamine coming – yet there's no real harm in binge-watching, and who's to say you shouldn't bask in some harmless pleasure?

The Bottom Line: Binge-watching is an enjoyable way to immerse yourself in a specific TV show, but it might not be the healthiest activity in which to partake and may actually ruin the experience of a show for you. What do you think? Do you prefer to binge-watch a show (or one, or two or three…) or stagger your viewings?

THE PERSPECTIVE ON FOX NEWS

Original debate written by Andrew Vitelli

Fox News was launched in 1996, created as an alternative to news stations like CNN. The station quickly became a favorite among conservative viewers and soon shot past its rivals in the ratings. While it has been plagued in recent years with controversy[175] surrounding numerous and continual sexual harassment cases [176]against some of its biggest names, the network has long drawn criticism over its right-wing tilt.

Is Fox News bringing much-needed balance to a one-sided media universe, or is it simply a propaganda mouthpiece? We take a look at three arguments for each position.

Fox News Provides Necessary Balance
The media really does have a liberal bias

While it has become a cliché to criticize the mainstream media's liberal bias, it is also a stretch to say such a bias does not exist. According to the Pew Research Center[177], left wing views dominate most newsrooms, which can be attributed to the fact that only 7%[178] of journalists self-identify as Republican[179]. And while professionalism demands a degree of neutrality, it is unrealistic to think ideology does not come through. Just look at the effect of the media bubble[180] after the 2016 presidential elections. Donald Trump's victory took most of the country by surprise, likely as a result of the media[181] letting its left-leaning views obscure the 45th president's widespread support.

Right-leaning Americans need a voice

In a 2004 Pew survey[182], conservatives outnumbered liberals by more than two to one. Though the gap is narrowing today[183], self-identifying conservatives still outnumber self-identifying liberals. But while 41% of Americans don't trust the mass media[184], conservatives trust it even less. Still, they have to get their news somewhere, and 88% of conservatives surveyed rely on Fox News.[185]

Additionally, recent years have seen the rise of numerous far-right networks, from Breitbart News to the conspiracy theory-filled Infowars[186]. (The ascent of the late Radio host Rush Limbaughs[187] predates the network's launch.) With this in mind, Fox News is much closer to the mainstream media and features Emmy Award-winning journalists, like Chris Wallace. The news station has even, on many occasions, criticized former President Trump[188] and given coverage to many non-Trump-friendly issues. Fox News also depends on major companies for advertising – which, as the firing of former host Bill O'Reilly shows[189], helps maintain accountability. So, say what you will about the network, relative to the current media landscape, Fox is the natural home to the moderate conservative.

Fox News is not to blame for radicalism

To say that Fox News is responsible for the beliefs of its viewers is to reverse cause and effect. Right-leaning voters have always been attracted to politicians and pundits who buck the liberal mainstream, from President Nixon to Barry Goldwater to George Wallace.[190] The news channel did not create these viewers, it just appeals to them. Fox is also not the powerhouse liberals imagine[191]. While it has historically dominated cable news in the ratings contest[192] (though MSNBC has caught up since Trump's 2016 election), that is a small market. Its primetime programming boasted 2.4 million viewers [193]in 2018, which seems significant, but not compared to any episode of The Big Bang Theory, for example, which had anywhere from over 18 million viewers[194] that same year.

Fox News Has Harmed Political Debate

At Fox News, ideology comes first

Having a conservative voice among the news channels to question assumed wisdom and counter perceived bias makes sense in theory. But at Fox News, winning over conservative viewers has sometimes led the network to promote baseless conspiracy theories which may mislead its viewers. These include since-retracted claims calling the coronavirus a Democratic-backed impeachment scam[195], and bogus accusations that Dominion Voting Systems[196] rigged the 2020 election.

Perhaps more damaging is the reflexive partisanship, which in recent years manifested itself in a constant criticism of Democrats and seemingly uncritical defense[197] of former President Trump. Plus, the former president's hiring in the summer of 2018 of former Fox executive Bill Shine[198] to head White House communications strengthens the perception that the network and Republican party are closely linked. Shine[199] left the post in March 2019 in March 2019 to reportedly join the Trump's 2020 re-election campaign[200]. Let's also take note that it was Fox News' Tucker Carlson[201] who reportedly convinced former President Trump not to go to war with Iran in June 2019.

It creates an 'echo chamber'

Conservatives have long disagreed with the mainstream media's liberal tilt[202]. But before the launch of Fox News, they were at least forced to engage with the news seen by a major share of Americans. With many right-leaning viewers now getting their information from Fox News (along with the rise of partisan online media sites), though, they are not exposed to the viewpoints many Americans take for granted. Not only does this stop conservatives from challenging their own perspective[203], it also limits their ability to persuade[204] and engage others. After all, one must understand the other side in order to offer a compelling argument. And biased media can sway voters; not for nothing we have the "Fox News Effect[205]."

It is perceived by some as low-quality journalism

The difference between Fox News and other networks is not simply where they fall on the political spectrum. Some consider Fox to be less committed

[206]to accuracy and journalistic standards than its competitors. Politifact, a non-partisan fact-checking website, rated[207] more than 150 statements made on Fox News by pundits or their guests in 2015. Sixty percent were rated Mostly False, False, or Pants on Fire. This compares to just 27 percent for CNN, and 41 percent for MSNBC, the network's liberal competitor. Fox News has also never won a Peabody Award (though other Fox affiliates, including FX, have). There's a place for punditry, but at other networks, it takes a backseat to journalism. This is not necessarily the case at Fox News.

The Bottom Line: No one can question the impact that Fox News has had on the worlds of American broadcast news and politics in the last two-plus decades. Is this a positive development? Has diversifying the news landscape helped hold traditional media accountable? And how will the network continue to evolve?

THROWBACK TV: SEINFELD OR FRIENDS?

Original debate written by Rachel Segal

If you're a Gen Xer, you probably spent every Thursday evening in the 1990s and early 2000's watching *Friends* and *Seinfeld*, two shows that broke – and re-set – the mold for "Must-See TV[208]." With constant reruns of both today, especially with streaming options on Netflix and a long-awaited *Friends* reunion, fans of all ages can get in on the debate about which laugh-out-loud sitcom is better. Both shows invited us into an intimate circle of friends whom we collectively got to know, though it is up for debate as to which group was more cynical and neurotic[209]. Either way, the characters in both shows consistently drew big laughs – and still do today, even 25+ years[210] (*Friends*) and 30+ years[211] (*Seinfeld*) later.

Here are three arguments as to why *Seinfeld* is the better sitcom and another three why *Friends* should earn the distinction.

Why Seinfeld Is Better Than Friends
Seinfeld is innovative

Seinfeld revolutionized television[212], which is quite impressive for a show "about nothing[213]." But it's precisely because the show's story lines were about different aspects (and complaints) of everyday life, ranging from the mundane to the controversial, that *Seinfeld* made such a lasting impact. The show was especially groundbreaking by boldly and sophisticatedly turning taboo issues, never before addressed on television, into comic gold. (Before *Seinfeld*, had anyone ever dared discuss in public "being a master of their domain[214]"?)

It redefined the use of characters

Seinfeld was unique in that it made its secondary characters[215] a central part of what viewers loved about the show. The (blessedly) long list of secondary characters that had recurring appearances are so funny and memorable that they feel as if they are regulars. Unlike other sitcoms before and since, *Seinfeld*'s secondary characters weren't necessarily just about advancing the story but also about providing laughs, which is equally important.

The show was also the first of its kind to go against the grain of typical feel-good sitcoms to nurture the rise of the antihero[216]. *Seinfeld* pioneered the idea that main characters don't have to be good or likable. They can be superficial, peculiar, painfully honest or downright immoral and still make audiences laugh and root for them (like being relieved when your fiancé dies[217].) Because the show didn't have emotional glue, it needed to – and succeeded at – being funny at every turn.

Seinfeld had a distinctive and rich world that fueled a fandom culture around the show

Seinfeld's rich catalogue of unique references served as a cultural hotbed for viewers to bond with each other over the show. For example, before the actor Michael Richard's racist rant[218] in a comedy club changed public opinion, his character of Kramer was a cult figure. And to this day, there are popular tours around New York City to see various *Seinfeld* hot spots[219].

Also, no other sitcom in TV history has produced such a long list of catchphrases[220] that have made such a lasting, cross-generational impression on pop-culture lexicon. The show not only invented new concepts ("close talker[221]," "low talker[222]," "double-dip[223]," among many more) but also gave us phrases and terms[224] that have contributed to our modern-day vernacular, like "yada, yada, yada[225]."

Why Friends Is Better Than Seinfeld

Friends is the epitome of a classic sitcom

Friends[226] wasn't as innovative as *Seinfeld*, but it took on the possibly harder task of reinventing[227] the wheel. The humor in *Friends* managed to appeal to a much broader audience. The show's writing and production teams turned a simple premise into one of the most successful shows[228] ever produced as it was relatable[229] on many levels; audiences could see themselves in the main characters as they navigated their path into adulthood. (It was also fun to aspire to Monica, Rachel and Phoebe[230]'s beauty and style, Joey's coolness, Chandler's wit and Ross's sweetness.)

Sure, many aspects were unrealistic (whose NY apartment[231] is as big as Monica's?), but issues of dating, connecting and falling out with friends, job stress, the fears of becoming independent and settling down, etc. are all universally familiar. And the producers tackled all of these subjects candidly, with light, topical humor and clever dialogue that never offended viewers. Plus, the cast's genuine rapport[232] and excellent comedic timing made the show an enduring – and endearing – legacy. It is the quintessential classic sitcom, which is why it remains so popular today.

The show's character development showed depth and heart

Unlike *Seinfeld*, which purposely scoffed at character development, *Friends* let viewers grow with its characters. We followed and rooted for them as they matured, fell in and out of love, got pregnant[233], made mistakes and learned from them (how many divorces[234] did Ross have?). *Friends* was skillfully unique in that it was a fun, light comedy that succeeded to have its characters evoke feeling about life's struggles rather than just laughter (A perfect example is Monica and Chandler's fertility issues[235]).

Friends is easily translatable and therefore more influential

The fact that *Seinfeld* is almost impossible to replicate renders *Friends* the more influential series, given that it has set the bar and path[236] for the creation of more successful sitcoms. Without *Friends*, there would be no *How I Met Your Mother*, *New Girl* or even *The Big Bang Theory*, among others. Given the premise of *Friends* (see argument #1), which had 40-50 more episodes than *Seinfeld*, the show has also aged better than *Seinfeld*. Besides, the numbers don't lie: Netflix recently paid some $100m[237] to stream the series for 12 months (after which it can be found on HBO Max), citing that it was the second-most watched program among American viewers in 2018.

The Bottom Line: The *Seinfeld* vs. *Friends* debate boils down to the following question: Which is more commendable – inventing something new or successfully reinventing a classic sitcom formula?

WHICH IS BETTER: *STAR WARS* VS. *STAR TREK*?

Original debate written by Metin Bilman

Whether you're boldly going where no man has gone before or you're already in a galaxy far, far away, you've probably heard the age-old debate about which of science fiction's two biggest franchises is better. Geeks, freaks, scientists and even casual fans have long been arguing in every corner of the galaxy about *Star Wars*[238] and *Star Trek*[239]. Which is better and why? They both have spawned multiple spin-offs, (including for TV[240]), prequels, video games, cartoons[241], merchandise lines (Baby Yoda[242], anyone?), catch phrases (like "May the 4th be with you[243]!"), and even religions[244]!

Following are three arguments why *Star Wars* is better and three arguments why *Star Trek* is better. (With all due respect to the Last Jedi, Mandalorian or the USS Discovery, this debate is all about the original installments of each franchise.)

Why *Star Wars* Is Better

It's the most successful franchise in the world

Star Wars' massive span of galaxies, aliens, spaceships, tactical maneuvers and plot points assure there is something to satisfy many types of fans. The franchise's first installment became one of the biggest blockbusters ever, not just because so many people went to see the movie, but also because so many fans went to see it over and over again. It was also the first movie that created merchandise mania[245], a craze to follow many summer movies in the years to come.

By the way, did you know that even George Lucas didn't believe[246] that the movie would be such a success? On the evening of the movie's premiere, he didn't even bother to attend. Instead, he was in Hawaii with his best friend Steven Spielberg, brainstorming an idea for another movie. That movie was *Raiders of the Lost Ark*.

It's epic

You've got to hand it to George Lucas[247], who was inspired by Akira Kurosawa's *Hidden Fortress*[248], for creating a fable-like battle between darkness and light. The story is a very effective embodiment of good vs. evil. Darth Vader is the ultimate unstoppable force, and Luke Skywalker, with his naïve looks and belief in the goodness of mankind, triumphs against his father's attempts to lure him to the Dark Side. Moreover, despite it being set in the future and in a galaxy "far, far away," the use of medieval symbols, such as knighthood, swords, princesses and wise magicians, gives the *Star Wars* franchise the sense of a legend.

It made sci-fi inspiring

From lightsabers to dogfights in space, from exotic planets to the cynical yet lovable characters[249] – mainly the superb Han Solo[250] – the franchise is visually striking and stimulating to the imagination. *Star Wars* made science fiction cool and approachable, and inspired countless movies to follow. Could you imagine the dynamics among *The Avengers* gang or the *Guardians of the Galaxy* without being inspired by that of Han, Luke and Leia[251]? Could you picture what *The Matrix* would look like without taking costume ideas from Darth Vader?

Furthermore, the spectacular special effects used in *Star Wars* spawned ILM[252] (industrial lights and magic), created by George Lucas, which has forever changed movie special effects – both practical and computer-generated.

Why *Star Trek* Is Better

It's grounded in reality

When Gene Roddenberry[253] created *Star Trek*, he wanted to be as grounded as possible in reality, or "future reality." This is evident in that *Star Trek* deals with dilemmas that could very well become reality in the coming centuries, when humanity will exhaust Earth's resources and make its curious and necessary journey to outer space.

Star Trek debuted in 1966, just five years after Yuri Gagarin[254] was the first man to journey into outer space and two years before the moon landing. At that time in history, the race to space was as real as it gets. The quest to explore strange new worlds, gapping the difference between mankind and other species, was the key theme in all of the show's incarnations.

It's not afraid to deal with burning issues

When it came out in the 1960's, *Star Trek* tried to tackle issues of gender, race, socioeconomic differences and war. As it first aired during the Vietnam War, the peak of the Civil Rights movement, and the Cold War, the show tried – and often succeeded – in addressing these issues and educating its viewers for the better. Nichelle Nichols[255], who played Uhura in the series, was the first woman to have an interracial onscreen kiss on television. While protest quickly ensued, Nichols recalls being stopped one day on the street by a fan of the show who complimented the controversial kiss and encouraged her to keep taking chances. That fan was Martin Luther King[256].

It allows for complexity

Star Trek tries to educate its viewers about diplomacy and understanding[257] the other side in a conflict instead of resorting to war. This is why every villain has a reason for his furious grudge and mischievous actions. The show weaves this reasoning through the conflict and outcome, even if the villain sometimes dies. The Enterprise crew will always prefer reasoning – even at the cost of losing – for the sake of goodwill and of spreading the kindness of the human species across the galaxy.

The Bottom Line: *Star Wars* is a massive outwardly adventure while *Star Trek* aspires to use science fiction as a metaphor for our reality. On a given night, whose characters would you like to explore the universe with?

SOCIETY CHAPTER

- The perspective on animal testing
- Is the death penalty justified or should it be abolished?
- The perspective on fracking
- Social welfare: do its advantages outweigh its disadvantages?
- The perspective on the royal family
- Can people change their minds?
- The perspective on political correctness
- Can the use of torture be justified?
- Should we negotiate with terrorists?
- The perspective on circumcision
- Should we depend on fossil fuels or renewable energy?
- The perspective on abortion
- Does reverse racism exist in America?
- Should prostitution be legalized?
- Should the burqa be banned?
- Should convicted criminals have the right to vote?
- The perspective on surrogacy
- The perspective on unions
- Do vegans have the moral high ground?
- Are whistleblowers heroes or traitors?
- Should women serve in combat units?

THE PERSPECTIVE ON ANIMAL TESTING

Original debate written by Chaya Benyamin

People don't like getting sick, and they like discussions about how treatments for illness are developed even less. Humanity has long been uncomfortable with animal testing. Evocative pictures of caged animals make it easy to forget the frequently laudable ends that are met through animal testing. When heartstrings are being tugged, it's also easy to forget to ask: To what extent should ethical concerns about respecting animal life dictate the extent to which science and industry can advance?

Let's explore three reasons in support of animal testing, and three reasons against it.

It's Time to Leave Animal Testing Behind
Animal testing doesn't guarantee safety for human use

The FDA requires[1] all chemical materials, like cleaning products and cosmetics, to be tested on animals before introducing them to humans. The only trouble is that toxicity tests performed on animals predict problems for humans less than half the time[2] which is bad news for millions of mice, and for some humans too. Lack of correlation[3] between animal and human reactions have also been reported in clinical trials, some of which have caused human subjects to suffer permanent physiological damage[4]. If animal testing cannot give full guarantees of safety or results, is it really meeting its ends?

There are plenty of viable alternatives to animal testing

Improved imaging methods, in vitro, and computer models represent some of the many emerging options[5] for conducting research without animals. Governments, scientists, and even the commercial science industry agree that alternative approaches[6] are preferable. For commercial science enterprises, non-animal experiments have the dual benefit of cost efficiencies and less regulation. It stands to reason that the more the public nudges researchers[7] toward alternative testing measures, the more encouraged they'll be to find them.

Animal testing privileges humans over other species

Science has helped us to do away with a lot of useless ideas, and scientists would do well to ask themselves whether man's dominion over animals isn't one of them. The idea of man as lord of beasts is as old as Adam and Eve, and arguably, this idea of man's privilege has discouraged him from collaborating with his environment in favor of exploiting it. In a man-first paradigm, it is little wonder that humanity is wholly out of sync with its surroundings – we extract minerals from the Earth and, in return, inject it with poison. And why should we care? Man is in charge and the world is our oyster.

Animal Testing Is Still Necessary

The advances afforded to humanity through animal testing are undeniable

Who can identify the telltale limp of Polio survivors, or the panic that would ensue every summer when the disease would claim or cripple hundreds of young people each year? Polio[8], one of humanity's oldest and most pernicious killers, was eradicated with the help of animal testing, as was smallpox[9] and rubella. Plus, diabetes can now be controlled through insulin, which was discovered with the contribution of animal testing. Add to that new developments in HIV, cancer and diabetes treatments, and even electronic implants that can give patients the chance to activate paralyzed limbs, and it becomes clear that human medicine without animal subjects would be a mere shadow of itself. Animal research[10] is the primary vehicle for understanding how disease affects the human body. When we say no to animal testing, we also say no to deeper understanding and possibility.

Human medicine advances animal medicine

Animals and humans are often afflicted by the same infectious and congenital diseases[11]. Almost all of our pets die from diseases which are well known to us – the most common cause of sudden death in cats[12] is heart disease, the same disease that kills the most women[13] in the US every year. Medicines developed via animal testing for human use often end up benefitting[14] the very animal populations upon which they were first tested. (For example, monkeys, Ebola's first victims, could benefit from a developmental Ebola vaccination). The reflexive nature of advances and human sciences is expressed in the One Health Initiative[15], whose central premise connects human health to the health of animals as well as the environment. As such, animal testing is not merely subjugation of animal life to human life, but a necessary step in preserving Earth's biology writ large.

Lab animals lead fine lives

Lab animals are cared for by dedicated veterinarians who are committed to ensuring test animals have a high quality of life. Attending Veterinarian at University of Oklahoma Health Sciences Center, Wendy Williams, explains that by law[16], labs provide animals much more than their basic needs: "Animals must be free of pain or distress—which means they must receive pain medication, enrichment devices, social group housing, and other provisions to ensure they maintain health and welfare." In a nutshell, animal research labs are legally and ethically obligated to provide their test subjects with conditions that will allow them to live out their lives as any other member of the species would. Williams also points out that given the abundance of nutritious food, the safe environment and rigorous monitoring, lab animals also lead longer, healthier lives than most animals in the wild and even pets.

The Bottom Line: Researchers, laboratories, and governments take great pains to ensure that animal testing achieves the highest possible ethical standards. That being said, as a species for whom incarceration is one of the steepest punishments, we must continually investigate our motivations and justifications for using almost a million animals[17] in 2016 for animal testing across the US. In what cases do you think animal testing is justified?

IS THE DEATH PENALTY JUSTIFIED OR SHOULD IT BE ABOLISHED?

Original debate written by Chaya Benyamin

Throughout history, societies around the world have used the death penalty as a way to punish the most heinous crimes. While capital punishment is still practiced today, many countries[18] have abolished it. In fact, in the US, California's governor recently put a moratorium on the death penalty[19], temporarily stopping it altogether. Given the moral complexities and depth of emotions involved, the death penalty remains a controversial debate the world over.

The following are three arguments in support of the death penalty and three against it.

Arguments Supporting the Death Penalty

Prevents convicted killers from killing again

The death penalty guarantees that convicted murderers will never kill again. There have been countless cases where convicts sentenced to life in prison have murdered other inmates and/or prison guards. Convicts have also been known to successfully arrange murders from within prison, the most famous case being mobster Whitey Bulger[20], who apparently was killed by fellow inmates while incarcerated. There are also cases where convicts who have been released for parole after serving only part of their sentences – even life sentences – have murdered again[21] after returning to society. A death sentence is the only irrevocable penalty that protects innocent lives.

Maintains justice

For most people, life is sacred and innocent lives should be valued over the lives of killers. Innocent victims who have been murdered – and in some cases, tortured beforehand – had no choice in their untimely and cruel death or any opportunity to say goodbye to friends and family, prepare wills, or enjoy their last moments of life.

Meanwhile, convicted murderers sentenced to life in prison – and even those on death row – are still able to learn, read, write[22], paint, find religion, watch TV, listen to music, maintain relationships, and even appeal their sentence.

To many, capital punishment symbolizes justice and is the only way to adequately express society's revulsion of the murder of innocent lives. According to a 2020 Gallup Poll, the majority of Americans (55%[23]) think that legal executions fit the crime of what convicted killers deserve. The death penalty is a way to restore society's balance of justice – by showing that the most severe crimes are intolerable and will be punished in kind.

Historically recognized

Historians and constitutional lawyers seem to agree that by the time the Founding Fathers wrote and signed the U.S. Constitution[24] in 1787, and when the Bill of Rights were ratified and added in 1791, the death penalty was an acceptable and permissible form of punishment for pre-meditated murder.

The Constitution's 8th and 14th Amendments[25] recognize the death penalty BUT under due process of the law. This means that certain legal requirements must first be fulfilled before any state executions can be legally carried out – even as applied to the cruelest, most cold-blooded murderer[26]. While interpretations of the amendments pertaining to the death penalty have changed over the years, the Founding Fathers intended to allow for the death penalty from the very beginning and put in place a legal system to ensure due process.

Arguments against the Death Penalty

Not proven to deter crime

There's no concrete evidence[27] showing that the death penalty actually deters crime. Various studies comparing crime and murder rates in U.S. states[28] that have the death penalty versus those that don't found very little difference between the two. These inconclusive findings mean that capital punishment may or may not be a deterrent for crime. No definitive answer is reason enough to abolish it.

More expensive than imprisonment

Contrary to popular belief, the death penalty is actually more expensive[29] than keeping an inmate in prison, even for life. While the cost of the actual execution may be minimal, the overall costs surrounding a capital case (where the death penalty is a potential punishment) are enormously high. Sources say[30] that defending a death penalty case can cost around four times higher than defending a case not seeking death. Even in cases where a guilty plea cancels out the need for a trial, seeking the death penalty costs almost twice as much as cases that don't. And this is before factoring in appeals, which are more time-consuming and therefore cost more than life-sentence appeals, as well as higher prison costs for death-row inmates.

Does not bring closure

It seems logical that punishing a murderer or terrorist with the most severe punishment would bring closure and relief to victims' families. However, the opposite seems to be true. Studies[31] show that capital punishment does not bring comfort to those affected by violent and fatal crimes. In fact, punishing the perpetrator has been shown to make victims feel worse[32], as it forces them to think about the offender and the incident even more. Also, as capital cases can drag on for years due to endless court appeals, it can be difficult for victims' families to heal, thus delaying closure.

The Bottom Line: The death penalty has been used to maintain the balance of justice throughout history, punishing violent criminals in the severest way to ensure they won't kill again. On the other hand, with inconclusive evidence as to its deterrence of crime, the higher costs involved in pursuing capital cases, and the lack of relief and closure it brings to victims' families, the death penalty is not justified. Where do you stand on this controversial issue?

THE PERSPECTIVE ON FRACKING

Original debate written by Kira Goldring

"Fracking" is a technique used to extract gas and oil from shale rock, via drilling into the earth and using high-pressure water to force open fissures from which to take the gas. Less commonly known as hydraulic fracturing[33], this process has recently come under fire by environmentalists, who claim that fracking is more harmful to the earth than it is beneficial. Some countries have banned the process altogether, while others largely rely on fracking as their main energy source; the question is, who is right?

Here are three arguments supporting fracking, and three arguments against it.

Back the Frack

Jobs, jobs, jobs

Fracking technology has rejuvenated local economies and provided job security for people previously unemployed. Between 2005 and 2012, over 725,000 jobs[34] were created thanks to the introduction of fracking, which reduced the US unemployment rate by 0.5%. A nationwide study[35] found that communities benefit monetarily from having drilling sites in the vicinity, showing an average income increase of 6% and a 10% increase in employment for said communities. While having drilling sites nearby could be seen as a hassle, the economic benefits to surrounding communities makes it worth the inconvenience.

Cutting out coal

Until recently, coal was responsible for over 50% [36] of the US's electricity generation. But this dipped to less than 37% in 2012 thanks to fracking; America's carbon emissions have dropped[37] over 800 million tons as a result, which might help reduce the effects of climate change. Burning natural gases (made possible by fracking) instead of coal cuts almost every kind of air pollutant and C02 from the atmosphere, resulting in fewer harmful particles in the air.

Reduces foreign reliance on energy products

In the last few years, vast reserves of resources like oil and gas have suddenly been made available due to the creation of cost-effective extraction techniques, like fracking, which are completely transforming the US's perspective on energy. Thanks to fracking, America is now a leading natural gas producer,[38] in addition to increasing potential oil and gas exports. This has lowered US dependence on foreign sources for oil and gas; according to the U.S. Energy Information Administration (EIA), shale production from fracking helped reduce foreign petroleum imports by over 40%[39] since 2006. This significantly reduced the price of gas[40] and created a huge boom in domestic oil production.

What the Frack Are You Thinking?

Negative environmental impact

Extracting natural gas through fracking has dire environmental consequences. A 2014 study[41] on the environmental costs and benefits of fracking claims that fracking could potentially release toxic chemicals into the air and water, in addition to contaminating drinking water through surface spills and other means. Wastewater disposal[42] – a byproduct of fracking that gets injected into the ground – is partially responsible for a hundredfold increase in man-made earthquakes, threatening 3.5 million people a year. Additionally, there is evidence that fracking causes severe methane leaks[43], which traps heat in our atmosphere and can be devastating[44] for the climate.

Threatens property value

While fracking may have created job security for some, it has economic ramifications for communities surrounding the drilling sites. There are no laws in place to protect property owners, and the community members don't have a say – or a warning – when drilling projects pop up around their houses. This introduces increased noise pollution, light pollution and traffic. As a result of these disruptions, property values in the vicinity of drilling sites often decrease dramatically. Even the former CEO of Exxon (one of the largest oil and gas corporations in America), Rex Tillerson, claimed that drilling would do "irreparable harm[45]" to his property value, and he sued a water supply corporation[46] to stop construction of a water tower that was being built to supply drilling operations in the vicinity.

There are alternative solutions

Fracking isn't the only source to tap for energy, and therefore isn't necessary. Unlike finite resources like fossil fuels and shale rock, which eventually run out and negatively impact the environment, renewable energy[47] sources regenerate and can be used continuously. For example, solar energy[48] takes sunlight and allows it to be used for electricity, hot water, heat, etc. A study[49] published in the journal Science of the Total Environment ranked fracking between 4th-8th place in sustainability when compared to other energy resources. In comparison, renewable energy significantly reduces greenhouse gas[50] emissions, and is the cleaner pathway to energy consumption. And while renewable energy sources may be less immediately efficient than fracking, resources currently put towards fracking could be reallocated to renewable energy development to great effect.

....

The Bottom Line: Fracking allows for the acquisition of important resources and employs many people in the process, yet the potential costs to the environment and property values may be high enough to stop the endeavor altogether. What do you think? Should we keep drilling, or is it time to table fracking in favor of something else?

SOCIAL WELFARE: DO ITS ADVANTAGES OUTWEIGH ITS DISADVANTAGES?

Original debate written by Kira Goldring

America's first social welfare program[51] began with FDR, in response to the poverty resulting from the Great Depression. While nobly intended, his Work Progress Administration was met with derision by many of his political opponents, and the debate over government handouts has continued ever since. Well before the coronavirus pandemic hit, former President Trump signed an order[52] in 2018 calling on states to impose stricter criteria on welfare recipients. While the recent health crisis spurred the Trump administration to sign a $3 trillion aid package[53] to help shoulder the pandemic burden, these are highly unusual times.

This debate sets COVID-19 and its implications aside in examining three reasons why social welfare impedes productivity, and three reasons that it is necessary.

Social Welfare Discourages Productivity

The system is set up to be abused

Social welfare packages provide people with little incentive to work. For example, "Welfare Queen[54]" Linda Taylor cheated the system in the '70's and acquired over $150,000 a year from the government – a much higher "salary" than many make in their lifetime. There are less grand examples of others who may not want to permanently live off state handouts[55], but, like single mother Iris Swift admits, there are "a lot of advantages to staying on welfare." According to a Cato study, US welfare packages exceed the minimum wage[56] in benefits and salary in every state. If that's the case, why wouldn't people take advantage of the system when they get paid more not to work?

Short-sighted goals

While welfare may be helpful in getting individuals out of tight financial spots, it may do little to support future self-sustainment[57]. The government does a poor job[58] of weaning the needy off of welfare and teaching them how to enhance their employability or earning potential. Not to mention that high marginal tax rates[59] come into play when a household's income increases. The minute a family attempts to cross back over the poverty line, these tax rates are combined with benefit phase-outs, resulting in a loss of 50-60% of the family's initial income gain. This provides incentive to avoid jobs that pay highly enough for self-sustainment, promotions, and increased hours of work, subsequently trapping people in the cycle of poverty[60]

Psychologically unhealthy

Welfare benefits create a harmful culture of psychological dependence. A study[61] found that welfare recipients are deprived of positive feelings of self-worth after receiving handouts – feelings that are necessary to function in society at full capacity; lack of self-esteem[62] contributes to a lack of motivation and a diminished desire to move up in life. Research from a Yale University[63] study corroborates these findings. Even former President Obama – a staunch advocate for social benefits – cited his own anecdotal evidence of welfare programs encouraging this culture of dependency[64] and reducing motivation in their recipients.

Social Welfare Is Vital to Society

Improves the economy

Social insurance, such as unemployment benefits, create a risk-sharing economy[65] in which the threat of potential economic difficulties befalling any one person is protected by the majority. Take the Great Recession as an example, where unemployment rose by record levels, yet the poverty rate[66] only increased by 0.5%[67]. These social benefits also contribute to a more economically efficient society; for example, research found that increasing food stamps programs and public insurance in several states led to more entrepreneurship[68], because they made it less risky for would-be business owners to venture out on their own[69]. Unemployment benefits also provide people leeway to find jobs that match their skill sets, rather than snapping up the first available position. In other words, overall economic productivity increases as a result of government assistance.

Not what it looks like

Contrary to the argument that welfare disincentivizes people from working, welfare beneficiaries are often those who *cannot* work. A third of the people who received government assistance in 2015 were off it within the year. In 2018, the number of people registered for food stamps dropped 7 percent[70] year over year, following a 4.5 percent drop in 2017, showing a continued downward trend. Plus, most adults who qualify for TANF[71] (Temporary Assistance for Needy Families) for an extended period of time have physical and mental disabilities[72]. Additionally, a large percentage of children in the US[73] receive one of the six major forms of government assistance, and they participate in these programs longer than adults. Welfare benefits aren't for the lazy – they're for the needy.

Gives low-income children a chance

Aside from adults, social welfare can also brighten the future for poverty-stricken kids, ultimately halting the cycle of poverty in families at risk. A recent study[74] from Georgetown University and University of Chicago found that Mexico's Prospera – a cash-transfer system conditional on parents sending their children to school and staying up-to-date with doctors' appointments – led to greater increases in children's educational attainment long-term. These children grew up to work an average of nine more hours a week than their counterparts who weren't enrolled in the program, in addition to earning higher hourly wages. Another study found that kids who were covered by Medicaid[75] later earned more money and required less welfare assistance as adults. Poverty can be traumatic[76] for children, and welfare helps the next generation become less reliant on government support.

The Bottom Line: In times when the economy is not paralyzed by Covid-19[77], social welfare can easily be taken advantage of and may not leave its recipients with much motivation to provide for themselves. However, government assistance provides a hopeful future for individuals in need and the economy as a whole. Thinking back to pre-coronavirus times[78], do you think social welfare has benefited your community?

THE PERSPECTIVE ON THE ROYAL FAMILY

Original debate written by Chaya Benyamin

Elizabeth II, the current Queen of England, age 94, has held the throne for sixty-nine years [79]– the longest reign of any monarch in history. Despite – or maybe because of – Harry and Megan's controversial interview with Oprah that exposed unseen sides of the royal family, it seems as though the majority[80] of British subjects still support the British Monarchy. But in an era that increasingly values merit over birth (take Prince Will's marriage to middle-class Kate[81] and Prince Harry's marriage to former actress Meghan Markle[82], a Catholic, divorced American), the very concept of a monarchy seems outdated[83] at best and positively inegalitarian at worst.

So, is the British Monarchy a worthwhile institution or an unnecessary relic of times long gone? Here are three arguments in support of the British Monarchy and three against it.

God Save the Queen!

The royal family is a boon to the United Kingdom's economy

Step aside James Bond[84], the Windsor family is the UK's most popular and marketable brand, in good times as well as in bad[85]. Be it weddings[86] or births[87], the world is constantly watching as the Windsor family expands[88] and even, as of recently, gets smaller[89]. The prestige, popularity (and family drama) of the royal family earns the UK plenty of PR that drives tourism and business. Estimates from the British Tourism Council surmise that the Windsor family, worth an estimated $88 billion[90], generates over $770 million[91] in tourist spending annually. Additionally, the family's milestones (such as the weddings of Prince William[92] and Prince Harry[93] and the births of their children spur adjacent industries – injecting the economy with hundreds of millions of extra dollars from Britons eager to participate in the festivities – and the profits from their agricultural holdings[94] are deposited into the public's coffers.

The royal family has historically provided assurance to the nation in uncertain times

In times of upheaval, the English have always leaned on the Monarchy as a symbol of security in a changing world. Queen Elizabeth II's 1952 coronation[95] provides an excellent example. While Great Britain was recovering from the ravages of WWII, a country whose citizens were living on rations held an outsized ceremony to commemorate their new queen. In the Queen's prosperity, the people of England see their own prosperity, and the coronation a shining symbol of English perseverance. Moreover, there is something profoundly comforting in knowing that if the state's political institutions go berserk – or get sidelined by the coronavirus[96] – there is a stateswoman[97] or statesman prepared to take the reins. And not just any stateswoman – one whose entire family legacy hinges on her subjects' prosperity.

The Queen is an international unifier

As an a-political figurehead[98] (even in the heated times of Brexit[99] and especially during the anxiety-ridden pandemic[100]), the Queen, and by extension, the royal family, tend to unite Great Britain and its commonwealth around principles that transcend day-to-day politics, highlighting shared history and values and contributing to societal cohesion. This unifying effect stretches far beyond the UK's borders to the 2.2 billion subjects of the Commonwealth of Nations[101], a voluntary union of 54 nations dedicated to shared values like democracy and human rights. Headed by Queen Elizabeth II, the Commonwealth unites countries in history and trade, and provides a friendly platform to hold member states to high civic standards.

Magna Carta Her Out of Here!

Monarchy is unfair to monarchs

Being born a prince[102] or princess is very much an accident of birth. But is it a happy one? According to Princess Diana[103] and the Duchess of Sussex[104], no. Imagine a life where your every movement was carefully watched[105] and judged, where you were forbidden to have political conversations, refused medical treatment[106] – even when having suicidal thoughts. To put it bluntly, the life of royals is dictated by tradition and expectation; they don't enjoy the same basic freedoms[107] as their subjects. The UK has long passed the necessity[108] of an absolute ruler. It stands to reason that, if the royals' role in the governance of their society is largely ceremonial, then English society would be generous to release them of this burden, as Prince Harry and Meghan [109]have done.

The royal family ties England to a dark past that is best left behind

Sure, the majority of Britons express favor for the Queen. Of course, speaking against the Monarchy is technically an offense that can be punishable by life in prison[110]. Laws like the aforementioned Treason Felony Act reveal the pernicious nature of the British Monarchy's past, and to an extent, its present. Monarchies have long survived on the bread and blood[111] of their subjects, whom they regularly plundered and sent to wars on their behalf. Add to this the English Crown's long history of Colonialism[112] – its subjugation and pilfering of nearly a quarter of the planet's resources – and reveal a wholly inhumane enterprise. Is an institution that thrives upon degradation really an appropriate centerpiece of national pride? This is especially relevant to ask when long-held questionable attitudes about race still persist among the royal establishment, specifically regarding the skin color[113] of Prince Harry's son, Archie.

Monarchy is expensive

Weighed against the cost of security, travel, and yearly pensions (even for extended family!), the royal family's revenues are not quite as bountiful as they seem. The royal family cost taxpayers in the United Kingdom $86 million[114] in 2018/19 – a 41% increase over the previous year. That's quite a price tag for figureheads in a country strapped with over $2.2 trillion[115] in debt. Arguably, this money could be put to better use to improve the nation's ailing (some would even say failing) healthcare system[116], especially during a global pandemic, or spent on schools.

....

The Bottom Line: The Monarchy is English society's most exquisite display of romanticism – at once representing the grandness of the past and the promise of the future. However, it is both expensive to uphold and may be trapping the British in a past they no longer connect with (just ask Prince Harry[117]). Do you think the British Monarchy should be preserved, or, as Queen Elizabeth[118] nears her 95th birthday, is it time for a change?

CAN PEOPLE CHANGE THEIR MINDS?

Original debate written by Chaya Benyamin

Throughout the past two decades, the American public has gravitated toward opposite political poles[119]. A Pew poll[120] showed that record numbers of Americans have deemed their ideological counterparts "so misguided that they threaten the nation's well-being." The personalization of our newsfeeds[121] has decreased interaction with opposing viewpoints, and when exchanges do happen, they are increasingly ineffective. Today, 90%[122] of Americans feel the country is polarized. And the political, racial and cultural divisions[123] keep getting starker; even responses to the current health crisis[124] have become politically tinged and divided[125].

In such a divisive atmosphere, is idea-exchange even worthwhile anymore? Can people really change their minds? Below, we'll explore three reasons why we can, and three reasons why not.

Can People Change Their Minds? Yes.

Change is common

So, can people change their minds? You bet! In fact, the notion that people do not change their minds contradicts what we readily observe about the human experience. Many people who have eaten meat their whole lives have become vegetarians[126]. People change religions or take one up after a lifetime of atheism[127]. They change political parties, too; people tend to become more conservative[128] with age (and former NYC mayor Michael Bloomberg[129] has been a Republican, Independent and a Democrat, including even a 2020 Democratic presidential candidate[130]). There is no thought system in existence, no matter how deeply entrenched, that cannot ultimately be undone.

Win bees with honey, not vinegar

Positivity can go a long way in changing people's minds. A review of Reddit's ChangeMyMind[131] forum revealed that people who remained polite and practiced hedging – a linguistic tool used to make an argument appear less threatening ("it may be that") – succeeded more often in changing people's minds. Another study determined[132] that people are more likely to change their minds when they feel good about themselves. People who had practiced positive self-affirmation before entering an argument were more influenced by the argument than those who had only argued, without the benefit of the self-affirmation activity. Positivity opens the door to a flexible mind.

Change is a process

Change, in both behavior and thought, is often not the result of one brilliant counterargument, but a process that develops slowly over time. Science writer, Jennifer Oullette, likens changing one's mind to phase transitions[133] – the point at which a substance transforms from one state of matter (like liquid) to another (like gas). Liquid water can sit on an open flame for what seems like ages before the water turns to steam. Those expecting their opponent to announce an immediate reversal of their opinion would do well to remember that a watched pot never boils. Look at American food companies in the days after the George Floyd race protests. It has taken decades (if not longer) for brands like Uncle Ben's Rice, Aunt Jemima, Mrs. Butterworth and Cream of Wheat to take a stand against and change the use of African-American stereotypes in their marketing of food products[134]. It may take time, but change can come.

No, Minds Can't Be Changed
We're programmed to resist changes of heart

Evolutionarily-speaking, our survival hinges on our ability to cooperate with each other. The earliest humans increased their ability to cooperate by forming bonds based on shared ideas and beliefs, just like today. Our beliefs are a pronouncement of loyalty and identity[135]. When we declare loyalty, we increase our safety in two ways: First, by showing we are part of a large group that is not easy to threaten, and second, by increasing the likelihood that we will receive support from that group. As such, we have an innate resistance to changing our minds. Our propensity to lean somewhat blindly toward the beliefs of our peers (and reject the beliefs of others) is part of the evolutionary hardwiring[136] that has helped us to survive.

Facts fail

Countless studies[137] have revealed the discouraging truth that people don't often allow facts to intervene in their worldview. This is because belief and opinion are often tied to identity. For example, Christians organize their ethics and actions around the teachings of Jesus[138]. So, when someone challenges a core Christian belief (how did Jesus walk on water?), they are not just challenging an idea, but the foundation upon which a person has built her life. Given that views and identity are linked on the major issues (which differ from one person to another), it is unsurprising that many people will double down[139] on a certain belief when a fact challenges their worldview. For example, white nationalists, eager to prove their Aryan bona fides, have started utilizing genetic testing services to verify their "whiteness." When their results show that their ancestry is not exclusively white, instead of abandoning their belief in their whiteness (and in white superiority), they question the validity of the tests.[140]

In another example, supporters of the Standing Rock or Dakota Access Pipeline protest were so used to reports of police violence, that they readily believed the veracity[141] of a particularly egregious incident in which police allegedly burned down Indigenous activists' camps. A photo of tipis in flames circulated widely on Facebook before it became clear that no camps had been burned, and that the photo came from a 2007 HBO film.[142]

First impressions count the most

People tend to conform to the ideas they learned as children, not only because of the feelings of security generated at home, but also because first impressions make stronger imprints[143] on the brain than those that follow. Studies have found that a first impression, once formed, is hard to undo. This is especially true if a subject or person is first presented to you in a negative light. For example, one study that appeared in *Social Cognition* showed that people who observed someone who had made a bad first impression[144] were slow to believe she had changed for the better, even after weeks of seeing her perform kind acts.

....

The Bottom Line: People's natural and social impulses guide them away from change as much as they steer them toward it. What do you think? Are we hopelessly set in our ways, or always free to break into new mindsets? What do you think? Can people change their minds?

THE PERSPECTIVE ON POLITICAL CORRECTNESS

Original debate written by Zoe Jordan

Political correctness is intended as a tool of respect, avoiding language and actions that insult or exclude people who are already marginalized. For instance, when we say 'Native Americans' instead of 'Indians,' a name given by a mistaken Christopher Columbus, we are being politically correct. But when it comes to what is and is not acceptable, where do we draw the line, and who gets to draw it? Is PC culture making us more sensitive to others or afraid to speak to anyone who might think differently than we do?

Here are three arguments for political correctness, and three arguments against it.

PC Culture Benefits Us All
Changing language changes perception

The way we speak and the words we use influence the world around us. When we consider our choice of words, we are considering the impact they have on the people who hear them. Changing the common use of job titles like "policeman," "fireman" and "salesman" to "police officer," "firefighter" and "salesperson" has enabled more women to envision themselves[145] in these jobs. Refraining from using the word "retarded" to mean "stupid" is a basic show of respect for anybody who is cognitively impaired.

While PC culture may sometimes feel a bit forced or insincere, its intention is to be respectful and not to insult anyone. Even if we overdo it, it is a work in progress, which may take time to find a healthy balance that is easier to live up to. And if someone has to think twice to consider whether an intended compliment might come off sexist or offensive, is that such a bad thing? We all have sore spots[146] that we'd rather not have poked at.

PC culture isn't new

The moralizing and hand-wringing around the latest "frontier" of acceptable speech have always been part of public discourse. Just like every new technology poses new concerns[147], each advance or step forward in norms of social acceptability have always had nay-sayers and detractors who worry about censorship or limits to free speech.

Before women got the vote, anti-suffragists argued that women didn't even *want* to vote and that it would simply make the election process more costly and unwieldy. Before the GOP was formed to promote abolition, people worried that the end of slavery would devastate the cotton and tobacco trades[148]. New norms can take time to establish but, looking back, it's hard to imagine any other way.

PC culture promotes safer spaces for self-expression

If someone you love struggles with addiction and comes to the realization that it is time to seek help, they may attend a support group. The first thing they will want to know is that whoever they are and whatever they may have done, they won't be judged or labelled a "junkie" or a "drunk" but will be accepted and heard on their own terms. A functioning PC culture is part of creating a safe environment within which vulnerability can be exposed and people can grow and heal[149].

PC Culture Is Limiting at Best, Dangerous at Worst

PC culture is elitist and exclusionary

Political correctness, for all of its good intentions, is rather unpopular: no less than 80% of Americans think that it's a problem[150]. And if that doesn't seem representative of your milieu, it's probably time to check your privilege. While it claims to want to include everyone, calling someone out for using a "problematic" term or demanding that they adopt your speech norms is not only alienating and belittling, but a display of social cultural superiority[151]. After all, the most reliable determinants for someone's support of political correctness is their education and income[152]. So is this kind of sensitivity actually doing anything for minorities or is it just the virtue signaling[153] of the already-privileged?

PC culture threatens free speech

From cancelling controversial campus lectures to banning the use of certain words, PC culture can put a damper on self-expression and plurality of perspectives. While it does not *technically* stop free speech, the more insidious threat is that it leads to a culture of self-censorship and voluntary limitation[154] on speech. If people are not voicing the true extent of their thoughts and opinions, this in turn limits the scope of public discourse and deliberation.

PC culture can be particularly punishing online, where a bad joke, a misunderstood comment, or an actual mistake can literally ruin lives[155]. In a climate where an ill-conceived photo can garner negative responses, go viral, awaken a mob-mentality, get you fired and leave you unhireable, (think Lindsey Stone, of cemetery selfie infamy[156]), it's no wonder people may just clam up.

PC culture leads to less not more tolerance

Just because people aren't voicing their opinions does not mean they do not exist. On the contrary, without the chance to test or express ideas out loud, they just go untested, forced deeper underground, becoming more fixed and less flexible[157]. Rather than increase tolerance, PC culture's goal, it actually increases polarization by drumming up opposition; while some may relish the righteous feeling of "educating" someone, nobody wants to feel patronized or policed. In fact, many Americans' feeling of restriction was one of Trump's greatest selling points[158] since he positioned himself as the straight-talking antidote[159]; meanwhile trigger warnings and hypersensitivity to offense are making us feel more sensitive, and more triggered[160].

The Bottom Line: A culture of political correctness is meant to make society more respectful and inclusive as a way of encouraging diversity and equality, but it also leads to unintended effects, such as resentment or extremism. When it comes to PC speech, do the ends justify the means?

CAN THE USE OF TORTURE BE JUSTIFIED?

Original debate written by Kira Goldring

Officially a thing of the dark ages, torture is still used today. Many prisoners of war are tortured for information, as are suspects in malicious crimes. Yet, according to the Geneva Conventions[161], "torture, cruel or inhuman treatment and outrages upon personal dignity" are legally prohibited. Although this has been ratified by 194 countries[162], torture still occurs behind closed doors for a variety of security reasons.

Here are three reasons this strategy is purely abhorrent, and three reasons why there is a justifiable basis for torture.

Torture Is Abominable, No Matter the Circumstances

Pointless pain

Torture may be effective at getting people to talk, but it doesn't mean they're telling the truth. Take Khalid Sheikh Mohammed,[163] a terrorist involved in the 9/11 attacks, who was tortured by the CIA after his capture; his mid-torture "confessions" led to the arrest of many suspected terrorists – all whom were found to be innocent. According to two psychological surveys, people suffering from torture produce unreliable information[164], and the most effective way to get them to tell the truth is through building rapport. In fact, the US Senate Select Committee on Intelligence recently published a report[165] on the CIA's detention and interrogation program. After more than five years analyzing 6.3 million pages of documents, they found that the

CIA's enhanced use of interrogation techniques were ineffective in obtaining accurate information or gaining detainee cooperation.

Slippery slope

The minute the use of "enhanced interrogation techniques" is allowed on a prisoner, it's nearly impossible to draw the line as to what constitutes "too much" torture – and there's no telling how far[166] it will go. The psychological damage[167] that excessive torture can cause a victim is even worse than the physical damage; for example, Amir, a salesman who was brought to Abu Ghraib[168] prison in Iraq, was forced to remain naked in his cell for days, lay down in human excrement, and howl like a dog while being pulled on a leash. He was eventually let go without being charged, and now suffers from severe post-traumatic stress disorder[169]. No authority figure is equipped to decide what kinds of torture are acceptable without causing irreparable damage.

Entering the animal kingdom

When respectable law enforcement institutions use torture, they risk damaging their hard-earned reputations and moral upstanding. The use of torture is a rejection of a democracy's loyalty to abiding by societal rules and values. For example, torture directly contradicts the legal right[170] to remain silent, which suspects are afforded when questioned. Citizens in Western countries trust that they're living in a society where fair treatment [171]and basic respect for human rights are a given. Therefore, when these ideals are compromised by organized government, the "good guys" sink to the level of those who threaten the very principles they are fighting to protect and ordinary citizens lose trust in their authorities.

Torture Is a Justifiable Last Resort

The ends justify the means

Torture is acceptable if it can save the lives of fellow citizens in "ticking-bomb[172]" scenarios. Whether it's an issue of national security or the potential death of a kidnapped toddler, torture might be the only means of eliciting crucial information fast enough to rescue the people at risk. Although torture may not be legal, 63%[173] of Americans think that torturing suspected terrorists can be a justifiable way of extracting information from them. Imagine if someone with information on the 9/11 attacks[174] were to be captured, and torturing information out of him would have saved the lives of every Twin Tower victim; should his captors refrain from torturing him? The answer seems like a no-brainer.

All's fair in love and war

In times of war, armies may do whatever is necessary in order to save their country. By the very act of enlisting in military combat, a soldier has agreed to put his life on the line and die for his people if that's what's required of him — and suffering from torture can be a facet of that. Basic military training alone, specifically in elite units, can often involve some form of psychological or physical torture by the hands of a soldier's own army to help strengthen soldiers' immunity for worst-case scenarios. Such prisoner-of-war training exercises[175] are par for the course when countries are preparing for war. During actual war, all bets are off, and torture is often an unavoidable consequence.

It matters who you're up against

When facing enemies that don't subscribe to the rules of democracy and Western morals, governments may have to speak the language of their opponents to get results. Terrorist organizations like Al Qaeda don't think twice about torturing their captives, and even reportedly have a manual to show members exactly what to do. During the Vietnam war, the North Vietnamese government re-purposed the Hoa Lo Prison[176] in order to torture American POWs for information. If suspects (terrorists or otherwise) pose a threat to a nation and play by a different set of rules – rules that include the use of torture – the opposing government may have no choice but to do so as well. In fact, in some cases, torture may even be a deterrent to war, thus saving lives.

....

The Bottom Line: While a morally defunct and potentially inefficient way of gathering information, there may be good reason to use torture if it means saving lives. What do you think? Are there any scenarios in which using torture can be justifiable?

SHOULD WE NEGOTIATE WITH TERRORISTS?

Original debate written by Chaya Benyamin

One of the original thinkers of sociology, Max Weber[177], defined the modern state as "a human community which holds the claim for legitimate use of force within a given territory." To humanity's great chagrin, most terrorists have probably never read Weber, and thus go about their plots to influence politics with violence, mostly at the expense of civilians. Since Ronald Reagan's infamous pledge[178] to never negotiate with terrorists, the public has debated whether negotiations with terrorist groups are warranted or even advisable. In fact, in 2015, former President Obama announced a policy overhaul[179] publicly stating that the American government could start communicating and negotiate with hostage takers.

Below, we'll discuss three reasons for negotiating with terrorists, and three reasons for refusing to negotiate with them.

We Shouldn't Negotiate with Terrorists

Negotiating with terrorists isn't necessary

The shock and awe tactics employed by terrorists are intended to scare the public into believing that its powers are larger than they are and that its aims are an urgent matter. However (and with the utmost respect for the suffering of terror victims and their families), statistics reveal that losses of human life due to terror attacks are low in number[180]. Since 1975, just over 3,000 Americans have been killed in the US by foreign-born terror – that's a 1 in 45,808 chance of dying from terrorism[181]. For comparison, the odds of dying from heart disease or cancer are much higher: 1 in 7. In general, terrorists have no armies, minimal funding, and terrorist activities are generally unable to have a destabilizing impact on target countries. Victim countries maintain[182] their militaries, territory, and political systems. Negotiation is not merited when the state holds all the cards.

Terrorists do not represent the people they claim to represent

ETA[183], the militant Basque separatist movement, was formed with the goal of winning independence from Spain. The only problem was that violent resistance in general and the ETA in particular was never popular[184] among the Basques. Similarly, groups like al-Qaeda and ISIS claim to speak for all of Islam, when polling[185] from Muslim majority countries reveals that these groups couldn't be less popular.

Negotiating with such groups grants them legitimacy they do not have. It therefore does a disservice to the populations that these organizations pretend to represent by associating them with causes they, in fact, do not believe in.

Negotiating with terrorists undermines the rule of law

Terrorists are criminals, period. The tactics utilized by terrorist organizations and organized crime families, particularly drug cartels, are basically interchangeable[186]. Murder, extortion, kidnapping, drug trafficking, rape, and innumerable other acts committed by terrorists are already codified by law as criminal acts. Touting some purported grievance as the reason for these crimes in no way excuses them. Societies ruled by law expect their governments to pursue justice. Just as we would not negotiate with John Gotti[187] or El Chapo[188] over the nature of their crimes, we should not negotiate with terrorists in response to theirs.

We Should Negotiate with Terrorists

Negotiating with terrorists affirms the values of human life and community

Consider Israel's history of lopsided prisoner swaps[189] with terrorist groups. Israel once traded 4,700 detainees to the Palestinian Liberation Organization in exchange for six Israeli soldiers. That's a 783:1 ratio. The stakes were even higher in the 2011 prisoner exchange with Hamas[190], wherein 1,027 convicted terrorists were released in exchange for just one captive soldier (that's a 1,027:1 ratio for those keeping count). Is there anything more endearing to a country than the public proclamation that the life of one of its citizens is worth 1,000? Such negotiations send a clear message to the communities who benefit from them: You are part of this community, and your life has value.

Negotiating with terrorists can sometimes be a necessary evil

Let's talk about the world's most tenacious narco-terrorist, Columbia's cocaine kingpin, Pablo Escobar[191]. When extradition of narcotraffickers to the US became a Columbian imperative, Escobar sought to influence the policy with the tools at his disposal – namely, political assassinations, kidnappings, and bombings (lovely guy). Average citizens should not be forced to bear the consequences of terrorists' disagreement with the government. So, Columbia's decision to reverse its extradition law and even allow Escobar to serve out his prison sentence in a luxury prison[192] of his own design, was welcomed warmly by the public and was a necessary measure in ensuring public security.

Similarly, negotiations with terrorist organizations can serve as a starting point for a broader peace agreement, as secret and public negotiations between the government of the UK and the Irish Republican Army and the latter's subsequent disarmament and participation in politics demonstrates.

Negotiating with terrorists is preferable to the alternatives

Say what you will about terrorists, they are persistent. FARC guerillas[193] made Colombia's jungles untraversable for three decades. Al Qaeda has been in business since (gulp) 1988, and ISIS[194] has been around since 1999. The threat to public security is real, present, and potentially long term. Governments must therefore weigh the cost of non-negotiation, which can range from indiscriminate bombings, the kidnapping and torture of innocents, to biological warfare against potential gains of peace to be won through negotiation. Non-negotiation can also mean confrontation through violence. The only problem is that this kind of warfare is asymmetrical and generally more costly for governments than it is for terrorist groups. For instance, in 2011, it was estimated that America's "War on Terror" had cost $1 trillion[195], a number that rose to $5.6 trillion[196] as of 2018. So negotiations with terrorists may actually benefit national economic and security interests.

....

The Bottom Line: While the reasons for refusing to negotiate with terrorists are plain, this inflexible stance is not always feasible or necessarily desirable. But neither can a policy of negotiation always create positive results. With globalization and social media affording terrorists broader possibilities of influence, do you think governments should negotiate with them or refrain from doing so?

THE PERSPECTIVE ON CIRCUMCISION

Original debate written by Julian Bonte-Friedheim

Circumcision[197] is a ritual that has been performed by humans for thousands of years. It is a long-standing tradition in many societies due to practical, religious, health and cultural reasons, among others. The vast majority of male Americans are circumcised (80 percent according to the CDC[198]) whereas Europeans[199] have generally ended the practice. Why do we continue to circumcise our boys? Based on what we know now, are there good reasons for continuing doing so?

Here are three reasons against the practice of circumcision and three advocating it.

Arguments against Circumcision

It's non-consensual

Circumcising a newborn child is inherently done without his approval. They aren't old or self-aware enough to make a valid decision, much less communicate it. Just because the infant is too young to remember this incident doesn't mean it can't be traumatic. If every individual were able to make the choice as an adult, they would likely reconsider, given the significant pain that circumcision involves.

It can cause deep psychological trauma

Several studies[200] have indicated that circumcision may lead to profound psychological trauma. While the mind may not remember the pain (this procedure is often done without painkillers[201]), the body does. As it is a genital procedure it can lead to aftereffects as an adult, such as PTSD, higher sensitivity to pain[202], feelings of having been mutilated[203], violated, and feeling incomplete. Cutting off a piece of the body, albeit a very small one, can have a strong emotional effect, particularly in such an intimate area.

It can reduce sexual stimulation

The removal of the foreskin has been shown[204] to reduce sexual satisfaction. The foreskin contains nerve endings that are highly sensitive and it move[205] during sex in ways that can increase pleasure. Cutting it off dulls sensitivity in the 'head' of the penis. (This has led some men[206] to resort to "un-circumcision," which can be done with surgery and may increase pleasure.)

Arguments for Circumcision

It reduces the chance of contracting AIDS

According to the World Health Organization, circumcision reduces the chance of heterosexual men getting AIDS by 60%. The foreskin can be torn and inflamed during sex, increasing the chance of HIV entering the body. It can also trap fluids that contain the disease, making it more likely for the man to develop it. Additionally, the foreskin fosters the lingering of certain types of bacteria[207] that can raise the chance[208] of an AIDS infection.

It may help men last longer in bed

Circumcision may reduce[209] the chance of men ejaculating too early[210]. In fact, removing the foreskin can ensure that men last long enough for their partners to get off too. This is considerable given that premature ejaculation in men is an issue that may lead to sexual dissatisfaction[211] in their partners. It can also cause performance anxiety[212] that risks further worsening this problem. As such, circumcision can help enhance men's sexual performance and, thus, his relationship with his partner.

It helps boys fit in

A large majority of American babies are circumcised at birth[213]. This has been the case for many decades and is the norm in US hospitals. Medical and practical benefits aside, physically fitting in as a boy is a comfort during childhood and, especially, adolescence. While this behavior is most definitely not justified, boys bully and single each other out for far less significant reasons. Unfortunately, this has led to many boys and teens in America getting bullied[214]. Others around the world who are uncircumcised have also felt left out[215] and harassed[216]. Perhaps just fitting in is a good enough reason to get circumcised.

The Bottom Line: Circumcision has several up and down sides. many men that go through it don't notice a big difference. However, not remembering the procedure doesn't mean it didn't have an adverse effect on them. Would you circumcise your child?

SHOULD WE DEPEND ON FOSSIL FUELS OR RENEWABLE ENERGY?

Original debate written by Rachel Segal

With more focus on the environment, especially following extreme weather events such as the historic snowstorms in Texas[217], not to mention the UN's cautionary warnings[218] about global warming, the battle between fossil fuels (oil, natural gas and coal) and renewable energy (specifically solar and wind energy for this article) is increasingly relevant. Should the global economy continue depending on fossil fuels or should renewable energy replace them?

Here are three arguments in support of fossil fuels and three in support of renewable energy.

Why We Should Depend on Fossil Fuels

High energy density

Fossil fuels are the world's dominant energy source mainly because of their high energy density[219]. Energy density is the amount of energy stored in something. When it comes to fossil fuels, oil[220] – or more precisely, its fuel derivative, gasoline – has a very high energy density, especially compared to solar energy. This makes gasoline more efficient.

For example, a mere gallon of gas contains enough energy to charge an iPhone every day for almost 20 years[221] whereas solar panels are less dense, requiring more surface area and hours of sunlight to recharge each day. While solar energy has an efficiency rate of 15-22%, fossil fuels are 20-40% efficient.[222]

More economical: cheaper and safer to store and transport

Fossil fuels[223] are considered some of the planet's cheapest fuel sources. Sure, the process of extraction and refinement is expensive, but the return on investment more than makes up for it. Plus, today's innovative technologies[224] may now be able to use fossil fuels in ways that don't pollute.

Also, the constant state of fossil fuels' molecular composition means they don't form other compounds when stored in canisters for long periods. This makes them easy to store and safe to transport over long distances, either on trucks or pumped through pipes above and below ground. The same cannot be said about handling or transporting nuclear energy, whose risks outweigh its extremely high levels of energy density.

Source availability and reliability

Oil, natural gas and coal are reliable sources of energy because they are abundant and easily available[225]. In fact, fossil fuels can be found in almost every country and will not be depleted any time soon. Plus, with the speed at which technology[226] is constantly developing, fossil fuel extraction and refinery procedures have improved, making their availability even greater.

This reliability includes generating electricity, transporting fuels, and making byproducts, like plastics, cosmetics, and even medicine, for the world population's energy needs[227]. Fossil fuels also provide more reliable sources of electricity than solar and wind energy since they are not dependent on climactic conditions[228].

Why We Should Depend on Renewable Energy

Endless potential for technology and job creation

Unlike oil, natural gas and coal, solar and wind energy are technologies[229] – not fuel. This means they are not restricted by eventual depletion or an innovation cap. As research continues and technologies improve, there will be even more advances in renewable energy – and at lower costs.

And with technological growth comes job creation[230], not only in the US[231] but also worldwide. While fossil fuel technologies are mostly mechanized, the renewable energy industry is more about labor. According to the Environmental Defense Fund[232], jobs in the solar and wind power sectors have grown at about 20% annually in recent years. And this is just the beginning.

Stable Energy Prices

Renewable energy sources can be continually replenished through natural processes, unlike fossil fuels. This can, perhaps, limit the potential for political conflicts, wars and, especially, price volatility. Renewable energy is already providing affordable electricity across the United States[233]. The trend is soaring as costs to generate electricity from solar and wind power are steadily declining[234]. In fact, in 2019, US renewable energy consumption surpassed coal[235] for the first time in over 130 years.

While renewable energy facilities are costly to build, once built, operations are low-cost, especially as the fuel is free for most renewable technologies. This leads to relatively stable renewable energy prices over time. In contrast, fossil fuel prices are vulnerable to dramatic price swings. Increasing our reliance on renewable energy can also help protect consumers when fossil fuel prices jump.

No harmful impact on environment or health

The most obvious advantage of renewable energy is its environmental impact, or lack thereof. Solar and wind energy, among other renewable energies, are non-pollutants, producing little to no global warming emissions[236]. In contrast, fossil fuels[237] overload our atmosphere with carbon dioxide and other greenhouse gas emissions. These all trap heat[238], which steadily increases Earth's temperature and creates disastrous impacts[239] on our environment and climate.

Health-wise, the air and water pollution (even in our drinking water) emitted by coal and natural gas plants is linked to breathing problems, neurological damage[240], cancer, and heart attacks. Also, unlike fossil fuels, wind and solar energy don't need water to operate and therefore don't erode or pollute our water resources and ground.

The Bottom Line: The availability and high energy density of fossil fuels make them a more economical resource to depend on for energy. However, they significantly contribute to global warming whereas renewable energy is a non-pollutant with limitless technological potential and output. Should America continue relying on fossil fuels or switch entirely to renewable energy?

THE PERSPECTIVE ON ABORTION

Original debate written by Talia Klein Perez

Long understood as an extremely personal issue and procedure, abortion has increasingly become a matter of public and political debate. The fact that the Supreme Court legalized abortion[241] in America in 1973 and hundreds of thousands[242] of abortions are performed in the U.S. each year has done little to quell the matter. On the contrary, in recent years, legislators in more and more states[243] are introducing increasingly restrictive abortion laws [244]that openly challenge the legality of abortion. As anti-abortion laws sweep the US, it begs the question, if abortion should remain a viable option for women with unwanted pregnancies?

Here are three arguments in favor of abortion, and three arguments against it.

Three Reasons Abortion Should Be an Option
Making an adult decision
It is the parents' responsibility[245] to love, care and provide for their children[246] – those already in the world and those yet to be born. But, if a woman knows there is no way for her to give her child the physical, emotional and financial sustenance he or she needs to survive and thrive, it is the mother's right[247] and obligation to make a tough decision. This includes taking responsibility and preventing the unborn child from having a life of pain, suffering, sadness and neglect. It is far easier to continue with a pregnancy than it is to supply a living child with everything he or she requires. In fact, it is more responsible in such a case, and especially in cases of rape[248], to terminate the pregnancy than it would be to remain with child.

Legislation = safety

When any act or substance is declared illegal, taking part in it becomes inherently riskier[249] and less safe for all parties involved. The fact is, whether abortion is a legal option will not stop attempts to end unwanted or dangerous pregnancies by any means possible. The only difference is that legalizing abortion would enable women to do so safely[250], hygienically and with the least amount of risk to the woman and her fertility. Legal restrictions lead women to attempt termination[251] on their own or seek out the help of an unskilled service provider.

Women's right to reproductive choice is supported by many religious groups

While many Americans assume[252] that abortion negates religious tenets, Rev. Harry Knox, President of the Religious Coalition for Reproductive Choice[253] (RCRC), has explained that many religious groups are officially pro-choice. Despite interpretations of the bible indicating that abortion is forbidden, the holy texts themselves contain no direct prohibitions[254] against termination. Abortion is not likened to homicide in any religious scripture.

"Part of the conversation is not getting out there in this country," Knox explained in an interview[255] with ThinkProgress. "The truth is that most people of faith, like the majority of Americans overall, support access to contraception, comprehensive sexuality education, and reproductive health care — including abortion."

Three Reasons to Say No to Abortion

Potential for life

Whether or not you believe a fetus is already a life, it is undeniable that once conception occurs, potential for life exists[256]. Life is our strongest biological and psychological instinct, serving as the foundation for Maslow's hierarchy of needs[257]. In a world of uncertainties, the pursuit of life is the only definite. Putting a deliberate end to life goes against our biological and physical existence. Who are we to play God and decide what constitutes life or who deserves to live and die? Who are we to take charge of the future of a totally dependent unborn child and determine that his or her life is not worth living, no matter the circumstances?

Can lead to further medical complications

Women who undergo abortions can experience medical complications later on in life. A study[258] published in 2003 by the International Journal of Epidemiology estimated that roughly 15% of spontaneous miscarriages taking place during the first trimester of pregnancy occur in women who previously underwent induced abortion. An abortion can also double the risk of ectopic pregnancies[259] and can increase the prevalence of pelvic inflammatory disease and the incidence of breast cancer.

Legalized abortion must not take the place of birth control

Any time a couple engages in sexual intercourse, there is a chance of conception, even with regular contraceptive use. In England for instance, more than half of the women who had abortions at the British Pregnancy Advisory Service were using at least one form of birth control at the time of contraception. In fact, 18 out of every 100 women[260] who are using condoms (which are 82% effective) as their sole method of contraception will become pregnant during the first year of use.

While most women don't view abortion as a method of birth control[261], it does occur. True, pregnancies are no walk in the park. They involve hormonal and physiological change, putting undue strain on the woman's body[262], sometimes irreversibly. Preventing conception is one thing, but it is immoral to terminate a pregnancy for convenience's sake, especially since there are ways to prevent pregnancies in the first place.

....

The Bottom Line: Whether you're pro-choice or pro-life, religious or secular, rich or poor, never want to have children or can't imagine life without them, abortion is a deeply personal matter that is also subject to public debate. What's your perspective on this extremely hot topic? Would you support a friend who wanted to have an abortion?

DOES REVERSE RACISM EXIST IN AMERICA?

Original debate written by Jordan Stutts

Decades after the civil rights movement, racial tensions [263]still run high in America today. While abuses against minorities, especially at the hands of police[264], are a major issue demanding decisive action, some white Americans feel under attack as well. This has led to a conversation about whether "reverse racism" exists in America, and whether there is discrimination against white people from minorities. The idea of reverse racism is divisive, which is why it should be addressed.

Here are three arguments asserting that reverse racism does exist in the US and three more asserting that it does not.

Reverse Racism Is Real
Affirmative action is discrimination

Affirmative action[265], first introduced in 1961, is mostly recognized as preferential treatment toward minorities for college admissions[266] or corporate hiring. The key argument is that, historically, white Americans have exploited and done irreparable damage to African Americans, so preferential hiring, contracts and scholarships are a legislated attempt [267] to compensate for past wrongs. The University of Michigan, for example, uses a point system[268] for its admissions process, awarding an extra 20 points (out of 100) to some minorities. A lawsuit against Harvard [269]by Asian-American students who claim the university discriminates against them, and the subsequent appeal[270], also brings into focus the efficacy of such minority-based quota systems.

This idea of reverse discrimination, which can be seen as an unintended consequence of affirmative action, has been tested in court repeatedly. However, no clear answer[271] has emerged for what is considered fair. Opponents of the policy say affirmative action amounts to racial preference and has logged countless victims[272] in an attempt to manufacture equality. For instance, a two-year Department of Justice investigation into Yale University's[273] admissions process has found that the university discriminates against white and Asian-American applicants.

A political correctness double standard

Over half of the US population says that Americans are too easily offended by the language of others[274]. In fact, 80% of Americans[275] think that political correctness[276] is a problem. Some say that the pervasive outrage against political correctness and many Americans' perceptions that their communication was being restricted[277] by others helped usher in the Trump era[278], in which he resented and rejected[279] political correctness. And some Americans believe that there is a political correctness double standard, limiting what white people can say, while people of color may reprimand white people for past transgressions.

In the media as well, there is imbalanced coverage of crimes when they are perpetrated by whites against African Americans. In 2013, conservative African American writer Clarence McKee wrote that "all too often it appears that a black life means more if taken or harmed by a white person[280] than another black," citing little coverage of Chicago's black-on-black crime epidemic[281] versus the attention George Zimmerman's 2012 shooting of Trayvon Martin received.

Open racism against white people

During the heat of the 2016 US presidential campaign, white Americans said in a Washington Post poll that they believed anti-white racism[282] is a problem outweighing anti-black racism. While Donald Trump's first presidential campaign was noted for racial overtones against minorities, it seems to have elicited anti-white violence too. For instance, in the months following the election, several videos surfaced[283] showing violence against white people, presumed to be Trump supporters, at the hands of minorities. While violent events like the 2017 Charlottesville rally put a spotlight on the growing popularity of white nationalism[284], and do not diminish concerns regarding racism, they also show that feelings of white victimization[285] exist and are a significant driver in many Americans' behavior. With the growth of the alt-right[286], it is apparent that such feelings will continue even after Trump[287]'s presidency.

There Is No Such Thing as Reverse Racism

A level playing field is lacking and needed

A 2019 study by the National Bureau of Economic Research found that 43% of white students admitted to Harvard[288] were legacy students, recruited athletes, children of staff and faculty, or among those applicants whose parents or relatives donated to Harvard as opposed to less than 16% of Latino, Black, and Asian American students. Additionally, a 2003 study[289] conducted by the National Bureau of Economic Research found that individuals with a "white sounding" name were 50% more likely to get called back by a potential employer than someone with an "ethnic" sounding name. These statistics exist even with affirmative action in place. Until it is demonstrated that minorities have a fair shot in the US, this policy is a needed intervention.

Celebrating non-white culture is not racist

Since Black History Month[290] was established or Black Entertainment Television[291] (BET) was created, critics have asked why there is no white equivalent in US society. That is because celebrating non-white cultures is not antiwhite[292].. White people have been the majority race throughout American history, driving the cultural narrative. Besides, in pop culture, there exists what's called the "white savior complex[293]," where white characters in movies are depicted as good guys who save people of color from oppression (like in *The Help, Green Book,* and *The Blindside,* just to name a few[294].) This narrative is obviously not always the case, and networks like BET are an important cultural outlet for African Americans to tell and share their own stories.

The deck is stacked in favor of whites

Institutional racism is prejudice and bigotry against certain groups is ingrained in the way society functions. Discrimination against white people might exist in America to an extent, but not in the same way[295] that institutions[296] such as schools, employers and housing authorities have discriminated against other minorities – and still do today. Not to mention cases of police brutality[297] are significantly higher against blacks than whites, as the killing of Eric Garner[298] highlighted. Plus, white Americans benefitted more from separate-but-equal school systems and have less frequently experienced housing discrimination[299]. A Harvard University study[300] shows that labor discrimination still exists in the job market, with white people still more likely to be hired even for low-wage jobs.

....

The Bottom Line: Racial tensions in America are high, and some white people feel under attack, that their voices to speak out have been limited, and that government policies favor minorities. However, they have not been historically discriminated against in America, and statistics show that they have advantages over minorities in school and work. So, when discussing discrimination in America, do you think reverse racism is a conversation worth having?

SHOULD PROSTITUTION BE LEGALIZED?

Original debate written by Chaya Benyamin

The oldest profession is rigorously recorded in the Bible[301] depicting instances of prostitution by career professionals as well as prostitutes prompted by circumstance. Today, with over 40 million[302] prostitutes worldwide and between one and two million prostitutes in the US alone, it's not surprising that every country on the planet has laws governing it. Whether prostitution should be vigorously opposed or tacitly accepted is a subject of much debate, and it seems no one policy holds the monopoly on success or failure.

So, when it comes to prostitution, should we legalize it or keep it criminal? Here are both sides of this debate.

Keep It Criminal

Legalizing prostitution has failed to check its illegal counterpart

When the Netherlands legalized prostitution in 1988, one of its main objectives was to curtail human trafficking and the criminal prostitution enterprise. In spite of best intentions, illegal brothels still proliferate and prostitutes continue to suffer abuses[303] at the hands of pimps. Similarly, Nevada's illegal prostitution industry is estimated to be about four times as large[304] as its legal counterpart. If legalization does not in fact protect prostitutes, then it proves nothing more than a cynical revenue source for the government.

It reinforces the darkest attitudes of capitalism, in which people are reduced to commodities

How does one quantify value for an hour of her time? How about for a pound of her flesh? Exchanging money for sexual interaction, an interaction which is commonly regarded as both an expression and vehicle of intimacy, reduces this bond-solidifying act to mere transaction. And while some buyers voice disillusionment with the services rendered, others draw extreme satisfaction from the leverage one gains from paying for sex, allowing them to "do things with [prostitutes] that real women would not put up with[305]." But, let's not forget that prostitutes are as real human women. The essence of this statement, which was taken as part of an international research project researching men who buy sex, shows just how effective sex-for-pay is at removing all traces of humanity from its practitioners.

Prostitution promotes degrading attitudes toward women, and invites violence against them

The fact that sex workers are 80% female[306] cannot be overlooked, nor should the fact that a sizable portion of sex workers are coerced by physical means or by economic hardship. Female prostitutes are more likely to be raped or murdered than any other population[307]. One former prostitute recalls the violence she withstood both as a trafficking victim and as an independent contractor, stating[308]: "I've been shot five times, stabbed 13 times – I don't know why those men attacked me, all I know is that society made it comfortable for them to do so."

And so, by the necessity to protect themselves, either from physical harm or from destitution, an overwhelmingly female contingent of sex workers find themselves at the mercy of the men they serve. Cruelly, society blames women for the violence committed against them, often postulating how she might have brought the trouble on herself. Rape statistics in Nevada, where prostitution is legal in most counties, supports the notion that degradation of prostitutes translates to females writ large: rapes in Nevada are 25% higher[309] than the national average. The only way to oppose such attitudes (and realities) is to increase legal measures against those who perpetuate the prostitution industry.

Legalize It

Legalization circumvents the most dangerous aspects of prostitution

Criminalization of prostitution leaves prostitutes on the fringes of society, making them vulnerable to violence, poverty, and health risks. Decriminalization allows sex workers to call police in incidences of violence. In the Netherlands, decriminalizing prostitution gave sex workers access to social security and public health care. India's union of sex workers improved prostitutes' financial security by teaching them how to identify counterfeit bills[310].

Sexually transmitted infections are also statistically lower in areas where prostitution is decriminalized. In rural Nevada, where prostitution is legal (and condoms and regular HIV tests mandatory), there has not been one case of HIV/AIDS diagnosed in a registered sex worker since 1986[311]. Beyond all the practical benefits, legalizing prostitution brings sex workers into the fold of society, increasing their sense of belonging, thereby enhancing their feelings of responsibility toward others.

Legalization can harness the sex industry's potential to contribute to society

One formerly illicit trade that is now legal, marijuana, has done wonders for economic and social rejuvenation in Colorado. In 2015, the state has grossed nearly $1 billion in pot revenues[312] (approximately 15% of that became the state's through taxation), most of which has reportedly been funneled into the state's school system. At the city and county levels, Coloradans have used their share to ramp up public health initiatives and even to address homelessness[313]. Imagine how different prostitution would seem if a portion of its proceeds went to providing child-care support for working parents, or to supplement medical research that helps to cure disease, or to help fund drug rehabilitation programs.

Legalization reflects the victimless nature of consensual prostitution

The internet abounds with sex worker testimonials who attest to the satisfaction of a career in sex, and these personalities carefully draw a distinction between themselves and those who are coerced. One prostitute marvels at her great financial success, and draws feelings of "empowerment" from her work. Stories of satisfied practitioners and customers beg the question: Why isn't prostitution simply viewed as a normal business transaction? As the great variation in prostitution laws[314] across the globe reflects, the illicit nature of prostitution is by no means an objective reality. And even if the ethical parameters of prostitution are unclear, free societies should, in principle, avoid restricting business transactions which do not harm individuals or society.

The Bottom Line: Prostitution is not a hegemonic practice. Because it comes in so many mediums, and is practiced by willing and unwilling parties, governments are unlikely to effectively address the ills (or the benefits) that accompany prostitution with one-size-fits-all policies – nor should they try. What do you think?

SHOULD THE BURQA BE BANNED?

Original debate written by Chaya Benyamin

No symbol is more emblematic of the tension between East and West, and between assimilation and tradition, than the burqa[315], a full-face veil worn by Muslim women to preserve modesty. The garment has come under fire in recent years, being banned[316] in a number of countries across Europe[317] – in France, Belgium, Denmark and Germany, among others. (COVID-19[318] and related mask-wearing mandates have presented an interesting challenge to these countries' bans on full face coverings but hasn't stopped the arguably paradoxical mid-pandemic burqa-banning[319])

Proponents of banning the burqa argue the need for security and cultural cohesion, while human rights advocates[320] claim such legislation is discriminatory[321] and a violation of religious freedom. Should the West embrace the burqa as part of its guarantee of religious freedom, or does it have the right to restrict dress that it feels antithetical to its cultural values?

Below, we'll explore three arguments for banning the burqa, and three arguments against a ban.

The Burqa Should Be Banned

The veil is sexist

The veil can be seen by some as sexist in two directions. While assuming men to be fundamentally unable to control their sexual urges, the veil instils gender inequality by placing the responsibility of checking male impropriety solely upon women, for whom the consequences are great. Veils, like the burqa and niqab, which obscure the face, prevent the women who wear them from full participation in society. She cannot eat or dine in public.

She cannot be easily heard by others, and without faces to remember, she is easily forgotten. The sum of these factors is the overall diminishment of female personhood, a notion that has no place[322] in societies that place a premium on equality in general and gender equality in particular.

Muslims oppose the burqa too

Even in Muslim majority countries, many view the burqa as unwelcome encroachment of Saudi-brand, ultra-conservative Islam. Morocco's government officially cited security concerns as the reason for its 2017 ban on the sale and manufacture of the burqa[323] (terrorists have used the burqa to hide bombs and other weapons). However, the pretext of deterring the integration of Salafist[324] versions of Islam into Moroccan society is certainly present. In Egypt[325], where religious scholars and public officials have contested the necessity[326] to cover the face in the name of modesty, universities[327] and hospitals have banned the niqab, and the government has mulled over[328] banning them in public spaces entirely. Controversies surrounding full-face veils in the Muslim world[329] underscore their complex social, religious, and political implications – implications that dictate a need to regulate their use in the public sphere.

The burqa endangers Muslim women

Columnist Sabria Jawhar argued in the past that in light of Islamophobic incidents[330] in general the necessity for safety[331] overrides the necessity to dress according to one's cultural mores. Jawhar noted that rather than fulfilling its purpose to repel attention from Muslim women, in the West, the burqa and niqab produce the opposite effect – attracting unwanted attention and in many cases, harassment or violence[332], which has become more and more normalized on social media. Official burqa bans could help women who might be ambivalent about removing their burqas make a decision that will better ensure their safety. Those who protest that the victims of bad behavior should not be the ones to make concessions will kindly remember that the burqa itself is intended to help women ward off lascivious male gazes.

The Burqa Should Be Welcomed

Restricting religious dress is a violation of civil liberties

Contrary to popular belief, Muslim women in the West and the East alike (Saudi Arabia and Iran notwithstanding) choose the veil[333] as a religious prerogative. The rights to religious freedom and the freedom of expression are enshrined in the First Amendment of the Constitution[334], which promises "Congress shall make no law respecting an establishment of religion, or *prohibiting the free exercise thereof.*" The Legal Information Institute at Cornell Law School points out that the amendment protects "actions taken upon behalf of [religious] beliefs[335]" – which necessarily includes clothing. Just as we would not restrict a person's right to proclaim their faith in Jesus by wearing a cross, so too should Muslims be allowed to express their faith through dress.

A burqa ban will only fuel extremism

Banning symbols associated with extremism does not necessarily combat extremism. In Australia[336], there have been different bills introduced over the years to ban women from wearing the burqa in public. However, its national security agency, ASIO, concluded that the measure would only fuel radicalization[337] campaigns and further isolate vulnerable populations. The ASIO's conclusions have already been brought to bear in Asia: the USSR's studious repression of Islam in Central Asia[338] in the twentieth century gave way to Islamic revivalism that turned to radicalism in the twenty-first century, with groups like the Taliban and ISIS gaining influence in Afghanistan, Uzbekistan, and Tajikistan. Similarly, China's restrictions against public expressions of Islam like growing a beard or wearing a veil has been a significant catalyst for unrest[339] in the country's predominantly Muslim Xinjiang region.

Live and let live

Wearing a burqa is no more harmful than wearing a Marilynn Manson shirt. Sure, it might make some people uncomfortable, but it does nothing to threaten the safety, liberty, or freedom of any other individual. If anything, today in the middle of the pandemic, those women wearing a burqa may actually blend in[340], given that no one else's full face should be uncovered out in public. Furthermore, women in the West who wear burqas are a minority within a minority – Muslims in the US constitute less than 1.1 percent[341] of the total population. As such, no legislation is required to protect onlookers from a piece of cloth most Americans are unlikely to be confronted with in the first place.

....

The Bottom Line: As the East and West draw ever closer, governments will continue to be challenged to rethink the delicate balance[342] between secularism and religious freedom. It is a question of values and ultimately, we must choose which value gets priority over another. If given the choice to create policy, what would you choose?

SHOULD CONVICTED CRIMINALS HAVE THE RIGHT TO VOTE?

Original debate written by Kira Goldring

Is voting a basic human right, or is it a privilege like being allowed to drive and having quiet neighbors? The world is divided over this issue, with some countries[343] permanently disenfranchising[344] convicted criminals (i.e., removing their right to vote) while others permit felons to vote even while they're in prison. As the number of Americans who can't vote due to felony convictions is on the rise[345], it's important to ask ourselves if this is indeed the approach to criminal voting rights America should be taking.

This issue has been revisited by Democratic presidential candidates, with Bernie Sanders[346] arguing that convicted felons should be allowed to vote. Though controversial[347,] this is a necessary and timely conversation, as the US faces increased contention on matters of voter suppression, voter fraud and the meaning of universal suffrage.[348]

Here are three reasons why convicted criminals should have the right to vote, and three reasons why not.

Losing the Right to Vote Shouldn't Be a Consequence of Committing Crime

Voting restrictions may create a racial imbalance

Studies have shown that ethnic minorities[349] are more likely to go to jail than members of the majority population; for example, African American males in the U.S. are five times more likely[350] to be incarcerated than white males. If the votes of specific racial ethnicities[351] are minimized more than those of the majority, their political interests won't be represented proportionally. Stemming from this, felony disenfranchisement would essentially nullify the US Voting Rights Act[352] that sought to provide meaningful ballot representation[353] for society's minorities.

Disenfranchisement can be a roadblock to rehabilitation

Many former prisoners eventually rejoin society, and they may well become our future neighbors[354]. With that in mind, you better hope the guy next door is rehabilitated and intent on staying that way! Strain theory[355] in psychology contends that society puts pressure on individuals to achieve certain socially acceptable goals, and if they're unable to meet these expectations, it causes strain that can eventually lead to crime. In this vein, restricting felons' rights to vote[356] can serve to further alienate them from the normative population, producing the type of strain that can cause them to re-offend.

Voting sets an example for children

Most prisoners have children who are under the age of 18[357], and these kids have no way to fight for representation of their own political concerns or interests. The number one advocates for children are their parents, but these parents can't influence public policy regarding their children without being able to vote[358]. There is evidence that children whose parents have a criminal background are at higher risk[359] of becoming criminals themselves. Therefore, it's important for these children to know that their parents are voting[360], as it shows them a positive model of behavior for contributing to society and trying to make it better.

Crime Deserves Punishment, and Voting Is No Exception

Crime is a societal problem, and voting is a societal privilege

While crime is perpetrated by individuals, the impact is on society as a whole. Crime is expensive[361], costing taxpayers—and the government—billions of dollars[362] per year. Furthermore, the amount of resources and time allocated to court trials detracts from time spent towards community productivity[363], and none of this takes into account the hurtful impact of crime on its victims. As such, it doesn't seem right that felons who have such an extensive negative influence on the social order should be allowed to be involved in the decision-making process that contributes to that order. In violating the social contract[364] by committing crime, felons are giving up their privilege of participating in the forming of societal policy.

Criminals have a proven history of bad judgment

Not all sentences end with a period of jail time; some have repercussions that continue across a criminal's life. For example, in many US states, sex offenders aren't allowed within a certain proximity of schools, playgrounds, or daycare centers, even after they've done their time. The logic behind this is simple: We can't trust the judgment of convicted felons. Just like minors[365] and aren't trusted to vote, neither should convicted criminals. The same way we want to trust our candidates, we also must trust the people voting them in.

Jail is a loss of freedom

The threat of jail time isn't necessarily enough of a deterrent to those with a criminal streak, as evidenced by the number of repeat offenders[366] who return to jail (45% within five years[367] of release). By definition, jail is a loss of freedom[368], and this threat is enhanced when it includes the loss of democratic rights as well. While some may argue that many felons are mostly indifferent[369] to losing the right to vote, the message is a societal one as much as a personal one: Criminal behavior is intolerable, and losing your most basic rights is fair game as a punishment.

....

The Bottom Line: Many people deserve a second chance, but not when they pose a risk to society at large. What do you think? Should the right to vote be untouchable, or is it a privilege that has potential to be revoked?

THE PERSPECTIVE ON SURROGACY

Original debate written by Talia Klein Perez

For many individuals and couples, having a child is the ultimate self-actualization. However, for some, this path to realization and happiness is impossible due to infertility[370], other medical issues, age or relationship status. Using a surrogate mother[371] to carry a pregnancy to term is a way for these people to overcome their challenges and become parents. Although this may seem like a great solution, surrogacy also poses some controversy, especially with respect to women's rights, emotional involvement, and financial gains.

Here are three reasons why surrogacy is a good idea and three reasons why it may not be great as it seems.

Three Arguments in Favor of Surrogacy

Surrogacy creates families

Today, approximately 10% of American women [372]struggle with infertility. For people who cannot conceive due to infertility or medical conditions, surrogacy can be one of the only ways to create a family. Surrogacy can help single men and women and LGBT couples become parents, enabling at least one parent to be biologically linked to their child. Plus, having kids and forming a family has been positively linked with increased parental happiness[373], productivity[374] and longevity[375], for all family members. Some research even suggests that parents are happier than non-parents later in life[376], once their children move out. Basically, surrogacy can create the foundation for a happier, more fulfilled life.

Unlike adoption, surrogacy allows intended parents to be involved in the gestation process

To better understand surrogacy, we must look at the alternatives available to people hoping to become parents. One alternative is adoption. Despite there being many children around the world in desperate need of homes, it can take years[377] for a single child to be adopted. Then, adoptive parents must get to know a child who is already born and who biologically belongs to someone else. It may also be challenging to find out a comprehensive health history[378] of the adopted child, which may cause complications later in life for everyone involved. Clearly, adoption is not easy.

Surrogacy, on the other hand, ensures that intended parents can be involved[379] in their child's life from the get-go. Intended parents are updated on the surrogate's pregnancy, can attend scans and be present[380] when the baby, often theirs biologically, is born.

Surrogacy is an economic opportunity for women

In countries[381] that allow and support commercial surrogacy, surrogate mothers are fairly compensated for their time and the medical risk involved. These women are instructed about the process, what medical procedures are required and how they must conduct themselves throughout the gestational period. Contracts are signed to protect the surrogate and intended parents to ensure that all parties get what they want. For the intended parents, this means a baby. For the regulated surrogate – a base compensation of around $25,000[382] can be expected, though it can be more[383], and the absolving of her responsibility towards the child and its intended parents following childbirth. From an equality perspective, surrogate mothers are well informed and conscious of their choice. The act of surrogacy can therefore be viewed as an educated and informed economic opportunity[384].

Three Arguments against Surrogacy

Surrogacy can be used to exploit women

Surrogacy is problematic because it can be used by men to dominate and degrade women, particularly in third-world countries[385]. The woman's unique childbearing capabilities are recognized and used to bring money in. The issue of consent[386] is at times unclear. Countries like India[387] offer surrogacy services to Western countries at a fraction of the cost, which can be seen as exploiting women as baby-making machines for a pittance. The low price tag can be tempting to couples and individuals desperate to expand their families, driving them to enter into surrogacy agreements with third-world women, despite the way these contracts may affect these surrogates.

Surrogacy is a form of alienated labor

Surrogacy is a paid "job" that women perform, often while attempting to remain emotionally detached from the "product of their work." This would be fine in some work environments, but in the case of surrogacy, alienated labor [388] that culminates in physical reproductive labor can be psychologically and physically harmful for the surrogate mother. It can also turn the entire surrogacy process into a physical act lacking in emotional attachment This is because surrogates might be compelled to sell their bodies and their function for money, while attempting to distance themselves from the significance of their acts and shield themselves from potential postpartum heartbreak.

Surrogacy turns babies into commodities

When surrogacy is allowed, babies become commodities for trade[389], often between wealthy Westerners and impoverished families in developing countries. This international trade approach to babies, with its mixed legal systems, can leave those babies without protection or rights. A Thai baby born with autism caused parents to back out of a deal [390] and leave him with his surrogate mother. A twin baby was abandoned in India [391] by Australian parents with knowledge of the Indian Authorities. Such examples point out the inherent inequality and possible injustice that arise from international surrogacy.

....

The Bottom Line: Surrogacy can be the ultimate answer for people who cannot have children. Yet, it can also be a rabbit's hole full of ethical and commercial conundrums. Do you think surrogacy is a great way to create a family, or do you think those who want to have kids should seek other options, like adoption?

THE PERSPECTIVE ON UNIONS

Original debate written by Kira Goldring

Labor forces across the globe once experienced unsafe and unregulated working conditions which arose from the imbalance of power that existed between employers and employees. To even out this imbalance, workers came together and formed what we now know as unions[392.] While unions originated in the UK, they later became popular in the US with the onset of the Industrial Revolution. Today, unions play a huge role in American politics[393] and the economy, having secured fair working conditions for the common man. In fact, today, 65%[394] of Americans favor unions. However, alongside these positive social changes, there has been uncertainty over whether unions are yet another institution that leverages its own power at society's expense.

Here are three reasons unions have given rise to overall societal improvements, and three reasons unions have brought about more social harm than good.

Down with Unions!
Exploitation goes both ways

In many cases, unions – which were initially formed to protect the underdog[395] – have become the bullies on the playground. For example, in the wake of George Floyd's death, critics blame police unions[396] for protecting those officers who abused their authority. In addition, although unions are meant to control and prevent worker exploitation, sometimes the reverse ends up happening, where leaders exploit their own members. Unite Here, the former hotel and restaurant workers' union, pressured union members to publicly divulge personal information[397] about themselves (bordering on psychological abuse), because they believed it would attract newcomers to the union. Additionally, Philadelphia unions were filmed using intimidation, threats and violence[398] on numerous occasions to get their way. Workers deserve to be treated well, yet these institutions preserve the hierarchical power structure that has, in some instances, harmed these workers in the first place.

The road to hell is paved with good intentions

Unions may be well-intended, but their actions can hurt the general population. Most strikes[399], for example, negatively affect everybody – not just the people unions are trying to negotiate with. Teachers' strikes, even if understandable amid coronavirus safety concerns[400], still hurt children who are trying to learn and parents who need to find last-minute arrangements for their kids; a health workers' strike[401] could potentially endanger the lives of the sick. It seems that this hurting of the general public is a tool unions will use to get what they want. Moreover, union violence[402] has been used in the past, such as in the Occupy Oakland strike of 2011, which culminated in violent riots [403]that were later condoned by the US Supreme Court. Good intentions or not, public harm should not be an acceptable means for unions to achieve their goals.

Hinder companies all around

Studies have found that the high wages that union members enjoy mean some companies[404] are forced to either hire fewer workers[405] or drive up their prices, which restricts their competitive advantage in the market. Additionally, in some cases, individual worker effectiveness can become somewhat irrelevant under unions, because their contracts may limit the amount an employee can advance within a company. As a result, some unionized employees may not be motivated to work hard[406] – yet they are protected by their union from losing their job. By the same token, employees that want to excel find it difficult to do so in an environment that places importance on seniority rather than merit. It's hard enough for businesses to thrive without the added headaches of unmotivated workers and restricted competitive advantage, but union interference can make company success a much more difficult outcome.

Workers, Unite!

Workplace improvements

Imagine working for 16 hours a day, yet barely making enough money to buy yourself dinner. This was the reality for many in the US before the National Labor Union[407] was introduced in 1886. There was no minimum wage or standard of safety regulations until unions established a precedent with the Fair Labor Standards Act[408], which put limits on child labor and demanded fair pay for overtime work. The benefits[409] many in the workforce have come to rely on are also a result of past unions' work; dramatic improvements that we now take for granted, such as sick leave, paid vacation, including for Labor Day[410], which celebrates workers, and pension, were only introduced into the workforce after unions fought against the terrible conditions that plagued the working class.

Collective bargaining power

Unions give individual workers a collective voice[411] – one that can adequately negotiate on behalf of its constituents. Where the complaints of a single worker are more easily ignored, the strength in union numbers allows that worker to be heard. (This is important today, when educators[412] are facing hard choices and unintended consequences due to the coronavirus on schools and campuses.) This extends to all members of a unionized workplace[413], regardless of whether said members are in the union or not. For example, in 2018, low-cost airline[414] Ryanair pilot unions succeeded in their struggle[415] to improve pay and conditions across Europe.

In general, there is statistical evidence that this collective bargaining power works in union members' favor: As of 2018, 94% of union workers[416] had medical care benefits, which is 30% more than non-union workers, and 85% of union members have life insurance – almost double the amount of non-union members – with a 30% higher salary [417]on average to boot.

Protects minorities and women

Unions help balance racial wage inequality, giving minorities a fair chance in the American workforce. A study[418] found that, if union representation[419] were to endure at high levels, weekly wage gaps between black and white women would be reduced by up to 30%. In general, unionization raises African American[420] wages by over 16%[421]. Women, too, find a 23% increase in salaries when represented by unions, which significantly narrows the gender wage gap[422]. While there may still be discrimination in the workforce, unions are an important tool through which to level the playing field for all Americans, regardless of race or gender.

....

The Bottom Line: Do unions[423] help achieve an equal employee-employer balance so that everyone wins, or do they contribute to the exploitation they are meant to fight against?

DO VEGANS HAVE THE MORAL HIGH GROUND?

Original debate written by Chaya Benyamin

Few lifestyle choices straddle the realms of politics, health, and environment as effortlessly as veganism. The movement is aspirational, promising ethical, environmental and physical equilibrium in exchange for giving up meat and animal products. With the explosion of celebrity vegans[424] and global interest on the rise[425], it's time to ask whether the ethical promise of veganism will make it as enduring as the Enlightenment, or if it's a moral lightweight with the staying power of the South Beach diet?

Below, we'll explore three ways veganism holds the moral high ground, and three ways it falls short.

Vegans Are Not Morally Superior to the Rest of Us

Veganism is an arbitrary expression of ethics

Treating food consumption as an ethical matter suggests that vegans will make all consumer choices through the anti-suffering lens of veganism. But this is not always the case. Whereas we might give vegans a pass on using smart phones powered by conflict minerals[426] or for unknowingly wearing garments[427] sewn by child laborers, we cannot ignore that vegans seem wholly unconcerned with crop production's main victims: human beings. Agricultural slavery[428] is a widespread practice – it's even been reported in the US.

The vegan who praises herself for eating fresh tomatoes over chicken cutlets may not realize that her tomatoes were likely picked by a migrant worker with no social benefits, who may have received only a 50-cent-piece rate for 32 pounds of fruit, who may suffer exposure[429] to pesticides that have been associated with deformities in farm workers' offspring, and who may have been a victim of sexual harassment[430]. If one considers the human toil involved in producing plant-based diets, veganism has its own unintentional claims to cruelty.

Meat consumption isn't patently unethical

Biology drives all creatures to ensure their survival and continuation. Just as chimpanzees[431] use sticks to harvest army ants, humans use their intellect to domesticate animals and ensure continued access to meat, the availability of which has underscored the success of the human species. Although these processes transcend ethical questions (it's not unethical for a bird to hunt a worm, right?), humans have created laws[432] surrounding the welfare and slaughter of domestic livestock, and a fair amount of animal products induce no animal suffering whatsoever. Free range chickens will hardly be bothered by the removal of their unfertilized eggs from the fields they roam, and merino sheep[433], who cannot shed their wool, are doubtless relieved to be shorn each year.

Veganism is perceived as elitist

Successful execution of a vegan diet requires year-round access to a wide variety of produce, grains, and legumes, and the ability to purchase them. Unsurprising, the world's highest concentrations of vegans live in developed countries, where these items are imported from countries with far less nutritional variety. Vegans supplement their diets with "superfoods" like coconut water and acai fruit, while the people living in the locales from which these items originate sometimes thrive mainly on bananas[434]. For poor communities in developed and developing nations alike, animal products are important sources of vitamin and calorie intake – nutritional opportunities that the poor cannot afford to miss. Vegan claims to the moral high ground evaporate with the ideology's inability to be universally applied.

Vegans Have the Moral High Ground

Animals have conscious lives that deserve consideration

Any pet owner can attest to their animals' distinct preferences and personalities and preferences. And while we might expect intelligent animals like elephants or wolves to express complex emotions like empathy, science is helping us to understand that the animals we may have previously dismissed as dumb in fact have complex social and emotional lives[435], too. A study of dairy cows[436] showed they excreted higher levels of stress hormone when surrounded by unfamiliar animals. Another experiment revealed that hens[437] have some understanding of numbers and time. As science provides more evidence for animal cognition and consciousness, we must adjust our treatment toward them accordingly.

Veganism promotes conscious consumption

At its core, veganism asks us to pause and evaluate the consequences of our purchases. More than highlighting the necessity to treat living creatures with respect, veganism is an exercise in reconnecting the consumer with the origins of their food. This practice may well help humanity navigate an era in which consumerism is fast outpacing[438] the rate at which the planet can sustainably meet demands for food and other goods. Even if veganism alone is unlikely to remedy the suffering of farm factory animals or significantly impact the demand for low-cost animal products, raising awareness of the lifecycle of a consumed product (including one's wardrobe!) is a necessary step toward new practices.

Some industrial farming practices are truly cruel

Industrial animal farming may involve varying degrees of unkindnesses to animals. Livestock are subject to a range of painful mutilations[439], from branding to horn and tail removal to castration (most of the time, without anesthetic). In many instances, livestock and poultry are kept in appalling conditions[440], in enclosed, confined spaces that atrophy the animals' muscles and bones. Imagine never being able to stretch out your legs or arms. Never seeing the light of day, or being genetically bred[441] to be so fat that your organs quickly deteriorate under your own mass. These are the conditions in which many industrial farming animals live, and one does not need to believe that animals possess a complex psyche in order to understand that such conditions would cause any living creature to suffer.

....

The Bottom Line: As an ethical premise, veganism is not without its shortcomings; it's lofty and ultimately unlikely to yield an animal-product free economy. However, veganism does articulate a response to the unjust suffering of animals, as well as to the precariousness of consumerism run amok. While you might not see it as a moral high ground, do you think such efforts are commendable or mostly self-righteous?

ARE WHISTLEBLOWERS HEROES OR TRAITORS?

Original debate written by Chaya Benyamin

Whistleblowers have gained hero status in American popular culture. Thousands of editorials have been penned hailing the likes of Edward Snowden[442], Chelsea Manning[443], and Julian Assange[444] as defenders of democracy while others see them as traitors risking national security.. Are whistleblowers really the silver bullet for governmental and corporate accountability?

Below, let's explore some reasons for how whistleblowers[445] improve society, and how they disrupt it.

Whistleblowers Are Traitors

Whistleblowers' motives can be murky

Whistleblowers have a wide range of motives, and, surprise surprise, they aren't strictly altruistic. Corporate whistleblowers are offered handsome bounties[446] for reporting corporate fraud to the Securities and Exchange Commission. With the lure of multi-million-dollar payouts, it is little wonder that whistleblowers prefer to do reconnaissance for the government than to push for reform from within their organizations. Whistleblowing can also be politically or personally motivated. After spending time with infamous Julian Assange, filmmaker Alex Gibney[447] noted that the WikiLeaks founder was perpetually focused on "personal slights" and "payback." That Assange has used his leak platform to further his own political viewpoints and even to influence politics is hardly in question. WikiLeaks[448] and its classified "data dumping" has shown that it is more concerned with making news than reporting it, which redefines the point of whistleblowing[449].

Whistleblowers undermine national security

When Edward Snowden[450] signed on to be an NSA security contractor, he knew he would be made privy to state secrets employed to protect and advance the national interest. More than betraying his personal promise not to share these secrets, he compromised the agency's ability to do its job by disclosing operating procedures and vulnerabilities. This information led state and non-state actors, including Google[451], to redouble their efforts to prevent breeches. More worrying are reports that terror groups began altering their communication[452] methods to neutralize the intelligence gathering tactics specified in Snowden's disclosures. Without the ability to collect information, intelligence agencies simply cannot do their job.

Whistleblowers fuel vigilantism

Hollywood glorifies whistleblowers. Oliver Stone's Snowden[453] delivers a sympathetic (and wildly paranoid) rendition of Edward Snowden's disclosure of classified NSA documents. Julian Assange receives the same hero's treatment in The Fifth Estate[454]. The image of whistleblower as hero clouds the fact that whistleblowers are people who take power derived from legitimate offices and appropriate it to their cause. Snowden deemed himself wiser than publicly elected officials and their deputies to set national security policy. Assange knowingly endangered countless government operatives and informants when he refused to redact their names from leaked reports, and defended his actions by calling those named criminals. Not to mention, Assange played a key role in interfering[455] in the US 2016 presidential elections[456], interrupting democracy instead of championing it. Whistleblowers are not elected officials, they are vigilantes with a computer. The romanticization of their actions seems to correlate with a rise in whistleblowing, a practice which ultimately leaves government and businesses less secure.

Whistleblowers Are Heroes

Whistleblowers are motivated by loyalty

Enron[457] whistleblower Sherron Watkins didn't blow her whistle in public (not initially, at least) – she blew it to her bosses. Watkin's memos[458] to the company's founder, Kenneth Lay, point to a loyal employee, worried that Enron would be disgraced by the revelation of faulty accounting. Watkins wasn't a traitor – more like a sailor helping to bail water from a sinking ship. Another example: DEA agent Celerino Castillo remained loyal to his mission to neutralize the drug trade when he accused the CIA[459] of being complicit in it. Plus, Chelsea Manning[460] felt she was siding with all of humanity by showing the needless suffering of war victims, in her revelation of 250,000 classified cables. If loyalty is the modus operandi guiding these revelations, are they really betrayals?

Whistleblowers speak truth to power

In your average democracy, most citizens have limited power. As such, whistleblowers are theoretically essential in keeping business and government accountable[461]. Biochemist Jeffery Wigand [462]fearlessly exposed the tobacco industry's cover-up of its knowledge of the deadly link between cigarettes and lung cancer, leading to stricter regulation of the tobacco industry, awards for punitive damages across fifty states, and fewer cigarette-related deaths. Daniel Ellsberg[463] forced the US government to come clean about its covert operations in Vietnam in 1971, initiating an important public conversation regarding the use of force. Whistleblowers and the threat of a larger, vigilant public incentivize business and government to behave more ethically.

Whistleblowers encourage us to watch out for each other

Management expert Margaret Heffernan reports, rather shockingly, that 85%[464] of workers see wrong-doing at their places of employment, yet fail to report it. She points out that contrary to popular belief, whistleblowers, the 15% who go against the grain (and the fewer still who report incidences of greater consequence), are uncommonly loyal[465] and committed to their organizations. Whistleblowers point out wrongdoing at great personal cost[466], and they do so from the conviction that things must be set right, either for the good of their organization, the general public, or both. Whistleblowers challenge the 85% to stop accepting corporate or governmental corruption as a fact of life and to start speaking up for ourselves and each other.

....

The Bottom Line: Whistleblowing isn't as clear cut as it seems. The whistleblower is essentially engaged in an act of betrayal (merited or not), and has deemed his or herself judge and jury in matters of the public interest. Audacity notwithstanding, whistleblowers have in many cases pushed society forward, shedding light on pressing issues that directly affect unaware citizens.

SHOULD WOMEN SERVE IN COMBAT UNITS?

Original debate written by Kira Goldring

Until recently, women in the United States were only able to enlist in military support or intelligence[467] positions and couldn't physically serve in combat. In 2015, the U.S. Pentagon opened all combat jobs[468] to women, and in 2016, the ban on women serving in close combat roles in the British military was lifted[469]. (In other countries[470], like Israel[471], women have been allowed to serve in combat units[472] for much longer). While many people believe that allowing women to serve in combat units is a positive step towards gender equality, there are concerns that it is inappropriate, if not dangerous.

Here are three reasons why women should be able to serve in combat units, and three reasons why they should stick to other military units.

Women Deserve a Chance in Combat

The bar is high – for everyone

Just like men, women should be allowed to choose how they fight for their country based on their strengths. Joining a combat unit requires meeting high demands[473] regardless of gender; if there are women who are able to meet the same training standards[474] as men, they can only be an asset to their team. Having female troops in every combat role is crucial for intelligence gathering[475], because they're naturally able to navigate cultural differences when interacting with local populations.

If the military is looking for the creme de la creme to serve in their units, then why give up on 51% of the candidates upfront? In Israel, women not only serve in combat units but lead[476] them, too. India[477] has also jumped on the equality bandwagon; its Supreme Court recently passed a ruling allowing women to serve as army commanders. The army mirrors society, and having exceptional women in the army[478] is crucial to the way we want to see society. Any concern about having women in combat units stems from broader attitudes toward gender norms; these can't begin to be addressed unless change starts at the core: The military.

The monopoly on emotions

The stereotype that women are the more emotional gender is debunked in the military, where women hold their own[479]. A study on UK soldiers who fought in Iraq in 2006 showed a lack of gender differences[480] in veterans who had post-traumatic stress disorder. This suggests that combat doesn't pose a higher risk to women's mental health than it does to men's. In fact, psychological research has shown that female soldiers in combat may be more resilient [481] to its effects than male soldiers. Women don't need to be "protected" from the difficulties of combat units – they can take the heat.

Same job, different title

Many women in the military serve in support units like engineering, artillery, and medical support, and they make it to the battlefield just as much as those in combat units. For example, women fighting in Iraq and Afghanistan were often on the front lines[482], even though they weren't formally in combat roles. For example, female medics[483] in Nad Ali came under fire just as much as the male medics with them. One of the medics, Sgt. Chanelle Taylor, was the first soldier to kill an enemy up close in Afghanistan, and she provided invaluable insight to her command team. If women are already unofficially serving on the battlefield[484] – and excelling at it – they should get the credit they deserve and be allowed to serve in combat units.

Combat Units Should Be Restricted to Men

Potential to misbehave

Adding women to combat units may invite potential sexual assault[485] into the military. To many, it seems unrealistic to put men and women together in combat training environments, which can include confined spaces (like bunkers) with no privacy and expect no tension to arise between the sexes. This can lead to anything from distracting consensual relationships to sexual assault. In 2010, an estimated 19,000 women were sexually assaulted in the military, and military sexual trauma[486] is the leading cause of post-traumatic stress disorder in female veterans. At year-end 2017, reported sexual assaults in the military were at an all-time high[487]. In fiscal 2018, the US Defense Department found that there were 20,500 instances[488] of unwanted sexual contact across the Army, Marines, Navy and Airforce, a 38% increase compared to 2016. Adding women to combat units will only bump up these numbers and add an unnecessary element of distraction.

Political correctness has no place in the military

The Western world has made great strides when it comes to feminism[489], but gender equality shouldn't be a factor when people's lives are at risk. A yearlong Marine Corps study[490] found that all-male units were faster, more lethal, and able to evacuate quicker than integrated units of men and women. Sources claim that the military is easing fitness standards[491] because the female soldiers can't meet them; lowering such standards hurts the institution as a whole. Female soldiers also have higher potential to be targeted for attacks.[492] Enemies don't care about political correctness[493], and if letting women serve in combat units poses a threat to the safety of all soldiers, then providing equal opportunity to men and women must come second.

Don't fix what isn't broken

Until now, many militaries have been successful[494] without having women in combat units. That's not to say that women can't contribute to their country; over 90% of U.S. military jobs[495] are open to women, and they are just as instrumental to military success. However, commanders of co-ed combat units have added liabilities[496] to worry about when women are added to the mix. Not to mention that complexities begin even with something as seemingly simple as uniforms and gear[497], which have different requirements to fit women than men and which are in short supply for women. So, why mess with the military status quo when it's been working thus far?

....

The Bottom Line: While some women deserve to join military combat units and could have a lot to contribute, the mixing of the sexes has potential to compromise all soldiers' safety. Do you think women belong in combat units?

SPORTS CHAPTER

- Is Roger Federer the best tennis player of all time?
- Are the NFL "Concussion Rules" ruining the game?
- Messi or Ronaldo – who is truly the best?
- Should college athletes get paid?
- Should sports betting be legal?
- Should women compete against men in sports?
- Lebron vs. Jordan: Who's the greatest of all time?
- Should instant replays (VAR) be used in sports?
- Should the NHL ban fighting in hockey?

IS ROGER FEDERER THE BEST TENNIS PLAYER OF ALL TIME?

Original debate written by Elad De Piccioto

Roger Federer may not have won every Grand Slam throughout his career but that hardly overshadows his 20 Grand Slam[1] titles, nor does it quell the debate of whether or not he is the greatest tennis player to have ever played the game. Many tennis fans may argue that Djokovic[2], Pete Sampras, Rod Laver or Raphael Nadal (who also won 20 Grand Slams) should be considered the Greatest of All Times (or GOAT).

Here are three arguments for why Federer[3] beinisg the greatest tennis player[4], and three acknowledging that while he is great, he's not necessarily the greatest of all time.

Federer Is Great but Not the Greatest

Lack of competition

Roger Federer dominated the tennis courts between 2003 and 2007, winning 12 out of his 20 Slams. In seven out of those twelve Grand Slams, Federer beat Andy Roddick[5] (who admits he is one of the worst players to ever hold the no.1 ranking), Lleyton Hewitt, Mark Philippoussis, Marat Safin and Marcos Baghdatis, none of whom are considered elite players, and who weren't ranked highly when Federer won against them.

The average ranking of the players Federer faced in the finals during those years is 16.3. Back then, Djokovic`s average, for example, stood at 6.5, meaning Federer played against weaker players than Djokovic did in the finals at that time. Federer's decline in wins coincides with the emergence of Nadal and Djokovic. His impressive record of Grand Slam wins should be attributed mostly to his lack of competition[6] during those earlier years. Since 2007, Nadal and Djokovic[7] have each taken their fair share of Grand Slam titles – with Nadal on par with Federer since Roland Garros 2020.

Actually, Serena Williams is the best

When considering who deserves to be named as "the best tennis player of all time," gender[8] should be left out of the discussion (although it usually isn't). In which case Serena Williams[9] would be considered the game's best player ever. Even Federer himself has acknowledged[10] her dominance in the sport.

Both Williams and Federer have each won the most Grand Slam trophies worldwide, but Williams's record of 23 wins[11] is more impressive than Federer's 20. No one is close to flirting with Williams's domination and she holds a better Slam-Average[12] (Grand Slams entered/won ratio). So, when only referring to men's tennis, the claim that Federer is the GOAT may be legitimate, although worth a deeper discussion. However, when gender[13] is taken out of the equation, it has to be Williams!

It's impossible to compare over time

Comparisons across eras are insufficiently meaningful[14]. Training conditions and methods are becoming more professional as time goes on. Modern equipment and technology provide players with better equipment and different means of playing the game. Moreover, you can't tell which players competed in a stronger era.

For example, can you tell if Federer is better than Rod Laver or Pete Sampras? Sampras competed with stronger players, like Boris Becker[15], Andre Agassi[16] and Pat Rafter. Laver dominated the game no less than Federer, winning 11 Grand Slams despite the fact that he was not allowed to compete[17] for five years in the middle of his career. It can't be said conclusively that Federer is the best player to ever play the game—therefore, it shouldn't be said.

Federer Is the GOAT

Federer plays the most beautiful, elegant tennis ever

There are few things in sports as aesthetically pleasing as Federer's tennis game[18]. At his prime, his flair and creativity were phenomenal, while his movement is economical[19], in that he doesn't run as far or as much as his rivals. His single-handed backhand[20] is poetry; a thing of beauty; an all-time classic. In fact, every aspect of his game is executed effortlessly[21], with much style and grace.

American statesman Henry Clay once said: "Statistics are no substitute for judgment." Following this logic, if Federer's 20 Grand Slams are not good enough proof that he is the greatest player ever, many can argue that the way he plays[22] is.

The claim about lack of competition is ridiculous

Federer has ushered in the golden era of men's tennis[23]; he has competed against Djokovic and Nadal, two players who have to be included in any GOAT discussion. Moreover, Stan Wawrinka and Andy Murray are stronger than their three Grand Slam titles (each) would suggest. If anything, it's Federer's talent that prevented those players from winning more Grand Slams.

Federer's ability is likely what prevented Nadal from holding the record for most Grand Slam titles, as much as Nadal's ability with clay court serves prevented Federer from adding more wins to his record than he already has (excluding Federer's Wimbledon 2019 semi-finals win). The quality and strength of Federer's competition is unquestionable. In fact, it has been said that Federer's skills have forced his competitors[24] to up their game just to be able to compete with him.

Federer is the most versatile to ever play the game

Jimmy Connors, winner of seven Grand Slams, once told the BBC[25]: "[In the modern game] you're either a clay court specialist, a grass court specialist, or a hard-court specialist... or you're Roger Federer." Federer won Grand Slams using all serves. He is the best of his era on hard and grass courts. (He did lose 11 finals to Nadal on clay, which arguably shows that Federer is the second-best on clay when compared only to the Spaniard.)

Versatility is what separates Federer from the rest. As mentioned, his one-handed backhand is a classic, and his forehand is one of the greatest shots in tennis[26], according to Pete Sampras. He controls every element in today's tennis, such as the backhand smash[27] and skyhook, half-volley and jump smash. And if that's not enough, he has the character of a champion, as we all witnessed in the 2017 Australian Open final and 2019 Wimbledon men's semi-finals.

....

The Bottom Line: Roger Federer's skill, class, versatility and stylish game may make him the undisputed GOAT, yet the claims that he faces weak competition and that it's hard to compare players over time remain a strong argument for those who believe he is not the best tennis player ever. Do you think Federer is the true GOAT?

ARE THE NFL "CONCUSSION RULES" RUINING THE GAME?

Original debate written by Elad De Piccioto

It's well-known that football is an intense and often violent game. However, in recent years, research[28] has shown that the on-field violence we see has a steep price. Are the long-term effects of football collisions and tackles a price that we, and more importantly, the players[29] are willing to pay? It's been shown that frequent head injuries[30] can cause Chronic Traumatic Encephalopathy [31](CTE), a progressive degenerative disease. CTE can cause long-term debilitating symptoms, including depression, memory loss, and even dementia; it has also already led student and professional players to commit suicide[32].

As a result, in 2009, the NFL enacted the "NFL GameDay Concussion Protocol[33]." The protocol specifies a list of symptoms for detecting concussions and offers guidelines for sideline evaluation. If a player is diagnosed with a concussion, he is immediately removed from the pitch and cannot return to play until he is fully recovered. In 2016, disciplinary action was introduced for teams not properly adhering to the protocol. over the years since its introduction, the Protocol has been tweaked[34], most recently in 2018, when the NFL's Head, Neck and Spine Committee updated it to include several additional guidelines to protect players.

The question stands: Is the protocol ruining the game or is it protecting the players? Here are three claims for the Concussion Protocol, and three claims against it.

Why Fans Should Embrace the Concussion Protocol

The game will be changed, but for the better

Like everything in our lives, football also changes. But not all changes are bad. Look at what happened in the NBA: The rules changed – the game may have gotten "softer" but it also got faster, and players developed new skills. The same goes for the NFL: With less violent tackles[35], players' skills will develop gradually. The game will probably become faster. A new form of player will evolve (and maybe already has), possibly a hybrid type of player that is quicker, faster and smarter. If football were to evolve in this way, would you really stop watching it?

There is more to football than violent collisions!

You're at work, talking with a friend about last night's NFL game. When he says something like, "Football is a violent sport…" you probably explain that football is much more than violence – it's about strategy, athleticism, teamwork and more. Well, guess what? These aspects are going to remain part of the game even when there are no more helmet-to-helmet clashes. Claiming that the life-saving protocols are ruining the game[36] minimizes the essence of the sport you love so much.

The new rules help to protect football's integrity

Sports are about giving your best in every single moment. When a player suffers a concussion, he is not playing his best. His cognitive reasoning and functionality decrease; he will have problems processing information and concentrating. The baseline cognitive test[37] helps to ensure that all the players on the football field can actually play their best. Isn't that what football is all about?

Why Fans Should Reject the Concussion Protocol

Players aim for the legs, causing more injuries than ever

With new regulations, defensive players now go lower to avoid drawing penalties, fines, and suspensions. This tendency [38]has caused some horrific leg injuries, like those of Miami Dolphins' tight end Dustin Keller, or of

New England's Rob Gronkowski[39]. Though the long-term [40]impact of head injuries is indisputable, in the short-term, some players actually prefer head injuries over leg injuries: "That's tough to deal with [concussions], you may miss a game or two... But you still get to go home, walk home to your family," said Dustin Keller[41], Miami Dolphins tight end. In fact, just to avoid leg injuries, other NFL players told ESPN's "Outside the Lines"[42] that offensive players are actually asking defensive players to be hit high rather than low.

There is no changing football

Physical collisions, including ones that cause concussions, are an inherent part of football. Violence has always been a part of the NFL and that's not going to change, regardless of the rules, fines or suspensions that the league puts in place. Even after the Concussion Protocol was introduced, Miami Dolphins' linebacker Channing Crowder[43] told NFL.com: "If I get a chance to knock somebody out, I'm going to knock them out and take what they give me..." And he is not the only one with this attitude. Football's defense players have been trained all of their careers to tackle and to tackle hard. This attitude is what has made them who they are.

The new protocol can backfire, risking players' careers

Disqualification due to a concussion can damage players' careers, not just their lives. A bad concussion protocol (a long record of concussions, with substantial time that the player has been ruled out from the field) means a threat to a player's career. So NFL players who have dedicated their entire lives to the game will do anything to stay out of the concussion protocol, including lying to their doctors. The new Concussion Protocol[44] is well-intended but may inadvertently cause players to lie about their concussion symptoms, potentially exposing themselves to greater damage.

The Bottom Line: The "NFL GameDay Concussion Protocol" is designed to make the game safer for players but it has the potential to backfire and expose the players to greater head damage. Do you support the new rules?

MESSI OR RONALDO - WHO IS TRULY THE BEST?

Original debate written by Elad De Piccioto

The current era of soccer is dominated by two giants: Juventus, Real Madrid and Man UTD legend Cristiano Ronaldo and Paris Saint-Germain's Lionel Messi. These two nemeses have scooped almost every individual award over the past 15 years, and despite their advanced ages (36 and 33, respectively in 2021), they show no signs of slowing down. As there can be only one, which of them is it? The phenomenal Portuguese Ronaldo or the one-team man Lionel Messi?

Here are three arguments for each side.

Team Messi

Advanced statistics proves Messi is better

Both Ronaldo and Messi[45] have impressive stats, but a closer look proves that Messi makes better decisions and, more importantly, brings greater value to his team. Using a framework that was originally developed for baseball, The Economist[46] rated Messi and Ronaldo goals based on their context and importance. These stats, called Expected Points Added (EPA), rate goals by their added win probability. Meaning, a winning goal in the last minute of the game is rated higher than the fourth goal scored in a 4-0 win. Messi's EPA stands at 59.5 while Ronaldo's is 50.4.

Moreover, Messi makes better decisions. Using a complex algorithm, a company called GoodCall values a player's decision-making[47] and Efficiency Per Match (EPM). This entails valuing each pass, shot, chance created or a dribble made by players, and then rating the player's decision-making and efficiency. Messi's EPM (as of 2019) is 238, and he makes good decisions 0.63% of the time. Ronaldo's EPM is 118 and his decision making rate stands at only 0.43%.

Messi is a better team player

Messi is not only an incredible scorer and gifted playmaker, he also makes everyone around him a better player. A true leader, he brings his team together. Not only does he have more assists and key passes[48] than Ronaldo, he is always using his phenomenal vision to keep his teammates involved. He has great tactical intelligence, finding free spaces to move into, receiving the ball and then laying it off to a team-mate, to build attacks.

While Ronaldo is more of an executor, who plays high up the pitch and scores great goals when given the chance, Messi can do that just as well, but is also comfortable dropping deep and keeping possession of the ball with his team. From these positions, he can send his colleagues on dangerous runs with pin-point passes. This versatility makes him that much better than Ronaldo.

Messi's magic

Messi and Ronaldo differ mostly in their style. Ronaldo is a machine. He is an explosive player, with abnormal physical abilities and a huge amount of talent. Tall and strong and certainly one of the greatest players, Ronaldo doesn't possess Messi's magic.

The Argentine is a greater natural talent. He is a virtuoso, a magician. His dribbling is considered to be the best the game has ever seen, and he passes and shoots the ball with the precision of a brain surgeon. He makes eye-popping moves that leave people speechless and overwhelmed. Seeing him weave his way through a team's defense[49] and then put the ball past the keeper is just something special.

Team Ronaldo

Ronaldo is a more advanced player

Nowadays, soccer is more dynamic and athletic than ever. The game has become faster, stronger and more demanding in most aspects of physicality. While Messi might have more talent, Ronaldo's combination of physical and technical abilities just makes him better. He is 6"1 of pure Portuguese muscle[50]. This means he's very hard to push off the ball and, combined with his NBA star-like jumping ability, makes his headers a serious threat. Ronaldo's combination of dizzying pace, great dribbling and powerful shooting with either foot terrorizes defenses.

He is simply a better fit for today's game. His athleticism is second to none; he combines dizzying pace with powerful shooting and a jumping ability of an NBA star, which makes his headers a serious threat to the opposition. And he's doing it at the same level, even at 36. Ronaldo, more than Messi, is the ideal model of the next generation of players.

Messi has a better supporting cast

Messi has won more titles since he plays for a better team, not because he is a better player than Ronaldo. Throughout his entire career, Messi played for arguably the best side to ever play the game. Unlike Ronaldo's team experiences, Messi's Barcelona teammates know each other blindly, since most of them have played together since they were 10 years old, always the same style and formation. The move to PSG will be a testing ground for Messi's effect on his team.

This is not to say that Ronaldo's teammates were bad. They were great, but just not as great as Messi's during the better part of his career. For example, Messi has played with Neymar (who is arguably the next best player) and Luis Suarez, two of the best forwards of the century, as well as with Xavi Hernandez and Andrés Iniesta, two of the most dominating center-midfielders of our era. While Messi has the added value of an unforgettable team, Ronaldo is the driving factor of his. Messi is like Tim Duncan of the Spurs, while Ronaldo is like LeBron James in Cleveland.

The international paradigm

Ronaldo's international career puts him on a higher level than Messi. In fact, Messi has never won an international trophy. He lost finals in both the Copa America (the South America championship) and the World Cup. Meanwhile, Ronaldo led his Portugal side to win the 2016 European Championship. Even if Messi ever leads Argentina to win the Copa America, Ronaldo's international achievements will be considered greater. Unlike other sports, international trophies in soccer are the ultimate glory. His three World Cup trophies fixed Pele's stature as the best player ever, and Diego Maradona winning it for Argentina puts him before Messi. Only a victory at the 2022 World Cup in Qatar could change that.

....

The Bottom Line: Ronaldo or Messi? On the one hand, Messi is a better team player and simply more talented. On the other, Ronaldo is more complete with a better international career. Where do you stand, Team Messi or Team Ronaldo?

SHOULD COLLEGE ATHLETES GET PAID?

Original debate written by Elad De Piccioto

CBS Sports and Turner paid over $1 billion a year[51] [52]for broadcasting the NCAA March Madness basketball tournament up until 2023. Until now, the broadcasts' college sports stars had no chance of receiving much of that sum (at least not directly). However, the NCAA recently decided[53] to allow college athletes to financially benefit[54] from the use of their names, images and likenesses. This decision follows the move by several states[55], led by California[56], to pass laws allowing the same right, as been part of the longtime debate as to whether college athletes should be paid or not. The question arises primarily regarding football and basketball student-athletes, since they bring in the most money.

Here are three arguments for and three arguments against paying college athletes:

Three Reasons Why College Athletes Should Get Paid

Difficulty of implementation is no excuse

An important argument from those who oppose paying college athletes is the challenge of implementing such a move. The following are just some of the questions that pinpoint the complexities: Who will pay the college athletes (the NCAA or colleges)? How often will they receive pay? Will there be a salary cap? The main question regards the equitable application of paying college athletes, namely who will get paid and who won't. The details of the new NCAA rules are still being discussed[57], and will need input from different state legislators and sports associations.

However, since the debate was first sparked over the NCAA's income from broadcasting, the answer seems simple: Theoretically, the athletes to get paid should be the ones playing the sports that bring in the big money, namely, men's college basketball and football players. College basketball and football[58] players in particular are the ones who provide good entertainment for fans who are willing to pay to watch the games, so they deserve to get paid. This is capitalism, and that's how it works in America. In its ruling, the NCAA distinguished[59] between amateur and potential professional athletes, i.e., those most likely to be recruited by professional teams. Time will tell who ultimately benefits from this decision.

Athletes risk their bodies and are exposed to permanent damage

One of the best aspects of college sports is the players' enthusiasm. Their love and passion for their game is admirable and infectious. But there is a downside to it; in their fervor to play their best, many college athletes suffer serious injuries that sometimes end their career prematurely[60].

Setting aside the disturbing fact that a career-ending injury will end their scholarship, those college athletes put their bodies at risk of permanent damage, without pay. Hurting your knee might leave you limping for the rest of your life. Suffering concussions[61] can cause dementia and depression, not to mention CTE[62]. Those college athletes who put their bodies on the line at each training session and game they play deserve to be paid[63] for the health risks[64] they are taking.

There's big money involved in college sports anyway

It's common to think paying college athletes can detract from the purity of the game and ruin the magic. But it won't. The passion fans see on the court or field is not because there is no money involved.

Big companies are profiting off of branding college athletes[65], namely, asking them to wear brand apparel during games without paying them to do so. As such, these players feel used, and rightly so. The new rule[66] allowing them to get paid shows that the NCAA and fans are really concerned about preserving the purity of college sports.

Three Reasons Why College Athletes Should Not Get Paid

The difference for college athletes is marginal in term of money

If salaries were to replace scholarships in college sports, athletes would not earn much more. In fact, an impressive $100,000-a-year salary for a college athlete would grant him only a few hundred dollars more per year than a scholarship. According to Money.com, a full athletic scholarship at an NCAA Division I university is about $65,000 a year[67]. This includes tuition, room, board, and books (if you enroll at a college with high tuition). In contrast, a salary will be subjected to federal and state income taxes. Therefore, out of the $100,000, a net of $65,100 will remain for the student. The difference is marginal.

Earning big money too soon can be harmful

People argue that paying college athletes will help them develop a sense of financial awareness. However, in reality, poor investments, trusting unethical financial advisors and lavish spending habits are some of the main reasons professional athletes find themselves broke after they retire, according to ESPN documentary, "Broke."[68] Without sound financial education, young college athletes may not be equipped to handle so much money.

Paying big money means college students missing the point of college

College is about preparing oneself for real life. It is supposed to provide students with tools and abilities to succeed after graduation. In that manner, college athletes are no different than other college students who practice or intern in hospitals, law firms or advertising agencies for little to no money. So why should athletes get paid while others don't?

A lot of young adults today are impatient and lack the ability to delay gratification. College can teach them the lesson: in real life, you have to work hard and wait for your chance. Paying big money to any college student, athlete or academic, is far from ideal preparation for life.

....

The Bottom Line: Paying big money to college athletes defeats the purpose of college as a preparatory lesson for life. On the other hand, not paying athletes who risk serious long-term injuries seems wrong. Was the NCAA right to change the current practice?

SHOULD SPORTS BETTING BE LEGAL?

Original debate written by Elad De Piccioto

In 2018, the Supreme Court reversed a 26-year-old federal ban[69] on sports betting, enabling individual states to decide whether to allow wagers to be placed on baseball, basketball, football, hockey, among other sports games. Previously, sports betting had been prohibited nationwide, except in four states – Delaware, Nevada, Montana and Oregon. Ever since, 22 states have approved sports betting, with almost all the rest moving towards legislation[70].

Since a vast majority of the American people supported the legalization of sports betting (55% felt that betting on sports should be legal, only 35% opposed[71]), this change in the federal government's approach to the subject is not surprising.

Following are three reasons why the legalization of sports betting is positive and three more explaining why its negative.

In Support of Legalized Sports Betting:

It is already a thriving industry

Regardless of its legality, the betting industry has blossomed. Illegal sports betting is a multi-Billion-dollar industry (some estimates are as high as $150 billion[72]); anyone who wants to place a bet can do so easily online or through local office pools and offshore books. Now, after the Supreme Court decision, states will be more inclined[73] to consider or pass legislation to legalize sports betting, thus allowing people to continue betting but in a regulated and fairer environment. It will also prevent them from dealing with questionable bookies. Moreover, addicts will have fewer stigmas, which may make it easier for them to seek help.

It's the economy, stupid

Sports betting is good for the economy. Legalizing sports betting will obviously create huge state tax revenues. More importantly, it has the potential to create jobs (estimated between 125,000-152,000 jobs) for the American people. Researchers estimate that legalized, regulated sports betting could actually bring in a total of $6 billion in annual revenue[74] for states by 2023.

Moreover, it has potential to bring huge money into the United States and keep it there. Currently, most of the betting takes place online. It is more than likely that legalizing sports betting in America will trigger American telecommunications and tech companies to take over the international market[75].

Sports betting won't corrupt the leagues

Louis Brandeis, an American lawyer and Associate Justice on the US Supreme Court, once said: "Sunlight is said to be the best of disinfectants; electric light the most efficient policeman…" Meaning, legalized sports betting will actually make it harder to fix games. This is because once legalized, sports betting will be monitored, and any irregular activity will be easily detected. It is easier to fix games in an unmonitored environment, in which money flows under the radar. Therefore, the common belief that legalizing sports betting will corrupt sports is wrong.

Against Legalized Sports Betting

The house always wins

Many of those who argued for the legalization of sports betting claimed that it's more about skill than luck. They said that much like stock trading, it's about wittingly identifying opportunities and acting on them. But this assertion is wrong.

The human element has a huge impact on sports; the unexpected often happens, which can affect everyone from team owners down to the last player. Even where skill may improve odds of winning, people who bet on sports may not always possess the deep understanding of statistics required to win. People usually bet on sports based on a hunch, not knowledge. Sports betting is not about skills and it's not like stock trading; it's gambling, and as in gambling, the house always wins.

Legalizing sports betting won't make illegal betting disappear

The main reason people bet with bookies is not the lack of alternatives but availability and, most importantly, the generous line of credit that bookies offer. Bettors don't need to deposit money to bet with bookies, which makes it easier for them to bet with money they don't have. This is also the main reason wagers get into troubling debt situations. Moreover, bookies will offer better margins and betting rates for their customers since they won't pay taxes. Thus, legalizing sports betting won't eliminate illegal betting[76] and the problems that accompany it[77], but is likely to simply increase right alongside legal betting, especially if sports betting becomes widely advertised.

It will change the nature of American sports

Legalizing gambling on sports will gradually change American sports. As with everything that involves money, the sports industry will become even more commercialized than it is now. In a slow but consistent process, the focus of American sports will become betting rather than the game itself. Anyone who has ever gambled on a sporting event knows that once you place a bet, the focus of the game suddenly becomes money, not the game itself. And that's not what sports is about.

The Bottom Line: The Supreme Court's decision to overturn the federal ban on sports betting is reasonable, especially since it is already happening to a large extent, and states deserve to monetarily benefit from it. On the other hand, legalizing betting won't eliminate illegal betting and will negatively change the nature of sporting events. Do you support the legalization of sports betting? Would you place a bet on your favorite team?

SHOULD WOMEN COMPETE AGAINST MEN IN SPORTS?

Original debate written by Elad De Piccioto

The world champion US women's soccer team [78] is appealing[79] a court decision about a 2019 lawsuit[80] they brought against the United States Soccer Federation over gender discrimination, including pay equity and working conditions. This echoes the stance taken by the U.S. women's hockey team[81] who, in 2017, decided to sit out the International Ice Hockey Federation World Championship in Michigan in protest of the unfair discrimination ranging from pay to equipment to publicity between the sexes in the sport. These protests once again spark the subject of gender inequality in all professional sports[82], questioning everything from the gender wage gap between sports teams to whether or not sports should be gender-segregated at all.

Here are three reasons why women should be allowed to compete against men in professional sports, and three reasons why they shouldn't.

Women Should Compete against Men in Sports

The physicality argument is not valid for all sports

Sports are not all about physicality. Some sports highlight physical aspects while others highlight skills. Take tennis for example: Players who are stronger and more physically adept hold an advantage in some areas of the game, but players who are more talented skill-wise are better overall. Roger Federer, for example, isn't the most physical tennis player, but he is probably the most skilled player[83] out there. Also, nobody who has ever watched Serena Williams play tennis can deny that sheer skill is what has won her

23 Grand Slam titles[84] (although her muscles definitely help). Her skills are what has earned her the no. 1 ranking[85] of the Universal Tennis Ranking.

While men and women may differ in physicality, they do not differ in their skills. This is why former tennis star John McEnroe[86] faced backlash in 2017 when he dismissed Williams as the sport's greatest tennis player and, instead, clarified that she may be the sport's best female player. In professional sports – where the importance of skills outweighs the importance of physicality – everyone should compete equally.

Let nature do its thing

Women should be allowed to compete against men in professional sports since, like in men's sports, only women who are good enough will be drafted to a particular team and will get the chance to play. That's just the nature of competitive sports. It's the "natural selection" mechanism of sports that leaves the bad players out, regardless of their gender, physicality, race or religion.

It's society's duty to stop segregation in sports

The socialization of boys and girls with regards to sports differs in so many ways; they're often funneled into different directions, and their different abilities are heightened before biology makes its first mark. This is a result of historical prejudice[87], stereotypes[88] and of centuries of discrimination, which shouldn't be part of modern society.

Sports are a cultural institution. They are known to be catalysts of social trends and movements[89]. Just look at US Women's Soccer team co-captain, Megan Rapinoe[90], who is a leading voice fighting for equal pay, along with Olympic gold medalist Simone Biles[91], and many others. As long as we agree with this prejudicial casting[92], we take part in reinforcing it. Our society must not put up with it anymore. It's not just about sports; it's about how we view and value one another.

Women Shouldn't Compete against Men

There won't be a level playing field

What makes professional sports so popular is "the sweet tension of uncertainty of outcome," in the words of Warren Fraleigh[93], a professor of physical education. Involving women in certain sports could break this tension. In short sprints[94], even the most talented women are at a disadvantage when competing against the average male athlete. This is due to such differences[95] as muscle mass, innate strength, testosterone levels or socially constructed gender differences.

Women won't catch up to men

There is a serious claim that once women are allowed to compete with men, they will eventually catch up in terms of ability and performance. Allowing women to compete against men could inspire a huge leap in their abilities, and most of the American public[96] believes that top female athletes will eventually beat top males.

Yet this claim overlooks important aspects: First, men's sports will make a leap at the same time as women's, making it harder for women to catch up. Second, and most importantly, the performance gap between the sexes is just too wide (between 8-12%),[97] a gap that is impossible for women to bridge. The top women in 100m sprints and long jump[98] still lag about 10% behind their male counterparts. Additionally, women's best scores in swimming or athletics don't even reach the top 400 men's scores[99]. While women's physical abilities will likely advance and the performance gap will get narrower, it is highly unlikely to disappear altogether – putting men at an unfair advantage.

The change in sports may not be welcomed

It has been claimed[100] that "if new weight and length classes are introduced in many sports [and] if the rules are changed," women will be able to compete against men and win in several sports. Essentially, some feel it may be worth considering changing the games so that they accommodate women. However, it's hard to believe that the American public would want their favorite sports to change. When the NFL launched the "Concussion

Protocol[101]" in order to save players' lives, fans didn't like it and claimed this change would ruin football. Additionally, fans were aggravated by the MLB's ban on home plate collision[102], and they still have issues with instant replay[103] being used to make better judgment calls. In this vein, any change in sports that is made to accommodate women will likely see strong opposition by fans.

....

The Bottom Line: While women competing against men in professional sports would be a positive win against gender discrimination[104], it would reduce the uncertainty of outcomes and potentially change the nature of the games the world has already come to know and love. What do you think? Would you want to see women and men competing against one another?

LEBRON VS. JORDAN: WHO'S THE GREATEST OF ALL TIME?

Original debate written by Julian Bonte-Friedheim

Over recent years, LeBron James has been establishing himself as a contender for the greatest basketball player of all time. However, Michael Jordan has long held that title according to many basketball fans, not to mention Netflix and ESPN's ten-part documentary series[105] highlighting Jordan's contributions[106] to the Bull's successes. Two undoubted legends of the sport, both have written history with their achievements, becoming ambassadors of the NBA. But which of the two has been the bigger winner?

Here are three reasons for either of these giants being better than the other.

LeBron Has Taken Over

He lifts up a whole team

In basketball, many great players succeeded as parts of great teams. However, unlike Jordan, LeBron led an arguably average Cleveland Cavaliers to win the NBA championship[107] in 2016. In each subsequent season with them until he left to join the LA Lakers[108] in 2018, LeBron's leadership in getting the Cavs to the finals was also a truly special achievement[109]. While the Cavs ended up losing those finals, it was only because LeBron faced a stacked Golden State Warriors team with far more individual quality than the Cavs. In Cleveland, LeBron proved that he could be a true leader[110], making everyone else around him bring their A game.

Bigger, stronger and more defensive

Both LeBron and Jordan are amazing offensive players that can dominate games like few others. But LeBron also has the edge over Jordan in terms of defense. Around 25-30 pounds heavier, two inches taller and with a significantly longer wingspan, LeBron is much more of a physical presence[111] on the court. This enables him to defend all five positions on the floor, from point guards to power forwards. LeBron also leads his team to defend as a unit, making it that much more effective. If they had ever played each other, LeBron could have likely come out on top in terms of defense.

Team player

LeBron is a better passer[112] than Jordan ever was. He averages 7.9 assists per game[113], while the Bulls and Wizards star had only 5.3 assists[114] in an average game. Unlike Jordan, LeBron has no problem letting go of the ball and passing it to a teammate. His ability to read the game and involve his team when needed makes him that much harder to play against, rather than an individual who keeps the ball all the time. Providing teammates with key assists [115]are a big part of LeBron's game, whereas Jordan was always seen as more of a selfish player.

Jordan Was the Best

Amazing scorer

No one could split a defense to score the game-winning shot[116] like Jordan could. His dribbling[117], jumping[118], footwork[119] and lethal scoring ability made him a nightmare to defend against. His lightning-fast first step often left opponents in the dust while he created space to score. It took until 2019 for someone (Lebron[120]) to pass Jordan on the NBA's all-time scoring records for most points scored on average during a season (30.12 a game[121]). Offensively, Jordan was just unstoppable[122].

Clutch

Jordan is very likely to have been the most clutch player that ever played the game. This means that he was able to raise his game when the pressure was the highest. His game winner[123], during his last Chicago Bulls game to secure the championship and his second three-peat with the team, stands out. Jordan won the NBA finals MVP award six times[124], twice as much as any other player. He was also a king at scoring the game-winning shot in the final seconds of play. On the other hand, even if he has outgrown it, LeBron still struggles to shed his label as a 'choker[125],' for having fallen short in big moments[126]. Jordan is better because he always delivered the good when it really mattered.

Beyond Legendary

Jordan is probably the biggest brand ambassador[127] basketball and the NBA[128] ever had. He was a mythical player, who moved and scored in ways that set him apart. His fadeaway jump shot. His up-and-under [129]finish. His ability to make it look easy to slip by the other team's defense. Jordan's unique technique allowed him to jump in the air and 'hang' there[130] that many fractions of a second longer than others. He could pull off dazzling moves[131] that excited fans everywhere and brought many new ones to the sport. It was his almost alien talent that set him apart, landing him a role in the 1996 Looney Tunes movie Space Jam[132] and making him a global household name. (A Space Jam sequel featuring Lebron James was released in 2021, keeping the comparison alive.)

....

The Bottom Line: While Jordan was more of a flashy individual talent, LeBron is a fantastic team player. Every conversation about who is the greatest NBA player of all time will undoubtedly include these two iconic names[133]. Where do you stand? Do you prefer LeBron's team-spirit or Jordan's unique attacking ability?

SHOULD INSTANT REPLAYS (VAR) BE USED IN SPORTS?

Original debate written by Elad De Piccioto

The debate over the use of replays[134] is common to all sports. Although controversies and referee-related mistakes[135] have always been part of sports, everyone will agree that games are better off without them. However, the use of replays makes games longer and less continuous, and the fans don't seem to like it.

In 2018, FIFA introduced the video assistant referee (VAR) technology – An assistant referee who reviews decisions using video footage[136]. Ever since, it has been subject to criticism by soccer fans all over the world. So, what's the better option? Here are three arguments for the use of replays in sports, and three arguments against it.

Argument against Replays

Imperfections make perfection

Sports are one of those rare things in life where perfection isn't necessary. The imperfections in sports is part of what makes watching them so entertaining; it's what allows teams to score against others; it's what makes it possible for the underdog to win[137;] it's what amazes us over and over again. Mistakes are part of a game's lore. It's unreasonable to ask for error-free sports. Referees[138,] like players, are humans who make mistakes, and that's part of what makes sports so entertaining and, sometimes, even relatable.

They ruin sports' historical moments

No matter the sport, games often get condensed into one particular moment. While the final score of any sport is determined as a result of an entire game, there is usually one defining moment during a particular game. SMoreover, sometimes that defining moment is also the final play, which also determines the game's winner of the game. Think about the greatest sports' moments you've seen or personally experienced. Now, imagine that those moments were subjected to replays during the game itself, with everything coming to a pause so that the judges can check the monitors. Puff, that initial magic is gone. Those are the most special moments in sports[139], and using replays means ruining them for fans.

They won't eliminate controversies but will create new ones

Using more replays won't eliminate[140] controversies from sports, rather they will simply change the nature of the controversies[141]. No matter the sport, replays are not needed for most calls, especially the ones that referees can easily make based on what they saw. Instant replays[142] are needed during questionable incidents when the call is not obvious. However, even in those cases, replays are not necessarily helpful. For example, in "the Tuck Rule game[143]," even after reviewing the incident, officials made the wrong call (after making the right one on the football field...). More examples can be found in Soccer, where the use of replays and VAR have not completely eliminated referee mistakes from the popular game. Replays[144] don't make games any fairer.

Arguments for Replays

Technology is the way forward

Technology has taken over and transformed innumerable aspects of our lives. For example, 47% of US jobs[145], including medicine and accounting will be automated soon enough. Using replays in sports is just another aspect in which technology is changing older methods to make things better. In fact, technological developments in sports[146] have exploded in recent years, improving players' abilities. It's only natural that the latest technology leap will also increase the use of replays, affecting referee calls. It's the natural evolution of sports. Replays are here to make games fairer, and they should be embraced.

It's the right thing to do

Choosing between longer games with no referee mistakes or shorter games with controversies and referee mistakes is easy; it has to be the first option, simply because it's fairer[147]. Professional teams, players and coaches work hard all season (and pre-season) and don't deserve to be sent home over one bad call[148]. It should be prevented if possible. The damage caused by extending sports games by a few minutes is relatively small compared to the damage when a game or even a season is decided over a bad call. Thus, implementing replays is the right thing to do.

They won't make sports substantially slower

There are countless ways to prevent replays from substantially slowing down games[149]. For instance, replay use can be limited solely to cases which significantly affect match score, like it is used in the NBA and Soccer (where only goals, penalties & red cards are decided using replays) nowadays. Leagues can limit the time allowed for referees to make a decision based on replays, or limit the number of challenges a team is allowed to have during a game.

Moreover, it's possible that new technologies[150] are becoming available right now that can provide referees with the right call through the use of replays, before they even ask for it. Whether through technology or limitations set by various professional sports leagues, the use of replays won't significantly slow down sports.

....

The Bottom Line: Using replays in sports offers both advantages and disadvantages. They can eliminate referee mistakes but can cause other controversies. Do you think they enhance sports or take away some of the magic[151]?

SHOULD THE NHL BAN FIGHTING IN HOCKEY?

Original debate written by Elad De Piccioto

Hockey is the only major-league sport in which fighting is largely tolerated[152]. Although it has declined significantly in recent years, fighting in the NHL is still common. [153]In the NHL, unlike in the MLB, NFL or NBA, players are not automatically suspended for fighting[154]. However, with growing concern over head injuries in sports, it seems inevitable for the league to take serious steps towards banning fighting; even Congress demanded[155] that they address this in 2016. On the other hand, many hockey fans and the NHL commissioner still see fighting as part of the game.

Here are three reasons why fighting in hockey should be banned and three reasons why it shouldn't:

Fighting in Hockey Should Be Banned

Banning fighting won't affect hockey's popularity

The standard claim of those who advocate fighting in hockey is that it's a major element of the sport's popularity. However, a recent survey[156] by Yahoo Sports/YouGov shows that most NHL fans, even those who are very devoted, believe that a formal ban on fighting would have "no impact" on viewership. True NHL fans watch the game for the skills demonstrated, not for the potential fighting – a fact that has been validated by studies[157]. Thus, banning fighting in the NHL won't affect the league's popularity.

Fighting endangers players' lives

In addition to the traditional fighting injuries – including broken faces, hands, noses and eye sockets – fighting can cause serious head trauma[158]. Colton Orr, for example, suffered a concussion and was benched[159] for two NHL seasons. As we've seen in other sports, specifically the NFL, repeated concussions can cause serious damage[160] in the long term. Frequent head blows and concussions cause CTE[161] (Chronic Traumatic Encephalopathy), which leads to memory loss, depression, and dementia, among other issues. There's a growing discussion[162] about head injuries in sports, and it's about time the NHL follows the NFL's "Concussion Protocol[163]" and bans fighting, where the actual goal is to hit other players in the head.

No fighting is hockey's natural selection

Fighting in hockey has become irrelevant[164]. League owners want to eliminate it[165], since they prefer not to pay enforcers[166] (whose job is to deter and respond to violent play by the opposition). Plus, fights promote bans, which can lead to losing games, and every loss can impede a team's playoff spot in an extremely competitive and balanced league like the NHL. Most importantly, players want fighting eliminated; this was relayed by the Florida Panthers' veteran defenseman, Willie Mitchell[167], who said the league needed to do a "better job" defending players. As recent years have seen the lowest fights-per-game average[168] in the NHL compared to the past few decades, banning fighting is just stamping out something that will be gone by natural selection anyhow – so why not do it now?

Fighting in Hockey Shouldn't Be Banned

Fighting serves to limit violence in the NHL

Let's be realistic: Fighting won't vanish from hockey. If it is banned, it will keep coming back in different ways, since it's embedded in the sport's culture[169]. A ban on fighting may inspire players to turn their sticks into weapons or take "cheap shots" at their rivals when they get frustrated, which will spark fights anyway. As things are now, violence is regulated by fights, which serve as a "policing" factor in the NHL. Fighting, which is informally regulated[170], prevents reckless players from hurting skillful players during the game, thus making the game safer for players. In fact, the Bruins' Brad Marchand has taken to licking his opponents[171]; while hardly the most mature way to settle disputes, this current form of "fighting" is relatively harmless.

Fighting in hockey is a catharsis

Hockey is one of the most physical of all sports. Also, hockey fans are some of the most loyal sports fans, who love the physical and aggressive[172] aspect of the game. For them, fighting may not be ideal, but it's not a barbaric ritual either; rather, it's a situation where a player makes the ultimate sacrifice for his team. So, every once in a while, players fight. In our purist-civilized and politically correct society, perhaps we need to make room for this catharsis[173]. Hockey fighting allows fans – who often live through the players – to experience an old-school fight in a controlled, regulated environment. If you're going to ban fighting in hockey, you might as well ban most reality TV shows[174].

Hockey has come a long way; let it progress naturally

There is no comparison between today's hockey with that of the bloody era of the 80's[175]. Violence and fighting have been pushed to the margins for years; it's relatively rare nowadays, with the rate dropping to just 0.18 fights per game for the 2018-2019 seas[176]on, the first time the average dropped under 0.20.

Fighting is part of hockey's culture, and cultural change takes time. Instead of trying to bury the phenomena with regulations and suspensions that hurt the game, let the trend of fighting fade away naturally. The change is already happening; the process has already kicked off. So why quit cold turkey by banning fighting outright?

The Bottom Line: Fighting in hockey serves both as a catharsis for fans and as a restraint of other forms of violence by the players. On the other hand, fighting can cause serious damage to players, and banning it won't affect the sport's popularity. If you were to buy tickets to an NHL game, would you want to see fighting on the ice?

HISTORY CHAPTER

- The perspective on Diana, Princess of Wales
- The perspective on Christopher Columbus
- The bombings of Hiroshima and Nagasaki: Plain evil or necessary evil?
- The perspective on Che Guevara
- The perspective on Ronald Reagan

THE PERSPECTIVE ON DIANA, PRINCESS OF WALES

Original debate written by Chaya Benyamin

Dubbed the "most photographed woman in the world," Diana, Princess of Wales's rare mix of shyness, fashion sense[1], charity and turbulent personal life captivated the world until her tragic death in August of 1997. Decades after her death, discrepancies about Diana's legacy persist. She is described as warm but volatile, naïve yet calculating. With a tribute to the princess included in Prince Harry and Meghan Markle's nuptials[2], and her being a focal point of The Crown[3]'s fourth season on Netflix, Diana remains at the forefront of the world's attention.

While Great Britain and the rest of the world grapples with Diana's complicated legacy, let's review three reasons that support Diana's legacy as a royal angel, and three reasons she might be more accurately determined a fallen one.

The People's Princess

Model Mum

Unlike the young monarchs who came before them, Diana's sons, Princes William and Harry, spent loads of time with their mother. In contrast to her husband's mother, Queen Elizabeth II, Diana insisted her children accompany her[4] on royal tours abroad, even as infants. Diana made concerted efforts to engage her children with life outside of the palace walls, whether that meant enrolling them in local preschools, riding roller coasters with them at Disneyland, or taking them to visit homeless shelters[5] and hospitals.

William recalls[6], "She was very informal and really enjoyed the laughter and the fun...She understood that there was a real life outside of Palace walls."

The People's Princess

Diana had genuine deference[7] toward her subjects. Although born in the aristocracy, Diana shared none of the royal family's preoccupation with rank or class-based decorum. Before becoming engaged to the prince, she worked common jobs – as a kindergarten aide and even a house cleaner[8]. Diana would speak to people eye-to-eye, crouching down (unthinkable for royalty) to speak to children[9] or the infirm. The princess described herself as "much closer to people at the bottom than to people at the top," and backed up her words with support for over 100 charities[10]. She leveraged her celebrity to bring much-needed exposure to ubiquitous problems like homelessness, HIV/AIDS, and landmines. Her humility and dedication made her the queen of the people's hearts, and made the whole Crown[11] a bit dearer to all.

Wrong place, wrong time

It cannot be overlooked that Diana was a young girl of nineteen – a naïve[12] bride – when she became wife of the 32-year-old Prince of Wales. By all accounts, the marriage was fueled by Diana's whimsical ideas of love and marriage, combined with her juvenile crush on Prince Charles. (Diana was said to have kept pictures of him in her room as a girl.) The advent of Charles's affair [13]with his ex, Camilla, must have been world-shattering[14]. Add to this the pressure of royal life[15] – packed with endless public engagements, stiff protocols, and the unbridled prying of an ungenerous media that labeled Diana "unstable and unbalanced[16]" – and a sympathetic picture of a woman at the mercy of forces beyond her control begins to emerge.

Rebel Royale

She tarnished the Crown

Diana made a habit of publicly airing the details of her personal life and her opinions of her husband and in-laws, in direct opposition to the throne's proclivity for privacy. The princess initiated the clandestine interviews that became the centerpieces of the biography Diana: Her True Story. In the book, Diana blamed her bulimia, self-harm, and suicide attempts on the coldness of her husband and the royal family. Even the book's author questioned[17] Diana's motives, pondering in a later article whether she was trying to position herself as the innocent party in a doomed marriage. Her airing of dirty laundry continued in an interview with the BBC's Martin Bashir[18,] wherein Diana bashed the prince as a bad father and called him unfit to be king. Whatever Diana's qualms, discretion was her royal duty – one she betrayed.

Affairs of her own

Prince Charles was publicly demonized for his well-known affair with long-time sweetheart, Camilla Parker-Bowles. Lesser known are Diana's own string of indiscretions[19], beginning with her bodyguard, Barry Mannakkee, in 1985 – a tryst thought to predate[20] Charles's affair with Camilla. Major James Hewitt[21] followed, from 1986-1991. In a leaked phone conversation with another lover, James Gilbey, Diana is said to have bragged about spoiling Hewitt with a new wardrobe that cost her quite a bit. If Charles's public favor was won and lost on his level of marital fidelity, it is only fair to observe that Diana, too, fell short of this mark.

Difficult Diana

Diana's public demureness and composure stand in contrast to reports of her offered by friends and staffers. Long-time friend, designer Roberto Dovorik, described her as having something of a "split personality[22]," in that she could be reliable one moment and totally irrational the next. Her former security guard claimed[23] that she was prone to outbursts and sulking, and that she had the ability to make "life impossible for everyone." In the wake of the national backlash against Charles following their divorce, friends of the prince rushed to supply the press with accounts of her tempestuousness[24]. They alleged that she taunted Charles and forced him to renounce his friends. Whether driven by insecurity or circumstance, Diana's frenetic behavior surely played a role in the unraveling of her family life.

The Bottom Line: Should Diana be remembered[25] as an attention-seeking, manipulative problem-child, or as a shy princess-turned-lioness in the face of difficult circumstances?

THE PERSPECTIVE ON CHRISTOPHER COLUMBUS

Original debate written by Chaya Benyamin

The legacy of Christopher Columbus[26] is one of American history's most contested subjects. Columbus certainly opened the door to the Americas, but in initiating the world's first steps toward globalism[27], he also instituted a centuries-long slave trade and fostered colonial realities which would forever weaken his indigenous hosts. Spurred by the summer of 2020's George Floyd protests for racial justice[28] and in solidarity with Black Lives Matter, indigenous people[29] across the US recently called for the removal of statues [30]that honor Columbus. So Columbus Day begs the question, whether the man and all he represents deserve a national holiday.

Below, we'll explore three reasons to consider Christopher Columbus a national treasure and three reasons to deem him a national blemish.

Columbus the Destroyer

Columbus was brutal

From his first voyage West, Columbus displayed a propensity for cruelty and dehumanization[31]. Columbus's first report to Queen Isabella concluded that the Taino tribesmen of the West Indies were "dirty" and "fit to be ruled[32]." In keeping with his belief of native inferiority, Columbus established the New World's first ecomienda[33], a tribute system which amounted to slavery for the natives he "inherited"; Columbus then popularized this system of feudal peonage himself by gifting land grants to Spanish settlers.

Slavery wasn't Columbus's only pastime – Spanish missionary Bartalome de Casas lamented that Columbus literally threw people to the dogs[34]. Columbus's brutality was so well known that the Spanish crown deposed him for floggings and extrajudicial executions of Spanish settlers. This is to say that the monarchs who led the Spanish Inquisition and literally burned people at the stake[35], felt Columbus was too cruel for a title in the Spanish court. Think on that.

Columbus' success was accidental

Columbus's accomplishments were not owing to his capabilities but to his penchant for ineptitude and miscalculation[36]. Columbus's initial mission was to discover an express route to Asia via the Atlantic. For reasons which are obvious today, Columbus never did discover such a route, nor did he discover the gold, gems, or spices that he'd promised in abundance to his Spanish patrons. He had no talent for geography[37]. Columbus insisted Cuba was Japan[38]. He was convinced that the Bahamas were islands off the coast of India (hence, the geographical misnomer "West Indies"). Even his first colony was established by default when he was forced to leave behind castaway crewmen from his wrecked flagship Santa Maria[39].

Columbus initiated a painful era of subjugation and eradication for indigenous peoples

Contrary to the view of the New World as a sprawling expanse of untraversed wilderness, the Americas were home to millions of inhabitants. Columbus's arrival[40] signaled a dramatic upheaval, and they were quickly decimated by European diseases and warfare, enslavement, and cultural and political subjugation. It's estimated that within 20 years of Columbus's arrival to Hispaniola (today's Haiti), the native population had shrunk to 11,000 from 300,000[41]. This Columbus-style "Euroization" of native populations continued for centuries and ultimately resulted in the eradication[42] of hundreds of civilizations across the Western Hemisphere.

Columbus the Great Explorer

Columbus was merely a product of the times

Renaissance historian William J. Connell[43] points out that it would be remiss to judge Christopher Columbus' actions against modern standards. Whereas using war captives as slaves would be unthinkable today, it had been common practice in Europe since the time of Aristotle. And although modern societies deride any form of compelled conversion, for fifteenth-century Christians, bringing savages under Christ's dominion[44] was considered an act of mercy and piety. Columbus and his royal patroness, Queen Isabella[45], doubtless believed that they were saving the inhabitants of the New World from eternal damnation and bestowing upon them the gift of civilization.

Columbus ushered humanity into a new age

Through the course of his many voyages, and the news of his voyages, which inspired countless other expeditions, Columbus initiated the Columbian Exchange[46], the transfer of ideas, plants, animals, technologies, and cultures across the Atlantic divide. These interactions greatly impacted the peoples on both sides of the ocean. In fact, the introduction of New World plants into European and Asian diets was foundational to the population booms that followed. Columbus's voyages constituted the world's first steps toward globalization. This process has transformed humanity, sometimes introducing conflict, but has also engendered cooperation and meaningful exchanges that have encouraged positive developments for people in every corner of the globe.

Columbus was a self-made man

Christopher Columbus's auspicious rise to power and fame is a slice of pull-yourself-up-from-your-bootstraps Americana. Columbus[47] was born to a landless Italian wool worker and started working his way up on merchant ships as a teenager. He secured his own education, and studied[48] cartography, mathematics, astronomy and navigation along the sea shores where he worked. Columbus was imperturbable in his efforts to find a patron to sponsor the voyage. He pitched his idea to monarchs in Portugal, France, and England before finally securing the support[49] of Spain's Ferdinand and Isabella, who named him admiral and viceroy.

The Bottom Line: Christopher Columbus opened the world, connecting East and West forever, but the human suffering (and Columbus's seeming indifference to it) had real and lasting consequences for those he "discovered." Are his achievements enough to justify having a national holiday in his honor, or do his crimes warrant the repudiation of all things Columbus?

THE BOMBINGS OF HIROSHIMA AND NAGASAKI: PLAIN EVIL OR A NECESSARY EVIL?

Original debate written by Lee Mesika

Seventy-five years[50] ago, in August 1945, the decision was made to drop the atomic bomb on Japan[51], causing two cities, Hiroshima and Nagasaki, to become synonymous with nuclear destruction[52] – and the human aptitude for it. Given the atrocious war it brought to a halt, historians are still divided over the question: was this act plain evil or a necessary evil?

Here are three reasons for and against the bombing[53] of Hiroshima and Nagasaki.

Justified Evil

The bombings ended WWII

On August 15, 1945, Japan announced their surrender. This was just six days after the Nagasaki bombing, and nine days after the bombing of Hiroshima. World War II was finally over. After the Potsdam Declaration[54] (which defined the terms for Japanese surrender) between July 17 and August 2, 1945, the Japanese Supreme War Council[55] could not reach a consensus regarding whether or not to surrender[56]. America decided to drop the bombs – and could have had three more atomic bombs[57] ready by August 19, 1945. Japan's Emperor Hirohito was pushed by America's destructive bombings[58] to break the deadlock within his War Council and agree to the terms of the declaration. The bombings of Hiroshima and Nagasaki officially ended the Second World War.

Led to global nuclear disarmament programs

This was the first time nuclear weapons were put to use in actual combat. It was also the last time[59], since it showed the world just how devastating they are. After World War II, many nuclear disarmament movements[60] and international councils came into being with the purpose of banning these weapons of mass destruction[61]. These organizations led to treaties being signed[62] and sanctions being placed against countries around the world in order to prevent nuclear catastrophe from happening again. Such continued global unity against nuclear weapons still resonates today, and has strengthened American-led efforts to disarm North Korea[63].

Saved lives

Despite the number of Japanese casualties, many believe that by dropping the bombs on Hiroshima and Nagasaki, hundreds of thousands, if not millions, of lives around the world were saved[64]. By the end of the war, the total number of US Army troops[65] who were dead or missing in the Pacific and southeast Asia was 41,592, with an additional 145,706 ground troops wounded. Not to mention that around 9,000 British, Indian and Commonwealth soldiers[66] were killed or wounded in the Far East with another 130,000 captured. Meanwhile, the Marine Corps and Navy corpsmen[67] in this region suffered total casualties of 23,160 killed or missing and 67,199 wounded.

On the Japanese side, let's look at the results of a B-29 incendiary raid over Tokyo[68]. Just one of these raids (of which there were a few) killed about 125,000 people. This suggests that two of these raids would have been equivalent to the total amount of casualties that resulted from the atomic bombs. In the Potsdam Declaration, the countries against Japan stated that if Japan didn't surrender, it would face "prompt and utter destruction," so it's safe to say that if the war against Japan hadn't ended when it did, there would have been more such raids. Historians suggest that the 250,000 casualties from the atomic bombs could have easily reached millions[69] if they hadn't been dropped.

Pure Evil

Oh, the humanity

The bombs completely [70]destroyed both Hiroshima and Nagasaki. In Hiroshima, nearly 92% of the structures[71] in the city were either destroyed or damaged by blast and fire. These weren't the only impacts these bombs had. While the more-than-a-quarter-of-a-million death toll[72] was enormous, the bombing itself was only the beginning of the enormous suffering the survivors went through. About half of the deaths[73] came in the immediate weeks/years that followed, not necessarily on the day of the bombing. Many died in the following weeks as a result of the radiation. For those who did survive, many types of illnesses and cancers[74] developed after the bombing.

Civilian collateral damage

Most nations are in agreement that war should be fought between armies, not civilians. True, civilian casualties can't always be avoided, but Hiroshima and Nagasaki gave new meaning to "collateral damage[75]". In Hiroshima, the estimate of civilian deaths resulting from dropping "Little Boy"[76] stands around 80,000[77]. (This is in addition to around 20,000 Japanese soldiers[78] killed as a result of the bombing.) Meanwhile, Nagasaki's death toll is estimated between 40,000-80,000[79]. The civilian deaths in Nagasaki included an estimated[80] 6,200 out of the 7,500 employees of the Mitsubishi Munitions plant, and 24,000 other civilians (including 2,000 Koreans) who worked in other war factories and plants. (This is in addition to around 150 Japanese soldiers.) Estimates of the total number of deaths as a result of the bombings differ[81], and range from anywhere between 220,000 to over 260,000 people. But the number of civilians killed seems unreasonably high in relation to the number of soldiers killed.

They didn't prevent the Cold War

After World War II, tensions rose between the America and the Soviet Union. It is believed that America actually used the atomic bomb[82] against the Japanese to show the Soviets their strength[83]. This ended up backfiring on America, leading to an arms race in which the Soviets were able to build a bomb of their own by 1949. The world once again came close to nuclear brinkmanship[84] in 1962, during the faceoff between America and the Soviet Union off the shores of Cuba. Though tensions have since cooled with the fall of the Soviet Union, relations are still challenging[85] today between these two powers (just look at the Russian bounties[86] on US troops).

....

The Bottom Line: Many believe that the bombings of Hiroshima and Nagasaki were inhuman. However, war itself is inhumane. As the bombings ended WWII, do you think they were an act of plain evil or was this evil necessary?

THE PERSPECTIVE ON CHE GUEVARA

Original debate written by Malkie Khutoretsky

In 1950s Cuba, Argentinian-born Ernesto 'Che' Guevara[87] entered Cuba with a plan to unite the masses. Inspired by Marxist communism, medical student Guevara incited the masses to a communist revolution. He held firm ideals, the foremost of which was that change could only come through armed and violent revolution. For those familiar with the man behind the most reproduced face of our time face, the battle cry "Viva La Revolución" proclaims Guevara as a visionary and a revolutionary. But is he a worthy icon or a glorified thug and failure?

The following are three arguments in favor of Guevara's iconic status, and three against it.

Thug and Failure

'The Butcher of La Cabana'

Post-revolution Cuba saw human rights violations at the hands of Guevara, who was backed by the Castro brothers. Opposition to the Castro regime was taken to facilities like La Cabana[88], where opponents were said to have been tortured and executed without trial. Guevara instituted 'Corrective work camps', inspired by the Chinese and Soviet Labor Camps model. He believed that trial and judicial procedure were the tools of the democratic system, and in revolution there was only violent force. Guevara led Cuba out of the frying pan of classist imperialism and into the fire of violent totalitarian communism.

Repeated failure

Charisma cannot mask across-the-board failure. As Minister of Economics, Guevara destroyed the Peso; as Minister of Industry, Cuba's thriving economy fell[89]; as a revolutionary in Cuba, he was not even in charge[90]. Guevara left Cuba in 1965 bound for revolution in Congo[91], which, by his own admission,[92] was also a failure. Following a brief return to Cuba, Guevara embarked on his last revolutionary attempt in Bolivia, where he was captured by the CIA[93].

Turned Cuba from a player into a pawn

Relations between Cuba, the US and the Former USSR have barely just recovered from the toxic alliance between Cuba and The Soviet Union. Guevara's biographer recorded[94] him as the "Scion of the Soviet Union," and the Soviet Ambassador to Cuba called him "the vital link to Cuba." Guevara's vision of the future saw Cuba breaking free of its sugar export[95] and branching out into global industry. However, the Soviets did not hold the respect for Cuba's future that Guevara's vision called for, using them only as a pawn for closer proximity to the US. This allowed the Soviet Union missile trade, which led to the Cuban Missile Crisis of 1961 and, eventually, the Cold War. Guevara's efforts to ally with the Soviets actually created more problems[96] than solutions for Cuba, and in turn, the Western World.

Hero and Enduring Icon

The Latin American story of David and Goliath

In the face of imperialism, Che Guevara fought the battle for "the little guy." At that time, Cuba had been suffering under the violent and corrupt[97] dictatorship of the Batista government. It was a regime that divided the people, making the poor, poorer and the rich, richer. Guevara, inspired by his journey[98] across Latin America, felt impassioned to lead the Latin American people to justice through Socialism. He thus entered Cuba with his new friends, the Castro brothers, and with a people's army of only 300, defeated[99] the governing Batista dictatorship's army. He heroically took control of Cuban territory for the people.

Facilitated lasting change

As a revolutionary physician, Guevara instituted initiatives that changed the face of healthcare[100] and education[101] in Cuba, which still remain in place to this day. Guevara established healthcare[102] as a human right, contrary to the capitalist view of a product for economic profit. Cuban life expectancy increased to 78 years, 18 years longer than the life expectancy of pre-revolution Cubans, and two years longer than the average American's lifespan. Infant mortality has also been reduced by 90%. Additionally, thanks to Guevara's Literacy Brigades[103] that were sent all over Cuba to educate the peasants, the literacy rate in Cuba jumped from 60% to 96[104]%.

Embodied a universal message

Guevara was a natural leader who gained popularity with his people and preached a universal message[105] of revolution through love and intention. He was the purest part of revolution: a man who did what he meant and meant what he did. His talk of educating the masses and caring for them turned into real policies[106] that still make a difference today. To a population that was weighed down by a dictatorship, he embodied – and gave voice to – hope. For university students around the world, he still remains a symbol of the romantic notion[107] that change is possible. It's not hard to find articles written at the time of his death which paint Guevara as a martyr[108], having died with his reputation intact, as a Liberator.

The Bottom Line: Pop history has seemed to distort the legacy of Che Guevara, presenting him as a successful hero. While he preached the change that Cuba needed, he also left a ravaged country in his wake. Is it time to reconsider the hero status of Ernesto Che Guevara?

THE PERSPECTIVE ON RONALD REAGAN

Original debate written by Andrew Vitelli

It has been thirty years since Ronald Reagan[109] completed his second term as US president. The Gipper, who was first elected in 1980 and re-elected four years later, is held up by most Republicans as the gold standard of the office, especially for his role in standing up to the Soviets. To Democrats, however, Reagan is remembered more for the Iran-Contra scandal than for ending the Cold War.

Here are three arguments that Reagan was the greatest US president since World War II and three more asserting that he was an irresponsible and heartless leader who benefited from circumstances outside of his control.

Reagan Brought an American Rebirth

Reagan ended the Cold War

While the Berlin Wall[110] fell during George H.W. Bush's first year in office, it was President Reagan's strong foreign policy and tough stance[111] towards the Soviet Union that helped the US win the Cold War. Upon taking office, Reagan launched a military buildup aimed at reassuring the country's allies, forcing the USSR to the negotiating table, and ensuring that the US could prevail in the event of war. Defense spending rose[112] from 5.5 percent of GDP in 1979 to 6.8 percent in 1986.

Reagan also recommitted the US to stopping the spread of Soviet-style Marxism around the globe[113]. In Afghanistan, he upped his predecessor's support for anti-Soviet forces, leading the USSR to flee. At the same time, he was restrained in the use of military force. While many of Reagan's actions – including his Strategic Defense Initiative, a missile defense system dubbed "Star Wars" by critics – were mocked at the time, Reagan had the last laugh. His commitment to "peace through strength" was vindicated with the collapse of the Soviet Union.

He restarted the economy

Under Reagan's predecessor, Jimmy Carter, the country had suffered from years of stagflation, inflation without economic growth. When Reagan took office, he brought a new economic approach, lowering taxes and lifting burdensome regulations. While it took a couple years to get going, Reagan's economy was a model of strength. From 1983 to 1988, annual GDP growth never dipped below 3.5 percent[114] (for context, the last time the US hit that mark was 2004). In 1984, growth reached a whopping 7.3 percent, the highest mark since 1951. Unemployment fell from over 10 percent in 1983 to just above 5 percent when Reagan's term ended. While Reagan did run a deficit, the severity is often exaggerated. Barack Obama and George W. Bush added more to the debt in 2009 alone than Reagan did in eight years in office.

He worked across the aisle

It may be hard to imagine Trump and House minority leader Nancy Pelosi or Biden and Kevin McCarthy kicking off their shoes after work and knocking back a glass of whiskey together, but that is exactly how Reagan and House Speaker Tip O'Neill, a Democrat, ended their day[115]. And his aisle-crossing was not limited to happy hour. His immigration reform bill signed in 1986 allowed amnesty[116] for those who entered the country before 1982. He also worked with O'Neill on a deficit reduction bill that increased taxes[117].

Some of these actions were not popular among Reagan's base, but they won over the electorate at large. Reagan won both his elections by a landslide, and in his re-election came with the most electoral votes in history. And Americans' view of the Gipper has only improved with time.[118]

Reagan Was Fiscally and Militarily Irresponsible

His domestic policy was a disaster

Reagan is often credited with reviving the US economy, though his first term began with a 16-month recession. His true legacy, though, is one of expanding deficits caused by a growing defense budget and tax cuts that proved to be irresponsible. During Reagan's presidency, there were also a record eight government shutdowns[119], suggesting enduring political partisanship and battles.

When it came to responsible budgeting, Reagan was anything but a fiscal conservative. The budget deficit was just $79 billion Reagan's first year in office, around 1.5 percent of GDP. By 1983, the shortfall had reached $208 billion[120], or 5.6 percent of GDP. It would reach $221 billion in 1986. The national debt nearly tripled[121] to more than $2.6 billion when he left office. Had the US gone deeply into the red improving health care (these were the years of the AIDS crisis[122], which Reagan was infamously indifferent about) or fighting poverty[123], it may have been justifiable. But this was decidedly not the case.

His foreign policy was no better

While the collapse of the Soviet Union coincided with Reagan's term in office, it was caused not by Reagan's military buildup, tough talk or "Star Wars[124]" speech. The fundamental weakness of the Soviet economy and Mikhail Gorbachev's leadership played a much greater role[125] – Reagan was simply in office at the right time.

Reagan's actual foreign policy decisions brought about undesirable consequences. His military buildup led to huge deficits. His support for Nicaraguan Contras undermined that country's democracy[126] and stability (and led to the Iran-Contra scandal, detailed below). His intervention in Afghanistan helped pave the way for the Taliban and al Qaeda.[127] And his invasion of the tiny Caribbean island of Grenada, which included a mistaken bombing of a mental hospital[128], irked even US allies[129].

He betrayed Americans' trust with Iran-Contra

Few episodes have represented a betrayal of the American trust to the degree of the Iran-Contra affair[130]. In an attempt to free American hostages held by Lebanese terrorists and to support Nicaraguan Contras, Reagan's administration covertly sold weapons to Iran and funneled the proceeds to the Latin American rebels. The former was both illegal – there was an embargo against shipping arms to Iran – and a violation of his campaign pledge not to negotiate with terrorists. The latter violated a Congressional ban against operations in Nicaragua.

The operation was a failure; while three hostages were released, three more were soon abducted. When the operation came to light, it badly damaged Reagan's reputation and led to charges against 14 people in the administration, including Oliver North[131].

....

The Bottom Line: Since leaving office, Ronald Reagan has become a Republican icon. While his legacy is mixed, the Trump presidency has made some moderate Democrats nostalgic for the Reagan years, even though he remains a polarizing figure[132] more than a decade after his death.

FINANCE CHAPTER

- Should we raise taxes on the rich?
- Should we raise the minimum wage?
- The perspective on Bitcoin
- Are entrepreneurs born or made?
- The perspective on the American dream
- Should you fly traditional or low-cost airlines?
- Is home ownership still worthwhile?

SHOULD WE RAISE TAXES ON THE RICH?

Original debate written by Andrew Vitelli

Debate over taxes on the wealthiest Americans is nothing new, but it's as relevant a topic as ever. It was a major focus of the 2020 US presidential election campaign among democratic candidates[1], with discussion over the moral, fiscal and economic consequences of raising tax rates on high earners. President Joe Biden has made it known that he plans to increase top income tax rates[2]. and a group of 83 super-rich individuals themselves called for higher taxes on the wealthy to pay for Covid-19 recovery. [3]A recent poll shows that a majority of Americans [4]support the idea of America's wealthiest paying more taxes. But just because the majority of Americans want to tax the rich more doesn't necessarily mean it's right.

Here are three arguments for raising taxes on the rich, and three arguments against it.

We Should Tax the Rich More

It makes economic sense

Taxing the rich to pay for programs that help the poor and middle class (or on things like infrastructure or national defense, which benefit all Americans) makes common sense economically, especially during a pandemic[5]. Very simply, money allocated to programs such as affordable healthcare, Pell grants, food stamps, and Earned Income Tax Credit – or given to working- and middle-class Americans through tax cuts – will be redistributed into the economy and stimulate growth. Tax hikes on the rich would have little impact on their spending, since most of this income would likely have gone into savings.

History[6] bears this out. President Clinton raised the top marginal income tax rate from 31 to 39.6 percent and saw GDP growth top 4 percent every year in his second term. Meanwhile, President George W. Bush's tax cuts[7] were supposed to accelerate growth but, instead, they led to unimpressive growth[8] and eventually recession.

It's about fairness!

The rich[9], by definition, have a lot of money. In fact, the top 1 percent[10] in the US holds 15 times more wealth than the bottom 50 percent combined. Meanwhile, 34 million[11] Americans live in poverty, with half a million homeless on any given night.

Even with higher tax rates[12] (and fewer loopholes), the country's wealthiest will be fine; billionaires[13] like Bill Gates and conservative Mark Cuban, among others, attest to this, having said they would be willing to pay more in taxes. For the government to provide basic housing, nourishment, health care and education to the rest of its citizens, the money must come from somewhere. For the most fortunate to fail to pay their fair share[14] would be a moral failure.

They're already low (compared to the past)

Let's take a look at tax rates over time. A tax reform bill[15] that became law in 2018 set new tax rates for Americans, lowering rates for most brackets, including the wealthy, by 1-4 percent. In fact, these tax cuts helped billionaires pay less taxes[16] than the working class. In 2015, that year's top tax rate was less than half the 91 percent[17] it was under President Eisenhower[18], a Republican. The top rate was consistently 70 percent or higher until the Reagan tax cuts[19] of the 1980s, and those cuts resulted in the national debt tripling in eight years.

We Shouldn't Tax the Rich More

It's about fairness!

First, let's define fairness. Fairness means that Americans reap the rewards of their labor, that what they earn inherently belongs to them and not to the government to redistribute as it sees fit, and that the path to prosperity is through hard work and success. Even through a flat tax[20], under which the rich pay the same tax rate as lower earners, the wealthy will still end up paying more in absolute terms since they have a higher amount of income to tax. But by any reasonable definition, the amount paid by the rich is already beyond their "fair share[21]." For example, in 2015, the top 1 percent earned 16.5 percent of income, but paid a staggering 43.6 percent[22] of federal income tax. Meanwhile, more than 44%[23] of Americans pay no federal income tax at all. Entrepreneurs and business owners should not be penalized for their success.

It makes no economic sense

Forcing a small slice of Americans to bear an inordinate burden of funding the government is not just immoral but also counterproductive[24]; it kills jobs, and sometimes even results in lower government revenue. Raising taxes on the rich[25] produces a disincentive for work and job creation, slowing both. If higher taxes discourage a business from opening or expanding, it is not just the rich who suffer but also the workers [26]who are not hired. Further, this means that tax hikes often do not have the intended effect of raising revenue. If high taxes slow down economic growth, the government ends up taxing a smaller amount of money at a higher rate. Sometimes, this means a tax hike actually leads to lower total revenues, but even in less extreme cases, tax hikes yield diminishing returns[27].

They're already high (compared to other developed countries)

In the past, before the Tax Cuts and Jobs Act[28] (TCJA) reduced the U.S. federal corporate income tax rate from 35 percent to 21 percent in 2018, the US was in bad company. Only the United Arab Emirates, an oil-rich Middle Eastern country with fewer people than Michigan, Puerto Rico, a

US territory, and Comoros had higher top corporate tax rates than seen in the US. Now, the US rates among the UK (20 percent), China (25 percent) and Canada (28 percent).

Before the corporate tax reduction, other countries had a competitive advantage[29] over the US when looking to attract businesses. This is no longer the case[30] and shows that raising tax rates may accelerate this trend, and every time a company moves overseas, it costs the US both jobs and tax revenue.

The Bottom Line: Those who favor higher taxes on the wealthy believe it makes economic sense and see virtue in some redistribution of wealth. Their free-market opponents not only see this as wrong-headed government intervention but also believe the economic consequences will hurt the rich and the poor alike. Do you think taxes should be raised on the rich, or should the status quo be preserved?

SHOULD WE RAISE THE MINIMUM WAGE?

Original debate written by Julian Bonte-Friedheim

The debate over raising the federal minimum wage divides the whole country. Some contend that raising it will hurt jobs and raise costs while others hold that at its current rate it won't let people earn enough to reasonably sustain themselves. The Biden administration hoped to include a minimum wage increase in the 2021 $1.9 trillion stimulus package but were barred by the Senate parliamentarian[31].

Is raising the minimum wage good or bad for the country as a whole?

Don't Raise the Federal Minimum Wage

It causes job losses

In a free market, salaries are as high as the jobs that earn them are valuable. By forcing companies to raise salaries higher than the output of such jobs, they will be forced to discontinue them. No longer able to make a profit, companies would have to send some workers home without any job at all, rather than giving them a steady income. Low-income workers would be at the highest risk of being fired since their work wouldn't be profitable any longer. A 2010 study[32] estimated that raising the minimum wage to $9.50 would end nearly 1.3 million jobs. This article[33] argues that Seattle has already started losing jobs due to its raised minimum wage.

It raises prices for consumers

By raising the minimum wage, we force businesses to make up for the loss of capital somehow. Often their only way to offset this deficit is by increasing prices for consumers[34]. If we force them to pay a higher minimum wage than they would have naturally, the prices for consumers of all goods and services go up. This will hurt consumption and business profits, from which the government will reap less taxes.

The market is best at determining wages

It is widely believed that America's free market model is a big reason for its economic successes. If a job requires little skill then the salary stays low. If a job is complicated, for example being a biological engineer, then the salary is appropriately high to encourage people to pursue that career. Not only is this fair it also encourages people to go for jobs that will benefit society. Market-determined wages make people work hard to become doctors or engineers, which provide a much-needed service.

Raise the Federal Minimum Wage

It will go right back into the economy

America's poor often can't afford to save their money, they need to spend it right away, so it goes towards businesses. Money being spent increases general cash flow and benefits the economy. According to research done at Per Capita[35] rich people are far more likely to save their money, putting it in the bank, where it serves the economy less. Raising the minimum wage helps businesses by allowing more Americans to buy their products.

It reduces income inequality

The 20 richest Americans own as much wealth as the bottom half of the country combined[36]. The US lags far behind other developed countries in terms of income inequality. The federal minimum wage of $7.25/h has not been raised since 2009[37]. Meanwhile the estimated living wage in the USA in 2019 was $16.54[38]. The plan to include a minimum wage increase to $15/h by 2025 in the 2021 COVID-19 stimulus package, was scrapped despite its potential impact: increasing the incomes of 27 million Americans and lifting nearly 1 million out of poverty[39]. Income inequality has been shown to fuel social tension[40] so reducing it is in everyone's best interest. Besides the morality of it, it would allow America to become a more equal and fair society.

It will benefit the children of poor families

Mahatma Ghandi once said: "A nation's greatness is measured by how it treats its weakest members." Studies have shown that children who grow up in poor households are far more likely to do badly at school[41], suffer from depression[42] and poorly integrate into society[43]. Through improving the living standards of poor children and giving their parents the disposable income needed for school supplies and tutors, a new generation of successful Americans can rise. Helping America's poor children is a long-term investment in the country's future.

The Bottom Line: Flat out raising the federal minimum wage to $15 an hour like some have proposed could have adverse effects that aren't obvious at first. Making such a drastic change could seriously hurt America's businesses and economic stability. On the other hand, with too many Americans are still below the poverty line, the US has to fix its gaping inequality problem. For better or worse, raising the minimum wage would put more money in the pockets of the poor, which would likely go back into the economy and improve their children's lives.

THE PERSPECTIVE ON BITCOIN

Original debate written by Kira Goldring

It's hard to go online these days without hearing the word "Bitcoin" mentioned at least once, whether for good (a surge in its worth[44]) or for bad (a recent scam[45] where hackers targeted high-profile leaders' Twitter accounts to ask for Bitcoin donations). Bitcoin is a virtual currency (cryptocurrency[46]) that is created online and unregulated by the government and banks. Only a limited amount of it has been created online, and every transaction of each Bitcoin is documented by a network of independent computers (using Blockchain technology[47]), which replaces the traditional middlemen (banks and governments) that have, thus far, regulated our money.

Emerging in 2009, Bitcoin was initially valued at near .008 cents. It skyrocketed to .08 cents in the span of five days, setting an upward trend for the next few years. While it hit highs of over $19,000[48] in 2017. In 2021, it was valued at over $52,000[49] at one point and under $33,000 at another, begging the question of whether Bitcoin could be the currency of the future or a bubble, unrelated to actual value.

Here are three reasons to stay away from Bitcoin and three reasons to embrace it as a currency.

Doomed to Fail, Bit by Bit
Risk > Reward

Many see the overall rise in Bitcoin prices as a bubble[50], due to its volatility[51]. In finance terms, a "bubble" is when the price of an asset far surpasses its fundamental value[52], implying that its preliminary spike in value will eventually crash and burn. For example, in 2008, the U.S. housing bubble popped[53], leading to an economic crisis[54], which became the Great Recession. In this vein, whenever Bitcoin prices drop, experts warn [55]that they will only continue to fall[56], especially in the long run, even after temporary recoveries. Also, Bitcoin takes money and power away from institutions that are used to being in charge – namely, banks and governments. It's reasonable to assume that given all the revenues they stand to lose, they won't take this lying down; they have all the resources in the world at their disposal to combat the success of virtual currency.

Getting your hands dirty

Attempts to regulate Bitcoin are underway (for example, the IRS is treating Bitcoin as property[57] and taxing it as such). Meanwhile, Bitcoin is both decentralized[58] – meaning it has no central role of management or authority – and unstable. Some may see its decentralization[59] as a good thing, but this opened it up for black market trading[60] in the past. In fact, in 2016, over 10% of Bitcoin transactions happened on The Silk Road, a hidden online service (which is now defunct) that allowed for trading drugs, illegal substances, and other illicit activities. Can we really allow ourselves to use Bitcoin if it might pave the way for criminal activity?

A shocking amount of energy

As of now, Bitcoin has the potential to become an environmental disaster[61]. While it may seem like it saves resources, the Bitcoin Energy Consumption Tracker[62] currently shows that Bitcoin consumes more than 75 Terawatt hours per year, and that number is only going up. To put that in perspective, that's the same level of energy consumption as Chile uses per year, and one Bitcoin transaction uses the same power consumption of an average US household over 22.17 days[63]. Currently, the amount of energy it takes to "mine[64]" (i.e., create) and use Bitcoin is unsustainable in the long term.

Who Wants to Be a Millionaire?

Cutting out the middleman

Bitcoin has allowed people to put their trust in technology instead of third-party mediators like banks and civil-law notaries. This is because it relies on blockchain technology[65], which is a complex mathematical model that instantly creates a virtual chain of recorded transactions when Bitcoin is transferred from one place to another. These transactions are easily verifiable, and will eliminate the possibility of human error, steep transaction fees, and long wait times[66] when transferring money. In other words, Bitcoin makes the whole process of using money more efficient by cutting out the middlemen who have had to oversee every transaction that takes place thus far. This is why mainstream payment firms like PayPal[67] are not only investing in it but adding it as an option to their platform.

Leaving paper in the past

Since more and more businesses have been moving online[68] – even before especially after the coronavirus pandemic hit – it's only logical that currency should do the same. Some people may be hesitant to adopt a technology that they don't fully understand, but time is marching on regardless. When cloud technology[69] first came around, many were put off by the idea, yet now it's a given [70]to use email, social media and online applications to store our memories and information. Similarly, people were skeptical of hospitality services like Airbnb, but it had over 41 million users[71] in the US alone in 2019. Bearing in mind that the amount of available Bitcoin is limited,[72] it may be beneficial to jump on the bandwagon instead of being left in the dust.

It's here. Get used to it

Bitcoin is catching on, regardless of any personal aversion to it. It is already considered as one of the world's top currencies [73]and is becoming more and more mainstream; Elon Musk's Tesla[74] invested $1.5 billion in Bitcoin while certain colleges[75] even accept it as payment. In fact, smaller banks have begun accepting Bitcoin[76], with the likes of JPMorgan and Goldman Sachs[77] pressured to follow suit. Even the U.S. Federal Reserve[78] is hinting at creating its own cryptocurrency, proving just how relevant Bitcoin already is to the future of currency.

Laypeople are also making money off of it; for example, anonymous Mr. Smith[79] invested $3,000 in Bitcoin a few months after it was created, and, pre-COVID-19, spent the $25 million he made flying first class around the world. Erik Finman dropped out of high school after investing in Bitcoin at $12 a coin. He then started his own company[80] at the age of 15 and is now boasting millions in investments. Like it or not, Bitcoin has already made its mark.

The Bottom Line: Bitcoin seems to have an enormous amount of exciting potential, but it may not be able to sustain itself as a currency – or an investment – for the long term. Have you thought about buying Bitcoin? Should people invest in it or stay as far away from it as possible?

ARE ENTREPRENEURS BORN OR MADE?

Original debate written by Chaya Benyamin

What makes an entrepreneur? Is entrepreneurial success the result of raw, natural talent and grit, or the result of study and experience? What is it, really, that separates Mark Zuckerberg[81] from Michael Bloomberg[82]? In this article, we'll explore three arguments explaining why entrepreneurs are made and three arguments demonstrating why entrepreneurs are simply born that way.

Baby, I Was Born This Way

Baby steps

So many stories of great entrepreneurs begin the same way, with the protagonist attempting to fill market gaps on the school yard. Zappos multi-millionaire Tony Hsieh[83] got his start in business selling bait worms at age nine. Meanwhile, Facebook CEO Mark Zuckerberg [84]had already been approached by Microsoft and AOL to sell his beta version of a Pandora-like music application that he invented while still in high school. Not every kid tries his or her hand managing a lemonade stand – those who do are probably born entrepreneurs.

Hyper hypomanics

Some researchers argue that entrepreneurism isn't merely a personality trait but something of a medical condition. Research finds that a great many entrepreneurs[85] suffer from hypomania[86] (a cousin disorder of both mania and manic depression), which is marked by sustained elation, hyperactivity, and grandiosity. Entrepreneurs self-report hypomanic symptoms as their norm, and their relatives had higher incidence of related diseases[87], suggesting that entrepreneurial tendencies, like hypomania, are indeed genetic.

We don't need no education

In a Northeastern University survey of over 200 US-based entrepreneurs[88], well over half of the survey participants cited "innate drive" as the main reason for embarking on independent business ventures, with only one percent of respondents noting education[89] or environment as influential factors. Indeed, some of the world's most prominent entrepreneurs (think Bill Gates[90], Steve Jobs[91], and even John D. Rockefeller) never earned more than a high school diploma. For born entrepreneurs, no training required.

If I Can Make It There, I'll Make It Anywhere

Necessity, the mother of entrepreneurship

People often become entrepreneurs not because of some inborn desire, but because life's circumstances compel them to do so. Consider immigrants, who for reasons ranging from language barriers to racial discrimination, are frequently blocked from the traditional job market, leading them to the highest rate of entrepreneurship[92] among any group in the US.

When a group of diverse individuals, such as immigrants to the US, collectively achieve a rate of 18%[93] business ownership and account for 30% of all small-business growth, it is not likely that they all share common genetic traits, but rather, circumstances that force them to establish businesses. While entrepreneurs of necessity don't enjoy the same prestige as Silicon Valley's opportunity entrepreneurs, they most certainly outnumber them, and their endeavors are no less impactful.

The B-school boost

What do Elon Musk[94] (PayPal; Tesla; SpaceX), Michael Bloomberg (Bloomberg L.P.) and Phil Knight (Nike) all have in common? They're all billionaire entrepreneurs with prestigious MBA degrees behind them. Getting the right education absolutely influences entrepreneurial success, helping people hone their leadership skills and identify viable business ideas. A Kaufman Foundation report[95] found that 95% of founders held a bachelor's degree, and 48% had higher degrees. Furthermore, higher education, especially in business, provides the kind of robust network that entrepreneurs need to get their ventures off the ground.

The start-up nation anomaly

Dubbed the "Start-Up Nation[96]" by journalists Dan Senor and Saul Singer, Israel, the country with the most venture tech dollars per capita and more tech startups than all of Europe and Asia combined, has media and business people worldwide pondering the secret of its entrepreneurial spirit[97]. Answers to this question would suggest that entrepreneurial instincts are an advent of Israeli culture[98]: "chutzpah" (most closely translated as moxie), leadership training acquired through mandatory military service, and a *carpe diem* mentality that enables a kind of communal willingness to fail are all reasons cited for the nation's entrepreneurial fervor. The existence of a nation where a quarter of the population is involved in entrepreneurial activities demonstrates that entrepreneurialism is more about environmental forces than personal traits.

....

The Bottom Line: Dedicated entrepreneurship programs[99] at top-ranked undergraduate and business schools would have us believe that entrepreneurship is a pie just about any person can take a bite of. However, the question still remains whether entrepreneurialism is learned or inherited. With so many examples of entrepreneurs both born and made, perhaps the only conclusion to draw is that the reasons that drive entrepreneurs are as varied as the markets they serve and the products they invent.

THE PERSPECTIVE ON THE AMERICAN DREAM

Original debate written by Jordan Stutts

The American dream, a national ethos of economic betterment, has been battered and bruised in the years following the Great Recession. The financial crisis has been declared over, but for many, this is a notion they've heard more than felt personally. Years of lackluster job growth and stalled wages and the latest blows from COVID-19 have left many wondering if the American dream is just that – a dream.

Here are three arguments for and against America still being the land of opportunity.

The Deck Is Stacked against You

Young people aren't doing as well as their parents

It is becoming harder for young people to reach a higher standard of living than their parents. One study shows that only half[100] of children born in the 1980s grew up to earn more than their parents, a steep drop from 90 percent of children born in 1940.

This is leading young people to delay traditional life milestones. In 2012, 20 percent of adults had never been married[101], compared to 9 percent in 1960. While the number of young adults living with their parents[102] was already up in recent years, the coronavirus pandemic has seen more 18- to 29-year-olds living at 'home' than ever. For the first time since the Great Depression[103], over half of young adults in the US are living with their parents, with some 2.6 million moving back between February and July of 2020.

Americans aren't earning more money

The ability to elevate one's social standing has been an important part of the American dream, but wage growth in the US has significantly stalled over the last few decades, and it currently lags behind job growth[104]. Economic Policy Institute research shows more than 90 percent[105] of American households between 1979 and 2007 saw their incomes grow at a slower rate than historical averages. Moreover, between 1979 and 2013, US productivity grew 8 times faster – 64.9 percent – than worker compensation did (at 8 percent). Meanwhile, a year after COVID-19 hit the US, many Americans are struggling, with 44% having been laid off or taken a pay cut[106]. Lower-income Americans have been hit hardest.[107]

Education doesn't mean a good job

The promise of working hard to get ahead in life is falling short for young people in the US investing in education. Unemployment rates continue to fall and are at an all-time low of 3.9%, but that doesn't necessarily mean good jobs are plentiful; data from the Federal Reserve Bank of New York shows that around 44 percent[108] of college graduates were employed in jobs that don't require a degree. What's more, studies[109] show that once college graduates take such a job, they are more likely to remain underemployed five years later.

Opportunities Still Exist

Americans continue to reinvent themselves

The new century ushered in changes that continue to ripple throughout the world, but America is in a great position to meet these changes. New industries, and the rebirth of traditional ones, are replacing the nearly 9 million jobs[110] erased during the Great Recession. Look no further than the tech industry. US cities consistently ranked as top job magnets[111] are places with thriving tech hubs: San Francisco, Austin, Raleigh, etc.

The US auto industry has also seen a massive turnaround from a decade ago. Vehicle production[112] fell below 6 million units in 2009, but has since rebounded to 12 million and remains consistently high. The energy industry has seen a renaissance as well. Advances in drilling technology, the increase in natural gas use and the growth of renewable energy employed 6.4 million[113] Americans in energy sector jobs last year – a growth of 5 percent, with 300,000 net new jobs. Besides, contrary to expectations, the stock market boomed in 2020, in spite if not because of the pandemic, setting record highs.[114]

Americans have more opportunities than they think

As American industries create new types of jobs, young people have more openings to enter the workforce than they might realize. Attaining an education has become easier as well; according to the US non-profit The College Board, $123.8 billion in scholarships and grants[115] were awarded in 2014-2015, and federal government grants[116] increased from $20.6 billion in 2005-2006 to $41.7 billion in 2015-2016.

To tackle student loan debt, now a collective $1.4 trillion nationwide, states like Oregon[117] and Tennessee are beginning to offer free tuition for community college, and New York recently passed legislation that significantly reduces the cost of four-year college tuition. Opportunities are also emerging from the rise of cheap or free online courses, with the number of students now topping 35 million[118] in 2015 – double from the year before.

The American Dream is what you make it

There was no mention of jobs or wages when historian James Truslow Adams first coined the phrase[119] "American Dream" in 1931. To him, the promise of America was "that dream of a land in which life should be better and richer and fuller for everyone." This is a less materialistic vision, and it can't be quantified by mere numbers shown in studies today.

For some, The American Dream is to reach new financial heights, and for others, it may be to own a business. Some dreamers want to shatter gender barriers, and others move to America with the single hope that their children can have a better chance in life. All of these dreams are possible in today's America, just like they were in Truslow's time.

The Bottom Line: Trends indicate that young people in the US have it harder than their parents did, yet they are still finding innovative ways to succeed. What does this mean for the American Dream? For you, does America signify the land of opportunity?

SHOULD YOU FLY TRADITIONAL OR LOW-COST AIRLINES?

Original debate written by Talia Klein Perez

Travelers today seem to have a wider variety of options than ever. In addition to the traditional or legacy airlines we're all familiar with, there are also a growing number of low-cost – or budget – airlines taking to the skies. While they may share some similarities, traditional and low-cost airlines[120] each offer distinct experiences. So, which is better for travelers?

Here are three reasons to fly low-cost and three reasons to stick with legacy carriers.

Three Reasons to Stick with Time-Tested Legacy Airlines

Increased responsibility

Major airlines are better equipped with resources to help passengers when needs arise, in comparison to their low-cost counterparts. In the event of flight delays, cancellations or luggage misplacement, traditional airlines have policies in place to offer passengers travel rerouting, refunds and compensation packages. This is something that low-cost airlines are not always able to do, as was seen with the 2018 Ryanair airline strike[121], during which hundreds of flights were cancelled. Another example is the case of Icelandic low-cost airline Wow Airlines, which left thousands of passengers stranded[122] at Kaflavik airport in March 2019 when it declared bankruptcy and suddenly ceased operations. While traditional airlines are not perfect[123], they try to stick to relatively strict flight schedules and allow passengers to view their plane seats ahead of time. Low-cost airlines, on the other hand, reserve the right[124] to make last-minute flight timing and seating changes, without due warning.

Better flight times and airports

Passengers flying legacy carriers are offered better flight times and choices of airports. Unlike low-cost airlines, traditional carriers provide nonstop flight service[125]s from their (multiple) larger hubs to many smaller destinations. What's more, as larger airlines have greater budgets, they can afford to pay steeper airport taxes, enabling them to obtain more optimal takeoff[126] and landing slots at more central airports.

You get what you pay for

Flying anywhere – even for just a few days – is an ordeal. Arriving at the airport hours in advance, undergoing personal and baggage security checks, passing through passport control and then traveling from the airport to your actual destination is time-consuming and exhausting. Therefore, having a good flight experience is key to having a successful vacation or business trip.

Positive in-flight experiences are more likely with traditional airlines, since you pay one fee for full service. For a set price, you can[127] check your luggage, enjoy in-flight catering, and watch television and movie programs broadcasted on the carrier's monitors. There are no hidden fees, taxes, insurance costs or other unexpected added expenses[128] to catch you by surprise[129] at check-in, which sometimes happens with low-cost airlines.

Three Reasons Low-Cost Flights Should Rule the Sky

Tickets are even cheaper than you think

The biggest advantage to flying low-cost is the ticket price – which is often 20-30% lower than that of larger airlines – but can be as much as 50-80% lower[130] when booking early. Intermediaries, like travel agents, are generally not used for booking, which cuts down on overall costs for the consumer. Low-cost flights also make off-peak[131] benefits available, like lower ticket prices for traveling on red-eye flights[132] when airport taxes are at their lowest

More money to spend at your destination

Low-cost airlines take a no-frills approach[133], which is how they are able to keep their fees so low. They save on luxuries, like reclining seats, which reduces initial plane purchase and maintenance costs. This translates into less expensive tickets. Plus, flight attendants on low-cost airlines often cover many roles, including ticketing, in-flight services and cleaning. Having a smaller staff also means companies can reduce their ticket prices.

While the in-flight experience may not be as comfortable[134] (to a degree) as with traditional airlines, travel is a means to an end. Who wouldn't prefer spending their hard-earned money on the reason(s) they are flying – be it hotel, shopping, or exotic destination – than on the flight itself? Plus, if taking one of the many red-eye flights that low-cost airlines offer, you'll also have fewer crowds to deal with at the airport, which leaves more time for sightseeing.

Newer, safer planes

Low-cost airlines tend to fly newer planes, which they can acquire at a large discount[135] when placing bulk orders. For instance, Ryanair bought 151 new planes of the same model (Boeing 737) during the post-9/11 air travel slump; the large size of the order is what made each plane so cheap. Many of the air carriers that budget airlines use are newly built or recently retrofitted[136] to meet current safety standards and requirements, and passengers are able to enjoy a smoother, safer flight. The planes are also more fuel-efficient[137]. In fact, the fuel efficiency of younger planes offsets the more expensive purchase price of newer models. That's how EasyJet has four-year-old planes and Spirit's vessels average 5.7 years. This, unfortunately, is not the case for many traditional airlines, which continue to fly planes that can be 20 years old or more![138]

The Bottom Line: Low-cost airlines get you to your destination at a fraction of the price, but also with a fraction of the services and amenities traditional airlines offer. Considering that budget carriers seek to improve their passengers' experience and legacy airlines look to lower overhead costs, how do you prefer to fly?

IS HOME OWNERSHIP STILL WORTHWHILE?

Original debate written by Chaya Benyamin

Homeownership has long been a symbol of financial security for individuals across the globe, and the US government has[139] implemented steps to help its citizens become homeowners. With entire television channels[140] devoted to the quest to own homes (and then make them cozy), the allure of homeownership is not likely to abate any time soon. However, following the mortgage crisis of 2008[141], which is estimated to have cost some 10 million homeowners[142] their homes, the appeal of homeownership has come under greater scrutiny. Plus, with natural disasters[143] on the rise and wreaking havoc on homes throughout America, is homeownership all it's cracked up to be?

Let's look at three disadvantages and advantages of homeownership.

Papa Was a Rollin' Stone

Homeownership is not a worthwhile investment

While home values don't often depreciate, they certainly can[144]. Moreover, home values don't often appreciate either. (Housing price increases are often perceived as a rise in the property value when the new price basically only accounts for inflation[145]). In reality, homeowners spend exorbitant amounts of money on interest; For instance, a $300,000 mortgage at the standard interest rate of 3.5% will cost nearly $653,000[146] over thirty years, to say nothing of the hundreds of thousands of dollars that homeowners spend on property taxes, home repairs, and upgrades that do not necessarily add[147] to the value of the house. Investors and economists[148] agree that the capital is better spent on products with a higher return on investment.

Homeownership ties you down

The word mortgage literally means death pledge[149]. How's that for final! More than tying homeowners (those with a mortgage, at least) to a lifetime of debt, homeownership locks the owner to a specific location, complicating relocations for professional or personal reasons. What's more, no one can promise that a home can be resold at the buying price. Being tied to one place can be especially problematic if your town or city is on the decline[150]. Take Detroit, for example. Once a bustling metropolis, in 2015, houses that once sold for tens of thousands of dollars went go to auction for one dollar[151]. Talk about a cautionary tale.

Widespread homeownership dampens the economy

Studies[152] have revealed a concerning connection between high rates of homeownership and unemployment; they also suggest that homeownership may undercut the formation of new businesses. This connection can be seen in Europe. Germany[153], a country with the second-lowest homeowner rate in the EU, is unsurprisingly Europe's economic powerhouse, dwarfing the economies of countries like Spain[154], which has high rates of homeownership. In light of different studies[155] that demonstrate how homeownership often functions to hold back individual workers and entire economies, it seems unreasonable for the US government to continue encouraging homeownership to the tune of $200 billion[156] in yearly revenues in the form of homeowners' subsidies and tax breaks[157].

Home Sweet Home

Homeownership garners stability

Unlike renters, who are frequently at the mercy of the market and their landlords (especially in minimally regulated markets[158] like the US), homeowners know exactly how much (adjustable interest-rate loans notwithstanding) their housing costs will be for the long-term. In 2016, rental rates rose four percent[159], four times the rate of inflation. Renters are forced to dig deeper into their pockets to stay in the same place year to year. This is a process which is both time consuming and costly. Rent fluctuations are especially onerous for retirees on fixed income, making the lifelong process of acquiring a home well worth the effort. More than avoiding unpredictable raises in rental fees, homeowners know which schools their children will attend, and they and their family have the ability to form deep ties with their neighbors and community. In this way, the stability[160] afforded to individuals and families through homeownership significantly increased quality of life.

Homeownership can help you weather a rainy day or accomplish other financial goals

If you have it, home equity[161] gains from a home's appreciation value minus monies owed, can be a powerful financial tool. Home equity loans and lines of credit can help[162] to turn a fixed asset into a liquid one. This can be a godsend if you need quick cash for unexpected home or car repairs, or if you suddenly have a medical crisis. Home equity can also help homeowners finance anticipated expenses like college tuition and vacations at significantly lower interest rates than those offered on student or personal loans. (Plus, the payments are tax deductible[163] – woohoo!). And homeownership can provide monthly dividends for those who decide to turn their homes into rentals. Even if you downsize to a smaller rental of your own, you'll pocket the difference each month, which can help turn into savings or even an extra vacation.

Home is where the heart is

If homeownership were merely about financial imperatives, there would probably be much fewer homeowners. But buying a home is much more than a financial transaction. Buying a home[164] first and foremost answers the human desire for rootedness and continuity. Homes provide a space for families to grow, convene throughout large spans of time, and create memories. A home can house a family through several generations and is a natural nexus of intergenerational bonding[165]. A house's market value may rise and fall, but a home is truly priceless.

The Bottom Line: In light of new research and market forces, the advantages of homeownership for individuals as well as economies may be overstated. While homes may not necessarily be the financial boon they were once thought to be, they still offer the benefits of security, stability, and familiarity. When we talk about what is possibly the biggest purchase of your lifetime, do you think a home should be it?

EDUCATION CHAPTER

- Redshirting: should parents delay kindergarten for a year?
- The perspective on school uniforms
- How great is 'great literature' if it needs to be studied to be understood?
- Should we allow smartphones in school?
- Should we distribute condoms in high schools?

REDSHIRTING: SHOULD PARENTS DELAY KINDERGARTEN FOR A YEAR?

Original debate written by Malkie Khutoretsky

While the 2020-2021 school year may look different[1] for many children due to the pandemic[2], the issue of "redshirting" remains a familiar issue. Redshirting is the practice of delaying enrollment of four- and five-year-old children into kindergarten. This delay is to allow an extra year for social, intellectual or physical development. The term was coined for those college athletes not yet ready to officially join the team but who were training and waiting in the wings for one year longer. In the US, the number of kindergartners over the age of five has more than tripled[3] in the past decade, a sign that parents are embracing redshirting in an attempt to engineer the age advantage. But does redshirting guarantee success, or does it cause more harm than good?

The following are three arguments against redshirting, and three for.

More Harm Than Good

Don't underestimate your child

Instead of letting children grow in their own space, which may include stumbles, we tend to try to eliminate all challenges from the get-go; even in harmless games, we are inclined to let our children win[4]. However, anticipating a child's growth, meaning setting high expectations[5] for them, is far more influential than coddling. Exposure to more mature peers has been proven to see younger students rise to the [6]challenge. The National Association of Early Childhood Specialists also suggests that the children being considered for redshirting are the very ones who would benefit from a focused, pedagogically[7] sound environment, like a kindergarten classroom.

Kindergarten should be an inclusive community of peers

With regard to identity, both the National Associations of Early Childhood Specialists and Education of Young Children oppose[8] redshirting in the belief that it "labels children as failures at the outset of their school experience." Such a label can also create a wedge[9] between redshirted children and their peers from the outset. As can the fact that from puberty to driving, your redshirted child may struggle[10] to find his or her identity among peers who may range from six months to a whole year younger than them.

False sense of achievement

In giving your child an additional year of development over their classmates, parents may unintentionally create a false reality or false sense of achievement[11] in which the redshirted kindergartner may appear to be ahead of the curve. However, while he or she might revel in bumped-up test[12] scores due to seemingly "advanced" fine and gross motor skills earlier on, studies [13]show that more often than not, late starters end up bored[14] and underachieving as their school years continue.

Using the Advantage of Time

Time is key to success

In Malcolm Gladwell's bestselling book, Outliers: The Story of Success[15], the term redshirting is reimagined to identify a parallel between the month we are born and our destined success. The theory is drawn that kids who are among the oldest in their clas[16]s have a developmental advantage that boosts the odds that they'll excel in school[17], on the sports field, and in many other aspects of life. In fact, researchers found that grade-schoolers who are among the oldest in their class have a competitive[18] advantage. The same study showed that high-school students who were among the oldest in their class were nearly 12% more likely to enroll in a four-year college or university and 15.4% less likely to get into trouble with the law while underage.

Smooth and healthy transitions

From as young as six months, children are typically exploring their attachment with their parents, specifically to their mother. Attachment is a very sensitive scale in that too much can result in poor social skills and too little can lead to risk-taking behavior. Many children, especially boys, are not emotionally prepared for the community of kindergarten. With another year of structured home[19] life or daycare, a child is able to more greatly form a personal identity that serves as a platform for healthy social interaction. They bring this confidence to kindergarten a year later and thrive socially and emotionally with a more stable backbone.

Avoiding unnecessary obstacles

Delaying kindergarten by just one year sees a reduction in hyperactivity by an average of 73%.[20] In fact, many children who just needed a chance to develop their skills are wrongly diagnosed[21] with learning disabilities. As such, older students may have a stronger chance of succeeding by being given the gift of time[22]. Whether this means more time in a familiar home environment or more time to adapt to structured surroundings at their own pace, redshirting could be all a child needs to feel prepared in motor skills, emotional maturity and mental capacity to succeed in kindergarten.

The Bottom Line: Every parent is looking to give their child a smooth, healthy transition into school. What do you think is the right decision regarding when children should start kindergarten? Is it better to not underestimate their abilities or to give them an extra year at home? Would you consider redshirting?

THE PERSPECTIVE ON SCHOOL UNIFORMS

Original debate written by Talia Klein Perez

Traditionally favored by private and parochial institutions, school uniforms are growing in popularity in the U.S. Nearly 22%[23] of American public and private schools currently have a uniform policy in place. Consequently, each year parents are forced to shell out money on school clothes in addition to their kids' regular wardrobes. Are uniforms conducive to the learning environment, or are they extraneous?

Here are three arguments in favor of school uniforms and three against:

Three Arguments in Favor of School Uniforms

Uniforms create a sense of equality among students

When school uniforms are required, all students are expected to dress the same, regardless of their style preferences or socioeconomic status. Uniforms can prevent envy and dissatisfaction among students, as there is no ogling[24] of designer dresses or mocking of thrift store rags. Instead of using children as walking billboards for various brands, creating an atmosphere of "haves" and "have-nots,"[25] uniforms ensure that everyone is dressed the same, creating an environment of equality. Plus, with uniforms, students save time and energy during the morning rush, giving them greater space to focus on their studies instead of on fashion.

Uniforms promote order within the school hierarchy

Learning is more likely to happen when there is a sense of decorum[26] and respect for authority in school. When school uniforms are mandatory, classrooms may become more disciplined and orderly, as uniforms remind students where they are and how they are supposed to behave. By demonstrating the school's expectation that high standards be met, through instituting uniforms, the hierarchy[27] of student – teacher – administrator is internalized more deeply. Consequently, attendance tends to rise[28], students tend to behave better, and teachers are therefore more able to do teach.

Uniforms promote students' safety

When uniformed students are off campus, they can be easily identified as belonging to a particular school. One related benefit is that teachers and strangers can readily spot them in a crowd[29], ensuring that no student goes missing while on field trips. Strangers also know that the uniformed students are minors[30] and should therefore not be flirted with, served alcohol, or engaged in any adult behavior. What's more, when students are required to wear uniforms, it becomes much easier to identify campus intruders[31], who stick out like sore thumbs, thereby increasing safety for students as they study.

Three Arguments against School Uniforms

School uniforms are an added expense

When school uniforms are mandatory, parents incur the added expense[32] of clothing that their children will have no use for outside of school. They still need to buy[33] regular clothes for their children to wear after hours, on the weekends and for casual dress days. For parents who would have sent their children to school in hand-me-downs or hand-crafted garments, as well as for parents banking on free public education, forking out funds for school uniforms can be unaffordable[34] and disconcerting.

Why not educate towards freedom of expression?

Schools teach students about the U.S. Constitution and its Amendments[35], so why not educate them to follow it? Everyone has a right to freedom of expression[36]. For example, in Tinker v. Des Moines Independent Community School [37](1969), the court said that a student's freedom of expression in school must be protected unless it would seriously interfere with disciplinary requirements. In a school setting, this can and should be extended to exhibiting individuality through clothing. Forcing all students to wear the same thing infringes on this right. It also stifles students' self-expression[38], which is a strong need during adolescence. Uniforms go against teens' natures and may drive them to express themselves through harsher means, such as body piercings, tattoos and rebellious behavior[39].

Uniforms can be impractical and uncomfortable

Uniforms may not be conducive[40] for spending long hours sitting at a classroom desk[41] and playing outdoors during recess. They are often designed to be worn by all body types, flattering none[42]. They can be restrictive and made of cheap canvas or polycottons[43] in unbecoming shades that may make students sweat in the summer and chill in the winter. This may be particularly true for girls, who often have to wear rigid skirts, while their male counterparts get to wear pants.

....

The Bottom Line: There are many reasons why school uniforms should be compulsory, but there are also many reasons why requiring students to dress a certain way simply is unfair to students and their parents. Do you think students are better or worse off wearing uniforms to school?

HOW GREAT IS 'GREAT LITERATURE' IF IT NEEDS TO BE STUDIED TO BE UNDERSTOOD?

Original debate written by Malkie Khutoretsky

Some readers enjoy picking apart Shakespeare[44] while others find inspiration in *To Kill A Mockingbird*. As schooling progresses, required reading expands to more complex literature, like Poe, Balzac, Frost, Mann and Plato, among others. These texts, often referred to as Great Literature[45], have been used by high schools and universities alike to encourage discussion and reflection. But what makes them so "great"?

From Dante's *Inferno* to Emily Bronte's *Wuthering Heights*, how great is Great Literature if it takes a high school or college course load[46] to decipher?

Here are three arguments in favor of studying great literature and three against.

It's Not That Great

Creating a gap where there should be a bridge

The study of Great Literature[47] divides us into two camps: those who get it, and those who don't. Whether it's the complex language or dynamic concepts, classic literature can alienate readers, especially if the only way to understand it is through a course load. Take *Ulysses*[48]. It's supposed to be genius, but if readers can't grasp it after hours of study, then they might think literature isn't for them. They may, therefore, lose touch with books and drift, instead, to more accessible and less challenging texts; they may even drift out of literature altogether – essentially making Great Literature literature's own worst enemy.

Dead-end lessons

A writer's job is to convey a story and engage the reader's mind, often through emotion. If the fiction writer has great ideas but doesn't engage the reader, then he or she has failed. Shakespeare[49] became Shakespeare because, in his time, he wrote melodramas for the masses. His emotional impact worked, as evidenced by the fact that all of the richness of his words had a receptive audience. Additionally, F. Scott Fitzgerald and Ernest Hemingway[50] introduced high concept through accessible vocabulary It might be that great literary works are not actually that great if they turn reading into (home) work.

Analysis diminishes legacy

Literature is solitary and meant for intimate consumption, not a class reading. One person writes it, one person reads it. The way that we personally experience art is its legacy. We may never definitively know what the Beatles' song "Lucy in the Sky with Diamonds[51]" is about or why the Edvard Munch[52] figure is screaming, but that is what makes them endure. Similarly, with Great Literature, people create the meaning they need and extract their experience from the rich layers of a truly great text. Readers who come back to the same text in different points in their lives will read it differently because *they* are different. Teachers telling readers what to think about *On the Road*, is probably not what Jack Kerouac[53] intended when he frantically wrote his great literary work.

They're Called 'Great' for a Reason

Discovering a common theme in humanity

Bookstores may be filled with bestsellers that contain neat little lessons, but the lessons discovered by taking time to truly understand Great Literature are, perhaps, the richer ones. From studying literature, we learn about ourselves[54] with greater perspective while learning to appreciate the many layers in art, and, indeed, life. There are supposedly only seven stories[55], or types of plots, in literature, and this is because the same things have always made humans tick. By deconstructing literature, we can place ourselves in these plots and identify a sense of purpose; we can challenge ourselves and our beliefs. Like great cuisine, Great Literature can't be gulped down, it needs to be digested slowly[56].

It's not just what you learn, but how

Great Literature asks its readers to locate its relevance and impact on society, both positive and negative. Literary criticism takes a piece of work and puts it under a magnifying glass. The process of studying is as beneficial to the reader as the work itself. By reading The Greats, you learn history, the norms of the time, as well as geography. As Henry James[57] once said: "It takes a great deal of history to produce a little literature." Plus, with text analysis, a reader can form a personal relationship with a body of work[58]. Socrates believed that "learning is seeking the truth in matters," and from him, we have adapted the Socratic method[59] of question-based learning.

Applying the fundamentals to real life

We use stories to talk about ourselves. That's how we share our lives (i.e., "How was your day at school?") That's how we sell an idea (i.e., "That commercial made me cry.") Knowing how a story works provides us with tools that are relevant to many aspects of our practical lives. Great Literature exposes students to a smorgasbord of emotions and literary devices. These devices, including time, space, allegory, etc., create a scene and a context. Mastering these devices may even help us live more ethical lives[60]. What's more, readers can get inspired by To Kill a Mockingbird[61]'s Atticus Finch and learn to stand up to society and hold one's ground.

....

The Bottom Line: For better or for worse, literature has bridged divides, inspired change and challenged our images of ourselves. Should the greatness of a text be measured by how great it is to read or by how complex it is? Should we keep going back to the classics for guidance or leave them in the past tense?

SHOULD WE ALLOW SMARTPHONES IN SCHOOL?

Original debate written by Alan Smithee

As many parents today know all too well, smartphones are not just for adults. The average age for a child getting their first smartphone is 10.3 years[62] (though Bill Gates[63] waited until his children were 14 before giving them smartphones). As the list of smartphone apps for kids[64] keeps expanding and communication between family members, friends and classmates (even teachers!) is increasingly centered around it, the gadget is becoming more of a necessity than an accessory. In the wake of COVID-19, kids' social and educational lives are more online than ever. Clearly smartphones are here to stay, so schools now need to decide whether to embrace them and make good use of them, or ban them altogether.

Here are three arguments for why we should ban phones from schools and three for why we should welcome them.

We Should Ban Smartphones from School

Less physical activity during recess

Kids spend most of their classroom time sitting down. Apart from gym class twice a week or so, the only time they get to stretch their legs and exercise is during recess. So what happens when you let children bring their phones to school? The obvious. Schoolkids who would otherwise be running around, playing ball, or just hanging on the monkey bars are now sitting with their noses glued to their tiny screens. These kids will miss out on exercising[65], which is not only good for their health but is also linked to improved cognitive function, better memory and better concentration[66].

Unwanted exposure

Parents rely on school staff to make sure their kids are safe at school. This includes safety from exposure to X-rated materials[67], such as porn and excessive violence. But even under close supervision, children can be exposed to such material on their own, or someone else's smartphone.. Not to mention what they see on smartphones while on the school bus[68] to and from school. While it's true that there are many parent-control apps[69] that filter and manage kids' usage of smartphones, kids are smart, digital natives; they enjoy the challenge of coming up with new ways to bypass these measures[70]. This can lead to an endless cat-and-mouse game of new measures and new workarounds.

The un-social network

For some children, screens are also used as a place of refuge[71]. Kids, especially socially awkward ones, sometimes lack the social skills required to make or interact with friends. They may shy away from social interactions if they feel out of place. But face-to-face interaction is a critical life skill[72]. When we interact with others, we are continuously processing wordless signals like facial expressions, tone of voice, and even the physical distance between us. Equipping children with smartphones may increase the chance that they will choose the phone over learning to socialize with other kids. This will make it harder[73] for them in the long term to face social situations as they grow up.

We Should Allow Smartphones in School

Interactive learning in classrooms

Many schools today don't have the equipment needed to make technology accessible for their students. This is where smartphones[74] as learning aids come into the picture. These everyday hand-held devices have more processing power than all of NASA's computers when they landed a man on the moon[75]. So, instead of dealing with computers, the teacher can simply ask the class to scan a QR code, or enter a www address that will take students directly to interactive content for the subject they are currently studying. With in-school education compromised by the pandemic and hybrid learning[76] now prevalent, digital education[77] is just another way for students to learn about the world around them and for teachers to communicate with them – on various digital platforms, all accessible by smartphones.

Keeping in touch

Back in the day, for parents to contact their children[78] at school, they would have to call the school secretary, dictate a note and have it passed to the teacher and then to the student. Such inefficient methods are no longer required; direct content allows students and parents increased flexibility and freedom in their after-school playdates, activities, and pick-up arrangements. Plus, given the record number of school shootings[79] occurring across America, smartphones give both students and their parents an added feeling of security, knowing that they can call and text each other at any moment.

That'll teach you

Children are growing up in a world dominated by smartphones. Instead of keeping this significant societal change outside of school and trying to pretend it doesn't exist, we are better off educating students in school about the benefits and risks of smartphone use (and overuse). This includes teaching children about digital and cyberbullying and its harmful effects and how to responsibly use various social media platforms that are accessible from their smartphones. Teachers can also encourage children to question information and sources[80] that they are exposed to on their smartphones, which is an especially important lesson in today's age of "fake news[81]."

....

The Bottom Line: Smartphones can make classrooms more in tune with the future lives of students, but can also pose a threat to their social and academic development. What would you say if your child asked to bring a smartphone to school?

SHOULD WE DISTRIBUTE CONDOMS IN HIGH SCHOOLS?

Original debate written by Rachel Segal

Sex education in school has always stirred debate. But sparks really start flying when discussing whether to provide free condoms in high schools. Proponents claim that making contraception readily available is a matter of safety,[82] while opponents say that morality is at risk in doing so. With 64% of pre-teens, teens and young adults (ages 13-24) actively searching for online porn[83] on a weekly basis, and 71% of them hiding this activity from their parents, it's safe to say that addressing sex education[84] – and contraception – with high schoolers remains an important topic.

Here are three reasons why it's important to make condoms accessible in high schools for students who need them and three reasons why doing so is a mistake.

Free Condoms Should Be Distributed in High Schools

Condoms help reduce the spread of STIs

Among U.S. high school students surveyed by the CDC[85] in 2019, 38% were sexually active. Of these, 27% had had sexual intercourse during the last three months and 46% of them didn't use a condom during their last sexual encounter. The same study also showed that half of the 20 million new STIs reported in the United States each year are among 15- to 24-year-olds, and that people aged 13-24 accounted for an estimated 21% of all new HIV diagnoses in 2018.

These numbers emphasize the importance of condom distribution in high schools for sexually active teenagers. If consistently used correctly, condoms[86] can be highly effective[87] in decreasing the probability of STI transmission and preventing HIV transmission. Whether we like it or not, U.S. high school students are already having sex. As long as this is the case, schools need to help them stay safe.

Condoms help prevent teenage pregnancy

While abstinence[88] is encouraged among high school students, parents aren't naïve. The numbers above strongly suggest that expecting abstinence is not realistic. The American Academy of Pediatrics (AAP) Committee on Adolescence knows this, and therefore has long advocated[89] access to condoms in schools[90] as part of comprehensive sex education programs to mitigate cases of unwanted pregnancies[91] (as well as AIDS and STIs).

Over the last 20 years, teen birth rates across the United States have been continuously declining[92]. According to Pew Research, the birth rate among 15- to 19-year-old females in 2018 was less than half of what it had been in 2008. Many factors have been linked to this decline, but especially prominent is the increase in contraception use[93] among teens. Even with recent pandemic disruption, teens spend the majority of their time at school, so it is the most natural and convenient place for sex education, including condom distribution.

Condoms make teens more sexually responsible

As teenagers are beginning to discover their sexual identities[94], providing condoms in high schools can help them establish the concept of safe sex as the norm and gives them the mandate to be responsible. Research shows that 60% of high schoolers[95] have had sex by the time they graduate. Therefore, introducing the idea of condom use into their conscience at such a formative age may help teens view contraception as second nature as opposed to something that either gender will have to continually negotiate with future partners.

Free Condoms Shouldn't Be Distributed in High Schools

It interferes with family and religious beliefs

By providing condoms to students, high schools are taking away the right of parents to decide whether their own teenage children should have access to contraception. To begin with, many parents[96] don't think that their adolescent children are yet emotionally or physically ready for sex. So having schools introduce condom use to their teenagers pressures both the parents and teens into having conversations about sex that may feel premature.

It may also interfere with a family's values or religious beliefs. For instance, the Catholic Church and other conservative faiths[97] oppose various forms of contraception. Parents who support the cause can provide condoms to their teenagers without having schools infringe on other families' timelines of talking about sex and/or religious freedoms.

They're not 100% effective, which gives a false sense of security

Condom distribution in high schools gives students a false sense of security when having sex. Since most teenagers lack experience with condom use, faulty implementation can be extremely ineffective. When used perfectly every single time, condoms are 98% effective[98] at preventing pregnancy. But people, especially teenagers, aren't perfect so typically condoms may be only about 85% effective. Not to mention the fact that vulnerable teenage girls still have less control over condom use.

It sends mixed messages and legitimizes sexual activity

In high schools that teach students about both abstinence and contraception use, these programs are sending mixed messages to students. If a school wants its students not to have sex, it shouldn't provide them with condoms to use during intercourse. Furthermore, making condoms available in schools might send the erroneous message to students that their teachers and parents are expecting them to engage in sexual activity.

The Bottom Line: Is it the providence and responsibility of a school or of the parents to educate their teenagers about safe sex when they feel the time is right? Or, in the words of TV's most iconic teen virgin, Donna Martin[99], from the original *90210*: "It's like if you have a swimming pool in your backyard, you can tell your children not to go in it, you can even build a fence around it, but if you know that they're going to find a way in to that water, don't you think you ought to teach those kids how to swim?"

HEALTH CHAPTER

- Are antidepressants a good solution?
- Is obesity a disease?
- Milk: Is it healthy or harmful to drink?
- Are vaccines safe or risky for your kids?
- Are vitamin supplements helpful or harmful?
- The perspective on cosmetic surgery

ARE ANTIDEPRESSANTS A GOOD SOLUTION?

Original debate written by Kira Goldring

Depression is a mood disorder that can negatively affect cognition, energy, self-esteem, and even everyday activities like eating and sleeping. Pre-Covid-19, it was estimated that over 300 million people worldwide [1]suffer from this debilitating condition, with 16.2 million adults suffering in the US alone. Numbers have understandably risen[2] since the onset of the pandemic. According to the US Census Bureau, a third of Americans currently show signs of anxiety and clinical depression.

In addition, celebrity depression-related suicides, like Kate Spade[3] and Anthony Bourdain[4], have brought depression more out into the open; the subject may have less of a stigma today. What's clear is that a solution to combat the breadth of mental illness is now needed more than ever. But are antidepressant drugs the answer, or are these pills capable of causing more harm than good?

Here are three arguments against using antidepressants to fight mental illness, and three arguments in favor of using antidepressants.

Find Another Way

Relapse is common

Antidepressants are often only a temporary solution to depression and may not consistently be helpful in getting rid of it long-term. Studies[5] show that the risk of relapse after discontinuing antidepressant medication is high; for one of the most common types of antidepressants (SSRIs), 26-45% [6]of people relapse after discontinuing the medication, and the relapse rate is even higher for people taking stronger antidepressants.

Time is of the essence

People with Major Depressive Disorder [7] often have a difficult time getting out of bed, let alone attending to their daily tasks. This kind of disorder needs immediate treatment, which antidepressants can't provide. While antidepressants may be helpful in the long run, they don't work fast enough. While it can take anywhere from six weeks to six months[8] for antidepressants to take effect, newer generations of SSRIs take about three weeks – which is still way too long to wait for someone who's feeling desperate and seeking professional help. Taking a pill for weeks without feeling a change may discourage a depressed person from continuing treatment or seeking further help. In contrast, seeing a therapist or implementing other lifestyle and behavioral changes[9] into their daily routine may bring about quicker results.

Not just your average side effects

Almost every drug poses a risk of negative side effects, but antidepressants up the stakes. Some antidepressants, such as benzodiazepines, have been found to be addictive and difficult to get off of. Fifty to 60%[10] of antidepressant users experience significant side effects[11], such as gastrointestinal and sexual complications, weight gain[12], nausea, insomnia and/or diarrhea. Even worse is the possibility of suicidal thoughts[13], which is a potential side effect of almost every antidepressant. The last thing a person with depression needs is another incentive to self-harm, and these potential side effects are too dangerous to warrant giving antidepressants a try.

We'll Take Two, Please

Balancing the scales

Antidepressants are a non-invasive way to "right the wrongs" that have transpired in a depressed person's brain. Depression has been linked to an imbalance of neurotransmitters[14] in the brain, meaning that the chemicals which are responsible for happiness, eating, sleeping, and other important biological functions are off-kilter. Antidepressants are small pills taken orally that seek to restore this imbalance. While a chemical imbalance is not the only potential cause of depression, studies show that 60-70%[15] of depressed patients who take antidepressants respond positively[16], with symptoms eventually remitting.

The unique effect of pills

For some, even the simple act of taking a pill can affect a positive change in mood, regardless of what the pill actually does. The placebo effect[17] – which is when a person positively or negatively responds to fake treatment when they believe that the treatment is real – is a good demonstrator of this. In fact, a study[18] of the placebo effect demonstrated that people with depression who show improvement while taking fake drugs get the most benefit when taking antidepressants. Just knowing that the pills are there provides comfort and can encourage your brain to fight depression along with the medicine.

Desperate times

When depression is severe enough, finding a cure can become a crucial next step to save a person's life. The pain of living with depression can often lead people to self-harm, and in some cases, to commit suicide[19]. There tends to be a stigma[20] against taking medication, which makes many weary of taking the plunge. However, antidepressants are one of the most effective treatments[21] for mental illnesses, and should be a resource that is well-considered. As one therapist[22] aptly says: "Depression without medication is like cleaning your house with a ball and chain on your ankle… When you take medication, you still have to clean the house, but without the ball and chain."

....

The Bottom Line: Some may feel discouraged from using antidepressants as they don't work quickly or necessarily provide a permanent solution, while others may find antidepressants a helpful resource with which to fight depression. What do you think? Would you encourage friends or family suffering from depression to seek treatment that includes antidepressants?

IS OBESITY A DISEASE?

Original debate written by Chaya Benyamin

Obesity worldwide and in America has been rising steadily since the 1970s. Recent years have seen its heyday, with more than one in three[23] [24]Americans (or 36% of the population) classified as overweight or obese. Amid what is considered to be a childhood obesity epidemic[25], Harvard researchers foresee that 57% of children[26] will be obese by the time they turn 35. This figure is likely to increase due to the pandemic and the negative effects[27] that social lockdowns are having on nutrition, eating habits and exercise in adults and children worldwide. In response to the growing number of individuals affected by obesity, medical organizations like the WHO have toyed with the idea of codifying obesity as a disease, and the American Medical Association[28] and Mayo Clinic[29] have already done so. But does calling obesity a disease really make it one?

Below, we'll discuss three reasons we should think of obesity as a disease, and three reasons we should not.

Is Obesity a Disease? No

Thinking of obesity as a disease can backfire

Yale disease prevention researcher, D.L. Katz[30], points out that in terming something a disease, one would expect remedies to lie within the realm of pharmacological treatment, clinical visits, or surgery. Therefore, classifying obesity as a disease may inadvertently steer treatment toward drugs and gastrointestinal surgeries, for a condition that can often be overcome (albeit less easily) through diet and exercise. Worse, it may diminish an obese person's sense of control[31] over their weight, and effectively discourage behavioral changes[32] that contribute to weight loss.

Obesity diagnosis is imprecise

Most health professionals diagnose obesity by calculating Body Mass Index[33] (BMI), which is an estimation of a person's body fat based on their weight and height. But BMI does not measure body fat directly, and as such, people who are not obese according to their body fat percentage are deemed obese with the BMI diagnostic. By this definition, fitness fanatics like Dwayne Johnson[34] (The Rock) and most NFL athletes are technically "obese." Worse, BMI is not an effective prognosticator of metabolic wellness; one study found that approximately one in four people with normal BMIs nevertheless had some kind of metabolic dysfunction.[35] Plus, when it comes to children, BMI[36] doesn't work well to identify health issues[37], especially mental health issues, that may contribute to a child's obesity.

Heavy people aren't necessarily ill

People of all shapes and sizes fall ill for reasons that have nothing to do with weight, and many people are in prime physical health despite being obese. The development of diseases like cardiovascular disease[38], stroke, and cancer depend on a great many factors beyond weight. A full third of people deemed obese indicate no increased risk[39] for diabetes or heart disease. Interestingly, while obesity is a risk factor in some diseases, it provides a safeguard against others. For example, obese women are less likely to develop osteoporosis[40], and another study showed that people deemed overweight by BMI measurements actually outlived[41] their counterparts in the normal BMI range.

Obesity Is a Disease

Obesity isn't a choice

Obesity is often caused by a number of underlying[42] genetic or metabolic[43] factors that cause people to gain weight or make them unable to lose it. Genes control everything from a person's ability to metabolize food to how full one feels after a meal. In some individuals, genetic factors[44] can influence obesity by as much as 80%. Those who have greater genetic disposition toward obesity are not usually able to lose weight or maintain weight loss through diet and exercise alone. Studies have shown that for long-term success, chronically obese patients indeed require intervention beyond incorporating healthy diet and exercise into one's lifestyle. Bariatric and other forms of gastric surgeries[45] show the best results for long-term weight management.

Treating obesity as a disease makes economic sense

Obesity is positively correlated with diseases that are highly expensive to treat, like kidney disease[46]. Dialysis, a common treatment for kidney failure, costs tens of thousands of dollars per year, per patient. With nearly 500,000 individuals on dialysis[47] in the US, it constitutes a significant cost burden for individuals, insurance companies, and the government. Defining obesity as a disease would help allocate the funds to treat and prevent it. Cost-effective treatments – like consultations with a nutritionist, physical therapy, or even bariatric surgery – can help to circumvent cases (and therefore costs) of the diseases with which obesity is associated. As the saying goes, an ounce of prevention is worth a pound of cure. As such, there are federal, evidenced-based dietary guidelines[48] in the works for infants, pregnant women and young children in an effort to prevent obesity.

Obesity as a disease encourages treatment

While being overweight or obese can have a number of negative effects[49] on overall health[50] and quality of life, especially increasing the risk of Covid-related death[51], obesity is hardly a focus of medicine. Medical schools tend to focus on pathology, devoting little time to the impact of nutrition and activity on health. This leaves physicians ill-equipped to advise their patients on such matters. So regarding obesity as a disease may enhance physicians' values and learning on the topic. Since there is deep stigma associated with obesity, designating it as a disease rather than a consequence of poor lifestyle may encourage those affected to seek medical assistance, instead of avoiding appointments for fear of humiliation. It may provide doctors the opportunity to address health concerns diplomatically and accurately, instead of equating obesity with poor choices which makes patients feel fat-shamed[52] or want to avoid the issue altogether.

The Bottom Line: Can obesity be kept at bay through healthy lifestyle choices[53], or does it require more comprehensive medical interventions for a sustainable cure? With adult and childhood obesity cases rising across the globe, and increasing the risk of Covid-related hospitalizations[54], now is the crucial moment to decide: Is obesity a disease or not?

MILK: IS IT HEALTHY OR HARMFUL TO DRINK?

Original debate written by Rachel Segal

Most of us grew up hearing that milk "does a body good[55]." No one questioned this sentiment, what with parents, doctors and teachers all echoing the same message, directly and indirectly. However, over the years, more and more research has emerged leading us to re-evaluate milk's attributes and starring role in our lives. Is it the key to good health or a health risk? Plus, with so many plant-based beverage alternatives[56] flooding the market, who's to say that cow's milk truly is the best option?

Here are three arguments for drinking "moo juice" and three suggesting we should reconsider how much of it we drink.

Bottom's Up!
It packs a single punch of needed nutrients

Our bodies need calcium, vitamin D and potassium to function properly. In fact, new research suggests that a lack of vitamin D[57] may make you more vulnerable to the coronavirus. There's no better single source for all three of these nutrients than milk. (For the record, vitamin D is added to fortified milk). Plus, it also contains carbs, fats, proteins and other minerals, all of which are a must for growing children, not to mention for aging adults – and everyone in between. True, milk isn't the only source for all of these required nutrients. As Americans don't eat enough[58] fruits and vegetables to meet the federal daily dietary guidelines[59], wouldn't it be easier to get yourself – and especially your kids – to gulp down an extra glass of milk each day[60] than to eat more vegetables?

Prevents osteoporosis

Put simply, osteoporosis[61] is the weakening of our bones. Each year, osteoporosis leads to millions of bone fractures[62]. Increased calcium intake can help prevent or minimize its effects, as calcium is essential for building and maintaining our bones. Preventing osteoporosis depends on two things: strengthening your bone density early on in life and limiting the amount of bone loss in adulthood. How? By regular exercise and, especially, by getting enough calcium and vitamin D – particularly in the form of the milk. Dairy products[63] have higher concentrations per serving of highly absorbable calcium than vegetables[64], beans and other alternatives.

It can help with weight loss

Milk contains a naturally high level of high-quality protein. In fact, it actually contains two types of protein, called whey and casein. By drinking just one cup, you'll get 8 grams of protein, which is more than double the amount most whole grains and fruits and veggies offer per serving. Why does this matter? Protein[65] plays a big role when it comes to losing and maintaining weight. Among other amazing things, it helps reduce our hunger and appetite. So, one glass can cut off the urge to snack or overeat.

Actually, We Don't Need So Much Milk

Can lead to increased health risks

Decades of research[66] asserts that milk may contribute to health problems as opposed to preventing them. Some sources believe that the beverage's high fat content[67] can lead to an increased risk of Type 1 diabetes as well as coronary heart disease, heart attacks or strokes. Other research suggests that milk may lead to an increased risk of cancer[68] due to the levels of IGF-1 growth hormones found in milk. While this hormone is normally found in our blood, higher levels of it may stimulate certain cancer cells.

Then, there's a milk allergy[69], which can be life-threatening. Symptoms range from wheezing to vomiting to a possibly fatal anaphylactic reaction. To a lesser degree, there's also lactose intolerance[70]. The dairy beverage has also been associated with causing ear infections, coughs, and bloated, upset and gassy tummies. Last but not least, teenagers should be aware that various studies[71] draw a distinct connection between drinking milk and increased acne.

Not proven vital for bone health

While milk has traditionally been considered the go-to source for maintaining bone health, recent voices suggest otherwise. For example, a 2011 scientific review[72] found that drinking it did not reduce the risk of fractures in women. In fact, a 2014 study[73] suggested that women who consumed large amounts of the dairy beverage may actually have a higher risk of fractures and death compared to others who drink less.

After infancy, we are not meant to digest dairy

As humans, we are not genetically programmed[74] to drink milk after infancy. In fact, our gene that is required to break down milk sugar (lactose) turns off during weaning. Some researchers argue that a genetic mutation is the only reason we in the Western world (where dairying has been a longstanding tradition) can tolerate it as adults. But, on the whole, animals don't drink milk after being weaned and they manage without it, especially since calcium and vitamins can be found in other sources or supplements.

Today, consumers are increasingly turning toward plant-based beverages, which are gaining in popularity and market share. Referred to by some as alt-milk[75], these alternatives derive from oats, coconuts[76], soy[77], macadamia, rice and even peas, among other sources. They have become so popular that the global dairy alternatives market[78] was estimated to be worth US$22.6 billion in 2020 and expected to reach US$40.6 billion by 2026. So, it seems there may be a new trend taking off that our bodies prefer.

....

The Bottom Line: We have long been told that drinking milk is a great (and convenient) way to boost daily intake of vitamins, minerals and protect bone integrity. However, research brings all of this reasoning into question. Would you consider switching to plant-based beverages the next time you reach for your coffee or a plate of cookies?

ARE VACCINES SAFE OR RISKY FOR YOUR KIDS?

Original debate written by Kira Goldring

A lot of fact and fiction surround vaccines. The same goes for the risk they may or may not pose[79] to human beings. While this topic has long been a popular one all year round, especially during normal flu seasons, it's been particularly relevant lately given the new coronavirus vaccine[80], the fastest-developed[81] and fastest-approved[82] vaccine in history. (And let's not forget the unexpected measles outbreak[83] that occurred in 2019.) While vaccines protect against disease and illnesses, can they potentially harm our children?

Below, we'll explore three reasons why vaccines are safe for your kids, and three reasons why they may be risky. Please note that none of the arguments in this debate address the new coronavirus vaccine.

Vaccines Are Safe for Your Kids

Rewards outweigh possible side effects

While vaccinations aren't 100% foolproof, the rewards definitely outweigh the possible side effects[84], which, if they occur, are usually mild and temporary. For example, vaccinating your child can reduce his or her risk of flu-associated death[85] by 51%[86] among children with underlying high-risk medical conditions and by nearly 65% among healthy children. In contrast, an unvaccinated child[87] can contract a disease that is vaccine-preventable, such as measles[88]. Also, keep in mind that unvaccinated children can catch vaccine-preventable diseases from other kids or people who don't even show any symptoms. For instance, Hib meningitis[89] can be spread from people who have the bacteria in their bodies but aren't even sick. As you can't tell who in your surroundings is contagious[90], vaccinating your kids[91], especially against the regular flu[92], gives you one less thing to worry about in a world of unforeseen risks. This is especially relevant in 2020.[93]

Who would you trust, if not the experts

As parents, we tend to be instinctively overprotective of our kids, which is why we turn to experts[94] for help in determining what's safe or risky for children's health. Many major health organizations, such as the World Health Organization[95], CDC[96], and FDA[97], all say that vaccines are safe, relying on studies to back up their claims. Doctors, who have studied health for most of their lives, are overwhelmingly pro-vaccines[98] as well, with some supporting them so strongly that they go as far as dismissing families from their practice [99]if the parents refuse to vaccinate their kids. Of course, there are instances where doctors are wrong[100], but they are our best bet when it comes to safeguarding our children's health. After all, they have dedicated their lives to studying and practicing medicine, overseeing the health of countless patients.

Community immunity

An extended benefit of vaccination is its potential for causing "herd immunity[101]"- also known as community immunity. This is when a large enough portion of a community becomes immunized to a disease, thereby limiting the chance of an outbreak within the *entire* community. (It is still too soon to tell whether herd immunity works against COVID-19[102], because it is not yet clear whether someone who has been infected with the virus will be immune to it and, if so, for how long.)

In cases not related to COVID-19, such community protection can be important for infants, who are too young to be vaccinated. However, a critical number of people need to be vaccinated for this to work; for example, 42,000 people[103] in the United States came down with whooping cough in 2012 after most of the country failed to meet the herd immunity criteria for pertussis vaccinations (92-94%), which was the highest outbreak[104] in the previous 20 years. In other words, if your child isn't vaccinated, he or she can pose a public health risk[105] and increase the chances of disease outbreak where you live.

Vaccines May Be Risky for Your Kids

Fighting the wrong fight

Just because a vaccine has reduced the risk of disease in the past doesn't prove that it will apply in the future. Diseases can have many different strains, and vaccines may not always protect against the right ones. For example, according to the CDC, there are years that the flu vaccine has no benefit [106] during periods that the vaccine isn't matched well to circulating influenza viruses. Or take Gardasil[107], the HPV vaccine that only assists in protecting against 9 strains of HPV – out of over 100[108]. If these vaccines are indeed fighting against the wrong strains of disease, they could effectively be ineffective for our children.

The body can defend itself

Unfortunately, illness is an inevitable part of everyday life; it's next to impossible to ride out an estimated 80-year lifespan without at least catching a good bout of the stomach flu. Your kids are no exception to this rule, and their bodies will need to learn how to fight sickness on their own, the same way they may have to learn how to stand up to the bully on the playground. Kids are born with immune systems,[109] which naturally help the body fight off diseases. Yet, it has been argued that giving vaccines to children can potentially prevent the immune system from doing its job, making kids more susceptible to getting sick in the long-term.

Medicine can be worse than the disease

Like most preventative medicines, any vaccine can potentially cause side effects.[110] Some may include a low fever, fussiness, soreness, a temporary headache, loss of appetite or fatigue. While some of these side effects[111] are rare, like a severe allergic reaction or even a neurological side effect such as a seizure, they can be unpleasant or even fatal. For example, 1 in 30,000[112] people can develop thrombocytopenia[113] (a decrease in blood platelets which can cause a bleeding disorder) from the MMR vaccine, which protects against the measles[114]. Therefore, in certain cases, it can seem like the side effects could pose a more severe threat to your kids than the diseases themselves.

The Bottom Line: Some children's level of physical development may not be suited for receiving vaccines, but there are extreme and collective health risks associated with not vaccinating children. What do you think? Do you vaccinate your kids?

ARE VITAMIN SUPPLEMENTS HELPFUL OR HARMFUL?

Original debate written by Malkie Khutoretsky

Seventy-seven percent[115] of American adults supplement their diets with vitamin supplements. While a vitamin is a natural substance usually found in food, a supplement is a manufactured product that contains one or more vitamins combined with other ingredients, like amino acids. Whether through pills, powders or oils, consumers take vitamin supplements in the hopes of enhancing their nutrition, boosting their immune system, increasing mental health and improving general day-to-day function. Today, as COVID-19 keeps spreading, more and more people are turning to vitamin supplements[116] to help boost their immune systems[117]. But how much do we really know about our vitamin supplements? Are they helping our bodies as much as we think they are?

The following are three arguments against vitamin supplements and three supporting them.

Get Your Vitamins from Food, Not a Bottle

Health kick or marketing tool?

In 2018, the vitamin supplement industry, including vitamins, minerals, protein & amino acids, etc., was worth an estimated $140 billion[118], and it's projected to rise to $216.3 billion in the next five years. With the global wellness industry growing exponentially, (in 2019 alone, its estimated value was $4.75 trillion), it's no surprise that the vitamin supplement industry is also booming[119]; Americans reportedly spend $635 a year[120] on nutritional supplements. Influencers like Gwyneth Paltrow[121], among other celebrities-turned-health-gurus[122], promote vitamin supplements via social media with little accountability. This industry feeds off such misinformation:[123] supplements' listed ingredients as well as testing for safety and purity are frequently inaccurate. Despite claiming to be health-focused, supplements are like any other business, prioritizing sales. In fact, in some instances, the supplement industry even has hidden dangers[124].

Uninformed patients and doctors

Vitamins can interact with prescription medicine. As consumers don't tend to consider vitamin supplements as medicine, this can be problematic. At the doctor's office, patients who take vitamin supplements often say, when asked, that they're not taking any medicine regularly. But taking regular vitamin supplements is vital information that doctors need to know. For instance, B-12 supplements are recommended readily, specifically to the elderly[125], as is vitamin K, which helps prevent hip problems. However, these supplements can affect certain medications. Although vitamin K is useful in joint function, it acts against blood-thinning medication. These compounds, prescription or vitamin, are part of a delicate cocktail that the average person cannot navigate safely.

Vitamin toxicity

There's such a thing as taking too many vitamins. This is called vitamin toxicity[126]. Various supplements mix different vitamins together, among other ingredients. This is where things start to get tricky. Unknown levels[127] of large doses of antioxidants, as found in vitamins like A, B and C, can increase risk of heart failure and mortality. Also, too much vitamin D[128] can harm your kidneys; this is especially important to note today, when people are increasingly turning to vitamin D to help boost their immune system[129] against the coronavirus that causes COVID-19. Plus, in order to keep our immune system functioning, our body actually needs a certain amount of "free radicals[130]," which are the "bad cells" that vitamins fight. Therefore, ingesting too many vitamins may get rid of too many free radicals, unintentionally creating an imbalance within our bodies and doing the opposite of what we're trying to achieve.

Give Your Body a Boost

Accessible and efficient

A decade ago, Americans consumed 31%[131] more packaged foods than fresh foods. Today, highly processed foods[132] make up 70%[133] of the calories in the food Americans buy at their supermarkets. Coupled with the increasing price[134] of fruits and vegetables, the average American's diet lacks important vitamins and minerals. Our culture's need for quantity over quality has led to a distinct decline[135] in nutrients in our crops and fresh foods. For example, fresh salmon is famous for providing us with Omega-3[136]. However, the amount of Omega-3 that the body actually absorbs from farmed salmon compared to the amount of toxins[137] also found in it is hardly worth the price of the fish. Instead, an investment in vitamin supplements allows your body to directly absorb Omega-3, encouraging metabolic function, without exposing yourself to the hidden toxins. (That the supplements are cheaper than the salmon is just an added bonus.)

Catered to the individual

Fifty percent[138] of the average older adult has a vitamin and mineral intake that is less than the daily recommendation[139]. This is due to a decrease in food consumption; as we get older, we're unable to consume foods the way we once did. Whether this is due to lack of appetite or inability to process solid foods, vitamin supplements can often be one's only alternative[140] to maintaining a healthy diet. Additionally, pregnant women, or even women trying to get pregnant, are advised that supplementing[141] vitamin D enforces healthy fetal as well as maternal bones, and folic acid[142] can help prevent birth defects. Plus, zinc[143], the most effective mineral to aid healthy reproduction and a staple of a prenatal supplement kit, is not readily found in plant-based diets. This makes zinc supplements, among others, very beneficial to those on a vegetarian or vegan diet.

Mental health

While we think of vitamins as benefitting our physical health, they have a positive impact on our mental health[144] as well. A study in the American Journal of Psychiatry concluded that 27% of severely depressed women older than 65 were deficient in vitamin B-12. By these statistics, it would seem that more than one-quarter of all severe depression[145] could be treated with B-12 shots[146]. Let's not forget Magnesium, which is missing in 48%[147] of Americans' diets. Magnesium deficiency can be linked to stress and insomnia[148], which severely impact mental health, as well as type 2 diabetes. Vitamin supplements also lower blood pressure and increase healthy sleep patterns, both of which increase mental health and resilience.

The Bottom Line: Vitamin supplements have become a staple of the American home, especially today, when everyone is trying to ward off COVID-19[149]. They provide a quick and easy fix to the country's vitamin deficiency problem. However, with not enough regulation[150], the industry leaves us vulnerable to further harm. Are vitamin supplements helping or hurting society?

THE PERSPECTIVE ON COSMETIC SURGERY

Original debate written by Talia Klein Perez

Many Americans want to put their best face (and body) forward, believing that appearance is the key to success in life, love and at work. This realization has led men and women to undergo 17.2 million[151] cosmetic surgery (or plastic surgery) procedures in 2017, up 2% since the previous year. Yet, despite an estimated 132% rise[152] in people going under the knife to improve their appearances since 2000, cosmetic surgery remains highly stigmatized and its recipients are often deemed "fake." So, does cosmetic surgery provide the lift people seek, or is it an industry feeding on our most shallow needs?

Here are three arguments in favor of cosmetic surgery and three against it.

Three Arguments in Favor of Cosmetic Surgery

Cosmetic surgery can improve confidence levels

One of the biggest advantages of cosmetic surgery is enhancing one's appearance. For some, modifying a specific physical feature via cosmetic surgery can be a game changer, which improves confidence[153] levels and self-image. The link between positive body image and high self-esteem[154] is well known. People who love the way they look will feel better about themselves and experience an increase in confidence. Improving a person's physical appearance can be the boost he or she needs to see themselves differently, change the attitudes that govern their lives and feel more accepted[155] by the public.

And if a common medical procedure is all it takes for one to make a change for the better, why not do it?

Cosmetic surgery provides significant health benefits to a suffering population

In some cases, cosmetic surgery can improve a person's health[156]. A person suffering from chronic congestion due to a deviated septum can undergo rhinoplasty (a nose job) and breathe freely at last. A heavily endowed woman experiencing regular pain as a result of the extra pressure on her back and shoulders can have a breast reduction. With cosmetic surgery, skin cancer can be removed[157] and open wounds can be closed. Burn victims can begin to heal, and the removal of fat cells through liposuction can drastically reduce the chance of diabetes[158] in at-risk populations.

Cosmetic surgery helps people gain a competitive edge

There is an increasing pressure for men and women to look younger and more attractive to better compete in the working world. This is related to the Halo Effect,[159] a cognitive bias that most people harbor, inducing them to connect positive personality traits with physical attractiveness and provide these people with better opportunities. The trend of women, as well as a growing number of men, going under the knife in the hopes of looking younger and remaining relevant at work is on the rise. In fact, in a study formulated by the American Society of Plastic Surgeons (ASPS[160]), 73% believed that appearance and youthful looks are critical for getting hired, a promotion, or new clients. If this is truly the case, then cosmetic surgery isn't a folly, it's a true competitive advantage.

Three Arguments against Cosmetic Surgery

Cosmetic surgery does not deal with self-image issues at their source

Cosmetic surgery is a Band-Aid solution – it changes an aspect of a person's appearance that has been harming their mental wellbeing. But cosmetic surgery deals solely with aesthetics. It does not solve the problem at its root. As such, a person suffering from body dysmorphia[161], an anxiety disorder that causes a person to have a distorted idea of how they look, will continue to experience negative body image and negative self-perception, even after the offending body part has been reconstructed. In fact, a person can be left feeling even more lost[162] following surgery than he or she did before going under the knife. In such cases, psychological counseling[163] would be more beneficial and less physically risky.

Cosmetic surgery panders to society's image obsession and objectifies women

In an era where the Kardashians[164] reign supreme, image has become everything and people are obsessed with meeting the unrealistic standards set before them by celebrities. Cosmetic surgery procedures pander precisely to that, making it seem as though beauty and success are products available for purchase. The media[165] practically promotes cosmetic surgery, through its idyllic casting of "reality" television shows (ahem, Extreme Makeover). Moreover, cosmetic surgery objectifies the female form[166], often to fit a male of idea of how women should look. In 2016, 92%[167] of all cosmetic surgery procedures, including the most popular breast augmentations and Botox[168], were administered to women. This reflects an imbalance in the way society views the female form, especially as it ages, to fit mainstream standards of beauty.

Cosmetic surgery is unhealthy

People will pinch pennies and forego everyday possessions and experiences to afford the steep cost of cosmetic surgery procedures. This is so despite the fact that cosmetic surgery has potential for complications, severe pain and long recovery times. And in some cases, cosmetic surgery does not produce the results the patient desires, driving men and women to return for repeat procedures and essentially enslaving themselves to a vicious cycle of cosmetic surgeries. Famous examples include Michael Jackson[169] and Joan Rivers[170], who according to her daughter, "had a staggering 348 cosmetic operations over her life and was never happy with the way she looked."

The Bottom Line: Does cosmetic surgery provide us humans a way to improve our experience in life, or does it bandage over problems and keep us away from evolving as people? What do you think?

TECHNOLOGY CHAPTER

- The perspective on Jeff Bezos
- The perspective on digital marketing
- Can Facebook maintain dominance?
- The perspective on Steve Jobs
- IOS or Android – which smartphone is better?
- The perspective on Elon Musk
- The perspective on Google

THE PERSPECTIVE ON JEFF BEZOS

Original debate written by Kira Goldring

Most well-known as founder and CEO of Amazon, Jeff Bezos, who also co-owns the Washington Post, is the richest man[1] in the world. Less known is the fact that Bezos invested in Google[2] back in 1998, way before the company became the internet giant it is today. He's certainly business savvy and powerful – some may say even too powerful[3] – but does that make Bezos a true role model of our time, especially when it comes to climate change[4]? And where does he stand regarding antitrust issues?[5] Congress is now trying to get to the bottom of allegations against Amazon[6] that it allegedly uses collected data from its merchants to compete against them. If true, is this the practice of an admirable leader?

Here are three reasons to look up to Jeff Bezos, and three reasons he may not be the ideal role model.

Bezos Is Best

King of e-commerce

Bezos single-handedly created a kingdom of e-commerce[7], and his product is nothing short of genius. Surprisingly, Amazon began as an online bookstore[8], and didn't make a profit for its first 20 years. Many criticized its revenue model [9]and predicted that the company would eventually collapse. However, Bezos saw potential in the internet despite the dot-com bust [10]of 2003, which gave him the drive to stick to his guns.

As we all know, today, Amazon[11] sells everything from toothpicks to televisions, in addition to providing a robust platform for third-party sellers and touting services like Amazon Prime (which recently garnered 47

Emmy nominations[12] for Amazon original programs), Web Services[13] and Kindle – not to mention its 2017 acquisition of Whole Foods[14]. From a programming perspective, its level of integration is one of the most sophisticated systems[15] the world has ever seen (and is partially why it outshines its competitors). But it is Bezos's willingness to take risks[16] and visionary outlook that, arguably, have made Amazon grow into the (estimated) $1.5 trillion[17] empire it has become today. (Prior to the pandemic, even Bezos couldn't have predicted the swell in business[18] Amazon would experience because of and during the coronavirus-induced shutdowns and shelter-in-place restrictions). Its stock is even forecast to reach $5,000[19] by 2023, and in July 2020, they hit the $3000 mark[20].

Governs through frugality

Part of Amazon's success is due to the list of "Leadership Principles[21]" that governs it, which contain ideals such as, but not limited to, customer obsession[22] (as opposed to competitor obsession), learning, and, surprisingly, a commitment to frugality. Bezos contends that doing more with less breeds resourcefulness[23], self-sufficiency, and invention. For a company valued at over $1 trillion in the US market, one would think thriftiness would be less of a priority. Yet, Bezos's limited spending isn't just restricted to his enterprise; he drove a Honda Accord[24] up until 2013, and credits his past frugalness[25] for his own personal success. Though his recent purchase of a $165 million mansion[26] may seem contrary to frugality, the standards on which Amazon thrives are arguably the qualities of a good leader, and no one embodies them more than the company's CEO himself.

Creatively defies norms

Revolutionizing industries aside, Bezos creatively breaks all sorts of norms. He has been known to give away 4,500 bananas[27] every day to the needy of Seattle, among other efforts[28] and monetary contributions[29] to combat homelessness in that city. He's creating an organization devoted to tackling climate change and funding it with $10 billion[30] of his own money. His creativity also extends to the Washington Post, as he proposed a game[31] that would allow his readers to remove vowels from stories and let other readers restore them. Bezos also takes the concept of "thinking big" to new levels, as he is turning his childhood dream of space exploration[32] into a business venture[33] called Blue Origin[34] focused on space tourism[35]. As Bezos says[36], invention often "requires a long-term willingness to be understood," and this quality is what made Bezos one of the top innovators in the world.

Bezos Shouldn't Lead

Poor treatment of workers and others

Bezos has come under fire more than once for poorly treating his employees, both at Amazon and the Washington Post. He has been accused – by a writer of his own newspaper[37], no less – of freezing company pension plans, cutting retirement benefits, and withholding severance payments at the Post. A New York Times[38] article went after him in 2015, claiming that Amazon is a "bruising workplace;" there's evidence of employees being encouraged to rip each other's ideas apart in meetings, backstab one another by secretly sending feedback to their coworkers' bosses, and meet unreasonable standards (such as getting flack for failing to respond to work emails that have been sent after midnight).

It's also hard to ignore recent headlines about his alleged affair[39] with his friend's wife, which broke up his 25-year marriage[40] and resulted in the most expensive divorce in history[41], with Jeff paying his ex-wife $38 billion and a 4% stake in Amazon. Not to mention his recent testimony before Congress regarding alleged anti-competitive practices[42]. While no one is perfect, these attributes and suspicions don't make Bezos's character one to look up to.

Tax evasion

Among public accusations that have been leveled against Bezos are those that he has skirted sales taxes[43], while simultaneously collecting billions in subsidies from the US Post office — and these aren't off the mark. In 2017, the EU ruled that Amazon owed Luxembourg €250 million due to illegal tax advantages[44] that had allowed the corporation to get away with paying only a quarter of their revenue tax. In the same year, Amazon paid zero federal taxes[45], and has seemingly been exploiting tax loopholes at every level. Additionally, sales tax revenue hadn't been collected from Amazon third-party sellers in almost every state, prodding several states to go after Amazon[46] for the money.

What charity?

Until recently, Bezos exhibited a surprising lack[47] of philanthropic tendencies. True, in 2018, he pledged $2 billion[48] to address homelessness and education in Seattle, and more recently announced his intention to contribute $10 billion[49] to fight climate change. But, previously, his list of donations[50] fell far short compared to other tech-involved billionaires of his calibre, like Bill Gates,[51] Warren Buffet[52] and Mark Zuckerberg[53]. While it's true Bezos pledged $33 million[54] to fund 1000 Dreamers' college tuitions, this came on the heels of laying off hundreds of employees, and hiring temps[55] at low wages with no benefits – hardly philanthropic in spirit. Not to mention, pledging to fight climate change when Amazon remains an enormous polluter itself seems misguided[56].

....

The Bottom Line: Jeff Bezos is undoubtedly innovative, smart, and has a superb head for business, but what he has or hasn't done outside Amazon's success warrants scrutiny. Also interesting will be Bezos' future when he steps down from his CEO role in the second half of 2021. Do you think Bezos is an admirable role model?

THE PERSPECTIVE ON DIGITAL MARKETING

Original debate written by Daniel Ravner

I started out in marketing around 2005, when TheFacebook had just become Facebook; the email of choice was Hotmail. Marketing back then was what would be considered traditional marketing today. The industry was all about figuring out the client's brief (product launches, etc.) and coming up with a compelling, creative message to shout out to the world. Media (i.e., newspapers, television, banners) were secondary to that effort.

Things have changed since then.

The advent of analytics, performance marketing, pay per click (PPC), SEO, and the whole spectrum of data-driven advertising (which, for the sake of this debate, we'll bundle under "Digital Marketing") have created new ways to make an impact, measure it, and readjust, in a continuous loop. Media is now king, and the people who manage it make up the bulk of marketing professionals. In 2019, digital ad spending surpassed all other traditional ad venues put together[57].

These developments lead us to question: Is the move to digital marketing a long-awaited evolution? Have we become too reliant on quantifiable metrics or not nearly enough? Are advertisers today that much savvier or at more of an advantage than they were 15 years ago?

Here are three arguments against the hegemony of digital marketing and three for it.

The Case against Digital Marketing

The new normal

Sure, a decade ago, any marketer who knew how to work the new platforms of Facebook and Google had a major advantage over the established ad man, but those days are long gone. The analytical approach has created a reality where most marketers perform the same actions, on relatively few platforms. In his book Alchemy[58], Ogilvy vice-chairman Rory Sutherland asserts that if your entire marketing strategy is based on the logical and fairly established digital marketing venues, then your best-case scenario is reaching a crowded point, standing side by side with your competitors who have also followed the same logical and established routes. What's the point of marketing if it doesn't single you out?

The (real) secret of success

We assume that digital marketing took over traditional marketing because it provided a better result for those paying for it. However, there may be other factors that account for its success. Here are a couple such factors to consider:

The business world at large, and the hi-tech sector specifically, are characterized by leaders who come from one of two backgrounds: business or technology. For these analytical minds, Excel makes more sense than a creative hunch. A spreadsheet displaying CTR (click through rates) percentage over time is something they easily 'get'; hence, they welcome performance marketing. In other words, digital marketing is their default choice – not because it's necessarily better than traditional marketing but because it's more familiar.

This is also true for marketing agencies. With digital marketing, you have the playbook pretty much written before the client enters. The crucial know-how (CPC, CPA, CTR, etc.) relates to the media, not to the specific product. This is very different from traditional advertising, where you have to tailor a new strategy for each creative challenge. Also, with digital marketing, it's much easier to guarantee a 2-5 percent improvement year over year, which keeps the client happy.

People are strange

It doesn't matter if you're erecting a billboard or sending a mass newsletter. There is always one person at the other end of a marketing message. This person is a human being, and, as such, s/he is led by evolution, circumstance, mood, culture and subconscious to an equal or greater degree than logic. The basic idea here is that you can't use a rational tool to illicit action from an emotional and unpredictable being. (Ever tried to logically persuade someone from the opposite political agenda about your point of view? Did it work?)

Our attachment to our views despite evidence to the contrary is well documented[59]. This innate human "failure" also comes into play in the way we understand data. Big data means that there are enough facts to support more than one claim. We can more easily identify and demonstrate patterns we are partial to, or as the renowned economist Ronald H. Cause once said: "If you torture the data long enough, it will tell you anything."

The Case for Digital Marketing

You can't improve what you can't measure

Any advancement that you can measure, be it revenues, productivity or number of employees, is what drives business forward. Digital marketing provides a clear understanding of what works and what needs fixing[60]. It's astounding to think that for generations, marketing was so expensive (up front) and offered so little in the way of clear return on investment. The tools and technology that are now part of digital marketing allow us to reach the relevant people with the relevant message, while eliminating redundant costs. (How many viewers of a dog food ad on TV actually have a dog?)

It elevated the whole marketing industry

For a long while, marketing was seen as an important but not crucial function. It was the realm of the 'creative folks' and not of the people who actually built the business. Digital marketing matured the entire advertising industry and made marketing accountable. Unlike traditional marketing's elusive ROI, with digital marketing, it suddenly became clear where money was going and how much of it was earned in return – the same as any other business function. Marketing was invited to the big boys' table and, as a result, became more influential, more professional, enjoyed increased budgets and bigger staff.

It opened up opportunities

Traditional marketing was thought of as an operation that only takes effect once the product was ready to launch. In contrast, digital marketing (or more specifically product marketing) is thought of as part of an ongoing process in which feedback is collected and product improvements are made continuously. Through marketing data (i.e., how many people have reacted to a specific message or product), customers get to influence the products they consume.

This integration of marketing into the company's core business is key to the rise of many online giants. For companies like Booking.com, the optimization of marketing reach is what determines their revenue. The publishing industry's revenue is comprised of the gap between the cost of acquiring a user and the money that can be made during their stay on a website (ads, subscription, etc.). There is a whole subset of businesses that drive traffic to other sites for a portion of revenue. Their whole operation is nothing but online marketing.

Digital marketing also opened up new opportunities for small and medium business, where traditional marketing offered very few options for a local business. Digital marketing enhances the voice and precision of any interested individual for any budget and with minimal know-how.

The Bottom Line: Humans are more complex than marketing data (exclusively drawn from the past) would suggest. But data provides metrics that are crucial for managing advancement, suggesting there may be an advantage to combining both traditional and digital marketing.

CAN FACEBOOK MAINTAIN DOMINANCE?

Original debate written by Jordan Stutts

Facebook has become a household name around the world for revolutionizing communication. Its services have forever changed how people interact with each other and businesses. However, a string of controversies[61], specifically its role in the 2016 elections[62] and 2020 US Capitol riots[63], have raised questions about its dominance and influence over its 2.7 billion users[64] worldwide.

Here are three arguments for Facebook being so successful that its status can't be jeopardized and three more arguments that the company has already passed its high point.

Facebook Is in a League of Its Own That Can't Be Challenged

The true unicorn

In Silicon Valley terms, a 'unicorn' is a tech start-up company valued at over $1 Billion. Facebook has become the model of this success, launching in 2004 and earning $20 Billion[65] in revenues in 2020, a more-than 22% increase year over year. Though Facebook experienced a drop in advertising sales because of the coronavirus[66] and unrelated backlash from advertisers[67] who boycotted Mark Zuckerberg's slow response to banning misinformation and hate speech from the platform, the company is still planning for future growth beyond facebook.com through its growing dominance in the field of VR[68] and from payments and e-commerce, including its own currency[69].

Facebook has sustained its growth by acquiring other in-demand apps[70], like Instagram and WhatsApp, and building an all-in-one information empire. Its more than 2.6 billion[71] monthly users dwarf other social media giants including Instagram (around 1 billion) – which Facebook bought in 2012 – and Twitter (around 330 million[72]).

Facebook built a platform users don't want to leave

Facebook's real power over users is evident in its ability to keep them on its platform for longer and for a greater variety of needs. By knowing its users and showing them what they want, Facebook has developed a habit-forming product that keeps users online every time a user is looking for [73]distraction, an ego boost, or a social connection.

The company's endless tweaks to its algorithm[74] aim to maintain its appeal. Back in 2016, for example, the company changed the algorithms[75] running its News Feed so that "things posted by friends you care about are higher up" in the feed. Since then, changes in its algorithm have centered more on eliminating fake news[76] and hate speech, especially after the US Capitol riots[77].

Their efforts have worked: more people are turning to Facebook as their medium for news consumption. Pew research[78] shows that a third of Americans get their news from Facebook compared to YouTube at 23% among online sources.

The amount of personal information Facebook has is insane

While Facebook has been known to obtain sensitive device data from hundreds of thousands of users, the platform has long been collecting information its users willingly give to use its services, from age, location and gender to long-distance relationships and expectant parents. This is how Facebook makes its money[79]: from selling this information to advertisers targeting users based on what they're likely to buy. The Federal Trade Commission reports that Acxiom, one of Facebook's largest advertising partners, has 3,000 data segments[80] for almost every US consumer. With such targeting abilities over a massive user base, it's easy to see why advertisers are pouring in money[81] to obtain results that are harder to get from other platforms.

Nothing Lasts Forever

Security scandals

Facebook has come under fire more than once for security breaches. Considering the amount of user information Facebook has access to, these breaches – culminating in election scandals[82], which left Facebook $60 billion poorer – could have severe impacts on everything from identity theft to election fraud.

Data analytics firm Cambridge Analytica[83] obtained personal information of over 50 million Facebook users without their consent, and used it to target individuals to help Donald Trump win the 2016 election. As a result, Facebook negotiated a $5 billion settlement[84] with the Federal Trade Commission. While being the largest fine of its kind in history, many say that this punishment is still too lenient[85]. Additionally, Facebook reportedly gave data[86] on millions of its users to former President Obama's second election campaign, which could be a major violation of federal campaign finance law.

In light of all this, many people think that Facebook can't be trusted[87] with its users' personal information. One lone corporation should not have this much power at its disposal. To allay users' and critics' fears, the company has agreed to create a privacy committee[88] to protect user data, in addition to an external assessor, appointed by the company and the FTC.

Facebook can't control its content

Over recent years, several instances have eroded users' trust in Facebook. The launch of Facebook's live-streaming service[89] in 2015 resulted in unintended consequences[90] as people have begun using it to broadcast[91] mass killings, rapes, suicides and the riots at the US Capitol building[92]. Some question whether the live streaming has opened a social media Pandora's box[93], especially after a terrorist used Facebook's live-streaming while attacking mosques in Christchurch, New Zealand[94], and a German shooter[95] used Amazon's Twitch to live broadcast his mass attack on a synagogue in Germany. Despite changes to Facebook's algorithm to prevent the prevalence of fake news and hate speech, Facebook has still come under scrutiny for its inability to control[96] the proliferation of it on its site. An Ipsos Public

Affairs poll shows that 18% of respondents trust news[97] on Facebook most of the time, compared to 44% who said they almost never do.

Facebook faces competition from other online advertisers

Other tech giants such as Google and Amazon are looking to advertisements for growth, with the latter commanding over 10% of market share of the US digital advertising market in 2020[98], Google takin 28.9% of revenue share, and 25.2% to Facebook.

Furthermore, investors may be in search of the next unicorn. Enter TikTok: In 2019, the Chinese app was downloaded more than 738 million times[99], beating Facebook and Instagram. The app's growth continues, in the West and in China, where Facebook is not allowed to operate. In fact, in 2020, alone, TikTok had 500 million new users[100] sign up, which is half of all Instagram users.

The Bottom Line: Facebook controls an enormous amount of personal and public information, giving it an advantage in the market that is very hard to match. But maintaining that level of dominance is almost impossible, and Facebook is facing mass criticism for privacy issues, content issues[101] and influence that seem to be spiralling out of the company's control. Do you think Facebook will continue to grow, or is it already tumbling down from its peak?

THE PERSPECTIVE ON STEVE JOBS

Original debate written by Kira Goldring

Most well-known as the co-founder of Apple, billionaire Steve Jobs had many far-reaching accomplishments and achievements under his belt. Although he died in 2011, he remains a symbol of innovation, drive, charisma and success – but also one of aggression and, some would say, tyranny[102]. While he was a man of obvious importance, we have to ask ourselves: What kind of overall legacy did Jobs leave behind?

Here are three reasons why he may not have been the best source of inspiration for a new generation, and three reasons to follow in his footsteps.

Not the Jobs You'd Hoped For

Exploitation

Most consumers would agree that the ends don't justify the means if a child is being harmed in the making of a product. Yet, by its own admission[103], Apple regularly employed teenagers and children below the age of 16 in their factories in China in 2010. These children, among other Chinese employees, worked in sweatshop-like conditions; they were paid terribly low wages, forced to work fifteen-hour shifts, had no access to air conditioning and constantly endured bug infestations – all so they could create Apple phones and computers. It's no wonder that 11 workers committed suicide[104] that year. While seemingly responsive to the suicides, Jobs denied the existence of the factories' poor working conditions. However, since Jobs stepped down as CEO of Apple in 2011[105], the company has become much more socially responsible[106] – putting Jobs at the root of the corporation's exploitative past.

Hostile work environment

In Apple's early beginnings, while Jobs may have run the company effectively, he is said to have treated his own employees and coworkers poorly. He had an informal policy of belittling his workers[107], and the overall corporate culture was one of secrecy and intimidation. Over the years, staff members have anonymously testified to the constant tension[108] they felt working under Jobs; in fact, Jobs was ousted by Apple[109] in 1985, amidst complaints that he was too demanding of his workers. Although he was later rehired after Apple had financial trouble in 1997, his authoritarian style of leading never wavered. After the disastrous launch of MobileMe[110], for example, Jobs famously gathered the team who created it so he could shout expletives at them and publicly fire the manager[111] of the project.

The man behind the Mac

Work wasn't the only place where Jobs came off as rough around the edges. Philanthropy was not his strong suit; in fact, there is no public record of Jobs[112] having given anything to charity, despite the billions he had to his name when he died. On a personal level, his moral principles were found lacking more than once. For instance, in deciding whether or not to appoint him to a government position, an FBI file [113]was opened; the report concluded – based on testimonies of friends, acquaintances and employees – that Jobs lacked personal integrity[114]. His honesty was questioned numerous times, especially when he denied fathering a child[115] that he later admitted to be his. Jobs may have been a computer whiz, but his personal connections with people had something left to be desired.

Job(s) Well Done

Foresight

Steve Jobs was, simply put, a visionary. Similar to his longtime friend and rival, Bill Gates[116], Jobs envisioned a world that included personal computers for everyone. His brains and commitment[117] helped him bring this vision to life, leading to the creation of Apple. Today, Apple is close to becoming the world's first $1 trillion dollar company[118], whose laptops, iPhones, smart watches, and iPads reside in nearly two-thirds[119] of American households. Like with Apple, Jobs always played a few steps ahead, and he foresaw the potential futures of music, phones, digital content and tablet computing. As a result of this forward-thinking, he ultimately disrupted half a dozen industries[120] with his genius.

Perseverance

Few have the unique blend of creativity and perfectionism that characterized Steve Jobs – traits that made him a billionaire[121]. Yet, what put Jobs ahead of other revolutionaries was his blatant refusal to give up. The best example of this was when Jobs bought Pixar[122] in 1986, following a (temporary) dismissal from Apple. When Pixar came into financial trouble, just eight years after its acquisition, Jobs didn't sell the company; instead, he invested millions of his own[123] to keep Pixar afloat. His perseverance paid off: Pixar came out with the first computer-animated film – the famous "Toy Story[124]" – and the movie made the company $360 million. "Toy Story" was a hit, and, like Apple, Pixar went on to become a multi-billion dollar [125]company.

Inspiration

Jobs wasn't just a tech maven or business guru; he was an inspirational success story. Many remember the last few years of his life, in which he battled cancer and openly reassessed his life's priorities. He is still praised for his famous commencement address[126] at Stanford University, in which he managed to poignantly cover subjects like love, loss and death in fifteen minutes[127]. (The speech has since been viewed over 30 million times.) Jobs aired his struggles (such as being fired from his own company), triumphs, difficulties and successes, in an effort to convey a carpe diem-centered message to his audience. His final advice in the speech was to "Stay Hungry. Stay Foolish," and he encouraged listeners to view death as an opportunity to chase their dreams.

Jobs may no longer be alive, but his words of wisdom still resonate[128] today. Six movies[129] have been made about him. Tens of books[130] attest to his genius. And execs[131] in companies from Tesla to Disney revamped their companies for the better, thanks to Jobs's advice[132] to dream big.

The Bottom Line: Steve Jobs effected change across a myriad of industries, but the controversial means through which he ran his businesses and conducted himself rendered him a questionable character. What do you think? Has Jobs's legacy had a long-lasting impact on your life?

IOS OR ANDROID - WHICH SMARTPHONE IS BETTER?

Original debate written by Kira Goldring

More than 99% of the world's smartphones[133] are operated by either iOS[134] (Apple) or Android[135] (Google) and each OS is affiliated with its hardware, meaning the OS you want is worth considering when you buy your phone. But which operating system is the ultimate cell phone winner? Both are smart, both are sleek – and both have their drawbacks.

Below, we'll explore three reasons for choosing iOS for your communication needs, and three reasons to opt for Android.

Team Apple

Most Secure

"Macs don't get viruses," was the common trope[136] paraded around when Apple first introduced their distinguished computers – and this statement extended to iPhones. iOS products are far less susceptible to viruses than Android because of Apple's level of exclusivity. iPhone apps can only be installed from the Apple Mac Store, providing a level of control over the malware that gets through. This seems to work effectively, as a much higher percentage[137] of mobile malware[138] targets Android than iOS; Nokia's latest threat intelligence report indicated that Android devices are fifty times more likely[139] to be infected by malware than Apple devices. So, to answer whether iOS or Android, when choosing the right phone for you, it seems that iOS is the safer choice.

Need for speed

Despite the 2017 controversy[140] surrounding slowed iPhones, subsequent iPhones, like the iPhone 8 plus[141] and the iPhone X[142], utilized an A11 Bionic chip[143], providing incomparable power and speed to iOS devices and adding a 25% increase in speed[144] when compared to its predecessors. Apple's latest is the A14 Bionic chip, which outperformed the Galaxy[145] Note 20 Ultra in transcoding a short 4K video in 26 seconds compared to the latter's 73. So, in addition to speed, the phones also have some 5 extra hours of battery life and a significant performance boost. It's no wonder, then, that gamers also appreciate the steep speed difference between iPhones and Androids, as iPhones facilitate a smoother experience when playing augmented-reality (and other intensive) games.

Constantly updated

In the iOS or Android debate, the former far outshines the latter with regard to updating devices with the newest operating system, and it has proven to have better support for older phone models than does Android. For example, iOS 14 – which was officially released in September, 2020 – is already being run on 80% of iOS devices[146], and 86% of iOS devices introduced in the last four years. By contrast, as of the Android Studio[147]'s latest update, less than 1% of Androids are using the latest OS, Android 11.

Team Google

Variety and compatibility

The Android platform is an open-source system[148], which means you can have access to any apps[149] you want, regardless of the maker – over a million more[150] than iOS provides. Additionally, any phone carrier can create devices for Android, and users can download any available Android system. In contrast, as mentioned above, iOS is exclusive, mainly because it's a closed-source system. This locks you in to using everything Apple once you commit to iOS; your devices will only be compatible with other Apple products, you can only troubleshoot technical issues in an Apple Store, and your available apps are limited to whatever Apple decides you should have.

Price

When contemplating iOS or Android, both have what to offer in terms of quality, but Android provides the quality at lower cost[151]. For developers[152], publishing an unlimited number of apps through the Android marketplace is affordable at $25 – where iOS costs $99 for the same – and there is a higher percentage of free apps in Google Play Store than in the iOS App Store. This, combined with the fact that Android provides low-cost, quality handsets[153] that are hundreds of dollars cheaper than iPhone's newer models, makes the choice a simple one. The proof is in the numbers: Android holds almost 75%[154] of market share around the world.

User experience

Android is the future, holding court when it comes to voice interfaces and AI[155]. Google Assistant[156] (GA) far surpasses Siri as a virtual assistant, with more accurate responses to questions and tailor-made service; for example, GA can read text on images[157] and convert it into meaningful calendar updates, notes, etc., while Siri is still trying to piece together the answers to basic questions. Not to mention that Google, basically the infrastructure of the web, has a much bigger fountain of data from which to draw when perfecting their services. There doesn't seem to be much to consider when asking iOS or Android[158].

The Bottom Line: The tight-knit hardware/software combination of iOS clearly provides users with quality mobile devices, while Android's overall compatibility makes it cheaper and more easily customizable. So, iOS or Android? What kind of phone are you going to buy next?

THE PERSPECTIVE ON ELON MUSK

Original debate written by Kira Goldring

Few have as impressive a resume as tech giant (and recent SNL host[159]) Elon Musk. A household name and innovative billionaire, Musk co-founded PayPal, Tesla and Neurolink, has put forth numerous ground-breaking projects (anyone ready for a trip to the moon or to Mars[160]?), and has won scores of accolades and awards. He was even the inspiration for Robert Downey Jr.'s portrayal of Iron Man[161].

So, is Musk the superhero that the world has portrayed him as, or given a number of controversies[162] that have resulted in lawsuits, raised eyebrows[163], and his 2018 removal[164] as Tesla chairman, are we romanticizing who he is at our own peril?

Elon Musk Is a Hero

Transformed multiple industries for the better

Musk is a visionary[165], and his dreams alone have had a positive global impact. His car company Tesla[166] has steered the automotive industry towards semi-autonomous vehicles[167] and electric cars[168], globally reducing vehicle emissions. Because of Musk, analysts[169] now believe that over half the cars sold by 2040 will be electric. The public agrees with Musk's vision; a poll[170] taken before the coronavirus pandemic showed that almost 50% of people believe Tesla is the most innovative technology company in recent years. Demand[171] confirms this: Its Model 3 sedans became the world's best-selling all-electric vehicle model[172] in 2020.

Additionally, Musk has demonstrated that the space industry can be privatized, and for the better; his company SpaceX[173] has seen the successful return of rockets[174] back to Earth after being launched into space[175]. Its Dragon[176] more recently succeeded in delivering a capsule of supplies to the International Space Station. These show that privatization ventures may significantly reduce costs of space exploration.

No stranger to adversity

As a man with an unhappy childhood and unfortunate circumstances growing up, Musk is a role model for those of lesser means and difficult conditions. Having survived both bullying and emotional abuse,[177] he still managed to code and sell his first video game at 12 years old, and his creativity hasn't stopped since. His failures were many before his success; Musk was removed from his CEO position at two of his own companies[178], survived malaria, and oversaw three failed launches after the creation of SpaceX (which left the company almost bankrupt).

He also settled with the SEC[179] after being accused of misleading investors[180] and agreed to step down as Tesla chairman, pay a $20 million fine but to remain as CEO. More recently, a Los Angeles court found Musk not guilty of defamation[181] after he made a series of Tweets, calling a British diver who was part of the life-saving efforts of a Thai youth soccer team stranded in underwater caves a pedophile after the diver rejected Musk's offer of a submarine. No matter how wealthy, brilliant (or, at times, petulant[182], especially when told that he couldn't yet re-open his Tesla plant due statewide coronavirus stay-at-home orders), Musk's experiences with hardship and failure make him relatable to the common man.

It's not about the money

Aside from creating over 35,000 jobs worldwide[183], Musk has put his own money on the line to ensure his employees continue to have jobs. In fact, he invested $20 million[184] into saving Tesla after it was on the cusp of bankruptcy in 2015, and he has never taken a paycheck[185] from the company. Additionally, $100 million[186] of his own money went into funding SpaceX – a risky investment, as the space industry had never been privatized before. He has quietly donated[187] to charities and has reportedly pledged to give away at least half of his money when he dies. More recently, he put 5 homes[188] up for sale worth almost $100 million in total after pledging on

Twitter that he aims to own no physical possessions. Time will tell what he will do with the money from the sales.

Elon Musk Is Only Human

Ignoring the little guy

Musk may be worthy of his glory but getting to his end-goal has a price, and he is not necessarily the one paying it. In fact, some critics even go so far as saying that during the height of the pandemic, he played with his employees' lives[189] by re-opening his Tesla plant even after two Tesla workers tested positive[190] for COVID-19 and before California authorities recommended re-opening for business. Health risks aside, SpaceX staff have often been presented with impossible tasks[191], like pulling all-nighters[192] after working 12-hour days, in order to meet the deadlines Musk expects from them. His Tesla workers filed charges[193] in 2017 with the National Labor Board against him, citing coercion, hazardous working conditions, intimidation, illegal surveillance and prevention of worker communications as their main reasons for doing so.

Idealization is harmful to the collective

Social comparison theory[194] posits that human beings have an innate drive that leads them to compare themselves to other, more successful people. This can lead to negative self-esteem, envy, and unrealistic standards of success. Musk plays his own part in this comparison, creating the perception that he's the sole embodiment[195] of technological prowess. Yet, it's easy to forget that, in reality, Musk wouldn't have been able to get where he is without government funding[196], subsidies for electric cars, etc. It also helps to have a (now former) president's full and public support[197] and admiration[198].

Furthermore, Musk's elevation by the public to a capitalist idol[199] "has distorted the flow of capital and talent. Healthy markets don't take cues from the tweets of one man," writes American author and business professor Scott Galloway[200]. For example, Musk's outsized influence[201] on raising (or lowering, in the case of Dogecoin[202]) the value, popularity and production of cryptocurrency has masked the truth that the high level of carbon emissions[203] from increased mining of Bitcoin significantly reduces if not wipes out any carbon savings of Teslas.

There are other causes to focus on

A man of Musk's means, brilliance and stature has the power to significantly change the world for the better, yet he often devotes his resources towards projects that are arguably rooted in vanity. For example, his SpaceX Falcon Heavy Test Launch project – in which a Tesla sports car was launched into space – cost $90 million[204] to execute, and didn't contribute to any scientific or humanitarian gains. That money could have been used to further STEM research[205], launch satellites into orbit or end malaria, to name a few. Instead, it was used to begin a space race[206] with a car of Musk's own making, a project Musk defended as something "silly and fun."

Additionally, his Hyperloop[207] project – estimated to cost billions[208] – has been criticized as a parallel transportation network intended for catering to the rich[209]. With money and power often comes hubris, and it seems as though Musk isn't an exception to this rule. He has particularly shown arrogance with regard to the coronavirus and the stock market, as seen in some of his insensitive and even irresponsible comments[210] dismissing the dangers of COVID-19, and his careless (or deliberate?) Tweets causing tumult in the values of publicly traded companies[211], with real-life consequences for shareholders.

The Bottom line: Innovative and driven, Elon Musk has contributed immensely to the world of technological ingenuity. However, his celebrity-like persona may have given him personal and professional leeway, and thus has negative consequences[212] on society. Is Elon Musk someone you look up to?

THE PERSPECTIVE ON GOOGLE

Original debate written by Kira Goldring

Google: The world's encyclopedia, doctor, confessional and friend. Its creators, Larry Page and Sergey Brin, met at Stanford University, where Brin worked with Page on his doctoral thesis[213] regarding the World Wide Web. Their project later went on to become the heart and soul of the digital revolution – Google. With 77,500 searches[214] per second, or 2.5 trillion searches a year, Google Search Engine alone is one of the main doors to the internet. Celebrating its 22nd year[215], the tech giant is clearly powerful[216], but is Google too powerful, as the US government's lawsuit[217] against it claims? For instance, Google alone owns 90%[218] of the worldwide search market. And, how is this power affecting mankind? Does Google uphold its previous motto[219] of "don't be evil"?

Here are three reasons Google is a force for good, and three reasons it has too much power.

A Force for Good

Puts the world on equal footing

Google brings new meaning to globalization. Thanks to the last decade of the company's innovation and low-cost mobile broadband[220], developing countries[221] like India[222], among many others, have free access to information, to which much of the rest of the world is already privy. With Google Search operating in over 135 different languages[223] and Google Translate operating in 108 languages[224], the company's ability to provide accurate translations to so many international viewers means that every web page is territory to be charted equally by anyone around the globe. Also, because the company is privately owned[225], the speed at which it can impact developing nations is much faster than that of governments with complicated interests to protect. Plus, Google's annual Economic Impact reports assert that its search and advertising tools helped drive $385 billion [226]in US economic activity in 2019. It's ads and searches directly led to clicks for 16 million American businesses alone that same year.

Transformative – at no cost

Besides its search engine, the company's other platforms have also positively reshaped the ways in which we function – for no direct fee. YouTube[227] has transformed the music, television and advertising industries, putting a new, democratic spin[228] on the idea of celebrity. It recently introduced a console-free cloud-gaming platform[229]. Google's APIs for Android[230] has allowed people to develop their own apps and utilize them to grow revenue. Gmail, Chrome, Google Maps and Google Photos[231] have way over 2 billion[232] users combined, with Google Drive closing in on 1 billion users[233] itself. Just building and maintaining data centers to support such platforms costs upwards of $10 billion[234], but the company enables free use of every product. It has created scores and scores of free, useful tools [235]that have altered the way humans exist day to day.

Size matters

Google has immense access to research on every subject in any field, allowing them to advance science in a way no other company can. In 2010-2011, the company acquired[236] an average of more than one company per week[237] (Fitbit[238], anyone?). Its mere vastness and computational power[239] can be directed towards studying things like machine learning[240] and interactions between computers and humans – which is how they're on the way to creating self-driving cars[241]. A[242]lphabet Inc[243]. – Google's parent company – is tackling everything from home automation to drone delivery. Additionally, the company uses its wealth of information for humanitarian work, such as fighting child exploitation [244]and tracking flu trends[245] across populations, most recently helping with contract-tracing efforts to combat the spread of the coronavirus[246] and providing $6.5 million[247] in funding fact-checkers and nonprofits working to fight the spread of misinformation about the virus. It's undeniable that the company's power and prestige have greatly benefited the future of mankind.

Too Much Power

Complete control

Together with Facebook[248], Google controls nearly 70% [249] of the market in digital advertising; with its DFP (DoubleClick for Publishers), the company commands the infrastructure on which the majority of advertisements are managed. There are more than 2.9 million companies[250] that use one or more of Google's marketing services. After Google Search, the second largest search engine is Google-owned YouTube[251]. Because of this, it's the company's way or the highway. Hence, the US antitrust lawsuit against the tech giant.

This lawsuit aside, the company was under several antitrust probes[252] stemming from multiple countries, on the basis of it being a monopoly[253]. In 2018, they also faced Congressional scrutiny[254] for building what was perceived as a censored search engine for the Chinese market. Sure, there are alternative search engines like DuckDuckGo or Yahoo, but none have nearly the same reach – or overall offerings – as Google provides. So, is Google too powerful? The answer seems clear.

Goodbye, privacy

While people have the choice of whether to use Google's services, the fact is that it's expected, and difficult to survive the corporate or social worlds without it. Corporations rely on Google Calendar to share schedules between employees. Gmail has 1.5 billion users[255], which means the company has access to that many emails. Google Maps – which automatically comes with any Android phone – gives Google your exact location, at all times. None of this addresses the access the company has to your search history[256], from which they compile a profile[257] of you in order to target you with relevant advertisements. Is Google too powerful? Consider this: Its search engine market share is 90%[258]. The US government seems to think that Google is an illegal monopoly[259] and is consequently suing the tech giant[260] to break it up and halt alleged antitrust abuses.

While Facebook gets a lot of flak for data manipulation[261], you have to choose to be on one of their three platforms to have your data compromised; Google, on the other hand, is practically the whole web, with minimal competitors[262], so no place is safe[263] – not even your health records[264]! A 2019 hospital data-sharing deal[265] where Google partnered with a prominent US hospital network, acquiring patient information for tens of millions of patients without their consent is one manifestation of these privacy issues.

Undue influence in government and academia

Google has been accused of using its wealth to influence all levels of policymakers. This accusation seems to carry weight; the company has funded 330 papers on public policy[266] alone since 2005. Additionally, in trying to defend themselves against claims that Google tampered with a 2012 FTC investigation, the company admitted in 2015 to having influence[267] in Washington across a number of political domains. It's not only the government that's swayed by Google's authority; academic research teams haven't necessarily been aware of who the patrons are that sponsor their grants. A 2017 report[268] revealed that Google-funded studies suddenly increased when regulators threatened the company's business model – evidence of the level of Google's academic influence and power.

....

The Bottom Line: Google continuously offers the world tools through which anyone can thrive, in addition to many positive scientific and health advancements, especially in efforts to fight the coronavirus[269]. However, the level of control the company has across multiple domains and sectors is a cause for unease and may constitute an abuse of power and privacy[270]. So, is Google too powerful? Do you think it has the world's best interests in mind?

ACKNOWLEDGEMENTS

The Perspective is a startup. Like many startups, it needed an angel to become a reality, and we found ours in the shape of Jack Rimokh and the Rimokh Family Trust. We also want to thank Jae Park for being the connection between our angel and our workshop.

Another truth about startups is that anyone who is there from the start has to have the ability to be both its president and its intern. Rachel Segal has managed to be all of those things and more for The Perspective, since day one.

My gratitude for the writers featured in this book. Leading the pack is Julian Bonte-Friedheim, the master of trending perspectives, and following are: Chaya Benyamin, Zoe Jordan, Talia Klien Perez, Kira Goldring, Andrew Vitelli, Lee Mesika, Josh Gabbatiss, Steve Nash, Xygalatas Dimitris, Matin Bilman, Elad de Piccioto, Jordan Stutts and Malkie Khutoretsky.

Thank you to Dr. Gali Einav and Ofir Allen from Herzelia IDC Interdisciplinary Center, for believing in The Perspective enough to actually examine its effects through two academic research projects.

The younger and leaner the venture, the more meaningful is each member's contribution to its journey and success. This book is based on the work we've done on theperspective.com since 2017, which is filled with the imprint and wisdom of the following key members:

Design – Keren Soref
Development – Kiril Lavrishev
Legal – Ittai Tschernichovsky
Advisory board – Jacob Nizri, Gali Arnon, Yaki Gani, and Moran Saar

Monetization – Ono Magic

My wingman – Nadav Katz

Thank you is too small an expression to capture the degree of gratitude and connection I feel for my family, who always show up when it counts – and when it doesn't: Silvia and David Ravner, Liat, Yoav, Gidi, Tali, Anna, Miriam, Shalom, Sherry, Itamar, Revital, Glen, Aria and Ray. The same goes for my extended family, my friends, my Ramla crew, and my clients at Ravner.

Thank you, my Alex, Mila and Emmanuelle for always being the best answer to questions born in my best and worst moments.

To my partner, my heart, and best decision ever – Einat.

Lastly, thank you - The Perspective readers.

ENDNOTES

Politics

1 https://www.businessinsider.com/legal-marijuana-states-2018-1
2 https://www.vox.com/identities/2018/8/20/17938366/medical-marijuana-legalization-states-map
3 https://apnews.com/ae6205b0a71443afb61b9486adecef8a
4 https://edition.cnn.com/2018/06/20/health/canada-legalizes-marijuana/index.html
5 https://www.vice.com/en_us/article/gy4pa7/these-are-the-countries-most-likely-to-legalize-weed-next
6 https://www.canna-tech.co/cannatech/legal-cannabis-carbon-footprint/
7 http://www.cpr.org/news/story/nearly-4-percent-of-denver-s-electricity-is-now-devoted-to-marijuana
8 https://www.forbes.com/sites/debraborchardt/2016/09/22/cannabis-attracting-mainstream-research-analysts/
9 https://borgenproject.org/addiction-poverty-connected/
10 http://archive.boston.com/news/local/articles/2008/04/03/alcohol_more_available_in_poor_black_areas/
11 http://www.cde.ca.gov/fg/fr/eb/
12 http://www.politico.com/magazine/story/2016/05/what-works-colorado-denver-marijuana-pot-industry-legalization-neighborhoods-dispensaries-negative-213906
13 http://www.latimes.com/nation/la-oe-shapiro-marijuana-danger-20150104-story.html
14 https://www.usatoday.com/story/news/nation/2019/12/15/weed-psychosis-high-thc-cause-suicide-schizophrenia/4168315002/
15 https://www.childrenscolorado.org/conditions-and-advice/conditions-and-symptoms/conditions/acute-marijuana-intoxication/

16 http://health.usnews.com/health-news/patient-advice/articles/2016-10-12/marijuanas-public-health-pros-and-cons
17 https://luxury.rehabs.com/marijuana-rehab/addiction-statistics/
18 https://www.verywellmind.com/what-are-the-costs-of-drug-abuse-to-society-63037
19 https://www.cato.org/publications/tax-budget-bulletin/budgetary-effects-ending-drug-prohibition
20 https://www.cato.org/publications/tax-budget-bulletin/budgetary-effects-ending-drug-prohibition
21 https://www.forbes.com/sites/erikkain/2011/07/05/ten-years-after-decriminalization-drug-abuse-down-by-half-in-portugal/
22 http://www.foxnews.com/world/2010/12/26/portugals-drug-policy-pays-eyes-lessons.html
23 http://www.drugwarfacts.org/cms/Netherlands_v_US
24 https://www.scientificamerican.com/article/colorado-s-teen-marijuana-usage-dips-after-legalization/
25 https://www.boulderweekly.com/features/weed-between-the-lines/cannabis-use-drops-among-colorado-teens/
26 https://www.grandviewresearch.com/press-release/global-legal-marijuana-market
27 https://www.washingtonpost.com/news/wonk/wp/2016/10/27/the-marijuana-industry-created-over-18000-new-jobs-in-colorado-last-year/?utm_term=.8caf368960d0
28 http://www.cheatsheet.com/money-career/jobs-being-created-by-the-marijuana-industry.html/?a=viewall
29 https://www.nytimes.com/2016/09/08/us/veterans-back-on-patrol-this-time-to-protect-marijuana.html
30 https://www.sciencedirect.com/science/article/pii/S0165032718303100?via%3Dihub
31 http://www.quotationspage.com/quote/40429.html
32 https://en.wikipedia.org/wiki/Horseshoe_theory
33 http://www.latimes.com/local/lanow/la-me-berkeley-trump-20170416-story.html
34 https://www.nytimes.com/2017/08/13/us/charlottesville-virginia-overview.html
35 https://www.npr.org/2018/07/01/625095869/police-declare-a-riot-after-far-right-and-antifa-groups-clash-in-portland
36 https://www.cbsnews.com/video/authorities-suspect-white-supremacists-and-far-left-extremists-are-behind-violence-at-protests/
37 https://greatergood.berkeley.edu/article/item/suffering_may_lead_to_extreme_political_beliefs
38 https://www.theatlantic.com/science/archive/2017/08/the-worlds-worst-support-group/536850/

39 https://www.vice.com/en_us/article/7xqjv9/neo-nazis-are-giving-black-lives-matter-and-antifa-a-reason-to-work-together
40 https://www.abc.net.au/news/2020-06-07/police-brutality-caught-on-film-black-lives-matter/12330672
41 https://www.theatlantic.com/politics/archive/2015/09/the-rise-of-victimhood-culture/404794/
42 https://www.washingtonpost.com/outlook/2019/02/28/when-americans-loved-benito-mussolini/
43 https://www.theperspective.com/debates/politics/perspective-che-guevara/
44 https://www.youtube.com/watch?v=RIrcB1sAN8I
45 https://www.adl.org/education/resources/reports/dark-constant-rage-25-years-of-right-wing-terrorism-in-united-states
46 http://www.smithsonianmag.com/history/what-was-protest-group-students-democratic-society-five-questions-answered-180963138/
47 https://www.theguardian.com/world/2020/jun/06/what-is-antifa-trump-terrorist-designation
48 https://www.huffingtonpost.com/entry/boredom-and-political-extremism_us_5786491de4b03fc3ee4ea12c
49 https://www.nytimes.com/2017/08/04/education/edlife/antifa-collective-university-california-berkeley.html
50 https://qz.com/561848/its-not-the-poverty-in-the-middle-east-thats-driving-terrorism-its-the-politics/
51 https://www.scientificamerican.com/article/calling-truce-political-wars/
52 http://www2.ucsc.edu/whorulesamerica/change/left_and_right.html
53 https://www.theperspective.com/subjective-timeline/politics/rise-power-nazi-party/
54 https://www.cbsnews.com/news/marine-corps-to-remove-public-displays-of-confederate-battle-flag-2020-06-06/
55 http://www.bbc.com/news/world-us-canada-40966800
56 https://www.adl.org/resources/backgrounders/who-are-the-antifa
57 https://www.vox.com/2017/8/25/16189064/antifa-charlottesville-activism-mark-bray-interview
58 https://www.unhcr.org/refugee-statistics/
59 https://www.unhcr.org/refugee-statistics/
60 https://www.nytimes.com/2021/04/19/us/biden-refugees-psaki.html
61 https://www.reuters.com/world/americas/biden-keeps-us-refugee-cap-15000-rather-than-raise-it-official-2021-04-16/
62 https://www.amnesty.org/en/what-we-do/refugees-asylum-seekers-and-migrants/global-refugee-crisis-statistics-and-facts/
63 https://edition.cnn.com/2018/12/22/europe/france-strasbourg-attacker-intl/index.html
64 http://insider.foxnews.com/2016/06/16/cia-director-warns-isis-using-refugee-streams-move-operatives

65 https://www.theguardian.com/world/2016/mar/01/refugees-isis-nato-commander-terrorists
66 http://www.politico.eu/article/german-intelligence-warns-of-is-hit-squads-among-refugees/
67 http://cis.org/High-Cost-of-Resettling-Middle-Eastern-Refugees
68 https://www.washingtonpost.com/news/the-fix/wp/2015/11/30/heres-how-much-the-united-states-spends-on-refugees/?utm_term=.721e7e8e28a8
69 http://www.usdebtclock.org/
70 https://www.usnews.com/news/healthiest-communities/articles/2018-09-12/poverty-in-america-new-census-data-paint-an-unpleasant-picture
71 https://www.usatoday.com/story/news/nation/2018/05/24/fewer-americans-believe-united-states-should-accept-refugees/638663002/
72 http://www.jordantimes.com/news/local/jordan-cannot-take-any-more-syrian-refugees-%E2%80%94-officials
73 https://en.globes.co.il/en/article-israel-becomes-health-center-for-syrian-children-1001229351
74 https://www.unhcr.org/news/briefing/2017/12/5a2ffd534/un-partners-launch-plan-support-five-million-syrian-refugees-countries.html
75 http://www.arabnews.com/node/1235776/saudi-arabia
76 http://www.thedailybeast.com/the-middle-east-needs-to-take-care-of-its-own-refugees
77 https://hbr.org/2016/10/research-refugees-can-bolster-a-regions-economy
78 https://www.forbes.com/sites/stuartanderson/2016/10/02/3-reasons-why-immigrants-key-to-economic-growth/
79 https://www.worldvision.org/refugees-news-stories/forced-to-flee-top-countries-refugees-coming-from
80 https://www.brookings.edu/blog/future-development/2020/01/27/sharing-the-burden-of-the-global-refugee-crisis/
81 https://www.oecd.org/coronavirus/policy-responses/the-impact-of-coronavirus-covid-19-on-forcibly-displaced-persons-in-developing-countries-88ad26de/
82 https://www.motherjones.com/politics/2019/01/the-united-states-is-no-longer-the-world-leader-in-resettling-refugees/
83 https://www.americanprogress.org/issues/immigration/reports/2019/07/22/472378/restoring-rule-law-fair-humane-workable-immigration-system/
84 http://www.pewresearch.org/fact-tank/2017/01/30/key-facts-about-refugees-to-the-u-s/
85 http://thehill.com/blogs/pundits-blog/immigration/255237-anti-immigrant-activists-more-prone-to-terrorism-than-refugees
86 https://www.cvt.org/Refugee-Vetting-Process

87 http://www.heritage.org/immigration/commentary/how-the-refugee-vetting-process-works
88 https://www.concernusa.org/story/largest-refugee-crises/
89 https://socialnewsdaily.com/67878/will-china-finally-surpass-the-us-to-become-the-next-superpower/
90 https://www.bbc.com/news/world-asia-china-49891769
91 https://www.youtube.com/watch?v=bGTO437Oh6A
92 https://www.cnbc.com/2019/10/02/adidas-ceo-our-concern-is-whether-china-trade-war-hits-us-consumer.html
93 https://www.bbc.com/news/world-us-canada-47046264
94 http://www.worldstopexports.com/chinas-top-import-partners/
95 https://www.theatlantic.com/international/archive/2017/06/china-jinping-trump-america-first-keqiang/529014/
96 https://www.theguardian.com/world/2017/may/12/the-900bn-question-what-is-the-belt-and-road-initiative
97 https://www.cfr.org/backgrounder/chinas-massive-belt-and-road-initiative
98 https://www.bbc.com/news/business-56397602
99 https://www.investopedia.com/articles/investing/080615/china-owns-us-debt-how-much.asp
100 https://www.cnbc.com/2017/03/08/chinas-tech-giants-are-pouring-billions-into-us-start-ups.html
101 https://www.bloomberg.com/news/articles/2018-04-14/hainan-becomes-test-case-in-china-campaign-to-phase-out-gas-cars
102 http://www.bbc.com/news/business-43715084
103 https://www.bbc.com/news/business-45899310
104 https://www.forbes.com/sites/sarahsu/2018/04/13/how-effective-is-trumps-trade-strategy-for-china/
105 https://socialnewsdaily.com/67878/will-china-finally-surpass-the-us-to-become-the-next-superpower/
106 http://www.scmp.com/news/china/money-wealth/article/2042441/chinas-middle-class-rise-more-third-population-2030-research
107 https://www.forbes.com/sites/ywang/2018/01/11/try-try-and-try-again-facebook-and-google-plan-new-partnerships-to-break-into-china/
108 https://www.vanityfair.com/hollywood/2016/08/did-you-catch-the-ways-hollywood-pandered-to-china-this-year
109 https://www.nytimes.com/2019/05/07/arts/television/cbs-good-fight-chinese-censorship.html
110 https://www.investopedia.com/china-70-anniversary-future-4771950
111 http://www.wired.co.uk/article/how-china-became-tech-superpower-took-over-the-west
112 https://www.brookings.edu/wp-content/uploads/2019/05/ES_20190617_Klein_ChinaPayments.pdf
113 https://www.americanbanker.com/news/why-chinas-mobile-payments-revolution-matters-for-us-bankers

114 https://www.emarketer.com/content/global-historic-first-ecommerce-china-will-account-more-than-50-of-retail-sales
115 https://www.emarketer.com/content/us-ecommerce-growth-jumps-more-than-30-accelerating-online-shopping-shift-by-nearly-2-years
116 http://www.alibabagroup.com/en/global/home
117 https://www.tencent.com/en-us/index.html
118 https://www.businessofapps.com/data/tik-tok-statistics/
119 https://www.reuters.com/article/us-bytedance-tiktok-exclusive/exclusive-bytedance-investors-value-tiktok-at-50-billion-in-takeover-bid-sources-idUSKCN24U1M9
120 http://fortune.com/2017/11/21/china-innovation-dji/
121 https://foreignpolicy.com/2018/12/31/a-billion-bicyclists-can-be-wrong-china-business-bikeshare/
122 https://techcrunch.com/2019/07/14/china-micromobility-hellobike/
123 https://web.wechat.com/
124 https://www.nytimes.com/2017/12/25/opinion/america-dollar-trust-trump.html
125 https://www.forbes.com/sites/sarahsu/2017/02/02/why-china-wont-replace-the-u-s-as-the-worlds-superpower/
126 http://www.businessinsider.com/why-uber-failed-in-china-2016-8
127 https://www.cnbc.com/2018/04/11/china-to-allow-more-foreign-investment-in-financial-sector-by-year-end.html
128 https://www.france24.com/en/20190720-china-opens-finance-sector-more-foreign-investment
129 https://www.scmp.com/economy/china-economy/article/3023081/china-plans-allow-foreign-investment-vpn-services-part
130 https://www.cfr.org/backgrounder/chinas-repression-uyghurs-xinjiang
131 https://www.rte.ie/news/world/2021/0127/1192303-china-covid-latest/
132 https://www.bbc.com/news/world-asia-china-55355401
133 https://www.britannica.com/event/Bretton-Woods-Conference
134 https://www.theguardian.com/commentisfree/2015/mar/26/west-understand-china-trust-xi-jinping
135 https://www.scmp.com/economy/china-economy/article/3008471/chinas-population-peak-2023-five-years-earlier-official
136 https://www.ft.com/content/233b101e-7d51-11e9-81d2-f785092ab560
137 https://www.nytimes.com/2018/02/20/opinion/china-women-birth-rate-rights.html
138 https://www.channelnewsasia.com/news/cnainsider/leftover-men-china-get-married-gender-imbalance-one-child-policy-10485358
139 https://www.statista.com/statistics/282134/china-labor-force/
140 http://foreignpolicy.com/2018/02/01/chinas-middle-class-is-pulling-up-the-ladder-behind-itself/
141 https://wamu.org/story/20/09/18/how-many-people-in-the-u-s-own-guns/

142 https://gunsandamerica.org/story/20/06/01/gun-sales-continue-to-boom-during-the-pandemic/
143 http://www.smallarmssurvey.org/fileadmin/docs/T-Briefing-Papers/SAS-BP-Civilian-Firearms-Numbers.pdf
144 https://www.vice.com/en_us/article/bj3485/how-many-guns-are-there-in-america
145 https://www.cnn.com/2018/02/15/politics/guns-dont-know-how-many-america/index.html
146 https://www.washingtonpost.com/nation/2021/03/23/2020-shootings/
147 https://constitutingamerica.org/bill-of-rights/?gclid=EAIaIQobChMIqM-vjjqT94wIV2uDICh0psAMbEAAYAiAAEgJy9PD_BwE
148 https://www.law.cornell.edu/supct/html/07-290.ZS.html
149 https://www.nytimes.com/interactive/2017/11/06/opinion/how-to-reduce-shootings.html
150 https://www.washingtonpost.com/national/congress-moves-to-act-on-gun-control-amid-partisan-debate-about-background-checks/2019/02/13/340e26de-2fb7-11e9-8ad3-9a5b113ecd3c_story.html?utm_term=.f60bde94aea6
151 https://www.pewtrusts.org/en/research-and-analysis/blogs/stateline/2018/08/02/after-parkland-states-pass-50-new-gun-control-laws
152 https://edition.cnn.com/2016/03/10/health/gun-laws-background-checks-reduce-deaths/index.html
153 https://lawcenter.giffords.org/gun-laws/policy-areas/child-consumer-safety/design-safety-standards/
154 http://www.motherjones.com/politics/2013/01/high-capacity-magazines-mass-shootings
155 http://time.com/5160267/gun-used-florida-school-shooting-ar-15/
156 https://www.nbcnews.com/storyline/las-vegas-shooting/las-vegas-police-investigating-shooting-mandalay-bay-n806461
157 https://www.nbcnews.com/politics/politics-news/trump-administration-bans-bump-stocks-device-used-las-vegas-shooting-n949581
158 https://www.cincinnati.com/story/news/2019/08/05/ohio-shooting-videos-dayton-police-take-down-shooter-saved-literally-hundreds-lives/1919950001/
159 https://www.nbcnews.com/news/us-news/colorado-grocery-shooting-slain-boulder-officer-acted-heroically-chief-says-n1261788
160 http://www.leg.state.co.us/clics/clics2012a/commsumm.nsf/b4a3962433b52fa787256e5f00670a71/10498c3a3264be-7887257998006fe0d7/$FILE/HseJud0202AttachN.pdf
161 http://www.people-press.org/2014/12/10/growing-public-support-for-gun-rights/
162 http://www.pewsocialtrends.org/2017/06/22/americas-complex-relationship-with-guns/

163 https://www.washingtonpost.com/news/morning-mix/wp/2018/04/05/chicago-suburb-bans-assault-weapons-in-response-to-parkland-shooting/?noredirect=on&utm_term=.311a96daae6f
164 https://www.chicagotribune.com/news/local/breaking/ct-met-chicago-gun-laws-explainer-20171006-story.html
165 https://chicago.suntimes.com/crime/2020/11/18/21573378/chicago-homicides-700-murders-2020-gun-violence-shootings
166 https://chicago.suntimes.com/2020/12/30/22206618/chicago-gun-violence-homicides-policing-community-outreach-university-of-chicago-crime-lab-editorial
167 https://www.npr.org/2017/10/05/555580598/fact-check-is-chicago-proof-that-gun-laws-don-t-work
168 https://www.nytimes.com/2021/03/24/opinion/us-gun-violence.html
169 https://obamawhitehouse.archives.gov/issues/foreign-policy/iran-deal
170 https://www.npr.org/2018/06/12/619168996/read-the-joint-statement-from-president-donald-trump-and-kim-jong-un
171 https://www.bbc.com/news/world-asia-51689443
172 https://www.theperspective.com/perspectives/politics/is-the-israel-gulf-states-peace-deal-a-big-trump-victory/
173 https://www.nytimes.com/2020/08/13/us/politics/trump-israel-united-arab-emirates-uae.html
174 https://www.aljazeera.com/opinions/2020/10/31/trumps-normalisation-of-israel-has-nothing-to-do-with-peace
175 https://hbr.org/2016/11/what-so-many-people-dont-get-about-the-u-s-working-class
176 https://www.youtube.com/watch?v=GUzjYXVrPvM&ab_channel=NasDaily
177 https://theconversation.com/who-exactly-is-trumps-base-why-white-working-class-voters-could-be-key-to-the-us-election-147267
178 https://www.axios.com/trump-china-policy-special-report-154fa5c2-469d-4238-8d72-f0641abc0dfa.html
179 https://www.cfr.org/backgrounder/what-trans-pacific-partnership-tpp
180 https://www.bbc.com/news/world-44717074
181 https://www.sandiegouniontribune.com/columnists/story/2020-01-01/column-like-them-or-not-trump-policies-are-reducing-immigration
182 https://edition.cnn.com/2020/02/12/politics/amorality-presidency-donald-trump/index.html
183 https://www.reuters.com/article/us-usa-trump-cohen-idUSKCN1UD18D
184 https://www.npr.org/sections/thetwo-way/2017/03/31/522199535/judge-approves-25-million-settlement-of-trump-university-lawsuit
185 https://apnews.com/article/635b828ded6813ea66783869f32876c5
186 https://www.nytimes.com/interactive/2017/06/23/opinion/trumps-lies.html

187 https://edition.cnn.com/2021/02/22/opinions/trump-covid-big-lie-reiner/index.html
188 https://www.theguardian.com/business/2020/sep/12/us-corporations-sending-jobs-abroad-offshoring-pandemic
189 https://www.nsenergybusiness.com/features/trump-us-coal-industry/
190 https://www.bloomberg.com/graphics/2018-tax-plan-consequences/
191 https://www.brookings.edu/blog/up-front/2018/10/16/the-middle-class-needs-a-tax-cut-trump-didnt-give-it-to-them/
192 https://www.nytimes.com/2020/09/29/us/trump-750-taxes.html
193 https://www.bankrate.com/finance/taxes/tax-brackets.aspx
194 https://www.npr.org/2018/08/11/637665414/a-year-after-charlottesville-not-much-has-changed-for-trump
195 https://www.theguardian.com/society/2019/nov/12/hate-crimes-2018-latinos-transgender-fbi
196 https://www.youtube.com/watch?v=6YwKqDU8P7U
197 https://abcnews.go.com/US/president-trump-dozen-capitol-rioters-trumps-guidance/story?id=75757601
198 https://www.theguardian.com/us-news/2021/jan/08/capitol-attack-police-officer-five-deaths
199 https://www.nytimes.com/2021/02/13/us/politics/donald-trump-capitol-riot.html
200 https://www.youtube.com/watch?v=S3RzKKfNkTk
201 https://news.nationalgeographic.com/2018/03/gun-protest-march-of-our-lives/
202 https://www.youtube.com/watch?v=6_RdnVtfZPY
203 https://edition.cnn.com/us/live-news/george-floyd-protests-06-01-20/index.html
204 https://www.bbc.com/news/world-us-canada-55575260
205 https://www.channelnewsasia.com/news/world/us-capitol-protests-world-leaders-stunned-violence-election-13909836
206 http://www.pbs.org/wgbh/americanexperience/features/timeline/minewars/
207 https://www.theguardian.com/politics/guardianwitness-blog/2015/mar/05/miners-strike-30-years-on-i-fought-not-just-for-my-pit-but-for-the-community
208 http://www.scmp.com/news/china/policies-politics/article/1924126/miners-protest-ailing-chinese-coal-firm-heilongjiang
209 http://edition.cnn.com/2016/09/16/us/occupy-wall-street-protest-movements/
210 https://www.washingtonpost.com/
211 https://www.nbcnews.com/news/us-news/eric-garner-george-floyd-protests-reveal-how-little-has-changed-n1220501
212 https://www.history.com/this-day-in-history/womens-march
213 https://www.youtube.com/watch?v=PP-NBTnrOhM

214 https://time.com/national-school-walkout-gun-control-photos/
215 https://www.cbsnews.com/news/tea-party-protesters-rally-against-gangster-government/
216 https://www.scmp.com/news/hong-kong/politics/article/3014771/hong-kong-protests-go-global-marchers-take-streets-us
217 https://www.npr.org/2020/05/31/866428272/george-floyd-reverberates-globally-thousands-protest-in-germany-u-k-canada
218 https://www.nytimes.com/2020/04/18/us/texas-protests-stay-at-home.html
219 https://www.merriam-webster.com/words-at-play/intersectionality-meaning
220 https://womensmarch.com/press-releases/1/18-the-womens-march-puts-its-power-to-work-with-womens-agenda-platform-of-policies
221 https://www.washingtonpost.com/local/womens-march-on-washington-a-sea-of-pink-hatted-protesters-vow-to-resist-donald-trump/2017/01/21/ae4def62-dfdf-11e6-acdf-14da832ae861_story.html?utm_term=.bc711cc6f245
222 http://time.com/4649891/protest-donald-trump/
223 https://www.nonviolent-conflict.org/otpor-and-the-struggle-for-democracy-in-serbia-1998-2000/
224 http://www.bbc.com/news/world-middle-east-12324664
225 http://www.rollingstone.com/politics/news/trump-muslim-ban-why-civil-unrest-judicial-action-works-w463895
226 https://www.thenation.com/article/the-west-virginia-teachers-strike-shows-that-winning-big-requires-creating-a-crisis/
227 https://www.theguardian.com/us-news/2018/apr/07/resistance-now-teacher-protests-oklahoma
228 http://time.com/longform/never-again-movement/
229 https://www.nbcnews.com/feature/short-take/video/companies-cut-ties-with-nra-amid-backlash-after-parkland-shooting-1169108547978
230 https://www.theguardian.com/world/2019/jun/23/czech-republic-protesters-demand-prime-ministers-resignation
231 https://www.telegraph.co.uk/news/0/george-floyd-protests-why-riots-us-america/
232 https://www.vox.com/2020/5/31/21276031/george-floyd-protests-london-berlin
233 https://www.nytimes.com/2020/06/01/world/asia/george-floyd-protest-global.html
234 https://newrepublic.com/article/154248/depressing-reality-behind-hong-kongs-protests
235 https://www.nytimes.com/live/2021/01/06/us/washington-dc-protests
236 https://www.businessinsider.com/world-leaders-condemn-trump-and-his-supporters-violent-attempted-coup-2021-1

237 https://www.nbcnews.com/video/congress-confirms-biden-and-harris-electoral-college-win-99023429857
238 https://scholar.princeton.edu/sites/default/files/mgilens/files/gilens_and_page_2014_-testing_theories_of_american_politics.doc.pdf
239 https://www.theperspective.com/subjective-timeline/politics/the-kent-state-shooting/
240 http://www.nytimes.com/1995/06/02/opinion/l-did-protesters-really-stop-the-vietnam-war-004278.html
241 http://www.history.com/topics/vietnam-war/vietnam-war-protests
242 https://www.theguardian.com/uk-news/2016/jul/08/we-were-ignored-anti-war-protestors-remember-the-iraq-war-marches
243 https://www.bbc.com/news/world-us-canada-38724063
244 http://www.ncpolicywatch.com/2020/03/05/the-global-national-and-local-impacts-of-trumps-war-on-reproductive-freedom/
245 https://www.history.com/topics/black-history/civil-rights-movement
246 https://en.wikipedia.org/wiki/African-American_Civil_Rights_Movement_(1954%E2%80%931968)
247 https://en.wikipedia.org/wiki/Dakota_Access_Pipeline_protests
248 https://www.npr.org/2018/11/29/671701019/2-years-after-standing-rock-protests-north-dakota-oil-business-is-booming
249 https://grist.org/article/after-standing-rock-protesting-pipelines-can-get-you-a-decade-in-prison-and-100k-in-fines/
250 https://www.bbc.com/news/world-asia-china-49317695
251 https://www.nytimes.com/2020/05/29/world/asia/hong-kong-protest-future-china.html
252 https://www.researchgate.net/publication/298056897_The_Politics_of_Nonviolent_Action_A_Critical_Review
253 http://thefederalist.com/2016/07/12/black-lives-matters-violence-undermines-its-credibility/
254 https://www.nbcnews.com/politics/donald-trump/we-will-never-concede-trump-baselessly-asserts-voter-fraud-speech-n1253011
255 https://www.theperspective.com/debates/politics/left-support-antifa/
256 https://www.dailywire.com/news/20343/timeline-antifa-violence-january-%E2%80%93-august-2017-frank-camp
257 https://www.nationalreview.com/2017/08/charlottesville-alt-right-antifa-riot-violence/
258 http://thehill.com/blogs/pundits-blog/civil-rights/347524-charlottesvilles-polarizing-politics-shows-nobodys-right-if
259 https://www.nytimes.com/aponline/2020/05/30/us/ap-us-minneapolis-police-death-by-racism.html
260 https://www.cfr.org/timeline/trumps-foreign-policy-moments
261 https://www.cfr.org/interactive/global-conflict-tracker/conflict/north-korea-crisis

262   https://www.vox.com/world/2017/9/19/16227730/trump-afghanistan-3000-troops-mattis
263   https://edition.cnn.com/middleeast/live-news/us-iran-soleimani-tensions-live-intl-01-05-20/index.html
264   https://time.com/5954657/biden-troop-withdrawal-afghanistan/
265   https://www.youtube.com/watch?v=IuGRBFtkztE
266   http://www.reuters.com/article/us-iraq-war-anniversary-idUSBRE92D0PG20130314
267   https://www.cnbc.com/2019/11/20/us-spent-6point4-trillion-on-middle-east-wars-since-2001-study.html
268   https://www.history.com/topics/vietnam-war/vietnam-war-history
269   https://www.npr.org/2013/10/05/229561805/what-a-downed-black-hawk-in-somalia-taught-america
270   http://www.africanews.com/2016/04/11/obama-aftermath-of-gaddafi-overthrow-worst-mistake-as-president/
271   https://www.washingtonpost.com/business/2020/01/03/oil-prices-spike-dow-futures-dive-after-us-airstrike-kills-irans-top-military-leader/
272   https://learning.blogs.nytimes.com/2012/01/17/jan-17-1893-hawaiian-monarchy-overthrown-by-america-backed-businessmen/
273   https://www.vox.com/2017/4/6/15215132/us-syria-bombing-trump-assad-chemical-weapons
274   https://www.theguardian.com/world/2019/sep/26/syria-assad-chlorine-chemical-weapon
275   https://www.reuters.com/article/us-libya-gaddafi-finalhours/gaddafi-caught-like-rat-in-a-drain-humiliated-and-shot-idUSTRE79K43S20111021
276   https://www.insideover.com/war/libya-nine-years-after-the-overthrow-of-gaddafi.html
277   https://www.theatlantic.com/international/archive/2018/02/isis-libya-hiftar-al-qaeda-syria/552419/
278   https://www.aljazeera.com/indepth/interactive/2020/02/war-afghanistan-2001-invasion-2020-taliban-deal-200229142658305.html
279   http://www.theamericanconservative.com/articles/should-america-be-the-worlds-policeman/
280   http://www.un.org/en/sections/un-charter/chapter-vii/
281   https://www.history.com/news/crimea-russia-ukraine-annexation
282   https://www.history.com/news/russia-georgia-war-military-nato
283   https://foreignpolicy.com/2020/04/03/suleimani-iran-syria-influence-irgc-no-problem/
284   https://www.nytimes.com/2020/01/05/opinion/suleimani-iran-trump.html
285   https://www.washingtonpost.com/news/fact-checker/wp/2016/02/16/bill-clinton-and-the-missed-opportunities-to-kill-osama-bin-laden/?utm_term=.5169dbc1af6d

286 https://www.politico.eu/article/attacks-will-be-spectacular-cia-war-on-terror-bush-bin-laden/
287 https://abcnews.go.com/blogs/headlines/2014/04/20-years-after-rwanda-genocide-regret-and-remembrance
288 https://www.cfr.org/global-conflict-tracker/conflict/civil-war-syria
289 https://www.nationalreview.com/2015/05/why-america-was-indispensable-allies-winning-world-war-ii-victor-davis-hanson/
290 https://www.defense.gov/explore/story/Article/1728715/desert-storm-a-look-back/
291 https://www.theatlantic.com/international/archive/2012/04/bosnias-lesson-when-american-intervention-works-partly/256471/
292 https://academic.oup.com/irap/article/15/1/113/753219
293 https://www.cnbc.com/2020/01/21/davos-russia-and-putin-rising-all-over-the-middle-east-bill-browder-says.html
294 https://www.theatlantic.com/politics/archive/2019/05/whats-going-trump-and-iran-and-why-it-matters/589531/
295 https://www.nytimes.com/2019/05/08/us/politics/iran-nuclear-deal.html
296 https://www.nytimes.com/2020/01/03/world/middleeast/us-iran-war.html
297 https://www.youtube.com/watch?v=HBLlxoY7NmM
298 https://www.thesun.co.uk/news/9891426/vladimir-putin-party-loses-third-of-seats-moscow-election/
299 https://www.forbes.com/profile/vladimir-putin/
300 http://www.businessinsider.com/how-vladimir-putin-rose-to-power-2017-2
301 https://www.amazon.com/New-Tsar-Reign-Vladimir-Putin/dp/0345802799?tag=bisafetynet2-20
302 https://www.biography.com/people/vladimir-putin-9448807
303 https://www.theguardian.com/world/2018/mar/18/vladimir-putin-wins-russian-election-with-more-than-70-of-vote-exit-poll
304 http://www.pewglobal.org/2017/06/20/president-putin-russian-perspective/
305 https://www.statista.com/statistics/896181/putin-approval-rating-russia/
306 http://www.aljazeera.com/indepth/opinion/2014/03/why-do-russians-support-interv-2014328174257483544.html
307 https://www.britannica.com/place/Russia/The-Putin-presidency
308 https://www.hse.ru/data/351/229/1237/paper-Treisman.pdf
309 http://edition.cnn.com/videos/world/2017/12/13/russia-super-putin-exhibit-sebastian-pkg.cnn
310 https://www.themoscowtimes.com/2017/12/08/putin-crowned-superputin-at-new-art-exhibition-in-moscow-a59869
311 https://www.rt.com/op-edge/211447-putin-speech-annual-economy-sovereignty/

312 https://www.theguardian.com/world/2015/may/06/vladimir-putin-15-ways-he-changed-russia-world
313 https://www.washingtonpost.com/opinions/putin-won-in-ukraine/2015/09/07/02a0283c-5341-11e5-933e-7d06c647a395_story.html?utm_term=.cbbbd6ef3d0a
314 http://www.bbc.com/news/world-europe-28400218
315 https://www.theguardian.com/commentisfree/2014/jul/31/vladimir-putin-western-sanctions-russia-flight-mh17-state-propaganda
316 https://www.nytimes.com/2018/03/18/world/europe/election-russia-putin-president.html?hp&action=click&pgtype=Homepage&clickSource=story-heading&module=first-column-region&region=top-news&WT.nav=top-news
317 http://www.slate.com/articles/news_and_politics/cover_story/2017/01/how_vladimir_putin_engineered_russia_s_return_to_global_power.html
318 https://news.vice.com/story/putin-is-obsessed-with-keeping-his-daughters-identities-secret
319 https://www.usatoday.com/story/news/politics/2018/07/16/vladimir-putin-denies-meddling-2016-presidential-election/788219002/
320 https://www.voanews.com/a/comparing-trump-us-intel-community-when-to-comes-to-russia-meddling-in-us-election/4113414.html
321 https://www.dni.gov/files/documents/ICA_2017_01.pdf
322 https://www.occrp.org/personoftheyear/2014/
323 https://www.reportingproject.net/therussianlaundromat/
324 https://www.usatoday.com/story/news/world/2017/05/02/dozens-russian-deaths-cast-suspicion-vladimir-putin/100480734/
325 http://www.bbc.com/news/uk-43429152
326 https://news.un.org/en/story/2021/03/1086012
327 https://www.theguardian.com/world/2016/mar/22/millions-more-russians-living-in-poverty-as-economic-crisis-bites
328 https://www.usnews.com/news/world/articles/2017-02-17/vladimir-putin-could-be-worlds-richest-man-with-200-billion-net-worth-report-says
329 https://www.rferl.org/a/recession-sanctions-left-20-million-russians-living-poverty-2016-up-300000-2015/28413387.html
330 https://themoscowtimes.com/news/russian-life-expectancy-hits-record-high-58274
331 https://academic.oup.com/gerontologist/article/56/5/795/2605358
332 https://www.theguardian.com/commentisfree/2019/sep/08/the-observer-view-on-russia-subversion-of-democracy
333 https://www.nytimes.com/2019/09/06/world/europe/russia-lyubov-sobol-protests.html
334 https://time.com/5605456/russian-journalist-ivan-golunov-arrest/
335 https://www.theguardian.com/commentisfree/2020/mar/11/the-guardian-view-on-putins-power-games-fake-democracy

336 https://edition.cnn.com/2020/06/06/world/gallery/intl-george-floyd-protests/index.html
337 https://www.foxnews.com/us/america-protests-violent-riots-expected-to-continue
338 https://www.foxnews.com/us/america-protests-violent-riots-expected-to-continue
339 https://blacklivesmatter.com/
340 https://www.nytimes.com/interactive/2020/07/03/us/george-floyd-protests-crowd-size.html
341 https://www.nytimes.com/2016/07/16/us/all-lives-matter-black-lives-matter.html
342 https://www.youtube.com/watch?v=xd2He9Ngo9E
343 https://theestablishment.co/stop-making-black-people-fight-everyones-battles-cbcedc340a43
344 https://www.standard.co.uk/news/world/why-shouldnt-say-all-lives-matter-a4456686.html
345 https://www.cbsnews.com/news/all-lives-matter-black-lives-matter/
346 https://www.businessinsider.com/us-systemic-racism-in-charts-graphs-data-2020-6
347 https://www.rollingstone.com/politics/politics-news/no-justice-thousands-march-for-trayvon-martin-194667/
348 https://www.thecut.com/2020/07/breonna-taylor-louisville-shooting-police-what-we-know.html
349 https://www.vox.com/identities/2020/5/6/21249202/ahmaud-arbery-jogger-killed-in-georgia-video-shooting-grand-jury
350 https://www.youtube.com/watch?v=xvW6PLIDsbI
351 https://edition.cnn.com/2020/06/23/opinions/all-lives-matter-misses-the-big-picture-baker/index.html
352 http://www.latimes.com/nation/nationnow/la-na-stairwell-shooting-20160220-story.html
353 https://www.youtube.com/watch?v=P54sP0Nlngg
354 https://en.wikipedia.org/wiki/White_privilege
355 https://www.youtube.com/watch?v=vP4iY1TtS3s
356 https://tavaana.org/en/content/martin-luther-king-jr-fighting-equal-rights-america-0
357 https://www.israelhayom.com/2020/06/10/radical-groups-co-opt-black-lives-matter-movement-to-target-israel/
358 https://twitter.com/losotrosjudios/status/1266335730017632263
359 https://www.nytimes.com/2020/07/30/opinion/john-lewis-civil-rights-america.html
360 https://slate.com/news-and-politics/2017/06/how-single-payer-health-care-went-from-a-pipe-dream-to-mainstream.html
361 https://www.kff.org/health-reform/poll-finding/kff-election-tracking-poll-health-care-in-the-2018-midterms/

362 https://www.johnlocke.org/update/the-case-against-medicaid-expansion/?__cf_chl_jschl_tk__=239661fa28dd9164d203c5790f4ead8907490730-1618916454-0-AWmhmNynDbBoPy5bLucDqzSc25Xyc6lr1qbHU-U7GWhD0wr_5soq356JOwh860NzB4Qong-FthradPMM78Cw4jh-84K4qBFaRutJjkR9ZhDokX-TArltibBikc64NhIa2YUAj1WaZM-wf9uQSmZpRfna_dNY7eHmgaGljX_4mikprUmjYD0thz-iVkohPIJMc-3SpzbCgudrrmzJyFlpnAs4SwgIpQwIJxt-Vh97mx0EaGx5Gou0G6IN6_PQO5c0yywNsWryF4aZil4x4H2S5371Kws0iqu-_1ao-JaXY2MZ1O4-VhhPH07hstlpZG1sqrnML2AtaBgkttC_qOBmkbYnOa-biUJyadxydyVnWnUUKg97GL0N9zC87Jqf1I_niAJ0hI8nmP_vKJSn-2pEyu_4vEGwRhcrnZ_jvAHWwETL39jl0kjD4JMTc7RG5hNjP4c-9BaEOgGuLIcdyGdrF2C4aScwLFVkIVDyoPNCmInN2JiWu44pd-sWeFnx3tBHXJ-PXk-idIQ

363 https://www.medicareinteractive.org/get-answers/medicare-basics/medicare-coverage-overview/differences-between-medicare-and-medicaid

364 https://www.kff.org/infographic/employer-responsibility-under-the-affordable-care-act/

365 https://www.bustle.com/p/is-obamacare-still-around-a-2018-guide-to-the-us-health-care-system-10191878

366 https://www.cigna.com/assets/docs/about-cigna/informed-on-reform/employer-mandate-fact-sheet.pdf

367 https://pdfs.semanticscholar.org/aafa/cd8a244d57852cb69e972e-ca04e45bf3a172.pdf

368 https://www.healthsystemtracker.org/chart-collection/health-spending-u-s-compare-countries/

369 http://ajph.aphapublications.org/doi/full/10.2105/AJPH.2015.303157

370 https://www.theatlantic.com/health/archive/2014/06/us-health-care-most-expensive-and-worst-performing/372828/

371 http://www.commonwealthfund.org/interactives/2017/july/mirror-mirror/

372 https://www.theatlantic.com/health/archive/2017/07/us-worst-health-care-commonwealth-2017-report/533634/

373 https://www.citizen.org/article/coronavirus-shows-why-we-need-medicare-for-all/

374 https://www.oecd.org/berlin/47570143.pdf

375 http://www.politifact.com/truth-o-meter/statements/2015/jun/29/bernie-s/bernie-sanders-us-only-major-country-doesnt-guaran/

376 https://www.nytimes.com/2019/03/27/opinion/trump-obamacare-affordable-care-act.html?action=click&module=Opinion&pgtype=Homepage

377 http://www.cnn.com/2017/09/25/opinions/single-payer-failure-opinion-atlas/index.html

378 https://www.fraserinstitute.org/sites/default/files/waiting-your-turn-wait-times-for-health-care-in-canada-2016.pdf

379 https://www.merritthawkins.com/pdf/mha2009waittimesurvey.pdf

380 https://www.usnews.com/news/best-countries/articles/2016-08-03/canadians-increasingly-come-to-us-for-health-care
381 https://www.commonwealthfund.org/publications/issue-briefs/2015/oct/us-health-care-global-perspective
382 https://en.wikipedia.org/wiki/List_of_Nobel_laureates_in_Physiology_or_Medicine
383 http://www.nytimes.com/2006/10/05/business/05scene.html
384 https://www.forbes.com/sites/matthewherper/2011/03/23/the-most-innovative-countries-in-biology-and-medicine/
385 https://www.ncbi.nlm.nih.gov/pmc/articles/PMC2866602/
386 https://www.urban.org/sites/default/files/alfresco/publication-pdfs/2000785-The-Sanders-Single-Payer-Health-Care-Plan.pdf
387 https://www.urban.org/sites/default/files/alfresco/publication-pdfs/2000785-The-Sanders-Single-Payer-Health-Care-Plan.pdf
388 http://www.crfb.org/papers/adding-senator-sanderss-campaign-proposals-so-far
389 https://www.washingtonpost.com/opinions/single-payer-health-care-would-have-an-astonishingly-high-price-tag/2017/06/18/9c70dae6-52d2-11e7-be25-3a519335381c_story.html?utm_term=.4c773f2c9f6f
390 https://krugman.blogs.nytimes.com/2016/01/18/health-reform-is-hard/
391 https://www.npr.org/2020/08/16/898658570/protests-may-prompt-dialogue-on-racism-but-it-s-going-to-be-uncomfortable
392 https://www.newsweek.com/rush-limbaugh-kamala-harris-radio-show-1525554
393 https://washingtonmonthly.com/magazine/july-august-2020/what-makes-todays-dictators-different/
394 http://scholarship.law.wm.edu/cgi/viewcontent.cgi?article=2049&context=facpubs
395 https://www.thedailybeast.com/torch-wielding-white-nationalists-clash-with-counter-protestors-at-uva
396 https://www.tolerance.org/professional-development/strategies-for-reducing-racial-and-ethnic-prejudice-essential-principles
397 http://educateagainsthate.com/
398 http://www.chicagotribune.com/news/opinion/commentary/ct-perspec-free-speech-social-media-0921-story.html
399 http://scholarship.law.wm.edu/cgi/viewcontent.cgi?article=2049&context=facpubs
400 https://danielmiessler.com/blog/the-clash-of-extreme-left-and-extreme-right-will-create-a-new-centrism/
401 https://foreignpolicy.com/2020/07/03/america-founding-fathers-jefferson-washington-adams-race-civil-war/
402 http://www.nationalreview.com/article/436347/america-melting-pot-immigrant-culture-made-country-great

403 http://freespeechdebate.com/discuss/nineteen-arguments-for-hate-speech-bans-and-against-them/
404 https://www.nytimes.com/2017/07/14/opinion/sunday/when-is-speech-violence.html
405 https://www.ushmm.org/outreach/en/article.php?ModuleId=10007677
406 https://books.google.co.il/books?id=UJJyCwAAQBAJ&pg=PA211&lpg=PA211&dq=Jeremy+Waldron+value+neutral+state&source=bl&ots=aW5G_JVxn8&sig=vpIn1cQElkS8v8iZMMGxJQ2-s2s&hl=en&sa=X&ved=0ahUKEwj544yasvzWAhWL0RoKHdkcCdQQ6AEIPTAF
407 https://www.theodysseyonline.com/puerto-ricans-second-class-citizens-seeking-statehood
408 https://www.loc.gov/rr/hispanic/1898/jonesact.html
409 https://reliefweb.int/report/puerto-rico-united-states-america/hurricane-maria-one-year-later
410 https://townhall.com/tipsheet/sarahlee/2019/04/01/puerto-rico-threatens-trump-over-reduction-in-funding-while-quietly-passing-their-own-green-new-deal-n2544087
411 https://edition.cnn.com/2019/03/28/politics/house-puerto-rico-statehood/index.html
412 https://www.bls.gov/eag/eag.pr.htm
413 http://www.cnn.com/2017/06/12/americas/puerto-rico-statehood-referendum/index.html
414 https://www.census.gov/library/stories/2019/09/puerto-rico-outmigration-increases-poverty-declines.html
415 http://www.pewhispanic.org/2014/08/11/puerto-rican-population-declines-on-island-grows-on-u-s-mainland/
416 https://www.washingtonpost.com/news/worldviews/wp/2012/11/07/why-does-puerto-rico-want-statehood-anyway/?utm_term=.20edf0764c67
417 https://greengarageblog.org/17-big-pros-and-cons-of-puerto-rico-becoming-a-state
418 https://www.theodysseyonline.com/puerto-ricans-second-class-citizens-seeking-statehood
419 https://futureofworking.com/5-advantages-and-disadvantages-of-puerto-rico-becoming-a-state/
420 https://greengarageblog.org/17-big-pros-and-cons-of-puerto-rico-becoming-a-state
421 http://www.worldometers.info/world-population/puerto-rico-population/
422 https://www.law.cornell.edu/uscode/text/26/933
423 https://greengarageblog.org/17-big-pros-and-cons-of-puerto-rico-becoming-a-state
424 https://www.theodysseyonline.com/puerto-ricans-second-class-citizens-seeking-statehood

425	http://thehill.com/policy/finance/323187-sanders-offers-bill-aimed-at-preventing-corporate-tax-avoidance
426	https://www.usnews.com/news/world/articles/2018-07-05/puerto-rico-mayor-2-others-arrested-on-corruption-charges
427	https://abcnews.go.com/US/puerto-rico-votes-favor-statehood-island/story?id=74055630
428	https://www.tampabay.com/opinion/2021/04/20/puerto-ricans-voted-for-statehood-now-they-are-waiting-on-congress-column/
429	https://www.nytimes.com/2018/12/26/theater/hamilton-puerto-rico-lin-manuel-miranda.html
430	https://www.nytimes.com/2017/05/03/business/dealbook/puerto-rico-debt.html
431	https://www.bloomberg.com/news/articles/2021-02-24/puerto-rico-bondholders-cheer-deal-paving-way-to-end-bankruptcy
432	http://www.investopedia.com/terms/m/municipalbondfund.asp
433	https://www.nbcnews.com/news/latino/billions-puerto-rico-s-debt-might-be-invalid-federal-oversight-n958846
434	https://en.wikipedia.org/wiki/Puerto_Rican_government-debt_crisis
435	http://mentalfloss.com/article/13022/puerto-rico-verge-becoming-51st-state
436	https://www.wftv.com/news/local/hurricane-maria-victims-still-in-need-of-shelter-as-fema-help-ends/834066948
437	https://www.economist.com/blogs/graphicdetail/2017/08/daily-chart-19
438	https://edition.cnn.com/2019/03/28/politics/ricardo-rossell-donald-trump-puerto-rico-funding/index.html
439	http://nymag.com/daily/intelligencer/2018/09/brock-long-puerto-rico-hurricane-maria.html
440	https://www.huffingtonpost.com/maru-gonzalez/4-reasons-independence-is-the-right-path-for-puerto-rico_b_7907434.html
441	https://www.washingtonpost.com/news/wonk/wp/2015/03/01/this-is-the-best-explanation-of-gerrymandering-you-will-ever-see/?utm_term=.be1af513c09c
442	https://www.gpb.org/news/2020/11/05/georgia-today-how-racial-gerrymandering-divided-south-georgia-town
443	https://www.vox.com/2018/6/18/17474912/supreme-court-gerrymandering-gill-whitford-wisconsin
444	https://www.facingsouth.org/2020/11/north-carolina-election-results-show-persistence-partisan-gerrymandering
445	https://www.brennancenter.org/publication/extreme-maps
446	https://edition.cnn.com/2017/06/19/opinions/wisconsin-gerrymandering-scotus-douglas-opinion/index.html
447	https://www.isidewith.com/poll/318942016
448	https://www.ocregister.com/2017/07/28/california-redistricting-panel-an-example-for-u-s-2/

449 https://www.washingtonpost.com/graphics/2018/national/gerrymandering-in-california-where-do-you-draw-the-lines/?utm_term=.6d9d3f9bc720
450 https://www.citylab.com/equity/2016/10/the-big-sort-revisited/504830/
451 https://www.theguardian.com/commentisfree/2013/jan/03/gerrymandering-polarise-congress
452 https://fivethirtyeight.com/features/ending-gerrymandering-wont-fix-what-ails-america/
453 https://www.theguardian.com/law/2018/jun/18/supreme-court-sidesteps-ruling-in-partisan-gerrymandering-cases
454 https://www.washingtonpost.com/news/the-fix/wp/2018/03/28/marylands-redistricting-case-reminds-us-both-parties-gerrymander-a-lot/?utm_term=.fd25d72f0f84
455 https://www.theatlantic.com/politics/archive/2013/07/no-gerrymandering-not-destroying-democracy/312772/
456 https://www.theguardian.com/commentisfree/2013/jan/03/gerrymandering-polarise-congress
457 https://www.theguardian.com/commentisfree/2013/jan/03/gerrymandering-polarise-congress
458 https://fivethirtyeight.com/features/ending-gerrymandering-wont-fix-what-ails-america/
459 https://www.tandfonline.com/doi/abs/10.1080/24694452.2016.1191991?journalCode=raag21
460 https://fivethirtyeight.blogs.nytimes.com/2012/12/27/as-swing-districts-dwindle-can-a-divided-house-stand/
461 https://edition.cnn.com/2020/10/29/health/political-party-hate-study-wellness/index.html
462 https://www.un.org/un70/en/content/history/index.html
463 http://www.e-ir.info/2013/02/23/is-the-united-nations-an-effective-institution/
464 https://www.cnbc.com/2018/02/23/amnesty-ten-global-hotspots-for-major-human-rights-violations-in-2017.html
465 http://www.telegraph.co.uk/news/worldnews/africaandindianocean/centralafricanrepublic/10744412/After-the-Rwandan-genocide-20-years-ago-we-said-Never-Again.-Did-we-mean-it.html
466 http://www.foxnews.com/world/2017/09/23/un-peacekeepers-in-congo-hold-record-for-rape-sex-abuse.html
467 https://www.theguardian.com/world/2005/mar/25/unitednations
468 https://www.bbc.com/news/44537372
469 https://www.theatlantic.com/international/archive/2018/05/syria-is-now-in-charge-of-the-uns-disarmament-efforts-really/561386/
470 http://nationalpost.com/news/world/peacekeeper-babies-an-unintended-consequence-of-sending-in-the-united-nations

471 https://www.transparency.org/news/pressrelease/corruption_threatens_peacekeeping_success
472 https://www.nytimes.com/2017/06/26/world/americas/cholera-haiti-united-nations-peacekeepers-yemen.html
473 http://www.npr.org/sections/health-shots/2011/05/06/136049974/verdict-haitis-cholera-outbreak-originated-in-u-n-camp
474 http://www.npr.org/sections/thetwo-way/2016/08/18/490468640/u-n-admits-role-in-haiti-cholera-outbreak-that-has-killed-thousands
475 https://www.legalzoom.com/articles/what-kind-of-power-does-the-un-wield-internationally
476 http://www.un.org/en/sections/about-un/main-organs/
477 https://en.wikipedia.org/wiki/List_of_United_Nations_peacekeeping_missions
478 https://www.nytimes.com/2016/09/19/world/what-is-united-nations-un-explained.html
479 http://www.nytimes.com/2012/05/31/world/africa/charles-taylor-sentenced-to-50-years-for-war-crimes.html
480 http://www.un.org/en/universal-declaration-human-rights/
481 http://www.telegraph.co.uk/news/worldnews/europe/switzerland/11700969/UN-at-70-Five-greatest-successes-and-failures.html
482 https://news.un.org/en/story/2018/06/1012662
483 https://sdgs.un.org/goals
484 http://www.worldhunger.org/africa-hunger-poverty-facts/
485 http://www.un.org/sustainabledevelopment/blog/2015/07/what-progress-has-been-made-in-ending-global-poverty/
486 http://www.un.org/ga/search/view_doc.asp?symbol=A/69/700&Lang=E
487 http://www.npr.org/sections/parallels/2017/05/08/526078459/giving-up-nuclear-weapons-its-rare-but-its-happened
488 https://thediplomat.com/2015/04/kazakhstan-nuclear-weapons-free-for-20-years/
489 http://www.independent.co.uk/news/world/politics/g20-summit-120-countries-adopt-nuclear-weapons-ban-treaty-arms-war-prohibition-disarmament-a7828581.html
490 https://www.emirates247.com/news/world/obama-backs-un-secretary-general-for-new-term-2011-06-07-1.401600
491 https://www.businessinsider.com/snowden-leaks-timeline-2016-9
492 https://www.nytimes.com/2019/09/13/books/review-permanent-record-edward-snowden-memoir.html
493 https://www.nytimes.com/2019/08/01/books/edward-snowden-book.html
494 https://www.theguardian.com/world/interactive/2013/nov/01/snowden-nsa-files-surveillance-revelations-decoded
495 https://reclaimthenet.org/edward-snowden-surveillance-democracy/
496 https://www.lawfareblog.com/so-what-does-usa-freedom-act-do-anyway

497   https://faq.whatsapp.com/en/android/28030015/
498   https://www.theperspective.com/debates/politics/whistleblowers-heroes-traitors/
499   http://fortune.com/2017/10/03/edward-snowden-nsa-fisa-section-702/
500   http://www.cbc.ca/news/world/greenwald-the-investigators-1.3816510
501   http://edition.cnn.com/2016/05/30/politics/axe-files-axelrod-eric-holder/
502   https://www.theguardian.com/books/2019/aug/01/edward-snowden-memoir-to-reveal-whistleblowers-secrets-permanent-record
503   https://www.cjr.org/the_media_today/snowden-5-years.php
504   https://www.smh.com.au/world/north-america/five-years-on-us-government-still-counting-snowden-leak-costs-20180604-p4zj9d.html
505   https://www.bbc.com/news/world-us-canada-23123964
506   https://www.theguardian.com/commentisfree/2013/jun/22/snowden-espionage-charges
507   https://www.theguardian.com/commentisfree/2013/jun/22/snowden-espionage-charges

Living

1   https://www.youtube.com/watch?v=b-2fnZfK9Lg
2   https://www.cdc.gov/coronavirus/2019-ncov/prepare/managing-stress-anxiety.html
3   https://allthatsinteresting.com/worst-natural-disasters
4   https://www.ncbi.nlm.nih.gov/pmc/articles/PMC3126102/
5   https://www.forbes.com/sites/benjaminlaker/2020/03/13/how-to-be-positive-in-the-coronavirus-world/
6   https://slate.com/human-interest/2020/03/what-i-learned-about-self-quarantine-from-nine-months-of-chemotherapy.html
7   https://www.huffingtonpost.com/thai-nguyen/hacking-into-your-happy-c_b_6007660.html
8   https://www.theperspective.com/debates/antidepressants-good-solution/
9   http://journals.humankinetics.com/doi/abs/10.1123/jsep.33.6.884
10 https://www.sciencefocus.com/the-human-body/does-chocolate-make-you-happy/
11 https://positivepsychologyprogram.com/goal-setting/
12 http://www.nytimes.com/2011/11/22/science/a-serving-of-gratitude-brings-healthy-dividends.html
13 https://greatergood.berkeley.edu/pdfs/GratitudePDFs/2Wood-GratitudeWell-BeingReview.pdf
14 https://www.brainpickings.org/2014/02/18/martin-seligman-gratitude-visit-three-blessings/

15 https://www.psychologytoday.com/us/blog/emotional-nourishment/201711/why-random-acts-kindness-matter-your-well-being
16 https://www.forbes.com/sites/womensmedia/2016/12/21/how-to-train-your-brain-to-go-positive-instead-of-negative/
17 http://www.yourhormones.info/hormones/cortisol/
18 https://abc7.com/school-shootings-in-america-see-a-map-of-all-incidents-from-2010-2019/5697308/
19 https://www.ranker.com/list/worst-natural-disasters-2019/sammy-leary
20 https://www.bbc.com/news/world-51235105
21 http://www.pnas.org/content/114/32/8523
22 http://www.oecdbetterlifeindex.org/topics/life-satisfaction/
23 https://www.mayoclinic.org/diseases-conditions/seasonal-affective-disorder/basics/definition/con-20021047
24 http://www.spring.org.uk/2013/10/the-genetic-predisposition-to-focus-on-the-negative.php
25 https://www.encyclopedia.com/science/encyclopedias-almanacs-transcripts-and-maps/how-major-religions-view-afterlife
26 https://www.worldometers.info/coronavirus/?utm_campaign=homeAdUOA?Si
27 https://www.medicinenet.com/script/main/art.asp?articlekey=33438
28 https://www.indy100.com/article/is-there-an-afterlife-life-after-death-impossible-scientist-claims-8043746
29 https://www.thesun.co.uk/living/3177092/30-seconds-before-die/
30 https://www.express.co.uk/news/weird/1283735/Life-after-death-afterlife-account-NDE-near-death-experience-story
31 https://science.howstuffworks.com/science-vs-myth/afterlife/during-near-death-experience.htm
32 https://www.theperspective.com/debates/the-perspective-on-ayahuasca/
33 https://www.scientificamerican.com/article/new-clues-found-in-understanding-near-death-experiences/
34 https://pubmed.ncbi.nlm.nih.gov/30711788/
35 https://www.medicalnewstoday.com/articles/321792.php
36 https://www.express.co.uk/news/weird/1006439/life-after-death-what-happens-when-you-die-proof-of-afterlife
37 http://www.nderf.org/
38 https://www.amazon.com/Dying-Be-Me-Journey-Healing/dp/1401937535
39 https://www.youtube.com/watch?v=rhcJNJbRJ6U
40 https://iands.org/ndes/nde-stories/17-nde-accounts-from-beyond-the-light.html
41 https://www.express.co.uk/news/science/1005845/life-after-death-what-happens-when-you-die-soul-quantum
42 https://www.vice.com/en_us/article/vbmw89/near-death-experiences-have-a-freakish-amount-in-common

43 https://abcnews.go.com/GMA/DrJohnson/story?id=126449&page=1
44 https://abcnews.go.com/GMA/DrJohnson/story?id=126449&page=1
45 https://theculturetrip.com/north-america/mexico/articles/the-day-of-the-dead-mexico-s-mysterious-holiday/
46 https://www.imdb.com/title/tt2380307/
47 https://www.ancient.eu/Egyptian_Book_of_the_Dead/
48 http://www.viralnova.com/death-festivals/
49 https://www.tripsavvy.com/galungan-welcoming-the-spirits-home-to-bali-1629256
50 http://rsob.royalsocietypublishing.org/content/7/1/160267
51 https://royalsocietypublishing.org/doi/full/10.1098/rsob.160267
52 https://www.forbes.com/sites/startswithabang/2018/10/18/this-is-how-we-know-there-are-two-trillion-galaxies-in-the-universe/
53 https://www.usatoday.com/story/news/nation/2019/07/31/super-earth-potentially-habitable-planet-found-31-light-years-away/1884130001/
54 https://www.ranker.com/crowdranked-list/all-alien-movies-or-list-of-alien-movies
55 https://www.theverge.com/2019/7/5/20683399/stranger-things-season-3-review-duffer-brothers-finn-wolfhard-millie-bobby-brown-david-harbour
56 https://www.youtube.com/watch?v=t5Sd5c4o9UM
57 https://www.chemistryworld.com/news/meteorites-mechanical-energy-might-have-created-building-blocks-of-life/3008600.article
58 https://futurism.com/evolutionary-biology-intelligent-alien-life/
59 https://www.chemistryworld.com/feature/life-on-other-planets/3008503.article
60 https://www.space.com/25325-fermi-paradox.html
61 https://www.space.com/24054-how-old-is-the-universe.html
62 https://www.theatlantic.com/science/archive/2018/04/are-we-earths-only-civilization/557180/
63 https://gizmodo.com/5754347/how-far-in-space-can-radio-broadcasts-reach
64 http://www.businessinsider.com/why-aliens-have-not-contacted-humans-2015-9
65 https://cosmosmagazine.com/palaeontology/big-five-extinctions
66 http://www.astronomy.com/news/2016/01/the-aliens-are-silent-because-they-are-extinct
67 https://www.independent.co.uk/news/science/theres-a-compelling-reason-scientists-think-weve-never-found-aliens-and-it-suggests-humans-are-a7886066.html
68 http://sciencenordic.com/scientist-we-could-find-intelligent-life-space-within-two-decades
69 https://news.cornell.edu/stories/2019/07/tess-satellite-uncovers-its-first-nearby-super-earth

70	https://www.chemistryworld.com/feature/life-on-other-planets/3008503.article
71	https://www.wired.com/story/if-theres-life-on-saturns-moon-enceladus-it-might-look-like-this/
72	https://futurism.com/expert-well-find-alien-life-in-the-next-10-15-years-but-it-wont-be-intelligent/
73	https://www.nytimes.com/2017/12/16/us/politics/pentagon-program-ufo-harry-reid.html
74	https://www.washingtonpost.com/news/dr-gridlock/wp/2018/03/28/a-ufo-faa-recording-reveals-moment-two-pilots-report-unknown-object-flying-overhead/?utm_term=.405f70afc03d
75	https://www.youtube.com/watch?v=3RlbqOl_4NA
76	https://www.history.com/news/ufo-sightings-credible-modern
77	https://www.forbes.com/sites/startswithabang/2018/01/12/are-aliens-plentiful-but-were-just-missing-them/
78	https://www.pewresearch.org/fact-tank/2019/05/22/u-s-fertility-rate-explained/
79	http://www.pewsocialtrends.org/2015/05/07/childlessness/
80	https://www.carbonbrief.org/state-of-the-climate-first-quarter-of-2020-is-second-warmest-on-record
81	https://www.crisisgroup.org/global/10-conflicts-watch-2020
82	https://edition.cnn.com/2020/03/18/world/coronavirus-and-climate-crisis-response-intl-hnk/index.html
83	https://www.weforum.org/agenda/2020/06/us-race-economy-education-inequality/
84	https://inhabitat.com/runaway-carbon-emissions-threaten-two-thirds-of-the-earths-oxygen-supply/
85	https://www.crisisgroup.org/global/10-conflicts-watch-2020
86	http://www.ranker.com/list/childless-celebrities/celebrity-lists
87	https://en.wikipedia.org/wiki/Susan_B._Anthony
88	https://www.biography.com/people/nikola-tesla-9504443
89	http://money.cnn.com/2017/01/09/pf/cost-of-raising-a-child-2015/
90	https://www.usda.gov/media/blog/2017/01/13/cost-raising-child
91	https://qz.com/262645/people-without-kids-live-better-than-parents-on-all-fronts-except-one/
92	https://qz.com/912684/economists-quantified-what-sleep-deprivation-does-to-mothers-pay-and-productivity/
93	http://time.com/4673035/do-the-child-free-live-longer/
94	https://qz.com/802254/the-ultimate-efficiency-hack-have-kids/
95	http://nationalinterest.org/feature/chinas-self-inflicted-demographic-disaster-here-14216
96	https://www.bls.gov/iag/tgs/iag61.htm
97	http://ec.europa.eu/eurostat/statistics-explained/index.php/Educational_expenditure_statistics

98   http://www.today.com/parents/motherhood-brings-out-worst-us-best-1C9329506
99   http://time.com/4475048/which-came-first-chicken-egg/
100   https://www.theperspective.com/debates/living/perspective-time-linear-cyclical/
101   https://www.bonappetit.com/story/why-do-we-eat-eggs-for-breakfast
102   https://twitter.com/BillNye/status/296120258136248320
103   https://twitter.com/neiltyson/status/296100559423954944
104   https://www.mnn.com/earth-matters/animals/stories/finally-answered-which-came-first-the-chicken-or-the-egg
105   http://time.com/4475048/which-came-first-chicken-egg/
106   https://www.britannica.com/animal/Archaeopteryx
107   https://splice-bio.com/genetically-modified-chickens-lay-cancer-fighting-eggs/
108   https://www.ndtv.com/food/japanese-mutant-hens-are-laying-eggs-filled-with-cancer-drugs-1760992
109   https://www.neogen.com/neocenter/blog/chicken-eggs-may-lower-cost-of-cancer-treatment/
110   http://www.nbcnews.com/id/38238685/ns/technology_and_science-science/t/which-came-first-chicken-or-egg/
111   https://onlinelibrary.wiley.com/doi/abs/10.1002/anie.201000679
112   http://www.dailymail.co.uk/sciencetech/article-1294341/Chicken-really-DID-come-egg-say-scientists.html
113   https://www.theperspective.com/debates/living/should-the-bible-stories-be-regarded-as-history/
114   https://wcel.nwaonline.com/news/2020/feb/05/religion-the-year-2020-is-designated-as/
115   https://en.wikipedia.org/wiki/Book_of_Genesis
116   http://www.the-chicken-chick.com/caring-for-broody-hens-facilitating-egg/
117   https://www.independent.co.uk/environment/nature/what-does-a-hen-do-with-her-unfertilised-eggs-10100975.html
118   http://pages.vassar.edu/sensoryecology/smell-no-evil-birds-use-odd-smells-to-eject-foreign-eggs-from-a-host-nest/
119   http://abcnews.go.com/2020/story?id=124285
120   http://kidshealth.org/en/parents/medical-adopt.html
121   https://www.ncbi.nlm.nih.gov/pmc/articles/PMC4291307/
122   https://www.childandfamilyblog.com/social-emotional-learning/open-adoption-2/
123   http://www.umass.edu/ruddchair/research/mtarp/key-findings/outcomes-adopted-children-and-adolescents
124   https://www.ncbi.nlm.nih.gov/pmc/articles/PMC2638763/
125   http://www.umass.edu/ruddchair/research/mtarp/key-findings/outcomes-adopted-children-and-adolescents

126 https://www.adoptivefamilies.com/openness/understanding-open-adoption/
127 http://www.americaadopts.com/what-growing-up-in-an-open-adoption-has-taught-me/
128 https://www.franchisehelp.com/industry-reports/pet-care-industry-analysis-2018-cost-trends/
129 https://www.americanpetproducts.org/press_industrytrends.asp
130 https://www.theguardian.com/world/2020/apr/03/pets-helping-coronavirus-crisis-animals
131 https://www.wired.com/story/coronavirus-pet-adoption-boom/
132 https://3milliondogs.com/dogbook/10-unbelievable-jobs-that-dogs-do/
133 http://www.livescience.com/5613-dogs-smart-2-year-kids.html
134 https://www.sciencedirect.com/science/article/pii/S0148296307002214
135 https://www.scottsdalepethotel.com/why-dogs-are-so-protective-of-their-owners/
136 http://www.mnn.com/family/pets/stories/6-medical-conditions-that-dogs-can-sniff
137 https://well.blogs.nytimes.com/2011/03/14/forget-the-treadmill-get-a-dog/
138 https://phys.org/news/2015-09-cats-independent-dogs.html
139 https://www.independent.co.uk/news/science/this-is-how-your-cat-sees-you-9051965.html
140 https://www.indiegogo.com/projects/smart-kitty-automatic-litter-box-for-cats
141 https://www.washingtonpost.com/news/animalia/wp/2017/03/22/you-can-train-your-cat-to-use-the-toilet-just-dont-expect-it-to-flush/
142 http://www.dailyinfographic.com/the-healing-power-of-cat-purrs-infographic
143 https://www.independent.co.uk/life-style/health-and-families/coronavirus-pet-dog-can-you-catch-it-transmission-a9376926.html
144 https://edition.cnn.com/2017/02/10/health/move-personality-changes-partner/index.html
145 https://www.statista.com/statistics/269967/urbanization-in-the-united-states/
146 http://www.pewsocialtrends.org/2018/05/22/demographic-and-economic-trends-in-urban-suburban-and-rural-communities/
147 https://www.care.com/c/stories/9696/carecom-zillow-cost-of-living-comparison/
148 https://www.businessinsider.com/where-suburbs-are-cheaper-than-cities-2017-3
149 https://www.realtor.com/advice/finance/suburb-vs-city-where-is-cheaper/
150 https://www.theguardian.com/society/2018/jul/26/millennials-moving-suburbs-america-housing-crisis-urban-exodus

151 http://www.realtor.com/news/trends/home-values-grow-faster-in-cities-than-the-suburbs/
152 https://www.pinterest.com/pin/348888302354728732/
153 https://ny.curbed.com/micro-apartments-nyc
154 https://undark.org/2016/05/31/psychology-living-small-spaces/
155 https://www.theatlantic.com/health/archive/2013/12/the-health-risks-of-small-apartments/282150/
156 https://www.theguardian.com/commentisfree/2017/mar/13/warning-living-city-seriously-damage-health
157 https://grist.org/justice/does-city-living-spread-coronavirus-its-complicated/
158 https://www.theguardian.com/tv-and-radio/2017/may/27/baltimore-15-years-after-the-wire
159 https://patch.com/illinois/chicago/chicago-saw-more-killings-any-city-isnt-most-dangerous
160 https://www.security.org/resources/police-brutality-statistics/
161 https://www.businessinsider.com/most-violent-city-every-us-state-fbi-2018-4
162 https://ucr.fbi.gov/crime-in-the-u.s/2015/crime-in-the-u.s.-2015/tables/table-6
163 https://ovc.ncjrs.gov/ncvrw2016/content/section-6/PDF/2016NCVRW_6_UrbanRural-508.pdf
164 https://www.theperspective.com/debates/living/america-still-land-opportunity/
165 https://www.history.com/topics/immigration/u-s-immigration-before-1965
166 http://www.english-online.at/geography/world-population/urban-areas.htm
167 https://www.thoughtco.com/largest-cities-throughout-history-4068071
168 https://www.pbs.org/newshour/world/half-worlds-population-live-urban-areas-un-report-finds
169 https://en.wikipedia.org/wiki/List_of_Chinatowns
170 https://en.wikipedia.org/wiki/Little_Italy
171 https://en.wikipedia.org/wiki/Little_India_(location)
172 https://www.businessinsider.com/average-cost-car-insurance-in-every-state-ranked-2018-3
173 https://www.thoughtco.com/public-transit-or-drive-cost-2798677
174 https://en.wikipedia.org/wiki/History_of_the_New_York_City_Subway
175 https://en.wikipedia.org/wiki/Trams_in_Europe
176 https://en.wikipedia.org/wiki/Pacoima,_Los_Angeles
177 https://theculturetrip.com/north-america/usa/articles/12-best-us-cities-for-culture/
178 https://www.6sqft.com/city-kids-why-these-parents-pick-city-living-over-the-suburbs/

179 https://www.usnews.com/news/world-report/articles/2020-06-26/north-korea-threatens-us-with-nuclear-attack
180 https://www.usatoday.com/story/news/nation/2020/06/07/black-lives-matters-police-departments-have-long-history-racism/3128167001/
181 https://www.bbc.com/news/world-us-canada-52932611
182 https://slate.com/news-and-politics/2018/10/charlottesville-violence-was-premeditated.html
183 https://en.wikipedia.org/wiki/Unite_the_Right_rally
184 https://foreignpolicy.com/2019/03/18/syrias-civil-war-is-now-3-civil-wars/
185 https://edition.cnn.com/interactive/2018/02/us/florida-school-shooting-cnnphotos/
186 https://www.nbcnews.com/las-vegas-shooting
187 https://edition.cnn.com/2020/06/28/us/louisville-breonna-taylor-protest-park-shooting/index.html
188 https://www.usatoday.com/story/news/2018/10/28/pittsburgh-shooting-squirrel-hill-neighbors-left-reeling-mourning/1801363002/
189 https://edition.cnn.com/asia/live-news/new-zealand-christchurch-shooting-intl/index.html
190 https://www.lawfareblog.com/christchurch-shooting-domestic-terrorism-goes-international
191 https://www.youtube.com/watch?v=dQn1-mLkIHw
192 https://www.ncbi.nlm.nih.gov/pubmed/10601982
193 http://www.penguinrandomhouse.com/books/290730/the-blank-slate-by-steven-pinker/
194 https://www.socialsciencespace.com/2012/11/podcast-steven-pinker-on-violence-and-human-nature/
195 https://www.ncbi.nlm.nih.gov/pubmed/22477166
196 https://www.newyorker.com/magazine/2000/10/09/the-fierce-anthropologist-2
197 https://plato.stanford.edu/entries/hobbes-moral/
198 https://www.edge.org/conversation/steven_pinker-a-history-of-violence-edge-master-class-2011
199 https://www.sciencemag.org/news/2016/09/why-do-we-kill-controversial-study-blames-our-distant-ancestors
200 https://www.scientificamerican.com/article/the-decline-of-violence/
201 https://evolution-institute.org/article/no-room-for-a-gentle-ape/
202 https://www.dailymail.co.uk/sciencetech/article-4463722/Bonobos-closely-related-humans-chimps.html
203 https://www.youtube.com/watch?v=66IeDfeGbzA
204 https://greatergood.berkeley.edu/article/item/worlds_without_war
205 https://www.smithsonianmag.com/innovation/why-was-this-man-an-outcast-among-anthropologists-22930097/

206 https://www.washingtonpost.com/nation/2018/10/01/it-seemed-last-forever-one-year-later-mystery-las-vegas-massacre-remains/?utm_term=.fe231b2d2e41
207 https://www.history.com/topics/1990s/oklahoma-city-bombing
208 https://www.youtube.com/watch?v=mHjH1sl1o9s
209 https://www.youtube.com/watch?v=6X7cVDxYd6A
210 https://abcnews.go.com/US/anatomy-las-vegas-mass-shooting-deadliest-modern-us/story?id=59797324
211 https://edition.cnn.com/2020/02/14/us/parkland-shooting-marjory-stoneman-douglas-2-years/index.html
212 https://www.theguardian.com/world/2019/mar/21/christchurch-shooting-ardern-friday-prayer-mosque-reopen-gun-laws
213 https://www.theperspective.com/debates/politics/bombings-hiroshima-nagasaki-necessary-evil-just-evil/
214 https://www.youtube.com/watch?v=nHFTtz3uucY
215 http://time.com/4158007/american-fear-history/
216 https://www.rollingstone.com/politics/features/why-were-living-in-the-age-of-fear-w443554
217 https://www.chapman.edu/wilkinson/research-centers/babbie-center/_files/fear-of-2020-election-blog-updated.pdf
218 https://www.ncbi.nlm.nih.gov/pmc/articles/PMC7425672/
219 https://www.chapman.edu/wilkinson/research-centers/babbie-center/survey-american-fears.aspx
220 https://www.bbc.com/future/article/20200401-covid-19-how-fear-of-coronavirus-is-changing-our-psychology
221 https://www.business-standard.com/article/current-affairs/coronavirus-mutation-is-the-fear-justified-and-where-does-it-come-from-120121600265_1.html
222 https://deadline.com/2014/06/new-study-tv-violence-makes-people-more-afraid-of-crime-but-not-afraid-there-is-more-crime-792399/
223 https://www.fbi.gov/news/stories/2019-preliminary-semiannual-uniform-crime-report-released-012120
224 https://www.edge.org/response-detail/26696
225 https://www.who.int/csr/disease/ebola/one-year-report/virus-origin/en/
226 https://www.wired.com/2014/10/ebolanoia/
227 https://en.wikipedia.org/wiki/Ebola_virus_cases_in_the_United_States
228 https://www.huffingtonpost.com/douglas-labier/personal-development_b_2664129.html
229 https://www.huffingtonpost.com/catherine-chen-phd/afraid-of-disappointing-your-parents-heres-how-to-move-on_b_7678486.html
230 http://www.sciencemag.org/careers/2016/02/how-fear-can-limit-your-career-potential
231 http://www.sciencemag.org/careers/2008/02/no-youre-not-impostor
232 https://www.youtube.com/watch?v=h7v-GG3SEWQ

233 https://www.elitedaily.com/dating/fear-not-finding-love/1203713
234 https://www.telegraph.co.uk/women/sex/divorce/11710646/The-D-Word-Is-fear-the-only-thing-keeping-me-from-divorce.html
235 https://www.theperspective.com/debates/the-perspective-on-divorce/
236 https://www.nytimes.com/2020/05/25/health/coronavirus-cancer-heart-treatment.html
237 https://www.psychologytoday.com/us/blog/the-human-experience/201610/the-impact-death-our-everyday-lives
238 https://academyofideas.com/2015/11/fear-and-social-control/
239 https://www.theperspective.com/subjective-timeline/politics/rise-power-nazi-party/
240 https://www.theperspective.com/debates/politics/stalin-hero-villain/
241 https://www.livestrong.com/article/122357-cognitive-effects-anxiety/
242 https://www.dw.com/en/coronavirus-misinformation/a-54529310
243 https://www.sciencedirect.com/topics/neuroscience/fear-conditioning
244 https://www.youtube.com/watch?v=w1sHAGAuceE
245 https://www.cnbc.com/2020/02/27/coronavirus-raises-worries-about-a-broad-slowdown-in-air-travel.html
246 https://www.eurekalert.org/pub_releases/2014-07/uomh-lts072414.php
247 https://blogs.scientificamerican.com/mind-guest-blog/to-feel-meaningful-is-to-feel-immortal/
248 https://www.drweil.com/blog/spontaneous-happiness/the-legacy-of-music/
249 https://www.youtube.com/watch?v=tQlv5bxsVcE
250 https://www.psychologytoday.com/us/articles/201011/stealth-super-powers
251 https://www.scientificamerican.com/article/extreme-fear-superhuman/
252 https://medium.com/philonomist/when-is-it-ok-to-lie-ce56ca952984
253 https://www.psychologytoday.com/us/blog/happiness-in-world/201402/why-be-honest
254 https://www.theglobeandmail.com/life/the-hot-button/think-you-can-ease-your-conscience-with-by-telling-a-bit-of-the-truth-think-again/article16464794/
255 https://news.nd.edu/news/study-telling-fewer-lies-linked-to-better-health-relationships/
256 http://time.com/4540707/lying-lies-brain/
257 https://www.psychologytoday.com/us/blog/happiness-in-world/201402/why-be-honest
258 http://www.abc.net.au/news/2016-10-26/fear-trust--social-contract-society-on-permanent-alert/7959304
259 https://www.theperspective.com/debates/living/can-people-change-minds/
260 https://www.aarp.org/health/drugs-supplements/info-2020/covid-vaccine-myths.html

261 https://www.cnn.com/2016/03/04/us/flint-water-crisis-fast-facts/index.html
262 https://www.washingtonpost.com/national/health-science/flints-water-crisis-reveals-government-failures-at-every-level/2016/01/23/03705f0c-c11e-11e5-bcda-62a36b394160_story.html?utm_term=.0b895aa0f119
263 http://www.oprah.com/spirit/when-to-lie-when-to-tell-the-truth/all
264 https://www.theperspective.com/debates/businessandtechnology/perspective-twitter-life-enhancing-life-disabling-tool/
265 https://www.theodysseyonline.com/open-letter-those-overshare-social-media
266 http://www.sensationalcolor.com/color-meaning/color-words-phrases/white-lies-2122
267 https://www.psychologytoday.com/us/blog/we-can-work-it-out/201310/why-honesty-isnt-always-the-best-policy
268 https://newatlas.com/santa-survey-belief-father-christmas-children/57788/
269 https://www.theperspective.com/subjective-timeline/politics/cuban-missile-crisis/
270 https://www.inc.com/will-yakowicz/honesty-is-not-the-best-policy.html
271 https://thehill.com/changing-america/well-being/prevention-cures/489813-majority-of-americans-staying-home-as-much-as
272 https://www.theguardian.com/world/2020/mar/17/pause-reflect-and-stay-home-how-to-look-after-yourself-and-others-in-self-isolation
273 https://www.youtube.com/watch?v=Ph6U3mFBkO4
274 https://www.imdb.com/title/tt0088763/
275 https://www.youtube.com/watch?v=SR5BfQ4rEqQ
276 https://www.livescience.com/50941-second-law-thermodynamics.html
277 https://www.timeanddate.com/time/international-atomic-time.html
278 https://www.vice.com/en_us/article/gymn5m/there-is-more-than-one-kind-of-deja-vu
279 https://eclipse.gsfc.nasa.gov/SEhelp/calendars.html
280 https://www.independent.co.uk/news/science/archaeology/news/found-after-10000-years-the-world-s-first-calendar-8708322.html
281 https://www.theguardian.com/lifeandstyle/2020/mar/17/silver-linings-how-to-stay-positive-during-the-coronavirus-crisis
282 https://www.algemeiner.com/2014/01/28/jewish-and-chinese-calendars-are-more-similar-than-you-think/
283 https://www.theperspective.com/debates/living/finally-embrace-religion-finally-let-go/
284 http://www.history.com/topics/mahatma-gandhi
285 https://www.nobelprize.org/nobel_prizes/peace/laureates/1964/king-bio.html
286 https://www.biography.com/people/desmond-tutu-9512516

287 https://apnews.com/article/ruth-bader-ginsburg-race-and-ethnicity-discrimination-us-supreme-court-courts-1a8a92b60bd08a3ac-05c29a787ff399e
288 https://www.pewresearch.org/fact-tank/2020/04/30/few-americans-say-their-house-of-worship-is-open-but-a-quarter-say-their-religious-faith-has-grown-amid-pandemic/
289 https://artscolumbia.org/artists/michelangelo/michelangelo-and-religion-20889/
290 https://www.telegraph.co.uk/technology/2020/04/10/religion-goes-digital-churches-mosques-synagogues-turn-video/
291 https://qz.com/1815328/religions-are-embracing-live-streaming-and-conference-calls/
292 https://www.psypost.org/2013/06/painful-and-extreme-rituals-enhance-social-cohesion-and-charity-18516
293 https://www.sciencenews.org/article/rise-human-civilization-tied-belief-punitive-gods
294 https://en.wikipedia.org/wiki/On_the_Jews_and_Their_Lies
295 https://www.washingtonpost.com/news/worldviews/wp/2016/06/13/here-are-the-10-countries-where-homosexuality-may-be-punished-by-death-2/?utm_term=.29392ff388cb
296 https://www.nytimes.com/2017/08/07/health/atheists-religion-study.html
297 https://www.dw.com/en/germany-halle-synagogue-shooting-suspect-charged-with-double-murder/a-53201696
298 https://www.sciencedaily.com/releases/2007/02/070223143009.htm
299 https://www.youtube.com/watch?v=_0B1sMfxWYw&list=PLUc3xWze-J0RQTqVMZK0c0K-tw7ew3yAAL&index=8&t=0s
300 https://www.theatlantic.com/national/archive/2011/11/drinking-the-kool-aid-a-survivor-remembers-jim-jones/248723/
301 https://www.vox.com/2018/4/19/17246732/waco-tragedy-explained-david-koresh-mount-carmel-branch-davidian-cult-25-year-anniversary
302 https://www.pewresearch.org/social-trends/2020/12/09/how-the-coronavirus-outbreak-has-and-hasnt-changed-the-way-americans-work/
303 https://www.naco.org/featured-resources/future-work-rise-gig-economy
304 https://www.bbc.com/news/business-56192048
305 https://www.shrm.org/hr-today/news/hr-news/pages/flex-work-overtime.aspx
306 https://www.nytimes.com/2020/03/10/technology/working-from-home.html
307 https://www.inc.com/geoffrey-james/is-your-personality-type-right-for-working-remotely.html
308 https://www.workforce.com/2016/06/21/the-history-of-retirement-benefits/
309 https://qz.com/work/1360865/freelancers-facing-discrimination-have-fewer-legal-options/

310 http://www.oreilly.com/iot/free/files/serving-workers-gig-economy.pdf
311 http://business.time.com/2012/07/17/work-from-home-and-you-might-miss-a-raise-2/
312 http://blogs.wsj.com/atwork/2012/07/13/working-from-home-beware-a-career-hit/
313 https://www.flexjobs.com/blog/post/hidden-costs-of-freelancing/
314 http://www.forbes.com/sites/victorlipman/2016/05/02/are-remote-workers-happier-and-more-productive-new-survey-offers-answers/
315 https://remote.co/10-stats-about-remote-work/
316 https://hbr.org/2014/01/to-raise-productivity-let-more-employees-work-from-home
317 https://www.forbes.com/sites/andrealoubier/2017/07/20/benefits-of-telecommuting-for-the-future-of-work/
318 https://www.monster.com/career-advice/article/the-benefits-of-working-from-home
319 https://fortune.com/2020/03/10/coronavirus-remote-flexible-work-from-home/
320 https://www.forbes.com/sites/andrealoubier/2017/07/20/benefits-of-telecommuting-for-the-future-of-work/
321 https://hbr.org/2016/10/who-wins-in-the-gig-economy-and-who-loses
322 https://www.thebalancesmb.com/work-from-home-jobs-for-the-disabled-3969566
323 https://garage.ext.hp.com/us/en/modern-life/remote-workers-flex-work-increase-productivity.html
324 https://www.owllabs.com/blog/remote-work-statistics
325 http://www.forbes.com/sites/forbescoachescouncil/2017/01/04/the-gig-economy-your-ticket-to-sourcing-top-talent/2/
326 https://www.forbes.com/sites/andrealoubier/2017/07/20/benefits-of-telecommuting-for-the-future-of-work/
327 https://blog.mavenlink.com/how-the-rise-of-the-remote-worker-will-change-the-economy-forever

Entertainment

1 https://www.eonline.com/news/783227/all-the-records-harry-potter-has-broken-since-the-first-book-was-published
2 https://www.cinemablend.com/new/Harry-Potter-Deathly-Hallows-Part-2-Shatters-Midnight-Box-Office-Record-With-43-5-Million-25707.html
3 https://www.boxofficemojo.com/chart/top_opening_weekend/?area=XWW
4 https://www.cnet.com/news/why-watching-the-original-star-wars-again-was-a-bad-idea/
5 https://www.youtube.com/watch?v=OpJyVZCmPc8

6	http://mashable.com/2016/07/30/harry-potter-films-versus-books-debate/
7	https://www.bustle.com/articles/111507-8-reasons-the-harry-potter-books-are-better-than-the-movies
8	https://www.quora.com/Is-Hermione-Granger-necessarily-white
9	https://www.theguardian.com/stage/2016/feb/26/noma-dumezweni-hermione-harry-potter-and-the-cursed-child-palace-theatre
10	https://www.harrypottertheplay.com/
11	https://www.youtube.com/watch?v=6gxYEcNPkQo
12	https://consequenceofsound.net/2016/11/are-the-harry-potter-books-or-films-better/full-post/
13	https://www.theatlantic.com/entertainment/archive/2011/07/how-the-harry-potter-movies-succeeded-where-the-books-failed/241884/
14	https://wizardsandwhatnot.com/2017/01/16/molly-weasley-julie-waters/
15	https://www.youtube.com/watch?v=tc9nVR6jOxU
16	https://screenrant.com/harry-potter-book-changes-better-than-movies/
17	https://www.youtube.com/watch?v=YOVS9yn2R7c&t=2s
18	https://www.youtube.com/watch?v=eAHDS5Rn4kg
19	https://www.inverse.com/article/24076-harry-potter-visual-effects-quidditch-dragons-fantastic-beasts
20	https://screenrant.com/harry-potter-book-changes-better-than-movies/
21	https://www.youtube.com/watch?v=YKfJkhda-IE
22	https://www.pottermore.com/explore-the-story/blast-ended-skrewts
23	https://www.youtube.com/watch?v=twHLFlqZ8T8
24	https://edition.cnn.com/2019/03/04/media/reliable-sources-03-03-18/index.html
25	https://www.vox.com/culture/2019/1/30/18192932/lifetime-surviving-r-kelly-documentary-sexual-abuse
26	https://edition.cnn.com/2018/04/26/us/bill-cosby-trial/index.html
27	https://www.vox.com/culture/2017/8/17/16156902/roman-polanski-child-rape-charges-explained-samantha-geimer-robin-m
28	https://www.usatoday.com/pages/interactives/news/harvery-weinstein-timeline/
29	http://www.bbc.com/news/entertainment-arts-41884878
30	https://en.wikipedia.org/wiki/Wagner_controversies
31	http://www.telegraph.co.uk/news/worldnews/europe/italy/1396127/Red-blooded-Caravaggio-killed-love-rival-in-bungled-castration-attempt.html
32	https://en.wikipedia.org/wiki/Charles_Dickens
33	https://edition.cnn.com/2018/04/26/us/bill-cosby-trial/index.html
34	https://www.bet.com/celebrities/exclusives/cosby-show-op-ed.html
35	https://en.wikipedia.org/wiki/Roman_Polanski_sexual_abuse_case
36	http://variety.com/2018/scene/news/ronan-farrow-metoo-woody-allen-point-honors-1202749105/

37 https://www.bustle.com/p/should-we-watch-the-hundreds-of-films-produced-by-harvey-weinstein-female-film-critics-weigh-in-2894326
38 https://en.wikipedia.org/wiki/List_of_Presidents_of_the_United_States_who_owned_slaves
39 https://www.fastcompany.com/90289033/damning-documentary-gives-r-kelly-a-spotify-bump-and-he-still-has-a-record-contract
40 https://www.rollingstone.com/music/music-lists/timeline-of-chris-browns-history-of-violence-towards-women-103402/
41 https://www.theatlantic.com/entertainment/archive/2016/11/mel-gibson-is-not-sorry/506225/
42 https://en.wikipedia.org/wiki/Pablo_Picasso
43 https://www.theguardian.com/culture/2001/nov/22/artsfeatures.highereducation
44 http://www.snopes.com/history/american/mlking.asp
45 http://www.chicagotribune.com/redeye/redeye-history-sexual-abuse-allegations-woody-allen-20160719-story.html
46 https://kristof.blogs.nytimes.com/2014/02/01/an-open-letter-from-dylan-farrow/?mtrref=www.google.com&gwh=4FE25DB7ADD21859A090BE29C83F7950&gwt=pay&assetType=opinion
47 https://jezebel.com/louis-c-k-releases-statement-these-stories-are-true-1820338955
48 https://www.vox.com/2019/1/9/18172273/louis-ck-comeback-parkland-aziz-ansari-metoo
49 https://www.dailymail.co.uk/tvshowbiz/article-469646/I-felt-raped-Brando.html
50 https://www.elle.com/culture/movies-tv/news/a41202/bertolucci-last-tango-in-paris-rape-scene-non-consensual/
51 https://newsone.com/3784655/r-kelly-sexual-misconduct-under-age-girls-timeline/
52 https://www.vanityfair.com/hollywood/2019/02/leaving-neverland-michael-jackson-documentary-allegations
53 https://www.insider.com/investigator-says-uk-tabloid-paid-for-meghan-markles-private-information-2021-3
54 https://www.pride.com/celebrities/2019/9/15/ellen-degeneres-and-brad-pitt-dated-same-woman-who
55 http://www.cracked.com/article_20413_5-heartwarming-stories-to-restore-your-faith-in-celebrities.html
56 https://www.theperspective.com/debates/entertainment/gwyneth-paltrow-admired-ignored/
57 https://goop.com/
58 https://www.adnews.com.au/opinion/taylor-swift-the-brilliance-of-her-branding

59   https://www.buzzfeed.com/annehelenpetersen/debbie-reynolds-legendary-gossip-game?utm_term=.lokrQQ9eKN
60   https://www.oprahmag.com/life/a22676555/oprah-changing-perspective/
61   http://biography.yourdictionary.com/articles/why-did-martha-stewart-go-to-jail.html
62   https://en.mediamass.net/people/hugh-grant/highest-paid.html
63   https://www.bbc.com/news/entertainment-arts-41594672
64   https://www.theperspective.com/debates/entertainment/artists-seriously-questionable-morals-deserve-fame/
65   https://www.theguardian.com/film/2018/may/04/johnny-depp-hollywood-star-actor-fall
66   https://www.buzzfeednews.com/article/michaelblackmon/felicity-huffman-emmys-shade
67   https://www.scu.edu/ethics/focus-areas/internet-ethics/resources/why-we-care-about-privacy/
68   https://www.theperspective.com/debates/businessandtechnology/the-perspective-on-big-data/
69   https://www.theatlantic.com/technology/archive/2013/02/why-does-privacy-matter-one-scholars-answer/273521/
70   http://www.businessinsider.com/life-of-melinda-gates-2016-3
71   https://www.bustle.com/articles/64444-people-love-celebrity-gossip-and-theres-a-totally-valid-scientific-reason-why
72   https://theweek.com/articles/484520/3-billion-celebrity-gossip-industry-by-numbers
73   https://www.forbes.com/sites/marketshare/2013/05/24/the-30-most-popular-celebrity-gossip-sites-and-why-big-brands-love-them/
74   https://www.youtube.com/watch?v=yRZZpk_9k8E
75   https://www.cbsnews.com/news/tony-awards-2016-hamilton-wins-11-awards-but-doesnt-break-record/
76   https://www.youtube.com/watch?v=V3bNmhbvU2o
77   https://www.nytimes.com/2016/06/09/theater/hamilton-raises-ticket-prices-the-best-seats-will-now-cost-849.html
78   https://www.wsj.com/articles/a-hamilton-ticket-for-849-experts-call-that-a-bargain-11559860459
79   https://www.seattletimes.com/entertainment/theater/how-did-hamilton-tickets-get-so-expensive-and-what-does-that-mean-for-future-big-events/
80   https://entertainment.inquirer.net/385244/after-the-success-of-hamilton-are-musicals-the-remedy-to-hollywoods-pandemic-woes
81   https://www.thedailybeast.com/hamilton-is-broadways-most-expensive-showever
82   https://www.allmusicals.com/h/hamilton.htm
83   https://www.theatlantic.com/entertainment/archive/2015/12/hamilton-cast-album-best-album-of-2015/420975/

84	http://www.hollywoodreporter.com/features/hamiltons-lin-manuel-miranda-finding-814657
85	http://www.newyorker.com/culture/cultural-comment/why-donald-trump-and-jeb-bush-should-see-hamilton
86	https://www.theperspective.com/debates/living/america-still-land-opportunity/
87	https://time.com/5858556/hamilton-disney-plus/
88	http://howlround.com/why-hamilton-is-not-the-revolution-you-think-it-is
89	https://slate.com/culture/2016/04/a-hamilton-critic-on-why-the-musical-isnt-so-revolutionary.html
90	https://www.playbill.com/article/broadway-will-officially-remain-closed-through-2020
91	http://www.newsweek.com/hamilton-broadway-whats-all-fuss-about-360491
92	http://mentalfloss.com/article/69574/hamilton-uses-hip-hop-fit-more-20000-words-25-hours
93	https://www.broadwayleague.com/research/research-reports/
94	https://edition.cnn.com/travel/article/titanic-2-launch-2022/index.html
95	https://www.youtube.com/watch?v=jKyvc-zF8ks
96	https://www.scienceabc.com/humans/movies/jack-also-fit-floating-raft-alongwith-rose-saved-titanic-disaster.html
97	https://c.tribune.com.pk/2016/02/jack-and-kate1.gif
98	https://tribune.com.pk/story/1039288/kate-winslet-finally-admits-rose-could-have-saved-jack/
99	https://www.youtube.com/watch?v=JVgkvaDHmto
100	https://www.theguardian.com/commentisfree/2016/feb/04/kate-winslet-rose-jack-titanic
101	https://www.huffingtonpost.com/entry/neil-degrasse-tyson-problem-with-that-titanic-plot-hole_us_59d117afe4b09538b508e57e
102	https://www.buzzfeed.com/michaelblackmon/there-was-no-space-on-the-raft?utm_term=.opYmJbn7o
103	http://www.mirror.co.uk/news/weird-news/jack-titanic-would-never-fit-9728203
104	https://www.independent.co.uk/arts-entertainment/films/news/james-cameron-explains-why-rose-didnt-share-the-door-with-jack-in-titanic-a8078061.html
105	https://www.newsweek.com/titanic-movie-anniversary-could-jack-have-survived-scientists-weigh-751758
106	http://www.thedailybeast.com/james-cameron-on-the-trump-administration-these-people-are-insane
107	https://www.telegraph.co.uk/travel/news/titanic-ii-headquarters-paris/
108	https://archive.thinkprogress.org/keeping-up-with-the-kardashians-addresses-bruce-jenner-s-transition-with-real-emotion-b8f200f721d0/

109 https://www.themarshallproject.org/records/5944-kim-kardashian
110 https://www.vanityfair.com/style/2020/09/why-is-keeping-up-with-the-kardashians-ending
111 https://www.marketwatch.com/story/kylie-jenner-can-make-more-money-in-one-instagram-post-than-many-people-earn-in-a-lifetime-2019-07-23
112 https://www.elle.com/uk/life-and-culture/culture/articles/g32620/kardashian-grandchildren-list/
113 https://www.vogue.com/article/kim-kardashian-gestational-surrogate-third-child-preeclampsia-kanye-west
114 https://edition.cnn.com/2020/03/04/politics/trump-kim-kardashian-west-white-house/index.html
115 https://www.forbes.com/sites/sarabliss/2019/04/18/kim-kardashian-is-becoming-a-lawyer-what-her-move-can-teach-you-about-making-a-career-leap/
116 https://www.instyle.com/celebrity/kardashians-raise-awareness
117 https://www.thesun.co.uk/living/3196659/this-is-the-real-story-behind-kim-kardashians-sex-tape-and-how-it-made-her-a-star/
118 https://www.vanityfair.com/style/2016/10/solving-kim-kardashian-west-paris-robbery
119 https://www.hellomagazine.com/healthandbeauty/mother-and-baby/2020021284648/kim-kardashian-told-she-suffered-miscarriage/
120 https://www.insider.com/khloe-kardashian-tristan-thompson-cheating-scandal-timeline-2018-4
121 http://www.usmagazine.com/celebrity-news/news/khloe-kardashian-lamar-odoms-divorce-almost-finalized-w455065
122 https://www.bbc.com/news/entertainment-arts-53501482
123 https://www.washingtonpost.com/news/early-lead/wp/2017/07/27/lamar-odom-says-he-shook-hands-with-death-but-is-now-sober/?utm_term=.9cac46b94662
124 https://www.businessinsider.com/kardashian-reaction-to-bruce-jenner-becoming-woman-2015-4
125 https://www.vanityfair.com/hollywood/2015/06/caitlyn-jenner-bruce-cover-annie-leibovitz
126 https://www.nytimes.com/interactive/2019/02/21/magazine/women-corporate-america.html
127 https://www.nytimes.com/2020/09/09/style/kardashians-ending-takeaways.html?action=click&module=Editors%20Picks&pgtype=Homepage
128 http://www.etonline.com/news/165154_14_reasons_why_kris_jenner_is_the_ultimate_momager_and_deserves_to_trademark_that_phrase
129 https://people.com/style/proof-that-everything-the-kardashian-jenners-touch-turns-to-gold/
130 https://www.insider.com/how-the-kardashian-jenner-family-built-their-empire-became-famous-net-worth-2019-3

131   http://www.kardashianbeauty.eu/
132   https://wwd.com/fashion-news/fashion-scoops/kardashian-jenner-west-fashion-beauty-brands-in-works-1203407841/
133   https://twitter.com/KimKardashian?ref_src=twsrc%5Egoogle%7Ctwcamp%5Eserp%7Ctwgr%5Eauthor
134   http://www.independent.ie/style/voices/selfie-society-are-the-kardashians-ruining-womanhood-35201655.html
135   https://www.thedailybeast.com/the-dangerous-kardashian-effect-and-the-profound-impact-of-the-superficial
136   https://www.allure.com/story/kim-kardashian-west-skin-care-staples
137   https://www.vogue.co.uk/article/kim-kardashian-north-west-corset
138   https://www.independent.co.uk/voices/kim-kardashian-diet-suppressant-lollipops-flat-tummy-eating-disorders-feminism-a8355746.html
139   https://www.wired.com/2017/04/pepsi-ad-internet-response/
140   http://www.telegraph.co.uk/women/life/kim-kardashian-and-the-price-of-preening-narcissism/
141   https://www.theodysseyonline.com/the-female-narcissist-kim-kardashian
142   https://slate.com/culture/2015/05/selfish-kim-kardashian-wests-book-of-selfies-reviewed.html
143   https://www.thecut.com/2015/09/afternoon-with-the-kardashian-jenners.html
144   https://theindependent.sg/kris-jenner-is-a-narcissist-say-fans-who-have-been-watching-her-every-move/
145   https://www.nytimes.com/2015/09/27/books/review/selfish-by-kim-kardashian-west-and-more.html
146   https://www.psychologytoday.com/us/blog/communication-success/201704/8-life-setbacks-and-failures-narcissists
147   https://graziadaily.co.uk/celebrity/news/sarah-jessica-parker-feminist/
148   https://www.prnewswire.com/news-releases/deloitte-73-percent-of-americans-binge-watch-tv-millennial-binge-watchers-average-six-episodes-and-five-hours-per-viewing-300427152.html
149   https://www.iflscience.com/technology/netflix-data-on-viewers-habits-reveals-bingewatching-is-over-were-now-bingeracing/
150   https://www.latimes.com/entertainment-arts/tv/story/2020-03-19/coronavirus-streaming-binge-watch-overwhelming
151   https://www.theodysseyonline.com/the-stages-binge-watching
152   http://jcsm.aasm.org/viewabstract.aspx?pid=31062
153   https://markets.businessinsider.com/news/stocks/new-survey-88-of-us-adults-lose-sleep-due-to-binge-watching-1028656135
154   https://markets.businessinsider.com/news/stocks/new-survey-88-of-us-adults-lose-sleep-due-to-binge-watching-1028656135
155   https://www.dailymail.co.uk/health/article-6407903/Watching-2hours-12minutes-daytime-TV-lead-early-death-major-study-warns.html

156 https://alcalde.texasexes.org/2015/02/ut-study-links-binge-watching-depression/
157 http://www.health.com/mind-body/6-ways-a-tv-binge-affects-your-body-and-how-to-fight-each-one
158 https://listverse.com/2020/03/14/top-10-ways-binge-watching-is-ruining-your-health/
159 https://www.nasdaq.com/articles/is-coronavirus-boosting-netflixs-subscriber-growth-2020-03-08
160 http://nordic.businessinsider.com/lost-creator-damon-lindelof-doesnt-like-netflix-style-binge-watching-2017-4/
161 https://www.theperspective.com/debates/entertainment/game-thrones-epic-epic-fail/
162 https://www.vox.com/culture/2019/5/17/18624767/game-of-thrones-series-finale-season-8-episode-5-the-bells-daenerys-dany-kings-landing-targaryen
163 https://www.vulture.com/2019/01/the-sopranos-ending-does-tony-die.html
164 https://www.theperspective.com/debates/living/the-perspective-on-millennials/
165 https://mic.com/articles/98948/6-ways-binge-watching-is-ruining-our-brains-bodies-and-probably-our-souls
166 https://www.smh.com.au/lifestyle/health-and-wellness/is-netflix-binge-watching-causing-antisocial-behaviour-20171030-gzaqo7.html
167 https://www.rd.com/culture/binge-watching-unhealthy/
168 https://www.surveymonkey.com/curiosity/best-netflix-binge-buddies-pets/
169 https://news.byu.edu/news/prescription-living-longer-spend-less-time-alone
170 https://www.sbs.com.au/guide/article/2017/03/20/does-binge-watching-ruin-tv
171 http://collider.com/best-tv-shows-to-binge-watch/
172 https://qz.com/970502/in-defense-of-binge-watching/
173 https://health.clevelandclinic.org/is-it-bad-for-you-to-binge-watch-tv-shows/
174 https://www.psychologytoday.com/us/basics/dopamine
175 https://www.salon.com/2019/12/11/bombshell-jay-roach-interview-roger-ailes-megyn-kelly-lionsgate/
176 https://www.usatoday.com/story/entertainment/celebrities/2019/12/11/why-fox-news-being-sued-again-over-alleged-sexual-harassment/4398373002/
177 https://www.pewresearch.org/politics/2004/05/23/iv-values-and-the-press/
178 https://www.politico.com/blogs/media/2014/05/survey-7-percent-of-reporters-identify-as-republican-188053

179 https://www.politico.com/magazine/story/2017/04/25/media-bubble-real-journalism-jobs-east-coast-215048
180 https://www.politico.com/magazine/story/2017/04/25/media-bubble-real-journalism-jobs-east-coast-215048
181 https://thehill.com/blogs/pundits-blog/presidential-campaign/305191-surprised-by-trumps-win-media-bias-hid-what
182 http://www.people-press.org/2004/05/23/iv-values-and-the-press/
183 https://news.gallup.com/poll/316094/conservatism-down-start-2020.aspx
184 https://news.gallup.com/poll/267047/americans-trust-mass-media-edges-down.aspx
185 https://www.journalism.org/2014/10/21/political-polarization-media-habits/
186 https://www.infowars.com/
187 https://www.businessinsider.com/who-is-rush-limbaugh-radio-host-life-2020-2
188 http://www.thewrap.com/11-times-fox-news-criticized-trump/5/
189 https://www.theatlantic.com/news/archive/2017/04/why-was-bill-oreilly-really-fired/523614/
190 http://www.politico.com/magazine/story/2015/05/fox-news-liberals-118235
191 http://nymag.com/news/frank-rich/fox-news-2014-2/
192 https://www.salon.com/2018/11/23/can-we-save-loved-ones-from-fox-news-i-dont-know-if-its-too-late-or-not/
193 https://www.foxnews.com/entertainment/fox-news-finishes-2018-as-most-watched-cable-network-as-hannity-dominates
194 https://www.statista.com/statistics/607266/big-bang-theory-viewers-season/
195 https://www.youtube.com/watch?v=OIFCVYlM-rU
196 https://www.nbcnews.com/tech/security/fox-news-hit-16-billion-lawsuit-election-fraud-claims-rcna520
197 http://thehill.com/homenews/administration/342286-fox-news-host-defends-trump-jr-id-meet-with-the-devil-for-opposition
198 https://www.telegraph.co.uk/news/2018/07/05/donald-trump-hires-bill-shine-former-fox-news-executive-head/
199 https://www.politico.com/story/2019/03/08/bill-shine-resigns-will-join-trump-campaign-1213083
200 https://www.reuters.com/article/us-usa-election-trump-shine/trumps-top-communications-aide-shine-resigns-moves-to-re-election-campaign-idUSKCN1QP1YM
201 https://www.salon.com/2019/06/19/president-trump-got-talked-out-of-war-with-iran-by-fox-news-host-tucker-carlson_partner/
202 http://www.politico.com/magazine/story/2017/04/25/media-bubble-real-journalism-jobs-east-coast-215048

203 https://www.nationalreview.com/2016/08/fox-news-conservative-media-echo-chamber-hurts-conservatives/
204 https://www.theperspective.com/debates/living/can-people-change-minds/
205 https://fs.blog/2017/07/filter-bubbles/
206 https://www.cjr.org/tow_center/fox-news-partisan-progaganda-research.php
207 https://www.politifact.com/punditfact/article/2015/jan/27/msnbc-fox-cnn-move-needle-our-truth-o-meter-scorec/
208 https://www.youtube.com/watch?v=imr88VuLxdc
209 https://www.vice.com/en_us/article/ppmpb8/the-terrible-legacy-of-friends
210 https://www.usatoday.com/story/entertainment/tv/2019/09/16/friends-25th-anniversary-why-we-cant-let-them-go/2154983001/
211 https://www.usatoday.com/story/entertainment/tv/2019/07/03/seinfeld-remains-relevant-30th-anniversary-first-episode/1633814001/
212 https://www.vox.com/2014/7/6/5874267/how-seinfeld-changed-tv-30th-anniversary
213 https://www.youtube.com/watch?v=jUWiv5r_CZw
214 https://www.youtube.com/watch?v=JUtJBqgwNgo
215 http://seinfeld.wikia.com/wiki/Minor_characters_in_Seinfeld
216 http://www.vulture.com/2014/06/how-seinfeld-paved-the-way-for-tony-soprano.html
217 https://www.youtube.com/watch?v=HNK0Pez0Sb4
218 https://www.theguardian.com/world/2006/nov/22/usa.danglaister
219 https://www.skyscanner.com/tips-and-inspiration/10-seinfeld-locations-master-your-domain-new-york-city
220 http://seinfeld.wikia.com/wiki/List_of_Seinfeld_sayings
221 https://www.youtube.com/watch?v=NGVSIkEi3mM
222 https://www.youtube.com/watch?v=vKWYg9qFOpA
223 https://www.youtube.com/watch?v=RfprRZQxWps
224 https://parade.com/895318/walterscott/iconic-seinfeld-sayings/
225 https://www.youtube.com/watch?v=O6kRqnfsBEc
226 https://www.nytimes.com/2019/09/05/arts/television/friends-tv-show.html?searchResultPosition=2
227 https://tv.avclub.com/how-friends-changed-the-sitcom-landscape-1798271378
228 https://www.bustle.com/articles/84245-14-sitcom-tropes-friends-did-better-than-any-other-show-out-there
229 https://www.theodysseyonline.com/why-tv-show-friends-so-relatable
230 https://www.nytimes.com/2019/09/05/arts/television/phoebe-buffay-friends.html?searchResultPosition=7
231 https://www.nytimes.com/2019/09/06/realestate/how-did-they-have-such-nice-apartments-on-friends.html?searchResultPosition=1

232 https://www.eonline.com/news/955197/why-the-friends-cast-has-stayed-tight-for-more-than-20-years
233 https://www.youtube.com/watch?v=1HkqeORgn_U
234 https://www.youtube.com/watch?v=yHygF2uEJ4s
235 https://www.youtube.com/watch?v=-X022EvmmqU
236 https://www.nytimes.com/2019/09/05/arts/television/friends-biggest-fans.html?searchResultPosition=4
237 https://www.economist.com/prospero/2019/09/20/why-friends-is-still-the-worlds-favourite-sitcom-25-years-on
238 https://www.starwars.com/
239 https://www.cbs.com/shows/star_trek/
240 https://time.com/5717734/mandalorian-star-wars-timeline/
241 https://www.npr.org/2020/08/17/903329391/in-star-trek-lower-decks-jokes-are-the-final-frontier
242 https://www.marketwatch.com/story/disney-is-giving-us-baby-yoda-toys-for-christmas-2019-11-22
243 https://www.cbsnews.com/news/may-the-fourth-be-with-you-star-wars-day-celebrations-set-for-may-4-on-unofficial-holiday-for-fans/
244 https://en.wikipedia.org/wiki/Jediism
245 https://www.syfy.com/syfywire/how-star-wars-used-the-force-of-fandom-to-create-a-merchandising-empire
246 https://www.thestar.com.my/lifestyle/entertainment/2015/12/07/george-lucas-thought-star-wars-was-going-to-fail
247 https://www.biography.com/news/george-lucas-star-wars-facts
248 https://www.youtube.com/watch?v=TEJ6CzG9zVc
249 https://www.bbc.com/news/entertainment-arts-48142765
250 https://www.cbr.com/solo-a-star-wars-story-harrison-ford-han-deepfake/
251 https://www.cinemablend.com/news/2467981/mark-hamill-is-still-upset-that-han-luke-and-leia-never-reunited-in-the-new-star-wars-trilogy
252 https://www.wired.com/2015/05/inside-ilm/
253 https://www.britannica.com/biography/Gene-Roddenberry
254 https://www.space.com/16159-first-man-in-space.html
255 https://sciencefiction.com/2019/05/06/an-indiegogo-campaign-has-launched-to-create-a-documentary-about-star-trek-pioneer-nichelle-nichols/
256 https://www.youtube.com/watch?v=pqoZ0C0cnRE
257 https://intl.startrek.com/news/how-star-treks-queer-fluidity-has-been-giving-fans-the-brighter-future-they-deserve

Society

1 https://www.fda.gov/cosmetics/scienceresearch/producttesting/ucm072268.htm

2   http://www.bbc.com/future/story/20130609-will-we-ever-end-animal-testing
3   https://www.livescience.com/46147-animal-data-unreliable-for-humans.html
4   http://news.sky.com/story/man-brain-dead-after-medical-trial-goes-wrong-10130769
5   https://www.peta.org/issues/animals-used-for-experimentation/alternatives-animal-testing/
6   https://en.wikipedia.org/wiki/The_Three_Rs_(animals)
7   http://www.bbc.com/future/story/20130609-will-we-ever-end-animal-testing
8   https://en.wikipedia.org/wiki/History_of_poliomyelitis
9   http://www.animalresearch.info/en/medical-advances/timeline/smallpox-eradicated-through-vaccination/
10 http://www.telegraph.co.uk/news/science/science-news/3353960/Should-we-experiment-on-animals-Yes.html
11 http://www.hsvma.org/zoobiquity_the_intersection_of_human_and_veterinary_medicine_121012?utm_source=bb121112&utm_medium=hsvmaweb&utm_campaign=advocacy
12 http://www.pethealthnetwork.com/cat-health/cat-diseases-conditions-a-z/heart-disease-most-common-cause-sudden-death-cats
13 https://www.goredforwomen.org/about-heart-disease/facts_about_heart_disease_in_women-sub-category/statistics-at-a-glance/
14 https://www.aalasfoundation.org/outreach/About-Animal-Research/benefits_to_people_and_animals
15 https://onehealthinitiative.com/
16 https://en.wikipedia.org/wiki/Animal_Welfare_Act_of_1966
17 https://speakingofresearch.com/2017/06/19/usda-publishes-2016-animal-research-statistics-7-rise-in-animal-use/
18 https://en.wikipedia.org/wiki/Capital_punishment_by_country
19 https://edition.cnn.com/2019/03/12/politics/gavin-newsom-california-death-penalty/index.html
20 https://www.nytimes.com/2018/10/30/us/whitey-bulger-killed-prison.html
21 https://www.ranker.com/list/paroled-murderers-who-killed-again/jacob-shelton
22 https://www.themarshallproject.org/2018/07/12/a-day-in-the-life-of-a-prisoner
23 https://deathpenaltyinfo.org/national-polls-and-studies
24 https://www.concordmonitor.com/The-death-penalty-and-the-Constitution-16397572
25 https://pdfs.semanticscholar.org/2237/6a5d331f5beddb-4685fabb556b727f698575.pdf

26	https://www.theperspective.com/debates/living/humans-inherently-violent/
27	https://theconversation.com/theres-no-evidence-that-death-penalty-is-a-deterrent-against-crime-43227
28	https://deathpenaltyinfo.org/deterrence-states-without-death-penalty-have-had-consistently-lower-murder-rates
29	https://deathpenaltyinfo.org/costs-death-penalty
30	http://www.forbes.com/sites/kellyphillipserb/2014/05/01/considering-the-death-penalty-your-tax-dollars-at-work/
31	http://edition.cnn.com/2015/05/20/opinions/marsh-tsarnaev-forgiveness/index.html
32	https://www.pbs.org/newshour/nation/death-penalty-bring-closure-victims-family
33	http://www.bbc.com/news/av/uk-england-lancashire-33230412/fracking-the-pros-and-cons-of-extracting-shale-gas
34	https://www.reuters.com/article/usa-fracking-employment-study/u-s-fracking-boom-added-725000-jobs-study-idUSL8N13159X20151106
35	https://news.uchicago.edu/article/2016/12/22/study-suggests-hydraulic-fracturing-boosts-local-economies
36	https://www.eia.gov/todayinenergy/detail.php?id=25392
37	https://www.theguardian.com/commentisfree/2013/jul/08/shale-gas-fracking-good-for-environment
38	https://www.cfr.org/backgrounder/hydraulic-fracturing-fracking
39	https://www.eia.gov/dnav/pet/hist/LeafHandler.ashx?n=pet&s=mttimus1&f=m
40	https://www.investopedia.com/ask/answers/012915/how-has-fracking-helped-us-decrease-dependence-foreign-oil.asp
41	https://www.annualreviews.org/doi/abs/10.1146/annurev-environ-031113-144051
42	http://time.com/4687456/earthquakes-fracking-wastewater-injection/
43	https://www.wired.com/beyond-the-beyond/2016/03/fracking-and-methane/
44	https://www.edf.org/methane-other-important-greenhouse-gas
45	http://www.resource-media.org/drilling-vs-the-american-dream-fracking-impacts-on-property-rights-and-home-values/
46	http://online.wsj.com/public/resources/documents/water20140220.pdf
47	http://www.renewableenergyworld.com/index/tech.html
48	http://www.renewableenergyworld.com/solar-energy/tech.html
49	https://www.sciencedirect.com/science/article/pii/S0048969717331984?via%3Dihub
50	https://www.eia.gov/energyexplained/?page=renewable_home
51	https://www.history.com/this-day-in-history/fdr-creates-the-wpa
52	https://www.vox.com/2018/4/10/17221292/trump-welfare-executive-order-work-requirements

53	https://www.npr.org/2020/03/26/821457551/whats-inside-the-senate-s-2-trillion-coronavirus-aid-package
54	https://newrepublic.com/article/154404/myth-welfare-queen
55	https://www.irishtimes.com/news/social-affairs/welfare-versus-work-does-it-pay-to-take-up-a-low-paid-job-1.1944722
56	https://www.nytimes.com/roomfordebate/2013/05/05/denmarks-work-life-balance/when-welfare-undermines-work-ethic
57	https://www.downsizinggovernment.org/labor/employment-training-programs
58	https://www.forbes.com/sites/jeffreydorfman/2016/10/13/welfare-offers-short-term-help-and-long-term-poverty/
59	https://www.cbo.gov/publication/50923
60	https://fee.org/articles/why-its-so-hard-to-escape-americas-anti-poverty-programs/
61	https://www.researchgate.net/publication/14265381_Welfare_Participation_and_Self-Esteem_in_Later_Life
62	https://www.nbcnews.com/better/business/why-low-self-esteem-may-be-hurting-your-career-ncna814156
63	https://www.jstor.org/stable/30011810?seq=1
64	https://www.dailysignal.com/2011/07/09/president-obama-admits-welfare-encourages-dependency/
65	https://www.cbsnews.com/news/how-social-welfare-benefits-help-the-economy/
66	https://nymag.com/intelligencer/2019/03/trump-white-house-welfare-cuts-poverty-council-economic-advisers-report.html
67	https://www.americanprogress.org/issues/economy/reports/2014/03/31/86693/the-safety-net-is-good-economic-policy/
68	https://www.theatlantic.com/politics/archive/2015/03/welfare-makes-america-more-entrepreneurial/388598/
69	https://www.theperspective.com/debates/the-perspective-on-entrepreneurs-born-or-made/
70	https://www.nytimes.com/2020/02/20/business/trump-welfare-poverty.html
71	https://www.acf.hhs.gov/ofa/programs/tanf
72	https://www.cbpp.org/research/family-income-support/temporary-assistance-for-needy-families
73	https://www.thoughtco.com/who-really-receives-welfare-4126592
74	http://www.nber.org/papers/w24248
75	https://www.ncbi.nlm.nih.gov/books/NBK230341/
76	https://www.theatlantic.com/business/archive/2016/04/total-inequality/476238/
77	https://www.weforum.org/agenda/2020/04/pandemics-coronavirus-covid19-economics-finance-stock-market-crisis/

78	https://theconversation.com/the-world-before-this-coronavirus-and-after-cannot-be-the-same-134905
79	https://www.express.co.uk/news/royal/1359557/queen-elizabeth-ii-reign-how-long-has-queen-been-on-throne-when-was-coronation-evg
80	https://www.statista.com/statistics/373081/uk-royal-tourism-admission-numbers-by-establishment/
81	http://www.telegraph.co.uk/news/uknews/theroyalfamily/8137234/Royal-wedding-Kate-Middleton-will-be-first-middle-class-queen-in-waiting.html
82	https://www.chicagotribune.com/news/opinion/page/ct-perspec-page-prince-harry-meghan-markle-royal-family-0520-20180518-story.html
83	https://www.nytimes.com/2020/01/09/world/europe/duchess-sussex-prince.html?action=click&module=Top%20Stories&pgtype=Homepage
84	https://www.theperspective.com/debates/entertainment/battle-bonds-connery-craig/
85	https://www.nytimes.com/live/2021/03/07/world/meghan-harry-oprah-interview
86	https://blogs.spectator.co.uk/2017/11/made-in-windsor-how-kate-william-harry-and-meghan-became-britains-biggest-reality-tv-show/
87	https://www.youtube.com/watch?v=c8QvRIXbv-8
88	https://www.hellomagazine.com/royalty/gallery/2019081376454/grandchildren-great-grandchildren-of-the-queen/12/
89	https://www.usatoday.com/story/entertainment/celebrities/2020/01/08/what-harry-meghan-mean-they-dont-want-senior-royals-anymore/2847084001/
90	https://www.businessinsider.com/british-royal-family-richest-people-2017-11
91	https://www.sundaypost.com/fp/they-cost-us-a-mint-but-bring-in-much-more/
92	https://www.harpersbazaar.com/wedding/photos/g1522/kate-middleton-prince-william-wedding-photos/
93	https://edition.cnn.com/interactive/2018/05/world/royal-wedding-cnn-photos/
94	https://www.theguardian.com/world/2002/may/16/qanda.jubilee
95	http://www.bbc.com/news/uk-18237280
96	https://www.nytimes.com/2020/04/05/world/europe/coronavirus-queen-elizabeth-speech.html
97	https://www.reuters.com/article/uk-britain-eu/queen-sends-a-brexit-message-to-uk-politicians-end-your-bickering-idUSKCN1PJ0QN
98	https://www.royal.uk/queen-and-government
99	https://www.nytimes.com/2019/01/25/world/europe/queen-elizabeth-brexit-britain.html

100 https://www.ctvnews.ca/world/queen-stresses-importance-of-friends-family-during-pandemic-1.5337314
101 http://thecommonwealth.org/sites/default/files/page/documents/CharteroftheCommonwealth.pdf
102 https://www.nytimes.com/2020/01/09/world/europe/prince-harry-meghan-markle.html
103 https://www.theperspective.com/debates/living/perspective-diana-princess-wales/
104 https://www.nytimes.com/2021/03/08/world/europe/recap-of-harry-meghan-oprah-interview.html
105 https://www.vanityfair.com/style/2020/01/meghan-and-harry-royal-uncoupling-media
106 https://www.cosmopolitan.com/entertainment/celebs/a35755552/meghan-markle-mental-health-royals/
107 https://time.com/4914324/princess-diana-anniversary-paparazzi-tabloid-media/
108 https://www.independent.co.uk/news/uk/british-republican-group-calls-for-referendum-on-monarchy-when-queen-dies-a6993216.html
109 https://people.com/royals/meghan-markle-prince-harry-step-down-royal-life-timeline/
110 https://en.wikipedia.org/wiki/Treason_Felony_Act_1848
111 https://www.historyextra.com/period/roman/9-of-the-worst-monarchs-in-history/
112 https://en.wikipedia.org/wiki/British_Empire
113 https://www.cbsnews.com/video/meghan-markle-royal-family-archie-skin-color-cbs-exclusive-interview/
114 https://www.forbes.com/sites/niallmccarthy/2019/07/01/the-royal-family-is-getting-increasingly-expensive-for-uk-taxpayers-infographic/
115 https://www.ukpublicspending.co.uk/uk_nationl_debt.php
116 https://www.dw.com/en/coronavirus-in-the-uk-nhs-faces-perfect-healthcare-storm/a-52741344
117 https://edition.cnn.com/2021/02/26/media/prince-harry-james-corden-interview-scli-intl-gbr/index.html
118 https://www.wessexscene.co.uk/politics/2020/07/28/the-future-of-the-british-monarchy-after-the-queen/
119 https://www.ap.org/explore/divided-america/
120 http://www.people-press.org/2014/06/12/political-polarization-in-the-american-public/
121 http://graphics.wsj.com/blue-feed-red-feed/
122 https://www.ncbi.nlm.nih.gov/pmc/articles/PMC7201237/
123 https://news.sky.com/donald-trump-midterms-2018
124 https://www.marketwatch.com/story/why-do-so-many-americans-refuse-to-wear-face-masks-it-may-have-nothing-to-do-with-politics-2020-06-16

125 https://www.pewresearch.org/science/2020/06/03/partisan-differences-over-the-pandemic-response-are-growing/
126 https://www.worldatlas.com/articles/countries-with-the-highest-rates-of-vegetarianism.html
127 http://www.christianitytoday.com/ct/2016/june/nicole-cliffe-how-god-messed-up-my-happy-atheist-life.html
128 https://www.cbc.ca/radio/ideas/conservative-with-age-why-your-political-stripes-change-over-time-1.4442808
129 http://content.time.com/time/specials/packages/article/0,28804,1894529_1894528_1894524,00.html
130 https://www.theguardian.com/us-news/2020/may/02/michael-bloomberg-expands-influence-network-within-democratic-party
131 https://www.washingtonpost.com/news/wonk/wp/2016/02/10/how-to-change-someones-mind-according-to-science/?utm_term=.8181bb40902d
132 https://www.psychologytoday.com/blog/how-risky-is-it-really/201007/why-changing-somebody-s-mind-or-yours-is-hard-do
133 https://blogs.scientificamerican.com/cocktail-party-physics/what-does-it-take-to-change-a-mind-a-phase-transition/
134 https://www.nytimes.com/2020/06/17/business/aunt-jemima-mrs-butterworth-uncle-ben.html?action=click&module=Top%20Stories&pgtype=Homepage
135 https://www.psychologytoday.com/blog/how-risky-is-it-really/201007/why-changing-somebody-s-mind-or-yours-is-hard-do
136 http://www.newyorker.com/magazine/2017/02/27/why-facts-dont-change-our-minds
137 http://www.newyorker.com/magazine/2017/02/27/why-facts-dont-change-our-minds
138 https://www.theperspective.com/debates/living/perspective-religion-good-bad-society/
139 https://www.scientificamerican.com/article/how-to-convince-someone-when-facts-fail/
140 http://www.businessinsider.com/white-nationalists-genetic-ancestry-tests-dont-like-results-2017-8
141 https://www.theguardian.com/media/2017/feb/06/liberal-fake-news-shift-trump-standing-rock
142 https://www.theguardian.com/media/2017/feb/06/liberal-fake-news-shift-trump-standing-rock
143 https://www.livescience.com/10429-impressions-difficult-change-study.html
144 https://www.fastcompany.com/3062605/why-its-such-a-challenge-to-change-a-bad-first-impression
145 https://humanities.byu.edu/sexist-job-titles-and-the-influence-of-language-on-gender-stereotypes/

146	https://www.psychologytoday.com/us/blog/stronger-the-broken-places/201907/sore-spots
147	https://lenwilson.us/11-examples-of-fear-and-suspicion-of-new-technology/
148	https://www.ushistory.org/us/27f.asp
149	https://www.healthline.com/health/mental-health/safe-spaces-college
150	https://www.theatlantic.com/ideas/archive/2018/10/large-majorities-dislike-political-correctness/572581/
151	https://brownpoliticalreview.org/2019/11/the-woke-the-elitist/
152	https://www.theatlantic.com/ideas/archive/2018/10/large-majorities-dislike-political-correctness/572581/
153	https://theconversation.com/virtue-signalling-a-slur-meant-to-imply-moral-grandstanding-that-might-not-be-all-bad-145546
154	https://www.brown.edu/Departments/Economics/Faculty/Glenn_Loury/louryhomepage/papers/Loury (Politcal Correctness).pdf
155	https://edition.cnn.com/2015/04/16/living/feat-public-shaming-ronson/index.html
156	https://www.reputationdefender.com/blog/social-media/how-social-media-can-ruin-your-online-reputation
157	https://hbr.org/2006/09/rethinking-political-correctness
158	https://www.wnycstudios.org/podcasts/takeaway/articles/could-trumps-attack-political-correctness-help-us-discuss-race
159	https://www.theguardian.com/us-news/2016/nov/30/political-correctness-how-the-right-invented-phantom-enemy-donald-trump
160	https://nymag.com/intelligencer/2015/01/not-a-very-pc-thing-to-say.html
161	https://www.icrc.org/en/war-and-law/treaties-customary-law/geneva-conventions
162	https://www.cfr.org/backgrounder/united-states-and-geneva-conventions
163	http://www.independent.co.uk/voices/comment/torture-it-didnt-work-then-it-doesnt-work-now-9923288.html
164	https://www.irishtimes.com/news/science/does-torture-work-trump-says-yes-but-science-says-no-1.3096064
165	https://edition.cnn.com/2015/01/29/us/cia-torture-report-fast-facts/index.html
166	https://www.theatlantic.com/politics/archive/2011/05/torture-opponents-were-right/238387/
167	http://edition.cnn.com/2009/HEALTH/05/22/torture.health.effects/index.html
168	https://www.newyorker.com/magazine/2004/05/10/torture-at-abu-ghraib
169	https://www.mayoclinic.org/diseases-conditions/post-traumatic-stress-disorder/symptoms-causes/syc-20355967
170	http://www.bbc.co.uk/ethics/torture/ethics/wrong_1.shtml

171 https://www.humanrightsfirst.org/resource/statement-national-security-intelligence-and-interrogation-professionals
172 https://blogs.spectator.co.uk/2014/12/there-are-certain-times-when-torture-can-be-justified/
173 https://www.huffingtonpost.com/entry/torture-suspected-terrorists-polls_us_56fbea2ce4b0a06d5804284f
174 http://www.history.com/topics/9-11-attacks
175 http://www.newsweek.com/ultimate-stress-test-special-forces-training-82749
176 https://www.ranker.com/list/hanoi-hilton-terrible-stories/christopher-myers
177 https://www.thoughtco.com/max-weber-relevance-to-sociology-3026500
178 https://www.history.com/topics/1980s/iran-contra-affair
179 https://www.nytimes.com/2015/06/25/world/middleeast/obama-softens-policy-on-hostage-negotiations-with-terrorist-groups.html
180 http://www.datagraver.com/case/people-killed-by-terrorism-per-year-in-western-europe-1970-2015
181 http://www.businessinsider.com/death-risk-statistics-terrorism-disease-accidents-2017-1
182 https://www.theguardian.com/books/2015/jan/31/terrorism-spectacle-how-states-respond-yuval-noah-harari-sapiens
183 https://www.britannica.com/topic/ETA
184 http://www.csmonitor.com/World/Europe/2011/1021/How-the-militant-ETA-lost-support-among-Basques
185 http://www.pewresearch.org/fact-tank/2015/11/17/in-nations-with-significant-muslim-populations-much-disdain-for-isis/
186 http://www.thedailybeast.com/articles/2015/12/09/terrorism-drug-trafficking-and-isis-when-wicked-worlds-collide.html
187 https://en.wikipedia.org/wiki/John_Gotti
188 https://en.wikipedia.org/wiki/Joaqu%C3%ADn_%22El_Chapo%22_Guzm%C3%A1n
189 https://en.wikipedia.org/wiki/List_of_Israeli_prisoner_exchanges
190 https://en.wikipedia.org/wiki/Gilad_Shalit_prisoner_exchange
191 https://www.britannica.com/list/pablo-escobar-8-interesting-facts-about-the-king-of-cocaine
192 http://www.nytimes.com/1992/07/23/world/colombian-drug-baron-escapes-luxurious-prison-after-gunfight.html
193 https://www.bbc.com/news/world-latin-america-36605769
194 https://ing.org/an-overview-of-isis/
195 http://nation.time.com/2011/06/29/the-5-trillion-war-on-terror/
196 https://www.thenation.com/article/americas-war-on-terror-has-cost-taxpayers-5-6-trillion/
197 http://www.urologyhealth.org/urologic-conditions/circumcision

198 https://matthewtontonoz.com/2015/01/05/why-is-circumcision-so-popular-in-america/
199 https://qz.com/885018/why-is-circumcision-so-popular-in-the-us/
200 https://www.psychologytoday.com/blog/moral-landscapes/201501/circumcision-s-psychological-damage
201 http://www.economist.com/node/21562905
202 https://www.psychologytoday.com/blog/moral-landscapes/201109/myths-about-circumcision-you-likely-believe
203 http://journals.sagepub.com/doi/abs/10.1177/135910530200700310
204 http://www.dailymail.co.uk/health/article-2279166/Circumcision-DOES-reduce-sexual-pleasure-making-manhood-sensitive.html
205 https://www.youtube.com/watch?v=yxFV4Fy7i7g
206 http://www.independent.co.uk/life-style/health-and-families/health-news/health-they-took-my-foreskin-and-i-want-it-back-some-men-feel-their-circumcision-at-birth-was-an-1458890.html
207 http://mbio.asm.org/content/4/2/e00076-13
208 http://www.realclearscience.com/articles/2013/04/17/why_does_circumcision_reduce_hiv_risk_106511.html
209 http://www.menshealth.co.uk/sex/5-ways-circumcision-will-change-your-life
210 http://www.healthline.com/health/mens-health/how-to-last-longer-in-bed
211 http://www.mirror.co.uk/lifestyle/sex-relationships/dear-coleen-husband-suffers-premature-6943792
212 http://www.webmd.com/men/tc/premature-ejaculation-topic-overview
213 https://www.babycenter.com/404_how-many-baby-boys-get-circumcised_10331716.bc
214 https://www.reuters.com/article/us-penis-surgery/surgery-may-not-stop-locker-room-taunts-about-penis-appearance-idUSKBN0M628Z20150310
215 http://www.iol.co.za/news/africa/bullied-for-not-being-circumcised-315024
216 https://www.thesun.co.uk/news/2615992/bullied-teenager-tried-to-circumcise-himself-with-machete-after-laughing-pals-said-hed-never-get-a-girlfriend/
217 https://www.theguardian.com/science/2021/feb/17/arctic-heating-winter-storms-climate-change
218 https://news.un.org/en/story/2018/10/1022492
219 https://en.wikipedia.org/wiki/Energy_density
220 https://www.brookings.edu/essay/why-are-fossil-fuels-so-hard-to-quit/
221 https://gizmodo.com/5870501/a-gallon-of-gas-can-power-an-iphone-for-20-years
222 https://www.consumeraffairs.com/solar-energy/solar-vs-fossil-fuels.html
223 https://ourworldindata.org/fossil-fuels
224 https://www.sciencedaily.com/releases/2018/01/180102134833.htm

225 https://www.energy.gov/science-innovation/energy-sources
226 https://www.mckinsey.com/industries/oil-and-gas/our-insights/how-tapping-connectivity-in-oil-and-gas-can-fuel-higher-performance
227 https://www.forbes.com/sites/rrapier/2020/06/20/bp-review-new-highs-in-global-energy-consumption-and-carbon-emissions-in-2019/?sh=1d6c-1cb866a1
228 https://www.newsweek.com/texas-wind-turbines-frozen-power-why-arctic-1570173
229 https://www.pewresearch.org/fact-tank/2020/01/15/renewable-energy-is-growing-fast-in-the-u-s-but-fossil-fuels-still-dominate/
230 https://www.irena.org/newsroom/pressreleases/2020/Sep/Renewable-Energy-Jobs-Continue-Growth-to-11-5-Million-Worldwide
231 https://www.usatoday.com/story/opinion/2021/02/16/climate-change-clean-energy-jobs-economic-stability-column/4451356001/
232 http://edfclimatecorps.org/sites/edfclimatecorps.org/files/the_growth_of_americas_clean_energy_and_sustainability_jobs.pdf
233 https://en.wikipedia.org/wiki/List_of_U.S._states_by_electricity_production_from_renewable_sources
234 https://www.theguardian.com/environment/2017/jun/06/spectacular-drop-in-renewable-energy-costs-leads-to-record-global-boost
235 https://www.eia.gov/todayinenergy/detail.php?id=43895
236 https://www.nationalgeographic.com/environment/article/renewable-energy
237 https://www.nytimes.com/2018/10/08/opinion/epa-climate-environment-trump.html?action=click&
238 https://www.nytimes.com/interactive/2018/10/07/climate/ipcc-report-half-degree.html?mtrref=www.google.com&gwh=067C3651637C12421E9138D764743514&gwt=pay
239 https://www.businessinsider.com/ipcc-climate-change-report-why-2-degree-warming-is-dangerous-2018-10
240 https://www.ucsusa.org/clean-energy/renewable-energy/public-benefits-of-renewable-power
241 http://www.emedicinehealth.com/abortion/article_em.htm
242 https://edition.cnn.com/2013/09/18/health/abortion-fast-facts/index.html
243 https://www.axios.com/abortion-restriction-states-passed-laws-8326c9aa-6631-4bd1-b02b-c6ba6cd0a335.html
244 https://www.vox.com/2019/5/16/18628002/abortion-ohio-alabama-georgia-law-bill-details
245 https://www.bustle.com/articles/17141-how-to-argue-pro-choice-11-arguments-against-abortion-access-debunked
246 http://www.slate.com/articles/double_x/doublex/2011/10/most_surprising_abortion_statistic_the_majority_of_women_who_ter.html

247 https://mashable.com/article/alabama-abortion-ban-alexandria-ocasio-cortez/
248 https://www.cbsnews.com/news/ohio-abortion-heartbeat-bill-pregnant-11-year-old-rape-victim-barred-abortion-after-new-ohio-abortion-bill-2019-05-13/
249 https://www.guttmacher.org/gpr/2009/11/facts-and-consequences-legality-incidence-and-safety-abortion-worldwide
250 https://www.plannedparenthood.org/learn/abortion
251 https://www.ncbi.nlm.nih.gov/books/NBK138200/
252 https://thinkprogress.org/religious-groups-take-a-stand-for-reproductive-rights-its-time-to-change-the-conversation-20ac5ec69a8f/
253 https://en.wikipedia.org/wiki/Religious_Coalition_for_Reproductive_Choice
254 https://en.wikipedia.org/wiki/Abortion_and_Christianity
255 https://thinkprogress.org/religious-groups-take-a-stand-for-reproductive-rights-its-time-to-change-the-conversation-20ac5ec69a8f/
256 http://www.bbc.co.uk/ethics/abortion/child/potential.shtml
257 https://www.google.co.il/url?sa=t&rct=j&q=&esrc=s&source=web&cd=13&cad=rja&uact=8&ved=0ahUKEwjz3fK2v6TWAhWGORQKHXQZCjsQFghdMAw&url=https%3A%2F%2Fwww.simplypsychology.org%2Fmaslow.html&usg=AFQjCNGqgMhHlTyc208qpXnChknZXIg5LQ
258 https://www.ncbi.nlm.nih.gov/pubmed/12777435
259 https://emedicine.medscape.com/article/2041923-overview
260 https://www.bpas.org/more-services-information/contraception/
261 https://www.bpas.org/about-our-charity/press-office/press-releases/women-cannot-control-fertility-through-contraception-alone-bpas-data-shows-1-in-4-women-having-an-abortion-were-using-most-effective-contraception/
262 http://www.healthline.com/health/pregnancy/body-changes-infographic
263 https://time.com/5907733/race-in-america-2020-election/
264 https://www.pnas.org/content/116/34/16793
265 https://www.theperspective.com/debates/living/is-affirmative-action-a-racist-policy/
266 https://www.newyorker.com/news/our-columnists/anti-asian-bias-not-affirmative-action-is-on-trial-in-the-harvard-case
267 https://www.aaaed.org/aaaed/About_Affirmative_Action__Diversity_and_Inclusion.asp
268 http://ns.umich.edu/new/releases/20237
269 https://www.thecrimson.com/article/2019/10/2/admissions-suit-decision/
270 https://www.thecrimson.com/article/2020/10/13/harvard-sffa-next-steps/
271 https://newsone.com/165891/many-whites-filing-reverse-discrimination-lawsuits/

272 http://www.heritage.org/poverty-and-inequality/report/discriminating-toward-equality-affirmative-action-and-the-diversity
273 https://www.bbc.com/news/world-us-canada-53774075
274 http://www.pewresearch.org/fact-tank/2016/07/20/in-political-correctness-debate-most-americans-think-too-many-people-are-easily-offended/
275 https://video.foxnews.com/v/5848502506001/?
276 https://theintercept.com/2020/07/18/political-correctness-destroying-america/
277 https://jspp.psychopen.eu/article/view/732
278 https://www.cambridgescholars.com/download/sample/65010
279 https://www.wnycstudios.org/podcasts/takeaway/articles/could-trumps-attack-political-correctness-help-us-discuss-race
280 http://www.newsmax.com/ClarenceVMcKee/Racial-politically-correct-crime/2013/12/31/id/544573/
281 https://www.theguardian.com/commentisfree/2013/jul/11/george-zimmerman-trial-black-crime
282 https://www.washingtonpost.com/posteverything/wp/2016/07/21/white-people-think-racism-is-getting-worse-against-white-people/?utm_term=.a4addbf8ce2d
283 https://www.washingtonpost.com/news/morning-mix/wp/2016/11/11/video-shows-group-beating-man-in-chicago-yelling-you-voted-trump-and-dont-vote-trump/?utm_term=.b18a5a2664a0
284 https://www.splcenter.org/20200810/when-alt-right-hit-streets-far-right-political-rallies-trump-era
285 https://www.vox.com/2018/8/10/17670992/study-white-americans-alt-right-racism-white-nationalists
286 https://www.theatlantic.com/politics/archive/2020/06/white-noise-documentary-alt-right/612898/
287 https://www.aljazeera.com/news/2020/8/25/trumps-far-right-legacy-will-remain-regardless-of-the-election
288 https://www.nbcnews.com/news/us-news/study-harvard-finds-43-percent-white-students-are-legacy-athletes-n1060361
289 http://www.nber.org/papers/w9873.pdf
290 https://www.history.com/topics/black-history/black-history-month
291 https://www.bet.com/
292 https://www.dailydot.com/via/reverse-racism-doesnt-exist/
293 http://www.revelist.com/movies/white-savior-movie-trope/5221/your-favorite-movies-probably-include-a-white-savior/1
294 https://www.glamour.com/story/the-help-white-savior-movies
295 http://www.huffingtonpost.com/entry/reverse-racism-isnt-a-thing_us_55d60a91e4b07addcb45da47
296 https://www.hrw.org/news/2020/06/02/us-address-structural-racism-underlying-protests

297 https://www.theguardian.com/us-news/2018/may/09/years-life-lost-us-police-violence-people-of-color
298 https://www.nytimes.com/2019/07/16/nyregion/eric-garner-case-death-daniel-pantaleo.html
299 https://www.washingtonpost.com/news/wonk/wp/2016/04/28/we-cant-forget-how-racist-institutions-shaped-homeownership-in-america/?utm_term=.49b39a90f48d
300 https://scholar.harvard.edu/files/bonikowski/files/pager-western-bonikowski-discrimination-in-a-low-wage-labor-market.pdf
301 https://books.google.co.il/books?id=SKBvqXL0jTQC&pg=PA60&lpg=PA60&dq=is+prostitution+sanctioned+in+the+bible&source=bl&ots=hij0L5rsDb&sig=U6VG0oKPO1e9_DxKIWg32mDw9oY&hl=en&sa=X&ved=0ahUKEwij762wm_vRAhVBuBQKHXZ8DPIQ6AEILzAE
302 https://prostitution.procon.org/view.answers.php?questionID=000095
303 http://www.ibtimes.co.uk/why-amsterdams-prostitution-laws-are-still-failing-protect-empower-women-1467733
304 https://www.cato-unbound.org/2013/12/12/dianne-post/how-we-treat-prostitution-measure-our-society
305 https://www.theguardian.com/society/2010/jan/15/why-men-use-prostitutes
306 https://prostitution.procon.org/view.answers.php?questionID=000095
307 https://www.cato-unbound.org/2013/12/06/dianne-post/prostitution-cannot-be-squared-human-rights-or-equality-women
308 https://www.bbc.com/news/magazine-33113238
309 https://www.cato-unbound.org/2013/12/12/dianne-post/how-we-treat-prostitution-measure-our-society
310 http://www.hindustantimes.com/kolkata/sex-workers-in-india-s-largest-red-light-area-all-set-to-get-moneywise-on-new-notes/story-ZLk81xGx5IuRHPIrqXCoVO.html
311 http://www.businessinsider.com/prostitution-legal-nevada-prostitutes-brothels-sex-2011-12?op=1/
312 http://www.npr.org/2016/10/01/496226348/where-does-colorados-marijuana-money-go
313 http://www.denverpost.com/2016/05/26/marijuana-sales-tax-revenue-huge-boon-for-colorado-cities/
314 http://prostitution.procon.org/view.resource.php?resourceID=000772
315 https://www.abc.net.au/news/2014-09-23/why-do-muslim-women-wear-a-burka-niqab-or-hijab/5761510?nw=0
316 https://www.dw.com/en/where-are-burqa-bans-in-europe/a-49843292
317 https://www.washingtonpost.com/world/2018/08/16/france-denmark-bans-full-face-muslim-veils-are-spreading-across-europe/
318 https://www.euronews.com/2020/09/23/has-covid-19-destroyed-the-case-for-banning-the-burqa-in-europe

319   https://foreignpolicy.com/2021/03/10/switzerland-europe-burqa-ban-referendum-coronavirus-face-masks-egerkinger-komitee/
320   https://www.dw.com/en/french-burqa-ban-violates-human-rights-rules-un-committee/a-46007469
321   https://www.thelocal.dk/20180801/women-defiant-as-danish-ban-on-full-face-veil-takes-effect
322   https://www.theguardian.com/world/2009/jun/22/islamic-veils-sarkozy-speech-france
323   http://theconversation.com/why-moroccos-burqa-ban-is-more-than-just-a-security-measure-72120
324   https://www.theweek.co.uk/world-news/6073/what-is-salafism-and-should-we-be-worried-by-it
325   http://www.independent.co.uk/news/world/africa/egypt-drafts-bill-to-ban-niqab-veil-in-public-places-a6920701.html
326   https://qz.com/633632/egyptian-lawmakers-want-to-ban-muslim-women-from-covering-their-faces/
327   https://www.arabnews.com/node/1618916/middle-east
328   https://www.dailymail.co.uk/news/article-6366629/EGYPT-considers-banning-burqa-crackdown-against-Islamic-extremists.html
329   https://www.bbc.com/news/world-middle-east-44411333
330   https://www.hrw.org/news/2017/05/11/hate-crimes-against-muslims-us-continue-rise-2016
331   http://www.huffingtonpost.com/sabria-jawhar/why-i-hate-the-burqa----a_b_669953.html
332   https://voxeu.org/article/jihadi-attacks-media-and-local-anti-muslim-hate-crime
333   http://www.csmonitor.com/World/Middle-East/2009/1213/Behind-the-veil-Why-Islam-s-most-visible-symbol-is-spreading
334   https://www.history.com/topics/united-states-constitution/first-amendment
335   https://www.law.cornell.edu/wex/free_exercise_clause
336   https://en.wikipedia.org/wiki/Burka_ban_in_Australia
337   http://www.dailymail.co.uk/news/article-2811599/ASIO-warns-banning-burqa-fuel-extremist-recruitment-radicalisation-Australia.html
338   http://www.heraldnet.com/news/ussrs-effort-to-destroy-islam-created-generation-of-radicals/
339   http://foreignpolicy.com/2015/02/09/is-china-making-its-own-terrorism-problem-worse-uighurs-islamic-state/
340   https://theconversation.com/muslim-women-who-cover-their-faces-find-greater-acceptance-among-coronavirus-masks-nobody-is-giving-me-dirty-looks-136021
341   https://en.wikipedia.org/wiki/Islam_in_the_United_States

342 https://www.pewresearch.org/fact-tank/2020/12/16/women-in-many-countries-face-harassment-for-clothing-deemed-too-religious-or-too-secular/
343 https://felonvoting.procon.org/view.resource.php?resourceID=000289
344 http://www.mncatholic.org/wp-content/uploads/2015/02/13.1211-MN-Disenfranchisement-FAQ.pdf
345 https://www.sentencingproject.org/publications/felony-disenfranchisement-a-primer/
346 https://www.vox.com/policy-and-politics/2019/5/13/18535423/prisoner-felon-voting-rights-bernie-sanders-2020
347 https://www.vox.com/2019/5/3/18528319/poll-felons-right-to-vote
348 https://www.brennancenter.org/issues/ensure-every-american-can-vote/vote-suppression
349 http://www.independent.co.uk/news/uk/home-news/ethnic-minorities-crime-victims-perpetrators-uk-race-report-a7993521.html
350 http://www.naacp.org/criminal-justice-fact-sheet/
351 https://www.nytimes.com/2014/11/19/opinion/the-racist-origins-of-felon-disenfranchisement.html
352 https://scholarlycommons.law.case.edu/cgi/viewcontent.cgi?referer=https://www.google.co.il/&httpsredir=1&article=2224&context=caselrev
353 https://www.miamiherald.com/news/politics-government/state-politics/article240525886.html
354 https://www.theguardian.com/commentisfree/2013/nov/01/prisoners-are-our-future-neighbours-so-is-rehabilitation-such-a-dangerous-idea
355 http://clydebankhigh.org.uk/New CHS Website/Files/modern studies/Adv Higher/CausesEffects of Crime/Articles-handouts/Strain Theory.pdf
356 https://www.nytimes.com/2019/04/11/opinion/voting-prisoners-felon-disenfranchisement.html
357 https://www.bjs.gov/index.cfm?ty=pbdetail&iid=823
358 https://www.peoplespolicyproject.org/projects/prisoner-voting/
359 http://www.nytimes.com/1982/01/08/us/study-says-criminal-tendencies-may-be-inherited.html
360 http://tucson.com/lifestyles/families/one-of-the-most-important-things-children-watch-their-parents/article_1b580878-eb3b-56b2-bf70-62aa3115652a.html
361 http://www.thetimesnews.com/news/20160503/state-by-state-how-much-does-it-cost-to-keep-someone-in-prison
362 https://eji.org/news/mass-incarceration-costs-182-billion-annually
363 http://law.jrank.org/pages/12125/Economic-Social-Effects-Crime.html
364 http://www.iep.utm.edu/soc-cont/
365 https://constitutioncenter.org/interactive-constitution/amendments/amendment-xxvi

366 https://www.themarshallproject.org/2016/03/09/seven-things-to-know-about-repeat-offenders
367 https://www.ussc.gov/sites/default/files/pdf/research-and-publications/research-publications/2016/recidivism_overview.pdf
368 https://prisonthehiddensentence.com/your-voice/some-rights-and-privileges-inmates-have-and-lose-when-incarcerated%EF%BB%BF%EF%BB%BF%EF%BB%BF%EF%BB%BF/
369 http://www.telegraph.co.uk/news/uknews/1536945/Prisoners-dont-care-about-their-right-to-vote.html
370 https://www.nichd.nih.gov/health/topics/infertility/conditioninfo/common
371 https://www.webmd.com/infertility-and-reproduction/guide/using-surrogate-mother
372 https://www.womenshealth.gov/a-z-topics/infertility
373 http://www.nwherald.com/2016/10/13/looking-at-the-research-having-children-makes-us-better-if-not-happier/agpuml/
374 https://www.today.com/parents/motherhood-brings-out-worst-us-best-1C9329506
375 http://time.com/4673035/do-the-child-free-live-longer/
376 https://edition.cnn.com/2019/08/19/health/parents-kids-happiness-study-scli-intl/index.html
377 https://www.rainbowkids.com/adoption-stories/why-does-it-take-so-long-to-adopt-a-child-1300
378 https://www.self.com/story/adoption-health-history-genetic-testing
379 https://surrogate.com/intended-parents/the-surrogacy-process/intended-parents-faq/
380 https://surrogate.com/intended-parents/raising-a-child-born-from-surrogacy/how-to-emotionally-transfer-a-baby-born-via-surrogacy/
381 https://en.wikipedia.org/wiki/Surrogacy_laws_by_country
382 https://surrogate.com/surrogates/becoming-a-surrogate/being-compensated-as-a-surrogate/
383 https://www.conceiveabilities.com/surrogates/surrogate-mother-pay/
384 https://poseidon01.ssrn.com/delivery.php?ID=355025009087122065127005093123072067014057084078086094127025002100031097068075096002097006055007116104052101090089023080017002112073005049029107099106115106005001085069094020025109083082067064031118109121003078087030028115118098013077124073115027083&EXT=pdf
385 https://www.theguardian.com/science/blog/2017/mar/28/cross-border-surrogacy-exploiting-low-income-women-as-biological-resources
386 http://onlinelibrary.wiley.com/doi/10.1111/japp.12138/pdf
387 http://www.nytimes.com/2011/10/05/world/asia/05iht-letter05.html?_r=1&

388 https://www.ncbi.nlm.nih.gov/pmc/articles/PMC1376831/pdf/jmedeth00299-0027.pdf
389 https://www.ncronline.org/news/opinion/surrogacy-laws-cruelly-treat-children-commodities
390 https://www.independent.co.uk/news/world/australasia/baby-gammy-australian-father-who-abandoned-down-syndrome-surrogate-child-now-tries-to-access-funds-10261916.html
391 https://www.abc.net.au/news/2015-04-13/australian-couple-abandon-baby-boy-in-india-surrogacy-case/6387206
392 https://www.investopedia.com/financial-edge/0113/the-history-of-unions-in-the-united-states.aspx
393 https://www.reuters.com/article/us-usa-election-law-enforcement/trump-wins-backing-of-largest-us-police-union-as-he-touts-law-and-order-idUSKBN25V22V
394 https://news.gallup.com/poll/318980/approval-labor-unions-remains-high.aspx
395 https://www.history.com/topics/labor
396 https://theconversation.com/why-police-unions-are-not-part-of-the-american-labor-movement-142538
397 https://www.nytimes.com/2009/11/19/business/19labor.html?mtrref=www.google.com
398 https://www.phillymag.com/articles/2012/10/25/busting-philly-unions-pestronk-brothers/
399 https://www.theperspective.com/debates/politics/do-protests-work/
400 https://www.forbes.com/sites/tommybeer/2020/08/16/teachers-organize-mass-sick-days-resignations-and-potential-strikes-over-schools-reopening/
401 https://www.ncbi.nlm.nih.gov/pmc/articles/PMC3346014/
402 http://workerfreedom.org/union-dirty-tricks-part-1
403 https://www.theblaze.com/news/2011/11/07/labor-union-violence-in-america-a-brief-history
404 https://www.foxnews.com/opinion/why-unions-are-harmful-to-workers
405 https://opentextbc.ca/principlesofeconomics/chapter/15-1-unions/
406 https://www.gazettextra.com/archives/con-labor-unions-add-to-costs-and-discourage-productivity/article_f5995e55-aab3-5e23-9add-dde68d07beea.html
407 https://www.investopedia.com/financial-edge/0113/the-history-of-unions-in-the-united-states.aspx
408 https://www.investopedia.com/terms/f/fair-labor-standards-act-flsa.asp
409 https://www.fool.com/investing/general/2014/11/22/unions-good-or-bad.aspx
410 https://www.refinery29.com/en-us/2020/09/10007185/labor-day-history-unions-2020
411 https://uwua.net/what-are-the-benefits-of-being-a-union-worker/

412 https://www.nea.org/advocating-for-change/new-from-nea/during-pandemic-unions-continue-advocacy
413 https://www.theguardian.com/commentisfree/2018/feb/26/janus-afscme-supreme-court-case-labor-unions-impact
414 https://www.theperspective.com/debates/businessandtechnology/fly-low-cost-traditional-airlines/
415 https://www.newsclick.in/Ryanair-Airlines-Pilots-Strike-UK
416 https://www.bls.gov/news.release/archives/ebs2_07202018.pdf
417 https://www.unionplus.org/page/benefits-union-membership
418 https://www.ncbi.nlm.nih.gov/pmc/articles/PMC4300995/
419 https://www.bls.gov/news.release/pdf/union2.pdf
420 https://www.jec.senate.gov/public/_cache/files/ccf4dbe2-810a-44f8-b3e7-14f7e5143ba6/economic-state-of-black-america-2020.pdf
421 https://cepr.net/images/stories/reports/black-workers-unions-2016-08.pdf?v=2
422 https://www.epi.org/blog/unions-help-narrow-the-gender-wage-gap/
423 https://www.nytimes.com/2020/09/06/opinion/labor-unions-republicans.html?action=click&module=Opinion&pgtype=Homepage
424 https://www.womenshealthmag.com/food/g19810291/vegan-celebrities/
425 https://www.theguardian.com/lifeandstyle/2018/apr/01/vegans-are-coming-millennials-health-climate-change-animal-welfare
426 https://www.washingtonpost.com/graphics/business/batteries/congo-cobalt-mining-for-lithium-ion-battery/
427 http://projects.aljazeera.com/2015/08/rana-plaza/
428 http://civileats.com/2016/10/25/did-slaves-produce-your-food-forced-labor/
429 http://www.npr.org/sections/thesalt/2011/09/08/140289240/shining-a-light-on-the-hidden-hardships-of-tomato-pickers
430 https://broadly.vice.com/en_us/article/9kgp7y/metoo-domestic-workers-farm-workers-organizing
431 http://www.dailymail.co.uk/sciencetech/article-2795672/chimpanzees-favourite-tools-hunting-ants-creatures-use-shrub-dig-dip-aggressive-prey.html
432 https://www.nal.usda.gov/awic/humane-methods-slaughter-act
433 https://www.buzzfeed.com/robstott/this-woolly-sheep-got-a-fabulous-makeover-and-it-broke-a-wor?utm_term=.lg6xVVn2a4
434 http://www.economist.com/node/21547771
435 https://www.ft.com/content/275ccb7a-b7db-11e7-bff8-f9946607a6ba
436 http://www.dailymail.co.uk/sciencetech/article-2011124/Cows-best-friends-stressed-separated.html
437 https://phys.org/news/2017-01-chickenthink-intelligent-complex.html
438 http://www.un.org/sustainabledevelopment/sustainable-consumption-production/
439 https://en.wikipedia.org/wiki/Cruelty_to_animals

440 http://www.huffingtonpost.com/bruce-friedrich/eggs-from-caged-hens_b_2458525.html
441 http://www.haaretz.com/israel-news/new-israeli-pioneers-search-for-humane-dairy-methods-1.465878
442 https://www.ft.com/content/9089dcac-d960-11e9-8f9b-77216ebe1f17
443 https://www.theguardian.com/us-news/2018/oct/07/chelsea-manning-wikileaks-whistleblowing-interview-carole-cadwalladr
444 https://www.bloomberg.com/opinion/articles/2019-04-11/julian-assange-a-hero-or-villain-why-not-both
445 https://www.politico.com/story/2019/09/19/trump-whistleblower-loophole-1505636
446 https://www.sec.gov/whistleblower/
447 https://www.nytimes.com/2016/08/08/opinion/can-we-trust-julian-assange-and-wikileaks.html
448 https://www.cbc.ca/news/opinion/assange-opinion-1.5096309
449 https://www.nytimes.com/2019/04/26/opinion/media-constitution-assange-leaks.html
450 https://www.theperspective.com/debates/politics/edward-snowden-hero-traitor/
451 http://foreignpolicy.com/2014/02/27/whistleblower-or-traitor/
452 http://www.independent.co.uk/voices/comment/dont-listen-to-edward-snowdens-supporters-his-leaks-have-been-a-gift-to-terrorists-10307959.html
453 http://www.imdb.com/title/tt3774114/videoplayer/vi3406935833?ref_=tt_ov_vi
454 http://www.imdb.com/title/tt1837703/videoplayer/vi2566236441?ref_=tt_ov_vi
455 https://www.washingtonpost.com/news/democracy-post/wp/2018/09/27/the-image-of-julian-assange-grows-darker-by-the-day/
456 https://www.vox.com/world/2016/11/8/13563750/wikileaks-2016-election-statement
457 https://edition.cnn.com/2013/07/02/us/enron-fast-facts/index.html
458 http://www.nbcnews.com/id/11839694/ns/business-corporate_scandals/t/enron-whistleblower-tells-crooked-company/
459 https://oig.justice.gov/special/9712/exsump3.htm
460 http://www.rollingstone.com/politics/news/bradley-manning-explains-his-motives-20130228
461 https://www.politico.com/story/2019/09/19/trump-whistleblower-loophole-1505636
462 https://www.youtube.com/watch?v=1_-Vu8LrUDk
463 https://www.youtube.com/watch?v=Kz3SmFUHbJ0
464 http://www.ted.com/talks/margaret_heffernan_the_dangers_of_willful_blindness

465 http://blog.ted.com/cherish-the-employees-who-bring-you-bad-news-says-margaret-heffernan/
466 http://www.huffingtonpost.com/2012/06/04/whistleblower-law-false-claims-act-awards-james-holzrichter_n_1563783.html
467 https://www.defenseone.com/ideas/2020/03/barred-combat-these-women-rose-top-military-intelligence/163614/
468 https://www.theatlantic.com/national/archive/2015/12/women-in-the-military/418680/
469 http://www.bbc.com/news/uk-36746917
470 https://in.news.yahoo.com/nine-countries-that-allow-women-in-combat-positions-081844202.html
471 https://en.wikipedia.org/wiki/Caracal_Battalion
472 https://www.timesofisrael.com/breaking-record-some-1000-women-join-idf-combat-units-this-summer/
473 https://www.washingtonpost.com/news/checkpoint/wp/2016/06/22/how-the-marines-new-physical-standards-for-combat-jobs-weed-out-men-and-women/?utm_term=.916f5ccb7c01
474 https://www.npr.org/2014/07/07/327716479/the-marines-are-looking-for-a-few-good-combat-ready-women
475 http://www.latimes.com/opinion/op-ed/la-oe-spencer-men-should-help-recruit-women-they-know-for-combat-20161012-snap-story.html
476 http://www.jpost.com/Israel-News/First-female-IAF-pilot-appointed-deputy-commander-in-combat-squadron-513492
477 https://www.aljazeera.com/indepth/opinion/equal-roles-women-indian-army-feminist-victory-200303152707759.html
478 https://www.cnas.org/publications/reports/an-update-on-the-status-of-women-in-combat
479 https://mwi.usma.edu/women-arent-problem-standards/
480 https://academic.oup.com/ije/article/36/2/327/723609
481 https://www.apa.org/monitor/2009/09/women-war
482 https://www.livescience.com/52998-women-combat-gender-differences.html
483 http://www.telegraph.co.uk/men/thinking-man/11896832/Should-women-be-allowed-to-fight-on-the-front-line.html
484 https://www.nationalgeographic.com/culture/2019/10/women-are-in-the-fight-on-todays-battlefields-feature/
485 https://www.protectourdefenders.com/factsheet/
486 https://www.popsci.com/science/article/2013-01/do-men-really-fall-apart-when-female-soldier-falls
487 https://www.wsj.com/articles/sexual-assault-in-military-isnt-going-away-as-a-problem-1514502528
488 https://www.nytimes.com/2019/05/02/us/military-sexual-assault.html
489 https://www.theperspective.com/debates/living/the-perspective-on-feminism/

490 https://www.npr.org/sections/thetwo-way/2015/09/10/439190586/marine-corps-study-finds-all-male-combat-units-faster-than-mixed-units
491 https://www.wsj.com/articles/women-dont-belong-in-combat-units-11547411638
492 http://www.nytimes.com/2005/12/20/world/middleeast/a-mission-that-ended-ininferno-for-3-women.html?_r=0
493 http://www.nationalreview.com/article/423888/women-combat-endanger-their-fellow-soldiers-lives-david-french
494 http://www.businessinsider.com/11-most-powerful-militaries-in-the-world-2014-4
495 http://nationalinterest.org/blog/the-skeptics/the-truth-about-women-ground-combat-roles-14904
496 https://www.nytimes.com/roomfordebate/2015/08/20/should-women-serve-in-combat-roles/maintain-the-combat-exclusion-for-women-in-the-military
497 https://www.militarytimes.com/news/your-military/2018/05/09/dunford-fix-to-womens-combat-gear-shortages-will-take-some-time/

Sport

1 https://www.theguardian.com/sport/video/2018/jan/28/australian-open-mens-final-federer-defeats-cilic-to-win-20th-grand-slam-title-video-highlights
2 https://metro.co.uk/2019/07/15/djokovic-wont-be-loved-while-federer-is-around-but-he-could-be-greatest-wimbledon-will-ever-see-10304424/
3 https://www.usatoday.com/story/sports/tennis/2019/03/08/roger-federer-interview-achievements-rivalries-retirement/3098975002/
4 http://www.sportbible.com/tennis/reactions-news-legends-roger-federer-voted-the-greatest-tennis-player-of-all-time-20190714
5 https://www.youtube.com/watch?v=DDKJR9R0VTU
6 https://metro.co.uk/2016/01/28/why-novak-djokovic-has-overtaken-roger-federer-as-the-greatest-tennis-player-of-all-time-5649557/
7 https://www.express.co.uk/sport/tennis/989167/Novak-Djokovic-saved-tennis-Roger-Federer-Rafael-Nadal
8 https://www.theperspective.com/debates/living/women-compete-men-sports/
9 http://www.tennis-x.com/grand-slam-finals/serena-williams.php
10 https://www.theguardian.com/sport/2018/may/23/roger-federer-serena-williams-greatest-ever-tennis-player
11 https://www.totalsportek.com/tennis/grand-slam-titles-winners-mens-women/
12 https://medium.com/@Alatenumo/the-greatest-serena-williams-or-roger-federer-18f6de442f5d

13 https://www.vox.com/culture/2017/6/27/15879520/john-mcenroe-serena-williams-greatest-controversy
14 http://more.bleacherreport.com/articles/317739-no-lists-is-it-reasonable-to-compare-tennis-players-of-different-eras
15 https://www.youtube.com/watch?v=lkEztZPwvT8
16 https://www.youtube.com/watch?v=KTFiecpgd-c
17 https://www.tennisfame.com/hall-of-famers/inductees/rod-laver/
18 https://www.youtube.com/watch?v=J8__TwOgTY0
19 http://edition.cnn.com/2016/06/28/tennis/roger-federer-tennis-wimbledon-statistics/
20 https://www.youtube.com/watch?v=TT1bn-1VikE
21 https://www.indiatoday.in/sports/tennis/story/wimbledon-2019-rafael-nadal-roger-federer-novac-djokovic-1568061-2019-07-13
22 https://www.youtube.com/watch?v=Y4KqWH3jb5M
23 http://www.telegraph.co.uk/sport/tennis/australianopen/9826014/Australian-Open-2013-Federer-Nadal-Djokovic-Murray-this-is-golden-era-of-mens-tennis-says-Andre-Agassi.html
24 https://www.express.co.uk/sport/tennis/1010132/Roger-Federer-Rafael-Nadal-Novak-Djokovic-Andy-Murray-tennis-news-US-Open
25 https://www.telegraph.co.uk/sport/tennis/wimbledon/5751523/Wimbledon-2009-Roger-Federer-what-they-say.html
26 http://edition.cnn.com/2016/06/28/tennis/roger-federer-tennis-wimbledon-statistics/
27 https://www.youtube.com/watch?v=u2vF9xnL-EU
28 https://www.scientificamerican.com/article/striking-evidence-linking-football-to-brain-disease-sparks-calls-for-more-research/
29 https://en.wikipedia.org/wiki/List_of_NFL_players_with_chronic_traumatic_encephalopathy
30 https://www.vox.com/science-and-health/2018/2/2/16956440/concussion-symptoms-cte-football-nfl-brain-damage-youth
31 https://www.webmd.com/brain/what-is-chronic-traumatic-encephalopathy-cte
32 https://lawofficeofmichaelwest.com/2017/07/list-former-football-players-committed-suicide-brain-injury-continues-grow/
33 https://www.playsmartplaysafe.com/newsroom/videos/nfl-head-neck-spine-committees-concussion-protocol-overview/
34 https://www.sbnation.com/nfl/2016/9/18/12940926/nfl-concussion-protocol-explained
35 https://www.nytimes.com/2018/09/06/sports/nfl-week-1-tackling-rule.html
36 https://www.theringer.com/nfl/2018/3/29/17174936/targeting-rule-change-history-ruining-football-roger-goodell
37 https://abcnews.go.com/Sports/story?id=99901&page=1

38 http://www.espn.com/blog/nflnation/post/_/id/106384/inside-slant-knee-injuries-on-rise-overall
39 http://www.espn.com/nfl/player/_/id/13229/rob-gronkowski
40 https://www.theraspecs.com/blog/nfl-long-term-damage-concussions-head-trauma/
41 https://bleacherreport.com/articles/2188997-nfl-players-plead-with-tacklers-to-aim-for-head-not-knees-in-otl-report
42 http://www.espn.com/espn/otl/story/_/id/11466663/nfl-players-grudgingly-adjust-new-tackling-rules-avoid-head-injuries
43 https://www.huffingtonpost.com/2010/10/21/channing-crowder-miami-do_n_771215.html
44 https://nflcommunications.com/Pages/NATIONAL-FOOTBALL-LEAGUE-AND-NATIONAL-FOOTBALL-LEAGUE-PLAYERS-ASSOCIATION-ANNOUNCE-NEW-POLICY-TO--ENFORCE-CONCUSSION-PROTOC.aspx
45 https://www.theperspective.com/debates/sports/premier-league-or-la-liga-which-is-the-best-soccer-league/
46 http://www.economist.com/blogs/gametheory/2015/03/statistical-analysis-football
47 https://www.soccerissue.com/ronaldo-vs-messi-who-makes-the-better-decisions-on-the-field/
48 https://www.thesun.co.uk/sport/football/2588980/cristiano-ronaldo-lionel-messi-who-is-better-stats-trophies/
49 https://www.youtube.com/watch?v=4cmPze0n0aM
50 https://www.gq.com/gallery/cristiano-ronaldo-alessandra-ambrosio-body-issue-photo-shoot
51 https://www.ncaa.com/news/basketball-men/article/2016-04-12/turner-cbs-and-ncaa-reach-long-term-multimedia-rights
52 https://www.sbnation.com/college-basketball/2016/4/12/11415764/ncaa-tournament-tv-broadcast-rights-money-payout-cbs-turner
53 https://www.ncaa.org/about/resources/media-center/news/board-governors-starts-process-enhance-name-image-and-likeness-opportunities
54 https://www.cbsnews.com/news/ncaa-players-can-get-paid-for-likeness-name-image-and-likeness-officials-say-today-2019-10-29/
55 https://www.theatlantic.com/ideas/archive/2019/10/ncaa-had-cut-student-athletes-better-deal/601036/
56 https://www.newsweek.com/ncaa-california-law-student-athletes-lebron-james-herschel-walker-1462385
57 https://www.ncaa.org/about/resources/media-center/news/board-governors-starts-process-enhance-name-image-and-likeness-opportunities
58 https://finance.zacks.com/much-money-college-sports-generate-10346.html
59 https://www.youtube.com/watch?v=cnA2TRV-974

60 https://www.foxsports.com/college-football/story/15-college-football-players-whose-careers-ended-too-soon-052417
61 https://www.forbes.com/sites/stevensalzberg/2017/08/09/will-this-be-the-end-of-college-football-it-should-be/
62 https://qz.com/1302232/the-fate-of-ncaa-football-is-tied-up-in-a-new-brain-injury-lawsuit/
63 https://www.forbes.com/sites/artcarden/2018/07/26/college-athletes-are-worth-millions-they-should-be-paid-like-it/
64 https://www.theperspective.com/debates/sports/are-nfl-concussion-rules-ruining-the-game/
65 https://www.nytimes.com/2017/10/03/opinion/how-the-ncaa-cheats-student-athletes.html
66 https://www.cnbc.com/2019/10/29/ncaa-allows-athletes-to-be-compensated-for-names-images.html
67 http://money.com/money/4241077/why-we-shouldnt-pay-college-athletes/
68 https://smartasset.com/retirement/should-student-athletes-be-paid
69 https://www.usatoday.com/story/sports/2018/05/14/supreme-court-sports-betting-paspa-law-new-jersey/440710002/
70 https://www.espn.com/chalk/story/_/id/19740480/the-united-states-sports-betting-where-all-50-states-stand-legalization
71 https://www.legalsportsreport.com/20010/sports-betting-poll-2018-results/
72 https://theconversation.com/market-for-illegal-sports-betting-in-us-is-not-really-a-150-billion-business-96618
73 https://www.playusa.com/sports-betting/
74 https://www.forbes.com/sites/darrenheitner/2017/09/27/how-legalized-sports-betting-could-bring-in-6-03-billion-annually-by-2023/
75 http://www.espn.com/chalk/story/_/id/17892685/the-future-sports-betting-how-sports-betting-legalized-united-states-the-marketplace-look-like
76 https://www.usatoday.com/story/opinion/2018/05/14/federal-sports-betting-ban-failed-american-gaming-association-editorials-debates/34909947/
77 https://www.usatoday.com/story/opinion/2018/05/14/supreme-court-sports-betting-ruling-feeds-states-gambling-addiction-editorials-debates/609179002/
78 https://www.vox.com/2019/7/7/20685183/us-womens-soccer-team-fifa-world-cup-title-2019-france-vs-netherlands
79 https://www.espn.com/espnw/sports/story/_/id/29402707/uswnt-players-hire-appeals-lawyers-equal-pay-lawsuit
80 https://www.espn.com/soccer/united-states-usaw/story/4071258/uswnt-lawsuit-versus-us-soccer-explained-defining-the-pay-gapswhats-at-stake-for-both-sides

81 http://money.cnn.com/2017/03/15/news/us-womens-hockey-fair-pay/index.html
82 https://www.ijf.org/news/show/gender-equity-means-pay-equity
83 https://www.theperspective.com/debates/sports/federer-best-tennis-player-time/
84 https://www.biography.com/people/serena-williams-9532901
85 https://www.forbes.com/sites/daniellerossingh/2019/02/28/why-serena-williams-is-no-1-in-new-universal-tennis-ranking-backed-by-larry-ellison/
86 https://www.vox.com/culture/2017/6/27/15879520/john-mcenroe-serena-williams-greatest-controversy
87 https://www.healthline.com/health-news/gender-stereotypes-ruin-sports-for-young-women
88 https://www.youtube.com/watch?v=XjJQBjWYDTs
89 https://www.theguardian.com/sport/2017/jul/29/womens-sport-activism-and-political-protest-planned-parenthood
90 https://www.independent.co.uk/sport/football/womens_football/us-women-uswnt-equal-pay-megan-rapinoe-a9495556.html
91 https://www.olympicchannel.com/en/stories/features/detail/top-10-moments-gender-equality-in-sport-intl-equal-pay-day/
92 https://www.youtube.com/watch?v=CtjqX-GJKXI
93 https://etda.libraries.psu.edu/files/final_submissions/16547
94 https://sportsscientists.com/2010/04/let-male-and-female-compete-together/
95 https://books.google.co.il/books?id=pZl5AgAAQBAJ&pg=PA102&lpg=PA102&dq=on+average+they+perform+poorly+in+comparison+with+men,+that+they+are+always+defeated+by+some+men.+This+will+be+discouraging+for+women+in+general+and+female+athletes+in+particular.&sourc
96 https://theconversation.com/will-women-ever-be-able-to-compete-against-men-in-olympic-events-64118
97 https://www.healthline.com/health-news/will-women-athletes-ever-be-able-to-compete-with-men
98 https://sportsscientists.com/2010/04/let-male-and-female-compete-together/
99 https://sportsscientists.com/2010/04/let-male-and-female-compete-together/
100 https://books.google.co.il/books?id=pZl5AgAAQBAJ&lpg=PA102&dq=on%20average%20they%20perform%20poorly%20in%20comparison%20with%20men%2C%20that%20they%20are%20always%20defeated%20by%20some%20men.%20This%20will%20be%20discouraging%20for%20women%20in%20general%20and%20female%20athletes%20in%20particular.&hl=iw&pg=PA107
101 https://www.theperspective.com/debates/sports/are-nfl-concussion-rules-ruining-the-game/

102 http://ftw.usatoday.com/2013/12/home-plate-collision-ban-reactions
103 https://www.theperspective.com/essentials/sports/let-watch-instant-replay-used-sports/
104 https://www.nytimes.com/2019/03/08/sports/women-sports-equality.html
105 https://www.youtube.com/watch?v=HsTQ6H4jNUE
106 https://www.cbssports.com/nba/news/the-last-dance-documentary-why-michael-jordans-mythical-stature-will-likely-never-be-seen-again/
107 https://www.theguardian.com/sport/blog/2016/jun/20/lebron-james-cleveland-cavaliers-nba-title-goat
108 https://www.espn.com/nba/story/_/id/23763553/lebron-james-joining-los-angeles-lakers-nba-free-agency-complete-coverage
109 https://www.theringer.com/nba/2018/6/5/17429314/lebron-james-cleveland-cavaliers-finals-teammates
110 https://lebronwire.usatoday.com/2019/11/24/los-angeles-lakers-off-to-best-start-ever-for-a-lebron-james-team/
111 https://www.cbssports.com/nba/news/phil-jackson-lebron-james-has-all-the-physical-attributes-to-be-better-than-michael-jordan/
112 https://www.cbssports.com/nba/news/lebron-james-ex-teammates-jokingly-congratulate-the-ball-hog-for-passing-michael-jordan-in-scoring/
113 https://www.basketball-reference.com/players/j/jamesle01.html
114 https://www.basketball-reference.com/players/j/jordami01.html
115 https://www.youtube.com/watch?v=VD7JQRTPrxE
116 https://www.youtube.com/watch?v=SE8F9E48jjs
117 https://www.youtube.com/watch?v=vDESGrXI8jE
118 https://www.youtube.com/watch?v=XDbDWmtCl1E
119 https://www.youtube.com/watch?v=8JUWdpnlFSU
120 https://www.si.com/nba/2019/03/07/lebron-james-michael-jordan-nba-career-points-list-eight-graphs
121 https://en.wikipedia.org/wiki/Michael_Jordan
122 https://www.youtube.com/watch?v=N9Z9JtNcCWY
123 https://www.youtube.com/watch?time_continue=22&v=vdPQ3QxDZ1s
124 https://www.basketball-reference.com/awards/finals_mvp.html
125 https://www.theguardian.com/sport/2014/jun/09/lebron-james-nba-heat-no-choker
126 https://www.youtube.com/watch?v=hIuxKHehuSk
127 https://www.indiewire.com/2020/04/the-last-dance-review-espn-michael-jordan-documentary-1202224350/
128 https://www.theperspective.com/debates/sports/magic-johnson-vs-larry-bird-better/
129 https://www.youtube.com/watch?v=IiSdb16N_Dg
130 https://www.youtube.com/watch?v=cWlCdvact5E
131 https://www.youtube.com/watch?v=LAr6oAKieHk&t=180s
132 https://www.youtube.com/watch?v=PJmy6WjFubo

133 https://www.nytimes.com/2020/04/20/sports/basketball/michael-jordan-last-dance-legacy-lebron.html
134 http://mentalfloss.com/article/26075/upon-further-review-brief-history-instant-replay
135 https://www.youtube.com/watch?v=tfUbbjZ80S0
136 https://en.wikipedia.org/wiki/Video
137 https://www.mensjournal.com/sports/15-greatest-underdog-sports-stories-all-time/
138 https://www.shortlist.com/entertainment/sport/the-15-worst-refereeing-mistakes-ever/74108
139 https://www.si.com/more-sports/2016/03/08/100-greatest-moments-sports-history
140 https://www.theatlantic.com/entertainment/archive/2016/05/the-myth-of-the-perfectly-officiated-game/483030/
141 https://dailytrojan.com/2018/05/22/t-time-instant-replay-is-ruining-sports/
142 https://www.youtube.com/watch?v=LjmaS8D2zIA
143 https://en.wikipedia.org/wiki/Tuck_Rule_Game
144 https://www.theatlantic.com/technology/archive/2018/07/world-cup-var-replay-technology/565001/
145 https://adage.com/article/digitalnext/5-jobs-robots/308094
146 https://www.thestatszone.com/development-of-video-technology-in-sport
147 https://www.washingtonpost.com/sports/nationals/mlb-instant-replay-improves-accuracy-adds-strategy/2014/03/07/bbdbec20-a625-11e3-8466-d34c451760b9_story.html?noredirect=on&utm_term=.beded7a3db9e
148 https://www.denverpost.com/2013/11/16/how-instant-replay-has-revolutioned-sports-on-tv/
149 https://www.vocativ.com/325264/is-instant-replay-slowing-down-baseball-nah/index.html
150 https://www.dealstreetasia.com/stories/softbank-sports-engagement-heed-108022/
151 https://www.theperspective.com/debates/sports/nfl-football-losing-appeal/
152 https://www.youtube.com/watch?v=ie-MWjkHXhU
153 https://www.espn.com/nhl/story/_/id/27283018/the-new-normal-why-fighting-nhl-dropped-historic-lows
154 https://www.nbcsports.com/video/edmonton-oilers-milan-lucic-fined-not-suspended-actions-vs-lightning
155 http://www.nydailynews.com/sports/hockey/u-s-senator-nhl-provide-steps-reduce-concussions-article-1.2685892
156 https://sports.yahoo.com/news/nhl-fighting-ban-wouldnt-impact-fan-viewership-survey-reveals-163849278.html

157 https://www.theguardian.com/sport/2015/nov/06/nfl-fighting-hockey-study
158 https://www.nytimes.com/2019/05/31/sports/nhl-concussions-hockey-boogaard.html
159 https://www.thestar.com/sports/hockey/2015/04/09/colton-orr-remnant-of-nhls-enforcer-past-arthur.html
160 https://neurotracker.net/5-risks-repetitive-head-impacts/
161 https://concussionfoundation.org/CTE-resources/what-is-CTE
162 https://www.nature.com/news/head-injuries-in-sport-must-be-taken-more-seriously-1.22471
163 https://www.theperspective.com/debates/are-nfl-concussion-rules-ruining-the-game/
164 https://www.chicagotribune.com/sports/blackhawks/ct-hockey-fighting-fading-spt-0207-20160206-story.html
165 https://www.theglobeandmail.com/sports/hockey/shifting-nhl-culture-knocks-games-enforcers-down-for-the-count/article23570987/
166 https://www.sportsnet.ca/hockey/nhl/a-look-at-the-decline-of-fighting-and-extinction-of-the-nhl-enforcer/
167 http://www.nydailynews.com/sports/hockey/nhl-finally-ban-fighting-good-article-1.2693523
168 https://www.tsn.ca/fighting-continues-to-fade-from-nhl-1.1216252
169 https://fisherpub.sjfc.edu/cgi/viewcontent.cgi?referer=https://www.google.co.il/&httpsredir=1&article=1061&context=sport_undergrad
170 http://www.cbc.ca/sports/hockey/nhl/nhl-safer-with-fighting-players-say-1.2416907
171 https://www.nytimes.com/2018/05/07/sports/hockey/brad-marchand-licking.html
172 https://www.thestar.com/sports/2009/03/17/hockey_fans_love_fighting_survey_says.html
173 http://fightland.vice.com/blog/the-art-of-the-hockey-fight
174 https://www.theperspective.com/debates/entertainment/the-perspective-on-reality-tv/
175 http://grantland.com/the-triangle/why-were-the-80s-so-insane-in-the-nhl/
176 https://www.espn.com/nhl/story/_/id/27283018/the-new-normal-why-fighting-nhl-dropped-historic-lows

History

1 https://www.latimes.com/lifestyle/story/2020-11-15/princess-diana-fashion-inspires-designers-style-icons
2 https://www.vanityfair.com/style/2018/05/royal-wedding-princess-diana-harry-meghan

3	https://www.nbcnews.com/news/world/princess-diana-debuts-netflix-s-crown-bbc-s-1995-interview-n1247837
4	https://beta.theglobeandmail.com/life/the-royals/how-the-royals-bring-up-baby/article12695893/?ref=http://www.theglobeandmail.com&page=all
5	https://www.youtube.com/watch?v=1aTE43vRG6c
6	http://people.com/royals/prince-william-prince-harry-princess-diana-parenting-style/
7	http://abcnews.go.com/International/rebel-royal-mum-dianas-legacy-parent/story?id=19241646
8	https://archive.nytimes.com/www.nytimes.com/books/first/s/smith-diana.html
9	https://www.sheknows.com/entertainment/articles/2060516/prince-harry-princess-diana-tradition-kneel-children/
10	https://www.harpersbazaar.com/culture/features/a9639085/princess-diana-charity-work/
11	https://www.youtube.com/watch?v=SMWUSgAXuHI
12	http://time.com/3583780/princess-diana-history/
13	https://www.townandcountrymag.com/society/a9961113/prince-charles-camilla-parker-bowles-relationship/
14	https://www.vanityfair.com/magazine/1993/02/princess-diana-revenge-anthony-holden-cover
15	https://www.theperspective.com/debates/living/perspective-royal-family/
16	http://www.bbc.co.uk/news/special/politics97/diana/panorama.html
17	http://www.dailymail.co.uk/femail/article-4590068/How-got-Diana-tapes-history.html
18	https://www.theguardian.com/media/2020/nov/13/bbc-finds-princess-diana-note-clearing-martin-bashir-wrongdoing
19	https://www.biography.com/news/princess-diana-lovers
20	http://www.dailymail.co.uk/femail/article-2142167/Penny-Junor-Ive-called-vile-evil-telling-truth-Diana-mentally-ill.html
21	https://www.bustle.com/entertainment/princess-diana-major-hewitt-relationship-affair-the-crown
22	http://www.nytimes.com/books/first/s/smith-diana.html
23	http://www.dailymail.co.uk/news/article-3728660/Pushed-endurance-Yes-Diana-difficult-woman-read-honest-account-loyal-bodyguard-true-provocations-face-marriage-decide-coped.html
24	http://www.dailymail.co.uk/news/article-4369674/Diana-s-emotional-instability-sent-Charles-therapy.html
25	https://www.youtube.com/watch?v=8SDO7naI-lw&list=PLrRD0_FimAroYrRFgTnYKhrjMRvVkJL6Z&index=313
26	http://www.latimes.com/opinion/op-ed/la-ol-patt-morrison-wey-gomez-20181003-htmlstory.html
27	https://en.wikipedia.org/wiki/Columbian_exchange

28   https://www.youtube.com/watch?v=jlYnQXheup4
29   https://whdh.com/news/in-solidarity-with-black-lives-matter-indigenous-people-call-for-removal-of-columbus-statue/
30   https://edition.cnn.com/2020/06/10/us/christopher-columbus-statues-down-trnd/index.html
31   https://progressive.org/dispatches/the-truth-about-christopher-columbus/
32   http://www.smithsonianmag.com/travel/columbus-confusion-about-the-new-world-140132422/
33   https://www.thoughtco.com/spains-american-colonies-encomienda-system-2136545
34   http://www.huffingtonpost.com/eric-kasum/columbus-day-a-bad-idea_b_742708.html
35   http://www.huffingtonpost.com/cullen-murphy/10-questions-about-the-inquisition_b_1224406.html
36   http://spectrum.ieee.org/tech-talk/at-work/test-and-measurement/columbuss-geographical-miscalculations
37   https://www.smithsonianmag.com/travel/columbus-confusion-about-the-new-world-140132422/
38   https://www.japantimes.co.jp/news/2013/07/27/national/history/what-if-columbus-had-reached-his-goal-japan/
39   http://www.npr.org/sections/thetwo-way/2014/05/13/312142316/christopher-columbus-ship-the-santa-maria-may-have-been-found
40   https://www.history.com/topics/exploration/columbus-controversy
41   http://www.nybooks.com/articles/2016/11/24/indians-slaves-and-mass-murder-the-hidden-history/
42   https://www.theguardian.com/commentisfree/2014/oct/13/christopher-columbus-slaughter-indigenous-people-history
43   http://www.nytimes.com/2000/10/08/nyregion/in-person-in-defense-of-columbus.html
44   http://www.smithsonianmag.com/travel/columbus-confusion-about-the-new-world-140132422/
45   http://historythings.com/queen-isabella-castile-queen-sponsored-columbus/
46   https://www.youtube.com/watch?v=UC5km6-o2oM
47   https://www.britannica.com/biography/Christopher-Columbus
48   http://www.history.com/topics/exploration/christopher-columbus
49   http://college.cengage.com/history/primary_sources/world/agree_columbus.htm
50   https://www.bbc.com/news/world-asia-53660059
51   https://www.theperspective.com/subjective-timeline/living/the-bombing-of-hiroshima-nagasaki/
52   https://www.nytimes.com/2020/08/06/world/asia/hiroshima-nagasaki-japan-photos.html

53 https://edition.cnn.com/2020/08/04/world/gallery/hiroshima-nagasaki-atomic-bomb/index.html
54 https://en.wikipedia.org/wiki/Potsdam_Declaration
55 https://en.wikipedia.org/wiki/Supreme_War_Council_(Japan)
56 https://nsarchive.gwu.edu/nukevault/ebb525-The-Atomic-Bomb-and-the-End-of-World-War-II/
57 http://www.japantimes.co.jp/opinion/2016/08/06/commentary/japan-surrender-world-war-ii/
58 https://www.npr.org/2018/08/06/636008863/last-surviving-crew-member-has-no-regrets-about-bombing-hiroshima
59 https://theprint.in/world/5-ways-1945-nuclear-attack-on-hiroshima-nagasaki-continues-to-impact-the-world/476458/
60 https://en.wikipedia.org/wiki/Nuclear_disarmament
61 https://en.wikipedia.org/wiki/Weapon_of_mass_destruction
62 https://en.wikipedia.org/wiki/Nuclear_disarmament
63 http://www.abc.net.au/news/2018-06-12/donald-trump-kim-jong-un-singapore-summit/9859210
64 http://thediplomat.com/2014/08/how-hiroshima-and-nagasaki-saved-millions-of-lives/
65 http://www.pwencycl.kgbudge.com/C/a/Casualties.htm
66 https://www.nam.ac.uk/explore/far-east-campaign
67 http://www.pwencycl.kgbudge.com/C/a/Casualties.htm
68 http://www.abc.net.au/news/2015-03-09/tokyo-wwii-firebombing-remembered-70-years-on/6287486
69 https://www.theatlantic.com/magazine/archive/1946/12/if-the-atomic-bomb-had-not-been-used/376238/
70 https://www.motherjones.com/politics/2005/08/hiroshima-cover/
71 http://www.cnduk.org/campaigns/global-abolition/hiroshima-a-nagasaki
72 https://thebulletin.org/2020/08/counting-the-dead-at-hiroshima-and-nagasaki/
73 https://www.warhistoryonline.com/world-war-ii/lasting-effects-wwii-atomic-bombings.html
74 http://atomicbombmuseum.org/3_health.shtml
75 https://www.sacbee.com/news/local/article244718857.html
76 https://en.wikipedia.org/wiki/Little_Boy
77 http://edition.cnn.com/2013/08/06/world/asia/btn-atomic-bombs/index.html
78 https://en.wikipedia.org/wiki/Atomic_bombings_of_Hiroshima_and_Nagasaki
79 http://www.bbc.co.uk/history/ww2peopleswar/timeline/factfiles/nonflash/a6652262.shtml
80 https://en.wikipedia.org/wiki/Nagasaki
81 https://thebulletin.org/2020/08/counting-the-dead-at-hiroshima-and-nagasaki/

82   http://www.ibtimes.co.uk/hiroshima-nagasaki-did-us-need-drop-atomic-bombs-japan-1513563
83   https://www.newscientist.com/article/dn7706-hiroshima-bomb-may-have-carried-hidden-agenda
84   https://www.theperspective.com/subjective-timeline/politics/cuban-missile-crisis/
85   https://www.brookings.edu/policy2020/votervital/why-are-us-russia-relations-so-challenging/
86   https://www.usatoday.com/story/news/world/2020/07/03/russian-bounties-us-troops-did-russia-cross-line-taliban/5354686002/
87   http://www.aljazeera.com/news/2017/10/che-guevara-171008111523876.html
88   https://562016739558899411.weebly.com/butcher-of-la-cabana.html
89   https://sociable.co/web/fidel-castro-appointed-che-guevara-bank/
90   https://pulitzercenter.org/education/global-perception-che-guevara
91   https://www.jacobinmag.com/2017/04/che-guevara-cuba-castro-congo-patrice-lumumba-colonialism
92   https://afrolegends.com/2017/10/09/ernesto-che-guevaras-contribution-to-africas-struggles-for-independence/
93   http://www.newsweek.com/how-did-che-die-cia-helped-military-ruled-bolivia-kill-marxist-revolutionary-680751
94   https://books.google.co.il/books?id=dwuN8y-SeYUC&pg=PT64&lpg=PT64&dq=che+guevara+the+vital+link+soviet+alliance&source=bl&ots=m-58KCRV4u&sig=svhDjTAZaxKrsS1el-HCQklFiFE&hl=en&sa=X&ved=0ahUKEwjMlb-ntaXZAhXPjqQKHet2ByYQ6AEIKjAA
95   https://www.theguardian.com/commentisfree/2007/oct/08/chepermanentrevolutionary
96   https://www.theguardian.com/world/2009/jan/01/fidel-castro-raul-cuba
97   https://www.britannica.com/biography/Fulgencio-Batista
98   https://www.theguardian.com/books/booksblog/2015/jul/31/the-motorcycle-diaries-by-ernesto-che-guevara-top-gear-and-marxism
99   http://www.peoplesworld.org/article/movement-that-changed-the-world-began-in-cuba-july-26-195/
100 https://www.workers.org/2009/world/cuba_0917/
101 https://562016739558899411.weebly.com/cuban-literacy-campaign.html
102 http://www.radford.edu/~junnever/law/cuba.htm
103 https://562016739558899411.weebly.com/cuban-literacy-campaign.html
104 http://www.truth-out.org/opinion/item/29502-so-close-and-yet-so-far-exploring-the-real-cuba
105 https://www.elephantjournal.com/2011/03/che-guevara-true-revolution-is-love/
106 http://www.radford.edu/~junnever/law/cuba.htm
107 https://www.theguardian.com/film/2004/jul/11/features.review

108 http://www.economist.com/node/9942074
109 https://www.nytimes.com/2019/01/10/opinion/reagan-trump-speech.html
110 https://www.theperspective.com/subjective-timeline/politics/rise-fall-berlin-wall/
111 http://www.usgovernmentspending.com/defense_spending
112 http://www.usgovernmentspending.com/defense_spending
113 https://millercenter.org/president/reagan/foreign-affairs
114 https://www.thebalance.com/us-gdp-by-year-3305543
115 https://campaignstops.blogs.nytimes.com/2012/10/05/frenemies-a-love-story/?mcubz=0&_r=0
116 http://www.npr.org/templates/story/story.php?storyId=128303672
117 https://www.newyorker.com/news/john-cassidy/can-donald-trump-learn-from-ronald-reagan-and-tip-oneill
118 http://www.gallup.com/poll/11887/ronald-reagan-from-peoples-perspective-gallup-poll-review.aspx
119 https://www.history.com/news/ronald-reagan-government-shutdown-reasons
120 https://www.thebalance.com/us-deficit-by-year-3306306
121 https://www.thebalance.com/national-debt-by-year-compared-to-gdp-and-major-events-3306287
122 http://www.sfgate.com/opinion/openforum/article/Reagan-s-AIDS-Legacy-Silence-equals-death-2751030.php
123 http://www.nybooks.com/articles/2017/06/22/america-the-forgotten-poor/
124 https://www.history.com/speeches/reagan-announces-star-wars
125 http://www.huffingtonpost.com/jonathan-weiler/why-ronald-reagan-didnt-r_b_819445.html
126 http://www.rollingstone.com/culture/features/contradiction-19870212
127 http://www.nytimes.com/2004/04/04/books/chapters/ghost-wars.html?mcubz=0&_r=0
128 http://america.aljazeera.com/articles/2013/10/25/invasion-grenadaronaldreagan.html
129 http://www.margaretthatcher.org/document/109427
130 http://www.pbs.org/wgbh/americanexperience/features/reagan-iran/
131 https://www.theguardian.com/us-news/2017/may/05/oliver-north-iran-contra-affair
132 http://www.huffingtonpost.com/entry/nixon-reagan-paved-way-for-gops-race-charged-health_us_58caee41e4b0537abd956ef8?utm_hp_ref=ronald-reagan

Finance

1. https://www.politico.com/2020-election/candidates-views-on-the-issues/tax-reform/wealth-taxes/
2. https://www2.deloitte.com/us/en/pages/tax/articles/biden-tax-policy-impact.html
3. https://www.theguardian.com/news/2020/jul/13/super-rich-call-for-higher-taxes-on-wealthy-to-pay-for-covid-19-recovery
4. https://www.reuters.com/article/us-usa-election-inequality-poll/majority-of-americans-favor-wealth-tax-on-very-rich-reuters-ipsos-poll-idUSKBN1Z9141
5. http://bostonreview.net/class-inequality-politics/mark-engler-andrew-elrod-covid-19-provides-all-more-reason-tax-rich
6. https://www.vox.com/2019/3/19/18240377/estate-tax-wealth-tax-70-percent-warren-sanders-aoc
7. https://www.brookings.edu/research/the-bush-tax-cut-one-year-later/
8. https://www.cbpp.org/research/federal-tax/the-legacy-of-the-2001-and-2003-bush-tax-cuts
9. https://www.forbes.com/forbes-400/
10. https://www.forbes.com/sites/tommybeer/2020/10/08/top-1-of-us-households-hold-15-times-more-wealth-than-bottom-50-combined/?sh=3a2505b15179
11. https://www.census.gov/library/publications/2020/demo/p60-270.html
12. https://www.gq.com/story/70-percent-tax-rate-explainer
13. https://www.businessinsider.com/billionaires-asking-for-wealth-tax-americans-disney-soros-buffett-dalio
14. https://www.nytimes.com/interactive/2019/04/15/magazine/melinda-gates-foundation-interview.html
15. https://www.usatoday.com/story/money/taxes/2018/01/20/a-foolish-take-how-tax-rates-on-the-rich-have-changed-over-time/109488076/
16. https://www.forbes.com/sites/camilomaldonado/2019/10/10/trump-tax-cuts-helped-billionaires-pay-less-taxes-than-the-working-class-in-2018/?sh=488df3483128
17. http://www.slate.com/blogs/moneybox/2015/04/15/top_tax_rates_why_it_s_absolutely_crazy_that_we_don_t_ask_millionaires_to.html
18. https://inequality.org/great-divide/have-the-rich-always-laughed-stiff-tax-rates-away/
19. https://qz.com/1144721/tax-bill-2017-the-reagan-corporate-tax-cut-didnt-work/
20. https://www.thebalance.com/flat-tax-pros-cons-examples-compared-to-fair-tax-3306329
21. https://inequality.org/great-divide/have-the-rich-always-laughed-stiff-tax-rates-away/

22 http://www.taxpolicycenter.org/model-estimates/baseline-distribution-tables-version-0515-1-model/share-federal-taxes-all-tax-8
23 https://www.marketwatch.com/story/81-million-americans-wont-pay-any-federal-income-taxes-this-year-heres-why-2018-04-16
24 https://www.telegraph.co.uk/news/politics/georgeosborne/9919152/Taxing-the-rich-may-be-good-politics-but-its-bad-economics.html
25 https://www.theguardian.com/public-leaders-network/2015/jan/23/rich-inequality-economist-christopher-pissarides-davos
26 https://fee.org/articles/why-a-billionaire-wealth-tax-would-hurt-the-working-poor-and-the-middle-class/
27 https://www.economicshelp.org/microessays/costs/diminishing-returns/
28 https://taxfoundation.org/us-corporate-income-tax-more-competitive/
29 https://www.cbo.gov/publication/52419
30 https://taxfoundation.org/publications/corporate-tax-rates-around-the-world/
31 https://edition.cnn.com/2021/02/25/politics/minimum-wage-covid-relief-senate-parliamentarian/index.html
32 https://object.cato.org/sites/cato.org/files/four_reasons_not_to_raise_the_minimum_wage.pdf
33 https://www.forbes.com/sites/timworstall/2016/07/26/seattles-minimum-wage-rise-is-reducing-employment-in-seattle-i-was-right-in-predicting-this/
34 http://www.heritage.org/jobs-and-labor/report/15-minimum-wages-will-substantially-raise-prices
35 https://www.theguardian.com/business/2015/jun/04/better-economic-growth-when-wealth-distributed-to-poor-instead-of-rich
36 http://www.dailymail.co.uk/news/article-3347520/The-richest-20-Americans-wealthy-half-entire-U-S-population.html
37 https://www.epi.org/publication/raising-the-federal-minimum-wage-to-15-by-2025-would-lift-the-pay-of-32-million-workers/
38 https://livingwage.mit.edu/articles/61-new-living-wage-data-for-now-available-on-the-tool
39 https://www.theguardian.com/us-news/2021/feb/27/us-minimum-wage-senate-explainer
40 http://www.cbsnews.com/news/social-tensions-growing-in-us-between-rich-poor/
41 https://theconversation.com/why-do-poor-children-perform-more-poorly-than-rich-ones-39281
42 http://www.dailymail.co.uk/health/article-2476615/Growing-poor-affects-brain-Children-difficult-childhoods-struggle-handle-emotions-later-life.html
43 https://psmag.com/economics/growing-up-poor-has-effects-on-your-children-even-if-you-escape-poverty

44	https://www.cnbc.com/2021/02/18/bitcoin-passed-50000-dollars-heres-what-you-need-to-know.html
45	https://www.bbc.com/news/technology-53425822
46	http://www.dummies.com/personal-finance/what-is-cryptocurrency/
47	https://blockgeeks.com/guides/what-is-blockchain-technology/
48	https://www.forbes.com/sites/johnkoetsier/2017/12/07/bitcoin-hits-almost-19k-coinbase-crashes-under-buying-pressure/
49	https://www.coindesk.com/price/bitcoin
50	https://www.channelnewsasia.com/news/commentary/bitcoin-tesla-elon-musk-cryptocurrency-stock-market-invest-price-14207768
51	https://www.coindesk.com/bitcoins-price-volatility-3-month-low
52	https://www.investopedia.com/articles/stocks/10/5-steps-of-a-bubble.asp?ad=dirN&qo=investopediaSiteSearch&qsrc=0&o=40186
53	https://www.realclearpolitics.com/articles/2015/02/02/what_caused_the_housing_bubble_125463.html
54	http://edition.cnn.com/2009/US/01/29/economic.crisis.explainer/index.html
55	https://www.forbes.com/sites/billybambrough/2020/03/16/bitcoin-is-back-in-free-fall-and-dropping-fast-heres-why/
56	https://finance.yahoo.com/news/one-of-bitcoins-biggest-strengths-could-also-present-its-biggest-risk-111832902.html
57	https://www.investopedia.com/university/definitive-bitcoin-tax-guide-dont-let-irs-snow-you/
58	https://bitcoinmagazine.com/articles/bitcoin-truly-decentralized-yes-important-1421967133/
59	https://www.clevelandfed.org/en/newsroom-and-events/publications/economic-commentary/2019-economic-commentaries/ec-201912-bitcoin-decentralized-network.aspx
60	https://www.vice.com/en_us/article/5gq3ga/bitcoin-testimonials-black-market-dispatches
61	https://www.inverse.com/article/39138-bitcoin-energy-consumption
62	https://digiconomist.net/bitcoin-energy-consumption
63	https://digiconomist.net/bitcoin-energy-consumption
64	https://spectrum.ieee.org/energy/policy/the-ridiculous-amount-of-energy-it-takes-to-run-bitcoin
65	https://builtin.com/blockchain
66	https://www.seeker.com/how-blockchain-will-eliminate-banks-and-democratize-money-2214709749.html
67	https://www.cnbc.com/2021/02/18/bitcoin-passed-50000-dollars-heres-what-you-need-to-know.html
68	https://www.bigcommerce.com/blog/ecommerce-trends/
69	http://www.computerweekly.com/feature/A-history-of-cloud-computing
70	https://www.wired.com/insights/2012/03/cloud-here-to-stay/
71	https://www.statista.com/statistics/346589/number-of-us-airbnb-users/

72 https://www.warriortrading.com/future-of-bitcoin/
73 https://timesofindia.indiatimes.com/readersblog/blockchaintalk/bitcoin-is-now-among-top-5-world-currencies-28657/
74 https://markets.businessinsider.com/currencies/news/tesla-buys-bitcoin-elon-musk-stock-accept-form-of-payment-2021-2-1030055107?utm_source=markets&utm_medium=ingest
75 https://www.usnews.com/education/blogs/student-loan-ranger/articles/2018-02-21/pros-cons-of-using-cryptocurrency-to-pay-for-college
76 https://www.cnbc.com/2021/05/05/bitcoin-is-coming-to-hundreds-of-us-banks-says-crypto-firm-nydig-.html
77 https://www.cnbc.com/2021/02/12/bitcoin-banks-closer-accepting-cryptocurrency-asset-class.html
78 https://www.wsj.com/articles/why-central-banks-want-to-create-their-own-digital-currencies-like-bitcoin-11603291131
79 https://www.forbes.com/sites/bishopjordan/2017/07/07/bitcoin-millionaire/
80 https://www.cnbc.com/2017/06/20/bitcoin-millionaire-erik-finman-says-going-to-college-isnt-worth-it.html
81 https://time.com/collection/100-most-influential-people-2019/5567848/mark-zuckerberg/
82 https://www.forbes.com/profile/michael-bloomberg/?sh=76c0cfb81417
83 https://thenextweb.com/entrepreneur/2012/03/10/entrepreneurs-are-born/
84 https://www.bloomberg.com/news/articles/2020-12-10/facebook-break-up-would-demolish-zuckerberg-s-social-media-empire
85 https://www.nytimes.com/2010/09/19/business/19entre.html
86 https://www.businessinsider.com/isnt-hypomanic-entrepreneur-redundant-2011-3
87 https://www.nytimes.com/2005/04/10/books/chapters/the-hypomanic-edge.html
88 https://www.inc.com/news/articles/200610/born.html
89 https://www.businessinsider.com/eric-barker-millionaires-bad-grades-gpa-2017-6
90 https://www.cnbc.com/2018/04/27/the-no-1-thing-bill-gates-wishes-hed-done-at-harvard.html
91 https://www.inc.com/quora/steve-jobs-and-bill-gates-dropped-out-of-school-so-why-shouldnt-i.html
92 https://hbr.org/2016/10/why-are-immigrants-more-entrepreneurial
93 https://www.inc.com/jessica-stillman/immigrants-play-an-outsize-role-in-small-business.html
94 https://www.theperspective.com/debates/businessandtechnology/perspective-elon-musk/
95 https://www.americanexpress.com/en-us/business/trends-and-insights/infographics/educated-successful-entrepreneurs/

96   https://freakonomics.com/2009/12/04/how-did-israel-become-start-up-nation/
97   https://www.startupnationcentral.org/
98   https://venturebeat.com/2017/10/06/israel-startup-nation-the-good-the-great-and-the-one-fatal-flaw/
99   https://www.princetonreview.com/press/top-entrepreneurial-press-release
100   http://www.equality-of-opportunity.org/papers/abs_mobility_paper.pdf
101   http://www.pewsocialtrends.org/2014/09/24/record-share-of-americans-have-never-married/
102   https://www.futurity.org/living-with-their-parents-young-adults-1752212-2/
103   https://www.pewresearch.org/fact-tank/2020/09/04/a-majority-of-young-adults-in-the-u-s-live-with-their-parents-for-the-first-time-since-the-great-depression/
104   https://www.nytimes.com/interactive/2018/02/01/business/economy/wages-salaries-job-market.html
105   http://www.epi.org/publication/why-americas-workers-need-faster-wage-growth/
106   https://www.cbsnews.com/news/financial-struggles-covid-pandemic-one-year/
107   https://www.pewresearch.org/social-trends/2020/09/24/economic-fallout-from-covid-19-continues-to-hit-lower-income-americans-the-hardest/
108   https://www.newyorkfed.org/research/college-labor-market/index.html
109   https://www.insidehighered.com/news/2018/05/23/college-graduates-whose-first-job-doesnt-require-bachelors-degree-often-stay
110   https://www.bls.gov/spotlight/2012/recession/pdf/recession_bls_spotlight.pdf
111   http://www.newgeography.com/content/005242-large-cities-rankings-2016-best-cities-job-growth
112   https://www.selectusa.gov/automotive-industry-united-states
113   https://energy.gov/downloads/2017-us-energy-and-employment-report
114   https://www.washingtonpost.com/business/2020/12/31/stock-market-record-2020/
115   https://bigfuture.collegeboard.org/pay-for-college/grants-scholarships
116   https://trends.collegeboard.org/student-aid
117   https://oregonstudentaid.gov/oregon-promise.aspx
118   http://monitor.icef.com/2016/01/mooc-enrolment-surpassed-35-million-in-2015/
119   https://www.nytimes.com/2016/12/08/opinion/the-american-dream-quantified-at-last.html?_r=1&mtrref=undefined&assetType=opinion
120   https://airwaysmag.com/airlines/how-low-cost-airlines-are-changing-the-face-of-air-travel/
121   https://www.bbc.co.uk/news/business-45139077
122   https://www.claimcompass.eu/blog/wow-air-bankrupcy/

123 http://edition.cnn.com/2017/04/10/travel/passenger-removed-united-flight-trnd/index.html
124 http://dollarsandsense.sg/what-are-the-pros-and-cons-of-flying-on-a-budget-airline/
125 https://thepointsguy.com/2016/05/low-cost-carrier-vs-major-airline/
126 https://www.economist.com/the-economist-explains/2017/12/04/how-landing-and-take-off-slots-are-allocated-at-congested-airports
127 https://www.quora.com/What-are-the-advantage-and-disadvantage-of-Low-cost-and-full-service-airlines
128 https://www.bustle.com/p/budget-airlines-could-end-up-costing-you-more-thanks-to-these-hidden-fees-16102903
129 http://dollarsandsense.sg/what-are-the-pros-and-cons-of-flying-on-a-budget-airline/
130 https://www.flightcentre.com.au/travel-news/business-travel/the-benefits-of-booking-early
131 http://dollarsandsense.sg/what-are-the-pros-and-cons-of-flying-on-a-budget-airline/
132 https://www.travelertips.org/red-eye-flight-advantages/1395/
133 https://www.thesun.co.uk/living/1232827/ever-wondered-how-budget-airlines-keep-their-prices-so-low-and-still-make-a-huge-profit-heres-the-answer/
134 https://www.businessinsider.com/why-flights-are-getting-more-uncomfortable-2018-5
135 https://www.youtube.com/watch?v=069y1MpOkQY
136 http://www.aviationtoday.com/2015/04/01/upgrade-or-replace-airline-influencers-examine-potential-roi/
137 https://www.fool.com/investing/general/2015/09/30/aircraft-retrofits-will-boost-deltas-fuel-efficien.aspx
138 http://www.airsafe.com/events/airlines/fleetage.htm
139 https://www.huduser.gov/portal/periodicals/em/fall12/highlight1.html
140 http://www.hgtv.com/
141 https://www.youtube.com/watch?v=xWBI8xVJIvw
142 https://www.businessinsider.com/heres-where-those-who-lost-homes-during-the-us-housing-crisis-are-now-2018-8
143 https://www.theatlantic.com/photo/2018/10/photos-incredible-devastation-left-hurricane-michael/572956/
144 https://www.bloomberg.com/news/articles/2018-07-26/american-housing-market-is-showing-signs-of-running-out-of-steam
145 https://www.forbes.com/sites/jamiehopkins/2014/09/25/why-housing-is-a-bad-long-term-investment-and-why-you-should-buy-anyways/
146 http://www.mortgagecalculator.org/
147 http://www.investopedia.com/financial-edge/0910/6-things-you-think-add-value-to-your-home---but-really-dont.aspx
148 http://marginalrevolution.com/marginalrevolution/2016/02/67635.html

149 http://www.businessinsider.com/mortgage-means-death-pledge-2016-3
150 https://247wallst.com/housing/2018/06/03/10-us-cities-where-home-prices-are-falling-the-most/
151 http://www.freep.com/story/money/real-estate/2015/07/12/detroit-home-values-rising/29169949/
152 https://piie.com/publications/wp/wp13-3.pdf
153 https://qz.com/167887/germany-has-one-of-the-worlds-lowest-home-ownership-rates/
154 https://en.wikipedia.org/wiki/List_of_sovereign_states_in_Europe_by_GDP_(nominal)
155 https://www.theatlantic.com/national/archive/2009/07/homeowner-ships-downsides/20368/
156 http://www.citylab.com/housing/2015/04/the-us-spends-far-more-on-homeowner-subsidies-than-it-does-on-affordable-housing/390666/
157 https://www.taxpolicycenter.org/briefing-book/what-are-tax-benefits-homeownership
158 https://www.brookings.edu/research/under-us-housing-policies-home-owners-mostly-win-while-renters-mostly-lose/
159 http://www.cnbc.com/2016/06/16/rents-now-top-list-of-fastest-rising-prices.html
160 https://www.huduser.gov/portal/pdredge/pdr-edge-featd-article-061917.html
161 https://en.wikipedia.org/wiki/Home_equity
162 https://www.cnbc.com/2017/07/31/benefits-of-a-home-equity-line-of-credit.html
163 http://www.foxbusiness.com/features/2014/03/06/5-things-need-to-know-about-home-equity-loans.html
164 https://www.thebalance.com/eight-reasons-to-buy-a-home-1798233
165 https://quod.lib.umich.edu/m/mfr/4919087.0004.101/--introduction-intergenerational-relationships-in-todays?rgn=main;view=fulltext

Education

1 https://www.forbes.com/sites/robynshulman/2020/06/18/3-ways-school-may-look-different-in-the-fall/
2 https://www.bbc.com/future/article/20200603-how-covid-19-is-changing-the-worlds-children
3 https://www.parents.com/kids/education/kindergarten/thrive-in-2025-holding-kids-back-for-success/
4 https://www.mirror.co.uk/lifestyle/family/should-you-your-child-win-8108970

5	https://www.nytimes.com/2020/08/13/parenting/praising-children.html?surface=home-living-vi&fellback=false&req_id=268557380&algo=identity&imp_id=761799349&action=click&module=Smarter%20Living&pgtype=Homepage
6	http://www.nber.org/papers/w13663
7	https://www.ncbi.nlm.nih.gov/books/NBK310550/
8	http://www.naeyc.org/files/naeyc/file/positions/Psunacc.pdf
9	https://slate.com/human-interest/2013/09/academic-redshirting-what-does-the-research-say-about-delaying-kindergarten.html
10	https://www.nytimes.com/2011/09/25/opinion/sunday/dont-delay-your-kindergartners-start.html
11	https://www.huffingtonpost.com/2014/01/06/children-praise_n_4549369.html
12	https://www.nytimes.com/2007/06/03/magazine/03kindergarten-t.html
13	http://www.slate.com/articles/double_x/the_kids/2013/09/academic_redshirting_what_does_the_research_say_about_delaying_kindergarten.html
14	https://www.cultofpedagogy.com/academic-redshirting/
15	https://www.goodreads.com/book/show/3228917-outliers
16	https://www.parents.com/kids/education/kindergarten/thrive-in-2025-holding-kids-back-for-success/
17	https://www.usnews.com/news/healthiest-communities/articles/2018-08-21/does-redshirting-benefit-kids-kindergarten-decision-looms
18	https://www.parents.com/kids/education/kindergarten/thrive-in-2025-holding-kids-back-for-success/
19	https://www.ncbi.nlm.nih.gov/pubmed/2805901
20	https://ed.stanford.edu/news/stanford-gse-research-finds-strong-evidence-mental-health-benefits-delaying-kindergarten
21	https://papers.ssrn.com/sol3/papers.cfm?abstract_id=1017099
22	https://www.nytimes.com/2010/08/22/fashion/22Cultural.html
23	https://qz.com/quartzy/1382336/school-uniforms-are-rapidly-on-the-rise-at-us-public-schools/
24	http://www.healthguidance.org/entry/15038/1/Pros-and-Cons-of-School-Uniforms.html
25	http://www.norwichbulletin.com/x1992967098/School-uniforms-will-promote-equality
26	https://www.thoughtco.com/pros-cons-of-school-uniforms-6760
27	http://www.healthguidance.org/entry/15038/1/Pros-and-Cons-of-School-Uniforms.html
28	http://debatewise.org/debates/3367-school-uniforms-should-be-mandatory/
29	https://www.thoughtco.com/pros-cons-of-school-uniforms-6760
30	http://www.healthguidance.org/entry/15038/1/Pros-and-Cons-of-School-Uniforms.html

31	https://www.schneier.com/blog/archives/2007/07/school_uniforms.html
32	https://school-uniforms.procon.org/
33	https://soapboxie.com/social-issues/The-Pros-and-Cons-of-School-Uniforms
34	https://www.publicschoolreview.com/blog/public-school-uniforms-the-pros-and-cons-for-your-child
35	https://www.theperspective.com/debates/politics/first-amendment-cover-racism-hate-speech/
36	http://debatewise.org/debates/3367-school-uniforms-should-be-mandatory/
37	https://www.thoughtco.com/pros-cons-of-school-uniforms-6760
38	http://www.healthguidance.org/entry/15038/1/Pros-and-Cons-of-School-Uniforms.html
39	https://theconversation.com/school-uniforms-a-blessing-or-a-curse-41967
40	https://prezi.com/qed_7mcem0li/the-disadvantages-on-school-uniforms/
41	https://soapboxie.com/social-issues/Arguments-against-school-uniforms
42	http://debatewise.org/debates/3367-school-uniforms-should-be-mandatory/
43	http://www.healthguidance.org/entry/15038/1/Pros-and-Cons-of-School-Uniforms.html
44	https://www.youtube.com/watch?v=t1lUN62yHBE
45	https://www.youtube.com/watch?v=mvkRT0_Un_4
46	https://www.theperspective.com/debates/living/is-college-worth-it/
47	https://medium.com/@spencerbaum/3-reasons-why-you-should-read-more-classic-literature-in-2019-e762cb5c910c
48	https://www.youtube.com/watch?v=X7FobPxu27M
49	http://www.bbc.co.uk/drama/shakespeare/60secondshakespeare/themes_index.shtml
50	https://booksonthewall.com/blog/hemingway-and-fitzgerald/
51	https://www.rollingstone.com/music/music-features/beatles-sgt-pepper-at-50-remembering-the-real-lucy-in-the-sky-with-diamonds-121628/
52	https://www.edvardmunch.org/the-scream.jsp
53	https://www.newyorker.com/culture/culture-desk/a-slightly-embarrassing-love-for-jack-kerouac
54	https://www.youtube.com/watch?v=9nJv8sxpUKU
55	https://www.futurelearn.com/courses/brand-storytelling/0/steps/11272
56	https://www.youtube.com/watch?v=arkGyHQmc-A
57	https://en.wikiquote.org/wiki/Henry_James
58	https://www.doingwhatmatters.com/teach-classic-literature-in-context/
59	http://www.criticalthinking.org/pages/the-role-of-socratic-questioning-in-thinking-teaching-amp-learning/522
60	https://phys.org/news/2009-02-classic-literature-personal-ethics.html
61	https://theconversation.com/how-the-moral-lessons-of-to-kill-a-mockingbird-endure-today-100763

62   https://techcrunch.com/2016/05/19/the-average-age-for-a-child-getting-their-first-smartphone-is-now-10-3-years/
63   https://www.inc.com/melanie-curtin/bill-gates-says-this-is-the-safest-age-to-give-a-child-a-smartphone.html
64   https://www.digitaltrends.com/mobile/best-apps-for-kids/
65   http://www.health.harvard.edu/press_releases/regular-exercise-releases-brain-chemicals-key-for-memory-concentration-and-mental-sharpness
66   https://www.healthambition.com/how-to-improve-concentration/
67   http://www.dailymail.co.uk/news/article-2093772/Smartphones-exposing-children-pornography-violence-1-2m-youngsters-admit-logging-on.html
68   https://protectyoungeyes.com/the-case-for-removing-cell-phones-from-the-school-bus/
69   https://www.tomsguide.com/us/best-parental-control-apps,review-2258.html
70   http://www.makeuseof.com/tag/7-ways-children-might-bypass-parental-control-software/
71   https://www.psychologytoday.com/blog/behind-online-behavior/201408/the-psychology-behind-social-media-interactions
72   https://www.psychologytoday.com/us/blog/the-wide-wide-world-psychology/201701/why-child-s-social-emotional-skills-are-so-important
73   https://medium.com/thrive-global/will-technology-ruin-your-childrens-development-663351c76974
74   https://www.teachermagazine.com.au/articles/mobile-phones-in-the-classroom-what-does-the-research-say
75   http://www.zmescience.com/research/technology/smartphone-power-compared-to-apollo-432/
76   https://www.mckinsey.com/industries/public-and-social-sector/our-insights/back-to-school-a-framework-for-remote-and-hybrid-learning-amid-covid-19
77   http://www.govtech.com/education/news/cellphones-in-classrooms-part-2.html
78   http://www.seattletimes.com/business/cellphones-help-kids-keep-in-touch-with-parents/
79   https://edition.cnn.com/2018/03/02/us/school-shootings-2018-list-trnd/index.html
80   https://qz.com/1175155/a-special-class-how-to-teach-kids-to-spot-fake-news/
81   https://www.theperspective.com/debates/businessandtechnology/fake-news-not-real-problem/
82   https://www.cdc.gov/healthyyouth/about/pdf/hivstd_prevention.pdf
83   https://www.moms.com/statistics-children-watching-adult-content/

84	https://www.nytimes.com/2018/02/07/magazine/teenagers-learning-online-porn-literacy-sex-education.html
85	https://www.cdc.gov/healthyyouth/sexualbehaviors/
86	https://www.plannedparenthood.org/learn/birth-control/condom/how-effective-are-condoms
87	https://www.cdc.gov/condomeffectiveness/brief.html
88	https://www.nytimes.com/2017/08/22/upshot/sex-education-based-on-abstinence-theres-a-real-absence-of-evidence.html
89	https://www.nbcnews.com/health/condoms-should-be-more-available-teens-doctors-say-8C11479236
90	https://www.sciencedirect.com/science/article/pii/S1054139X1730160X
91	https://opa.hhs.gov/reproductive-health?pregnancy-prevention/birth-control-methods/abstinence/index.html
92	https://www.pewresearch.org/fact-tank/2019/08/02/why-is-the-teen-birth-rate-falling/
93	https://www.cdc.gov/nchs/products/databriefs/db366.htm
94	https://www.youtube.com/watch?v=VMXdSkW6hns
95	https://www.huffpost.com/entry/parents-teens-sexually-active_l_5fd-8ca83c5b62f31c2008bab
96	https://www.livescience.com/6404-parents-teens-sex.html
97	https://www.thoughtco.com/contraception-birth-control-and-world-religions-248029
98	https://www.plannedparenthood.org/learn/birth-control/condom/how-effective-are-condoms
99	https://www.upworthy.com/meet-the-concerned-mom-who-doesnt-think-kids-need-sex-ed-then-watch-the-daily-shows-response

Health

1	https://www.healthline.com/health/depression/facts-statistics-infographic
2	https://www.massgeneral.org/news/coronavirus/depression-on-rise-during-covid-19
3	https://www.reuters.com/article/us-people-kate-spade/designer-kate-spade-suffered-depression-for-years-husband-says-idUSKCN1J2304
4	https://www.cheatsheet.com/health-fitness/easily-missed-signs-of-anthony-bourdains-depression.html/
5	https://www.ncbi.nlm.nih.gov/pmc/articles/PMC5244448/
6	https://www.psychiatryadvisor.com/home/topics/mood-disorders/depressive-disorder/relapse-risk-after-discontinuation-of-antidepressants-for-anxiety/
7	https://www.healthline.com/health/clinical-depression
8	https://www.sane.org/mental-health-and-illness/facts-and-guides/antidepressant-medication

9   https://www.healthyplace.com/depression/depression-treatment/lifestyle-and-behavior-changes-gsd/
10 https://www.frontiersin.org/articles/10.3389/fpsyg.2012.00117/full
11 https://www.webmd.com/depression/features/coping-with-side-effects-of-depression-treatment
12 https://www.prevention.com/mind-body/11-things-only-someone-on-antidepressants-understands
13 https://www.drugwatch.com/ssri/suicide/
14 https://www.swamh.com/poc/view_doc.php?type=doc&id=12999&cn=5
15 https://www.ncbi.nlm.nih.gov/pmc/articles/PMC3363299/
16 https://www.ncbi.nlm.nih.gov/books/NBK361016/
17 https://www.webmd.com/pain-management/what-is-the-placebo-effect
18 https://www.webmd.com/a-to-z-guides/news/20150930/placebo-effect-might-help-predict-response-to-depression-treatment
19 https://caps.ucsc.edu/resources/depression.html
20 https://www.psychologytoday.com/us/blog/nurturing-self-compassion/201806/why-we-need-stop-demonizing-antidepressants
21 https://health.clevelandclinic.org/theres-no-shame-in-taking-an-antidepressant/
22 https://greatist.com/live/how-antidepressants-helped-me-deal-with-depression
23 https://www.niddk.nih.gov/health-information/health-statistics/overweight-obesity
24 https://www.singlecare.com/blog/news/obesity-statistics/
25 https://www.usatoday.com/story/life/allthemoms/2019/04/08/first-dietary-guidelines-for-pregnant-women-babies-toddlers-coming-in-2020/3395978002/
26 https://www.nejm.org/doi/full/10.1056/NEJMoa1703860
27 https://www.ncbi.nlm.nih.gov/pmc/articles/PMC7540284/
28 https://www.medicalnewstoday.com/articles/262226.php
29 https://www.mayoclinic.org/diseases-conditions/obesity/symptoms-causes/syc-20375742
30 https://www.nature.com/nature/journal/v508/n7496_supp/full/508S57a.html
31 http://healthland.time.com/2013/06/19/viewpoint-why-defining-obesity-as-a-disease-may-do-more-harm-than-good/
32 https://www.forbes.com/sites/peterubel/2015/03/27/calling-obesity-a-disease-dooms-dieters/
33 https://www.nichd.nih.gov/health/topics/obesity/conditioninfo/pages/diagnosed.aspx
34 https://www.menshealth.com/weight-loss/a19537796/the-problem-with-bmi/
35 https://www.scientificamerican.com/article/the-bmi-is-outdated-but-it-still-works/

36 https://www.medscape.com/viewarticle/911393
37 https://www.sciencedaily.com/releases/2019/04/190402215621.htm
38 https://www.theperspective.com/debates/living/repairing-broken-heart-stents-bypass-surgery/
39 http://www.bbc.com/news/23011804
40 https://www.theatlantic.com/health/archive/2013/06/is-obesity-really-a-disease/277148/
41 https://www.scientificamerican.com/article/the-bmi-is-outdated-but-it-still-works/
42 https://www.livescience.com/21222-obesity-disease-debate.html
43 https://link.springer.com/chapter/10.1007/978-94-011-0583-5_3
44 http://www.health.harvard.edu/staying-healthy/why-people-become-overweight
45 http://www.cbsnews.com/news/diet-exercise-treatment-for-obese-patients/
46 https://www.kidney.org/atoz/content/obesewyska
47 https://www.kidney.org/news/newsroom/factsheets/End-Stage-Renal-Disease-in-the-US
48 https://www.usatoday.com/story/life/allthemoms/2019/04/08/first-dietary-guidelines-for-pregnant-women-babies-toddlers-coming-in-2020/3395978002/
49 https://asmbs.org/patients/disease-of-obesity
50 https://www.cbsnews.com/news/unhealthy-diet-now-kills-more-people-than-tobacco-and-high-blood-pressure-study-finds/
51 https://www.sciencemag.org/news/2020/09/why-covid-19-more-deadly-people-obesity-even-if-theyre-young
52 https://www.nbcnews.com/think/opinion/when-doctors-fat-shame-their-patients-everybody-loses-ncna1045921
53 https://www.forbes.com/sites/robdube/2019/04/08/eat-well-stress-less-lead-better-americas-healthy-heart-doc-shares-the-keys-to-a-balanced-life/
54 https://www.nytimes.com/2020/04/16/health/coronavirus-obesity-higher-risk.html
55 https://www.youtube.com/watch?v=zGu5G1v0yn8
56 https://www.nytimes.com/2018/08/31/business/milk-nut-juice-plant-beverage-label.html
57 https://www.i24news.tv/en/news/international/1595758992-lack-of-vitamin-d-could-make-you-more-vulnerable-to-coronavirus-researchers
58 https://time.com/5029164/fruit-vegetable-diet/
59 https://www.theperspective.com/debates/living/perspective-paleo-diet/
60 https://www.choosemyplate.gov/dairy
61 https://www.nof.org/patients/what-is-osteoporosis/
62 https://www.iofbonehealth.org/facts-statistics
63 https://ods.od.nih.gov/factsheets/Calcium-HealthProfessional/

64 https://www.theperspective.com/debates/living/vegans-moral-high-ground/
65 https://www.healthline.com/nutrition/how-protein-can-help-you-lose-weight
66 https://www.motherjones.com/environment/2015/11/dairy-industry-milk-federal-dietary-guidelines/
67 https://www.pcrm.org/health/diets/vegdiets/health-concerns-about-dairy-products
68 https://www.pcrm.org/health/cancer-resources/ask/ask-the-expert-dairy-products
69 https://www.mayoclinic.org/diseases-conditions/milk-allergy/symptoms-causes/syc-20375101
70 https://www.mayoclinic.org/diseases-conditions/lactose-intolerance/symptoms-causes/syc-20374232
71 http://www.skininc.com/skinscience/physiology/Long-term-Research-Links-Dairy-and-High-Sugar-Foods-to-Acne-200252611.html
72 https://www.ncbi.nlm.nih.gov/pubmed/20949604
73 https://www.washingtonpost.com/news/to-your-health/wp/2014/10/31/study-milk-may-not-be-very-good-for-bones-or-the-body/
74 https://www.forbes.com/sites/quora/2018/06/06/why-are-humans-the-only-species-that-drinks-milk-past-infancy/
75 https://www.marthastewart.com/1527050/alt-milk-cheat-sheet
76 https://www.healthline.com/nutrition/coconut-milk
77 https://www.theperspective.com/debates/living/how-healthy-is-soy/
78 https://www.marketsandmarkets.com/Market-Reports/dairy-alternative-plant-milk-beverages-market-677.html
79 https://www.businessinsider.com/study-shows-no-link-between-vaccines-and-autism-2019-3
80 https://www.nytimes.com/interactive/2020/science/coronavirus-vaccine-tracker.html
81 https://www.livescience.com/mrna-vaccines-future-vaccine-development.html
82 https://time.com/5917109/u-k-covid-vaccine-approved/
83 https://www.usatoday.com/story/news/health/2019/04/03/measles-outbreaks-anti-vax-opposition-prompts-states-reactive/3347503002/
84 https://www.cdc.gov/vaccines/parents/vaccine-decision/index.html
85 https://www.cdc.gov/flu/about/qa/vaccineeffect.htm
86 https://www.cdc.gov/media/releases/2017/p0403-flu-vaccine.html
87 https://www.cdc.gov/vaccines/hcp/patient-ed/conversations/downloads/not-vacc-risks-color-office.pdf
88 https://www.cdc.gov/features/measles/index.html
89 https://en.wikipedia.org/wiki/Haemophilus_meningitis
90 https://www.nytimes.com/2019/04/03/opinion/parenting-vaccines-measles.html

91   https://www.cdc.gov/flu/weekly/index.htm
92   https://www.cdc.gov/mmwr/volumes/69/rr/rr6908a1.htm?s_cid=rr6908a1_w
93   https://www.scientificamerican.com/article/a-flu-shot-might-reduce-coronavirus-infections-early-research-suggests/
94   https://www.shotsheard.org/
95   http://www.who.int/mediacentre/commentaries/2017/embrace-facts-vaccines/en/
96   https://www.cdc.gov/vaccinesafety/ensuringsafety/index.html
97   https://www.fda.gov/BiologicsBloodVaccines/Vaccines/
98   https://www.ncbi.nlm.nih.gov/pubmed/16263976
99   https://www.webmd.com/children/vaccines/news/20200915/more-than-1-in-3-us-pediatricians-dismiss-vaccine-refusing-families
100 https://www.nytimes.com/2019/04/03/health/measles-outbreaks-ukraine-israel.html
101 https://apic.org/monthly_alerts/herd-immunity/
102 https://www.mayoclinic.org/diseases-conditions/coronavirus/in-depth/herd-immunity-and-coronavirus/art-20486808
103 https://www.scientificamerican.com/article/too-many-children-go-unvaccinated/
104 http://www.nytimes.com/2011/12/28/opinion/for-the-herds-sake-vaccinate.html
105 https://www.telegraph.co.uk/news/2019/03/27/unvaccinated-children-banned-public-places-amid-new-york-measles/
106 https://www.cdc.gov/flu/about/qa/vaccineeffect.htm
107 https://en.wikipedia.org/wiki/Gardasil
108 https://www.healthline.com/health/sexually-transmitted-diseases/hpv-types
109 http://kidshealth.org/en/parents/immune.html
110 https://www.cdc.gov/vaccines/vac-gen/side-effects.htm
111 https://www.mayoclinic.org/healthy-lifestyle/infant-and-toddler-health/in-depth/vaccines/art-20048334
112 http://www.who.int/mental_health/media/en/28.pdf
113 https://www.mayoclinic.org/diseases-conditions/thrombocytopenia/symptoms-causes/syc-20378293
114 https://www.cdc.gov/measles/index.html
115 https://www.crnusa.org/newsroom/dietary-supplement-use-reaches-all-time-high
116 https://www.healthline.com/nutrition/immune-boosting-supplements
117 https://edition.cnn.com/2020/03/25/health/immunity-diet-food-coronavirus-drayer-wellness/index.html
118 https://www.prnewswire.com/news-releases/dietary-supplements-market-to-reach-usd-216-3-billion-by-2026--reports-and-data-300969115.html

119 https://www.cnbc.com/2019/10/30/instagram-vitamins-are-big-business-will-they-make-you-healthier.html
120 https://www.lek.com/sites/default/files/insights/pdf-attachments/Opps-in-Nutritional-Supp_web.pdf
121 http://www.dailymail.co.uk/femail/article-4328802/Gwyneth-Paltrow-released-Goop-vitamin-supplements.html
122 http://www.newsweek.com/why-health-advice-oprah-could-make-you-sick-80201
123 http://time.com/3741142/gnc-vitamin-shoppe-supplements/
124 https://www.nbcnews.com/health/health-news/hidden-dangers-lurk-over-counter-supplements-study-warns-n919731
125 https://www.ncbi.nlm.nih.gov/pmc/articles/PMC5130103/
126 https://www.webmd.com/diet/guide/effects-of-taking-too-many-vitamins
127 https://ods.od.nih.gov/factsheets/MVMS-HealthProfessional/
128 https://www.mayoclinic.org/healthy-lifestyle/nutrition-and-healthy-eating/expert-answers/vitamin-d-toxicity/faq-20058108
129 https://www.healthline.com/nutrition/vitamin-d-coronavirus
130 https://www.livescience.com/54901-free-radicals.html
131 https://www.nytimes.com/2010/04/04/business/04metrics.html
132 https://www.sciencedaily.com/releases/2015/03/150329141017.htm
133 https://www.marketplace.org/2013/03/12/processed-foods-make-70-percent-us-diet/
134 http://www.cbc.ca/news/business/food-fruits-vegetables-meat-prices-1.3455523
135 https://www.scientificamerican.com/article/soil-depletion-and-nutrition-loss/
136 https://www.hsph.harvard.edu/nutritionsource/omega-3-fats/
137 https://www.drweil.com/diet-nutrition/food-safety/how-dangerous-is-farmed-salmon/
138 https://www.ncbi.nlm.nih.gov/pmc/articles/PMC2682456/
139 https://www.nia.nih.gov/health/vitamins-and-minerals
140 https://www.healthline.com/health-news/food-three-groups-who-can-benefit-from-vitamins-121913
141 http://americanpregnancy.org/pregnancy-health/nutrients-vitamins-pregnancy/
142 https://www.webmd.com/baby/folic-acid-and-pregnancy
143 http://americanpregnancy.org/pregnancy-health/nutrients-vitamins-pregnancy/
144 https://www.everydayhealth.com/columns/therese-borchard-sanity-break/patient-approved-natural-supplements-depression/
145 https://www.theperspective.com/debates/living/antidepressants-good-solution/
146 https://www.ncbi.nlm.nih.gov/pmc/articles/PMC3856388/
147 https://ods.od.nih.gov/factsheets/Magnesium-HealthProfessional/

148   https://www.healthline.com/nutrition/magnesium-and-sleep
149   https://www.usatoday.com/story/news/factcheck/2020/03/24/coronavirus-fact-check-could-vitamin-c-cure-covid-19/2904303001/
150   https://www.self.com/story/fda-dietary-supplements-regulations
151   https://www.plasticsurgery.org/news/press-releases/new-statistics-reveal-the-shape-of-plastic-surgery
152   https://www.plasticsurgery.org/documents/News/Statistics/2016/cosmetic-procedure-trends-2016.pdf
153   https://www.livestrong.com/article/71935-pros-cons-cosmetic-surgery/
154   http://www.goodtherapy.org/learn-about-therapy/issues/body-image
155   http://www.thoughtsonlifeandlove.com/cosmetic-surgery-the-pros-and-cons/
156   http://www.normanrappaportmd.com/5-benefits-of-plastic-surgery/
157   https://www.ukessays.com/essays/beauty-therapy/advantages-and-disadvantages-of-plastic-surgery.php
158   http://makeoverga.com/9-ways-plastic-surgery-can-improve-your-health/
159   https://en.wikipedia.org/wiki/Halo_effect
160   http://www.reuters.com/article/us-plasticsurgery-recession-life/some-job-seekers-invest-in-plastic-surgery-to-compete-idUSTRE5366ZW20090408
161   https://www.ncbi.nlm.nih.gov/pmc/articles/PMC2861519/
162   https://www.webmd.com/beauty/news/20010711/when-surgery-cant-make-you-pretty
163   http://www.nytimes.com/2009/01/15/fashion/15skin.html
164   https://www.theperspective.com/debates/entertainment/kardashians-inspiring-damaging-women/
165   http://gulfnews.com/your-say/your-view/focus-cosmetic-surgery-1.813295
166   http://debatewise.org/debates/1442-is-cosmetic-surgery-good-or-bad/
167   https://www.plasticsurgery.org/documents/News/Statistics/2016/plastic-surgery-statistics-full-report-2016.pdf
168   https://www.theperspective.com/debates/living/the-perspective-on-botox/
169   https://abcnews.go.com/2020/MichaelJackson/story?id=7982236&page=1
170   http://www.news.com.au/entertainment/celebrity-life/joan-rivers-death-was-100-preventable-daughter-melissa-rivers-says/news-story/b7628acd043e3cf2a8d795e5ed511e36

Technology

1   https://www.forbes.com/profile/jeff-bezos/
2   http://moneyinc.com/jeff-bezos/view-all
3   https://www.cnet.com/news/jeff-bezos-the-press-shy-billionaire-to-face-the-harsh-spotlight-of-congress/

4   https://www.livescience.com/jeff-bezos-funds-climate-change-fight.html
5   https://www.cnbc.com/2020/07/28/jeff-bezos-and-amazon-on-a-collision-course-with-dc-for-years.html
6   https://www.vox.com/recode/2020/7/27/21340218/jeff-bezos-congress-testimony-antitrust-big-tech-ceos
7   https://www.theperspective.com/debates/businessandtechnology/e-commerce-pushing-us-forward-holding-us/
8   https://www.history.com/this-day-in-history/amazon-opens-for-business
9   http://www.businessinsider.com/analysts-wrong-about-amazon-profit-2015-1
10 https://www.cnbc.com/2017/10/27/how-amazon-founder-jeff-bezos-went-from-the-son-of-a-teen-mom-to-the-worlds-richest-person.html
11 https://www.theperspective.com/debates/businessandtechnology/amazon-good-bad-shopping-industry/
12 https://www.amazon.com/primeinsider/video/emmy-noms-jul19.html
13 https://aws.amazon.com/
14 https://www.theatlantic.com/business/archive/2017/06/why-amazon-bought-whole-foods/530652/
15 https://money.howstuffworks.com/amazon2.htm
16 https://www.cnbc.com/2017/10/27/how-amazon-founder-jeff-bezos-went-from-the-son-of-a-teen-mom-to-the-worlds-richest-person.html
17 https://www.usatoday.com/story/money/2020/07/06/amazon-stock-highest-price-company-worth/5384673002/
18 https://www.cnbc.com/2020/04/19/coronavirus-retail-closures-speed-the-rise-of-amazon.html
19 https://www.coinspeaker.com/amazon-stock-5000-2023/
20 https://www.usatoday.com/story/money/2020/07/06/amazon-stock-highest-price-company-worth/5384673002/
21 https://www.amazon.jobs/principles
22 https://www.cnbc.com/2017/10/27/how-amazon-founder-jeff-bezos-went-from-the-son-of-a-teen-mom-to-the-worlds-richest-person.html
23 https://www.inc.com/jessica-stillman/amazon-ceo-jeff-bezos-just-explained-origin-of-his-extraordinary-resourcefulness.html
24 https://www.businessinsider.com/bill-gates-jeff-bezos-cars-of-top-tech-moguls-2019-7
25 http://www.businessinsider.com/jeff-bezos-honda-reveals-reveals-why-hes-so-successful-2018-1
26 https://www.latimes.com/business/story/2020-02-18/jeff-bezos-net-worth-david-geffen-house
27 http://www.bbc.com/news/business-40304535
28 https://slate.com/business/2018/09/jeff-bezos-2-billion-donation-homelessness-preschool.html
29 https://www.vox.com/2018/9/13/17855950/jeff-bezos-donation-2-billion-philanthropy-charity-amazon-ceo

30 https://www.space.com/jeff-bezos-blue-origin-climate-change-fight.html
31 https://www.politico.com/magazine/story/2018/04/18/jeff-bezos-amazon-washington-post-217994
32 https://www.smithsonianmag.com/innovation/rocketeer-jeff-bezos-winner-smithsonians-technology-ingenuity-award-180961119/
33 https://www.geekwire.com/2016/interview-jeff-bezos/
34 https://www.blueorigin.com/our-mission
35 https://www.recode.net/2018/10/15/17980544/jeff-bezos-blue-origin-space-travel-2019-tourists
36 http://www.businessinsider.com/jeff-bezos-on-how-innovation-happens-2013-8
37 https://www.foxbusiness.com/features/washington-post-writer-slams-jeff-bezos-in-op-ed-for-mistreating-workers
38 https://www.nytimes.com/2015/08/16/technology/inside-amazon-wrestling-big-ideas-in-a-bruising-workplace.html?mcubz=0&mtrref=www.foxbusiness.com&gwh=CBC2CA283D664ADF33222C0C0CA60ECF&gwt=pay
39 https://www.usmagazine.com/celebrity-news/pictures/jeff-bezos-divorce-and-cheating-scandal-everything-we-know/
40 https://www.businessinsider.com/jeff-bezos-wife-mackenzie-2017-11
41 https://www.theguardian.com/technology/2019/jun/30/amazon-jeff-bezos-ex-wife-mackenzie-handed-38bn-in-divorce-settlement
42 https://techcrunch.com/2020/07/29/amazons-hardware-business-doesnt-escape-congressional-scrutiny/
43 https://www.vanityfair.com/news/2018/04/trump-war-with-amazon-and-the-washington-post-is-personal
44 https://www.theguardian.com/technology/2017/oct/04/amazon-eu-tax-irish-government-apple
45 https://newrepublic.com/article/147249/amazon-big-tax
46 https://www.nytimes.com/2017/11/15/technology/amazon-sales-tax.html?mtrref=newrepublic.com
47 https://www.inc.com/minda-zetlin/jeff-bezos-first-big-charitable-gift-is-diabolically-clever.html
48 https://www.reuters.com/article/us-bezos-philanthrophy/amazons-jeff-bezos-commits-2-billion-to-help-homeless-pre-schools-idUSKCN1LT2MN
49 https://www.vox.com/recode/2020/2/19/21143107/jeff-bezos-earth-fund-questions-climate
50 https://www.bloomberg.com/news/articles/2017-10-31/for-bezos-now-world-s-richest-philanthropy-is-saved-for-later
51 https://www.theperspective.com/debates/businessandtechnology/perspective-bill-gates/
52 https://markets.businessinsider.com/news/stocks/warren-buffett-leads-giving-list-donating-billions-charity-years-billionaires-2020-1-1028833145

53 https://www.theverge.com/2015/12/1/9831554/mark-zuckerberg-charity-45-billion
54 https://www.rollingstone.com/politics/amazon-jeff-bezos-richest-man-philanthropy-charity-w515535
55 https://www.rollingstone.com/politics/amazon-jeff-bezos-richest-man-philanthropy-charity-w515535
56 https://www.vox.com/future-perfect/2020/2/19/21142312/jeff-bezos-climate-change-ten-billion-philanthropy
57 https://blog.hubspot.com/marketing/digital-ad-spend-to-surpass-tv-print-2019
58 https://www.salesartillery.com/marketing-book-podcast/alchemy-rory-sutherland
59 https://www.newyorker.com/magazine/2017/02/27/why-facts-dont-change-our-minds
60 https://www.inc.com/jim-schleckser/measurable-marketing-why-you-need-to-go-digital.html
61 https://www.vpncrew.com/timeline-of-facebook-controversies-scandals-privacy-concerns-data-breaches/
62 https://money.cnn.com/2018/03/17/technology/facebook-cambridge-analytica-2016-election/index.html
63 https://www.nbcnews.com/tech/tech-news/some-pro-trump-extremsists-used-facebook-plan-capitol-attack-report-n1254794
64 https://www.statista.com/statistics/264810/number-of-monthly-active-facebook-users-worldwide/
65 https://www.statista.com/statistics/268604/annual-revenue-of-facebook/
66 https://variety.com/2020/digital/news/facebook-q1-2020-2-6-billion-users-ad-drop-coronavirus-1234593395/
67 https://www.nytimes.com/2020/06/29/business/dealbook/facebook-boycott-ads.html
68 https://www.socialmediatoday.com/news/facebook-outlines-five-years-of-vr-advances-from-oculus-infographic/597505/
69 https://www.cnbc.com/2021/04/20/facebook-backed-diem-aims-to-launch-digital-currency-pilot-in-2021.html
70 https://www.industryleadersmagazine.com/top-companies-owned-by-facebook/
71 https://zephoria.com/top-15-valuable-facebook-statistics/
72 https://www.oberlo.com/blog/twitter-statistics
73 http://www.businessinsider.com/science-behind-why-facebook-is-addictive-2014-11
74 https://wallaroomedia.com/facebook-newsfeed-algorithm-history/
75 https://newsroom.fb.com/news/2016/06/news-feed-fyi-helping-make-sure-you-dont-miss-stories-from-friends/
76 https://www.wired.com/story/facebook-click-gap-news-feed-changes/

77 https://www.nytimes.com/2021/02/10/technology/facebook-reduces-politics-feeds.html
78 https://www.journalism.org/2021/01/12/news-use-across-social-media-platforms-in-2020/
79 https://www.popularmechanics.com/technology/security/a21272151/facebook-data-money-value/
80 https://www.theatlantic.com/technology/archive/2014/05/why-americans-cant-find-out-what-big-data-knows-about-them/371758/
81 https://digiday.com/marketing/as-facebook-boycott-continues-heres-a-look-at-what-major-marketers-were-spending-on-facebook-and-instagram/
82 https://www.theguardian.com/technology/2018/mar/24/facebook-week-of-shame-data-breach-observer-revelations-zuckerberg-silence
83 https://www.theguardian.com/news/2018/mar/26/the-cambridge-analytica-files-the-story-so-far
84 https://www.ftc.gov/news-events/press-releases/2019/07/ftc-imposes-5-billion-penalty-sweeping-new-privacy-restrictions
85 https://www.theverge.com/2019/7/12/20692524/facebook-five-billion-ftc-fine-embarrassing-joke
86 http://www.foxnews.com/opinion/2018/03/26/did-facebook-s-favors-for-obama-campaign-constitute-violation-federal-law.html
87 https://www.nbcnews.com/think/opinion/facebook-can-t-be-trusted-protect-users-data-its-own-ncna950386
88 https://www.nytimes.com/2019/05/01/technology/facebook-ftc-settlement.html
89 https://live.fb.com/
90 https://www.washingtonpost.com/business/technology/facebook-wanted-visceral-live-video-its-getting-suicides-and-live-streaming-killers/2017/04/17/a6705662-239c-11e7-a1b3-faff0034e2de_story.html?utm_term=.2555b1c2e2a8
91 http://time.com/4756939/facebook-live-alabama-suicide-james-jeffrey/
92 https://www.theverge.com/2021/1/6/22217421/capitol-building-trump-mob-protest-live-stream-youtube-twitch-facebook
93 https://www.theguardian.com/technology/2017/jan/05/facebook-live-social-media-live-streaming
94 https://www.bbc.com/news/technology-47758455
95 https://www.cnbc.com/2019/10/09/the-german-synagogue-shooting-was-streamed-on-twitch.html
96 https://www.technologyreview.com/2018/04/12/143927/three-problems-with-facebooks-plan-to-kill-hate-speech-using-ai/
97 https://www.buzzfeed.com/craigsilverman/people-be-reading-but-not-trusting-news-on-facebook?utm_term=.anPZz3P2QV
98 https://www.emarketer.com/content/amazon-s-share-of-us-digital-ad-market-surpassed-10-2020

99   https://mashable.com/article/why-mark-zuckerberg-worried-about-tiktok/
100 https://techhq.com/2021/03/is-tiktok-a-threat-to-facebook-social-media-dominance/
101 https://www.businessinsider.com/facebook-civic-groups-internal-docs-capitol-riot-misinformation-hate-2021-2
102 https://www.inc.com/graham-winfrey/why-steve-jobs-was-mean-to-his-employees.html
103 https://www.telegraph.co.uk/technology/apple/8324867/Apples-child-labour-issues-worsen.html
104 http://www.dailymail.co.uk/news/article-1285980/Revealed-Inside-Chinese-suicide-sweatshop-workers-toil-34-hour-shifts-make-iPod.html
105 https://www.apple.com/newsroom/2011/08/24Steve-Jobs-Resigns-as-CEO-of-Apple/
106 http://money.cnn.com/2016/08/24/technology/apple-tim-cook-five-years/index.html
107 http://fortune.com/2011/08/25/how-apple-works-inside-the-worlds-biggest-startup/
108 http://uk.businessinsider.com/what-its-like-to-work-at-apple-2015-9/
109 https://abcnews.go.com/Technology/steve-jobs-fire-company/story?id=14683754
110 https://www.cultofmac.com/224411/mobileme-failures-were-all-steve-jobs-fault-says-former-apple-engineer/
111 http://www.businessinsider.com/steve-jobs-jerk-2011-10
112 https://dealbook.nytimes.com/2011/08/29/the-mystery-of-steve-jobss-public-giving/
113 https://www.wired.com/2012/02/steve-jobs-fbi-file/
114 https://www.thedailybeast.com/steve-jobss-fbi-file-calls-him-smart-tough-and-not-very-honest
115 http://gawker.com/5847344/what-everyone-is-too-polite-to-say-about-steve-jobs
116 https://www.theperspective.com/debates/businessandtechnology/perspective-bill-gates/
117 https://www.entrepreneur.com/article/197538
118 http://money.cnn.com/2018/06/05/investing/apple-trillion-dollar-market-value-amazon/index.html
119 https://www.macrumors.com/2017/10/10/americans-own-one-apple-product/
120 https://www.forbes.com/sites/gilpress/2012/10/10/what-has-steve-jobs-wrought/
121 http://www.businessinsider.com/steve-jobs-pixar-2011-10
122 https://mashable.com/2011/10/06/steve-jobs-next-pixar/
123 http://www.businessinsider.com/steve-jobs-pixar-2011-10
124 https://toystory.disney.com/
125 https://www.wnyc.org/story/pixar-steve-jobs-and-future-disney/

126 https://www.ted.com/talks/steve_jobs_how_to_live_before_you_die
127 https://www.forbes.com/sites/carminegallo/2015/06/12/why-steve-jobs-commencement-speech-still-inspires-10-years-later/2/
128 https://www.cbsnews.com/news/stanford-05-grads-recall-impact-of-jobs-speech/
129 https://www.inc.com/graham-winfrey/6-movies-that-explore-the-legacy-of-steve-jobs.html
130 https://www.inc.com/geoffrey-james/7-intriguing-books-about-steve-jobs.html
131 https://www.cnbc.com/2018/05/29/what-ex-apple-pepsi-ceo-john-sculley-learned-from-steve-jobs.html
132 https://www.entrepreneur.com/article/251476
133 https://gs.statcounter.com/os-market-share/mobile/worldwide
134 https://www.forbes.com/sites/gordonkelly/2020/01/11/apple-iphone-12-2020-design-upgrade-iphone-11-pro-max-upgrade/
135 https://www.pcmag.com/roundup/334207/the-best-android-phones
136 https://www.digitaltrends.com/computing/can-macs-get-viruses/
137 https://us.norton.com/internetsecurity-mobile-android-vs-ios-which-is-more-secure.html
138 https://www.extremetech.com/mobile/304577-malware-spotted-on-government-subsidized-android-phone
139 https://www.pandasecurity.com/en/mediacenter/mobile-security/android-more-infected-than-ios/
140 https://variety.com/2017/digital/news/apple-slow-iphone-backlash-1202647220/
141 https://www.gsmarena.com/apple_iphone_8_plus-8131.php
142 https://www.apple.com/il/iphone-x/
143 https://www.tomsguide.com/us/iphone-is-better-than-android,news-21307.html
144 https://mashable.com/2017/09/14/inside-apple-a11-bionic-and-silicon-team/
145 https://bgr.com/tech/iphone-12-pro-speed-test-vs-iphone-11-galaxy-note-20-pixel-5-5880157/
146 https://www.digitaltrends.com/mobile/android-vs-ios/
147 https://developer.android.com/studio
148 https://android.jlelse.eu/top-secrets-of-why-android-is-still-better-than-ios-in-2018-391b89a45a09
149 https://www.digitaltrends.com/mobile/android-vs-ios/
150 https://www.statista.com/statistics/276623/number-of-apps-available-in-leading-app-stores/
151 https://www.zdnet.com/article/11-things-my-android-phone-does-way-better-than-your-iphone/
152 https://thebroodle.com/android/why-do-users-still-prefer-android-over-ios/

153 https://www.digitaltrends.com/mobile/android-vs-ios/
154 https://gs.statcounter.com/os-market-share/mobile/worldwide
155 https://www.lifewire.com/iphone-vs-android-best-smartphone-2000309
156 https://www.youtube.com/watch?v=3KNVx1ciN_g
157 https://www.macworld.co.uk/feature/iosapps/siri-vs-google-assistant-3659249/
158 https://www.online-tech-tips.com/smart-home/siri-google-assistant-cortana-three-digital-assistants-compared/
159 https://www.vulture.com/article/snl-season-46-episode-18-saturday-night-live-recap-elon-musk-hosts.html
160 https://www.inverse.com/article/51291-spacex-here-s-the-timeline-for-getting-to-mars-and-starting-a-colony
161 https://www.todayifoundout.com/index.php/2011/08/robert-downey-jr-modeled-his-portrayal-of-tony-stark-after-elon-musk-one-of-the-founders-of-zip2-paypal-tesla-motors-and-spacex/
162 https://www.timesnownews.com/business-economy/world-news/article/elon-musks-top-5-controversies-from-smoking-weed-on-camera-to-calling-tesla-stock-too-high/705282
163 https://www.vox.com/2018/7/18/17576302/elon-musk-thai-cave-rescue-submarine
164 https://techcrunch.com/2018/09/29/elon-musk-agrees-to-resign-as-tesla-chairman-in-settlement-with-sec/?guccounter=1&guce_referrer=aHR0cHM6Ly93d3cuZ29vZ2xlLmNvbS8&guce_referrer_sig=AQAAAAJfvZ9DCbE7fcrJ1Wofe-kmiV3gS0cJue2y2yCnjQZp9lHlOBofJ0_swLupfCpC9vPYB4gJEHo8_4Gx1duKOOEUWSDrWXy1NO-lUv-GIl0xZ81dRpHbS-IbQWEQ2wA2Al41txbNfovoMLRGP_NCniqRdRH13QwSPL_JGNAskM7PJ
165 https://www.biography.com/business-figure/elon-musk
166 https://www.tesla.com/
167 https://www.businessinsider.com/tesla-first-car-roadster-history-revamping-owner-relationships-2019-12
168 https://www.theverge.com/2017/7/28/16059954/tesla-model-3-2017-auto-industry-influence-elon-musk
169 https://about.bnef.com/electric-vehicle-outlook/
170 https://singularityhub.com/2017/04/27/heres-why-people-think-tesla-is-the-most-innovative-company-today/
171 https://www.statista.com/statistics/502208/tesla-quarterly-vehicle-deliveries/
172 https://www.statista.com/statistics/502208/tesla-quarterly-vehicle-deliveries/
173 http://www.spacex.com/
174 https://mashable.com/2018/02/06/spacex-falcon-heavy-boosters/
175 https://www.theperspective.com/debates/businessandtechnology/is-there-life-outside-earth/

176 https://www.cnbc.com/2019/12/08/spacex-dragon-successfully-docks-with-the-international-space-station.html
177 http://www.businessinsider.com/elon-musks-childhood-was-excruciating-2015-5
178 https://yourstory.com/2016/06/elon-musk-failure/
179 https://money.cnn.com/2018/10/01/technology/business/tesla-stock/index.html
180 https://qz.com/1405467/the-us-government-is-suing-elon-musk-for-misleading-investors-about-taking-tesla-tsla-private/
181 https://www.wired.com/story/elon-musk-wins-defamation-suit-british-diver/
182 https://www.cnbc.com/2020/05/09/elon-musk-says-tesla-will-move-its-headquarters-amid-fremont-factory-shutdown-due-to-coronavirus.html
183 https://www.teslarati.com/elon-musk-king-job-creation/
184 https://www.inc.com/magazine/20101001/elon-musks-guide-to-the-galaxy.html
185 http://www.businessinsider.com/tesla-elon-musk-net-worth-2017-10
186 https://www.teslarati.com/elon-musk-ventures-investments-infographic/
187 https://www.inc.com/jessica-stillman/with-power-down-in-storm-battered-puerto-rico-elon-musk-is-quietly-stepping-in-to-help.html
188 https://www.thedailybeast.com/elon-musk-puts-five-homes-worth-dollar975-million-up-for-sale?ref=home
189 https://www.nbcnews.com/think/opinion/elon-musk-reopening-his-tesla-factory-game-him-he-s-ncna1204611
190 https://www.cnbc.com/2020/03/26/coronavirus-two-tesla-employees-test-positive-for-covid-19.html
191 http://www.businessinsider.com/elon-musk-spacex-culture-2017-11
192 https://www.inc.com/justin-bariso/elon-musk-sent-an-email-to-employees-at-120-in-morning-it-just-may-signal-end-of-tesla.html
193 https://capitalandmain.com/tesla-workers-file-charges-with-national-labor-board-as-battle-with-elon-musk-intensifies-0419
194 http://www2.psych.ubc.ca/~schaller/528Readings/Festinger1954.pdf
195 https://www.technologyreview.com/s/539861/techs-enduring-great-man-myth/
196 https://www.latimes.com/business/la-fi-hy-musk-subsidies-20150531-story.html
197 https://www.cnbc.com/2020/05/12/trump-sides-with-tesla-ceo-elon-musk-open-the-plant-now.html
198 https://www.cnbc.com/2020/01/22/trump-likens-elon-musk-to-thomas-edison-as-one-of-our-great-geniuses.html
199 https://www.profgalloway.com/the-martian/
200 https://www.profgalloway.com/the-martian/

201 https://www.blockchainresearchlab.org/wp-content/uploads/2020/05/BRL-Working-Paper-No-16-How-Elon-Musks-Twitter-activity-moves-cryptocurrency-markets.pdf
202 https://www.cnbc.com/2021/05/08/dogecoin-price-plummets-as-elon-musk-hosts-saturday-night-live-.html
203 https://digiconomist.net/bitcoin-energy-consumption
204 https://www.cnbc.com/2018/02/12/elon-musk-spacex-falcon-heavy-costs-150-million-at-most.html
205 https://www.salon.com/2018/02/12/why-sending-a-tesla-into-orbit-is-a-slap-in-the-face-to-science/
206 https://www.theguardian.com/commentisfree/2018/feb/07/elon-musk-spacex-launch-utterly-depressing
207 https://www.theverge.com/2019/7/22/20703423/tum-hyperloop-record-463-kmph-spacex-elon-musk-competition
208 https://www.forbes.com/sites/alexkonrad/2016/10/25/hyperloop-one-seeks-new-cash-amid-high-costs/
209 https://gizmodo.com/elon-musks-hyperloop-concept-is-now-even-more-hopelessl-1823675120
210 https://nypost.com/2020/04/18/elon-musk-is-tech-covidiot-no-1-during-coronavirus-pandemic/
211 https://www.bloomberg.com/news/articles/2021-02-11/how-elon-musks-s-tweets-moved-gamestop-gme-bitcoin-dogecoin-and-other-stocks
212 https://www.nytimes.com/2020/05/18/opinion/elon-musk-tesla-factory.html
213 https://www.wired.com/2005/08/battelle/
214 https://99firms.com/blog/google-search-statistics/
215 https://www.independent.co.uk/life-style/gadgets-and-tech/news/google-21-birthday-doodle-homepage-search-engine-history-internet-archive-a9121906.html
216 https://www.independent.co.uk/life-style/gadgets-and-tech/news/google-21-birthday-doodle-homepage-search-engine-history-internet-archive-a9121906.html
217 https://www.bbc.com/news/business-54619148
218 https://www.broadbandsearch.net/blog/google-statistics-facts
219 https://www.forbes.com/sites/forbestechcouncil/2018/01/05/what-googles-dont-be-evil-slogan-can-teach-you-about-creating-your-companys-motto/
220 https://www.forbes.com/sites/timworstall/2013/05/25/googles-excellent-plan-to-bring-wireless-internet-to-developing-countries/
221 https://www.wired.co.uk/article/google-project-loon-balloon-facebook-aquila-internet-africa
222 https://www.theverge.com/2020/2/17/21140698/google-station-discontinued-free-wifi-india-south-africa-railway-stations

223 https://www.datadial.net/blog/good-guy-google-nine-awesome-things-google-have-done-that-you-didnt-even-know-about/
224 https://www.theverge.com/2020/2/26/21154417/google-translate-new-languages-support-odia-tatar-turkmen-uyghur-kinyarwanda
225 https://som.yale.edu/news/news/google-chairman-eric-schmidt-discusses-globalization-technology
226 https://economicimpact.google.com/
227 https://www.blog.google/around-the-globe/google-europe/youtube-role-music-industry/
228 https://daily.jstor.org/how-youtube-has-changed-our-concept-of-celebrity/
229 https://stadia.google.com/
230 https://developers.google.com/android/
231 https://www.fastcompany.com/90380618/how-google-photos-joined-the-billion-user-club
232 https://www.theverge.com/2017/5/17/15654454/android-reaches-2-billion-monthly-active-users
233 https://www.theverge.com/2018/7/25/17613442/google-drive-one-billion-users
234 http://www.datacenterknowledge.com/google-data-center-faq-part-2
235 https://www.exabytes.digital/blog/10-must-free-google-tools-websites-2018
236 https://en.wikipedia.org/wiki/List_of_mergers_and_acquisitions_by_Alphabet
237 https://www.lifehack.org/articles/technology/13-interesting-facts-about-google-that-you-may-not-know.html
238 https://www.forbes.com/sites/kateoflahertyuk/2019/11/17/heres-why-the-google-fitbit-deal-mattersand-what-you-should-do/
239 https://research.google.com/pubs/GeneralScience.html
240 https://www.insidephilanthropy.com/grants-for-scientific-research/google-grants-for-science-research.html
241 https://waymo.com/
242 https://www.androidheadlines.com/2016/01/nine-companies-alphabet-inc.html
243 https://www.androidheadlines.com/2016/01/nine-companies-alphabet-inc.html
244 https://www.blog.google/technology/safety-security/continuing-fight-against-child-sexual-abuse-online/
245 https://www.lifewire.com/google-flu-trends-1616299
246 https://edition.cnn.com/2020/04/03/tech/coronavirus-google-data-sharing-intl-scli/index.html
247 https://blog.google/outreach-initiatives/google-news-initiative/covid-19-65-million-help-fight-coronavirus-misinformation/

248 https://www.theperspective.com/debates/businessandtechnology/the-perspective-on-facebook/
249 https://marketingland.com/almost-70-of-digital-ad-spending-going-to-google-facebook-amazon-says-analyst-firm-262565
250 https://review42.com/google-statistics-and-facts/
251 https://searchengineland.com/youtube-ranking-factors-getting-ranked-second-largest-search-engine-225533
252 https://www.theverge.com/2019/11/14/20965455/google-antitrust-investigation-probe-advertising-search-android
253 https://intpolicydigest.org/2018/02/18/is-google-a-monopoly/
254 https://www.wired.com/story/congress-google-project-dragonfly-questions/
255 https://expandedramblings.com/index.php/gmail-statistics/
256 https://www.theperspective.com/debates/businessandtechnology/the-perspective-on-big-data/
257 https://www.makeuseof.com/tag/stop-using-google-search/
258 https://review42.com/google-statistics-and-facts/
259 https://www.cnet.com/news/google-is-a-search-monopoly-justice-department-says-in-landmark-antitrust-lawsuit/
260 https://www.nytimes.com/2020/10/20/technology/google-lawsuit.html
261 https://www.theguardian.com/technology/2018/mar/17/facebook-cambridge-analytica-kogan-data-algorithm
262 https://edition.cnn.com/2020/10/20/tech/doj-google-antitrust-case/index.html
263 https://www.reuters.com/article/us-usa-internet-privacy/google-to-acknowledge-privacy-mistakes-as-us-seeks-input-idUSKCN1M52RG
264 https://www.vox.com/recode/2019/11/19/20971337/google-medical-records-ascension-reset-podcast
265 https://www.cnbc.com/2019/11/12/google-project-nightingale-hospital-data-deal-raises-privacy-fears.html
266 https://www.theguardian.com/technology/2017/jul/13/google-millions-academic-research-influence-opinion
267 https://www.theverge.com/2015/3/27/8302571/google-denies-ftc-influence
268 https://campaignforaccountability.org/new-report-reveals-googles-extensive-financial-support-for-academia/
269 https://www.financialexpress.com/industry/technology/how-google-maps-is-helping-fight-the-coronavirus-pandemic/2100209/
270 https://edition.cnn.com/2020/10/22/tech/doj-google-antitrust-analysis/index.html

Printed in Great Britain
by Amazon